ZAGAT
2014

New Jersey Restaurants

LOCAL EDITORS
Mary Ann Castronovo Fusco and Pat Tanner
STAFF EDITOR
Yoji Yamaguchi

Published and distributed by
Zagat Survey, LLC
76 Ninth Avenue
New York, NY 10011
T: 212.977.6000
E: feedback@zagat.com
www.zagat.com

ACKNOWLEDGMENTS

We're grateful to our local editors, Mary Ann Castronovo Fusco, a freelance editor and contributor to *New Jersey Monthly,* and Pat Tanner, a restaurant critic and feature writer for *New Jersey Monthly,* food blogger for dinewithpat.com and food columnist for *The Princeton Packet* and *U.S. 1.* We also sincerely thank the thousands of people who participated in this survey – this guide is really "theirs."

We also thank Anne Bauso (editor), Miranda Levenstein, Andrew Murphy, Catherine Quayle and Rosie Saferstein, as well as the following members of our staff: Brian Albert, Sean Beachell, Maryanne Bertollo, Reni Chin, Larry Cohn, Nicole Diaz, Kelly Dobkin, Jeff Freier, Alison Gainor, Michelle Golden, Justin Hartung, Marc Henson, Anna Hyclak, Ryutaro Ishikane, Aynsley Karps, Michele Laudig, Natalie Lebert, Mike Liao, Vivian Ma, Molly Moker, James Mulcahy, Polina Paley, Josh Siegel, Albry Smither, Amanda Spurlock, Chris Walsh, Jacqueline Wasilczyk, Art Yagci, Sharon Yates, Anna Zappia and Kyle Zolner.

ABOUT ZAGAT

In 1979, we asked friends to rate and review restaurants purely for fun. The term "user-generated content" had yet to be coined. That hobby grew into Zagat Survey; 34 years later, we have loyal surveyors around the globe and our content now includes nightlife, shopping, tourist attractions, golf and more. Along the way, we evolved from being a print publisher to a digital content provider. We also produce marketing tools for a wide range of corporate clients, and you can find us on Google+ and just about any other social media network.

Our reviews are based on public opinion surveys. The ratings reflect the average scores given by the survey participants who voted on each establishment. The text is based on quotes from, or paraphrasings of, the surveyors' comments. Phone numbers, addresses and other factual data were correct to the best of our knowledge when published in this guide.

JOIN IN

To improve our guides, we solicit your comments – positive or negative; it's vital that we hear your opinions. Just contact us at **nina-tim@zagat.com.**

Contents

Ratings & Symbols

Name	Symbols	Cuisine	Zagat Ratings			
			FOOD	DECOR	SERVICE	COST

Area, Address & Contact

Tim & Nina's 🌓 *Pizza*   ▽ 23 | 9 | 13 | $15

Atlantic City | 5678 Pacific Ave. (Atlantic Ave.) | 609-555-1212 | www.zagat.com

Review, surveyor comments in quotes

"Miles from the boardwalk but still not far enough away", this "never-closing" AC "eyesore" "single-handedly" started the "saltwater-taffy pizza craze" that's "sweeping the casino capital" like "a run of bad luck"; don't forget to "visit the all-you-can-stomach buffet" – "it's to die for" (or from) – but don't look for ambiance because "T & N don't know from design", or service, for that matter, which is not that surprising, given the "give-away" prices.

Ratings

Food, Decor & **Service** are rated on a 30-point scale.

26 – 30   extraordinary to perfection
21 – 25   very good to excellent
16 – 20   good to very good
11 – 15   fair to good
0 – 10   poor to fair
▽   low response | less reliable

Cost

The price of dinner with a drink and tip; lunch is usually 25% to 30% less. For unrated **newcomers,** the price range is as follows:

I $25 and below   E $41 to $65
M $26 to $40   VE $66 or above

Symbols

🌓   serves after 11 PM
🚫   closed on Sunday
Ⓜ   closed on Monday
⊄   cash only

Maps

Index maps show restaurants with the highest Food ratings and other notable places in those areas.

New Jersey at a Glance

- 1,112 restaurants covered
- 8,956 surveyors
- **Winners: Nicholas** (Food, Service, Most Popular), **Rat's** (Decor)
- **Top Newcomers: Ama Ristorante, Café 37** (tie)

SECOND ACTS: Some of the most notable second acts are taking place on the Sandy-ravaged Jersey Shore (see page 6 for an update). Meanwhile, Christine Nunn became the chef of Westwood American **Grange** after her Fair Lawn eatery **Picnic** closed in January of this year, and Mike Jurusz returned to his old post at the **Atlantic Bar & Grill,** newly renamed **Chef Mike's ABG.** And after selling her two South Jersey restaurants, veteran restaurateur Elena Wu is back on the scene with a new eponymous Asian spot in Voorhees, **Elena Wu Restaurant & Sushi Bar.**

TRENDS: New Jersey is home to an increasingly diverse dining scene. The state saw a surge in Cuban cuisine, from Hackensack's **Casual Habana Cafe** and Hoboken's **La Isla** to **A Little Bit of Cuba Dos** in Freehold and **Cubacán** in Asbury Park. Doing their best George Washingtons, more and more of Philadelphia's finest chefs are crossing the Delaware, including Iron Chef Jose Garces, who is opening another restaurant in Atlantic City's Revel Resort, joining his **Amada** and **Village Whiskey;** former **Fork** toque Terence Feury (**Tavro Thirteen** in Swedesboro); Joey Baldino, alum of Philly's iconic **Vetri** (**Zeppoli** in Collingswood); and, coming soon, Marc Vetri himself, with a Moorestown satellite of his **Osteria.** Seems like everything old is new again, with Whitehouse's venerable **The Ryland Inn** reopening after a five-year hiatus under new chef Anthony Bucco and stalwart **Saddle River Inn** transitioning from legendary chef-owner Hans Egg to the team of chef Jamie Knott (ex Montclair's **Fascino**) and manager David Madison. The site of Princeton landmark **Lahiere's** is now home to farm-to-table newcomer **Agricola,** which has added to a thriving locavore movement that includes Montclair Southern specialist **Escape** and vegan-friendly American **Local Seasonal Kitchen** in Ramsey.

MAC DADDIES: Creative takes on mac 'n' cheese headline the menu at a number of Jersey newcomers, including the Newark outpost of Brooklyn-based **Elbow Room,** Princeton's **North End Bistro** and **River Grille** in Chatham.

MOST SEARCHED ON ZAGAT.COM: Elements, River Palm Terrace, Chart House, Roots Steakhouse, Ryland Inn

HOT TOWNS: Atlantic City (**Amada, Village Whiskey**), Montclair (**Escape, J&K Steakhouse, Pig & Prince, Samba Montclair**), Princeton (**Agricola, Despaña, Mistral, North End Bistro**) and Ridgewood (**Café 37, Due, Lisa's Mediterranean Kitchen**).

New Jersey
August 22, 2013

Mary Ann Castronovo Fusco
Pat Tanner

A Post-Sandy Update

On October 29, 2012, Superstorm Sandy pounded New Jersey with 14-foot waves along the Shore. Restaurants throughout the state were badly damaged, some irreparably. The building housing **Matisse** on Belmar's boardwalk was condemned and eventually demolished. Highlands' **Bay Avenue Trattoria,** the third highest-rated Shore property in our previous Survey, had no plans to reopen as of press time.

STORMING BACK: Despite the challenges, many Jersey restaurants have managed to dry themselves off and come storming back. Flood damage prompted the highly rated **Drew's Bayshore Bistro** in Keyport to move into a new space nearby – on higher ground. Marilyn Schlossbach's **Langosta Lounge** on the Asbury Park boardwalk reopened in May, even though, as she says, "We're still fixing as we go." Also up and running are two other Asbury Park boardwalk staples, **Cubacán** and **Stella Marina**, as well as the original location of Atlantic City's legendary **White House** sub shop (founded in 1946) and Margate mainstay **Steve & Cookie's By the Bay.**

STILL ON THE MEND: Langosta's next-door sibling, **Pop's Garage,** is still undergoing construction (though its Shrewsbury branch is open). Likewise, the Highlands location of **Grimaldi's** and **Sallie Tee's Waterfront Grill** in Monmouth Beach's Channel Club Marina were in the process of rebuilding at press time, while **Anjelica's** in Sea Bright is anticipating a midsummer debut.

SERVING THEIR COMMUNITIES: Even as they struggled to get back on their feet, many restaurants rallied to help their communities. After flooding ruined the outdoor bar and basement of **Rooney's Oceanfront** in Long Branch, it rushed to reopen within days, providing meals for emergency responders and serving as a pickup spot for supplies donated to relief organizations. The restaurant released a statement: "We opened so that our friends and neighbors would have a warm place to go, enjoy a nice meal, watch some TV, charge their devices . . . to show there would be normalcy after this." Jersey City's **Maritime Parc** raised cash for the restoration of storm-ravaged Liberty State Park with a pie sale. Widespread power outages didn't keep **Charrito's** from serving free lunches to Hoboken residents. Though the flood waters that inundated the entire town of Moonachie also forced local institution **Bazzarelli** to close for two months, it was still able to hold a fund-raiser for volunteer first responders. "We've heard about so many things – flooding, power outages and road closures – but the good stories outnumber the bad," says Marilou Halvorsen, president of the New Jersey Restaurant Association (who, coincidentally, began her first day on the job on the day Hurricane Sandy hit). "Even in the aftermath of the storm, so many of those restaurants really became the dining room of the community."

Michele Laudig

Key Newcomers

Our editors' picks among this year's arrivals. See full list at p. 204.

Acanto Ristorante: Upscale Tenafly Italian with French and Greek influences

Agricola: Midpriced locavore American in Princeton

Ama Ristorante: Ocean views and upscale Tuscan fare in Sea Bright

Bellissimo's: Sprawling high-end Italian in Little Falls

Blue Fig Café: Moderately priced BYO Med in Moorestown

Burgerwood: Hamburger joint near the Englewood PAC

Café 37: Ridgewood BYO American from Latour alum Cesar Sotomayor

Central Kitchen: Midpriced American comfort food in Englewood Cliffs

Despaña: Princeton outpost of the NYC boutique retailer/tapas cafe

Due: Ridgewood's new upscale BYO Italian

Elbow Room: Newark outpost of the Bklyn mac 'n' cheese specialist

Escape: Locavore Lowcountry fare at this upscale Montclair BYO

G Grab & Go: Edison gourmet sandwich shop from DC chef Mike Isabella

Giulia's Kitchen: Italian-accented American comfort food in Cliffside Park

Grange: Westwood American from Christine Nunn (Picnic)

Local Seasonal Kitchen: Ramsey BYO serving locavore American fare

Mistral: BYO Eclectic small-plates specialist from the Elements team

Pig & Prince: American fare in a renovated Montclair train station

Tavro Thirteen: Upscale American in Swedesboro's Old Swedes Inn

---

ON THE HORIZON: Three restaurants are opening this year on the Hudson River waterfront in Edgewater: **Haven Riverfront Restaurant and Bar,** from the team behind Hoboken's **3 Forty Grill**; the Mediterranean **Orama**; and **Pier 115 Bar & Grill.** Restaurateur Chris Cannon's **Jockey Hollow Bar and Kitchen** will operate out of Morristown's historic Vail Mansion. A gastropub from Food Network's Aaron McCargo (*Big Daddy's House*) is set to debut in Camden in the fall. Philadelphia's **Farm & Fisherman** will have a satellite in Cherry Hill on the former site of **Andreotti's Viennese Cafe,** while Philly legend Marc Vetri is launching a branch of his **Osteria** in Moorestown.

Most Popular

This list is plotted on the map at the back of this book.

1. Nicholas | *American*
2. Ninety Acres/Natirar | *Amer.*
3. CulinAriane | *American*
4. Amanda's | *American*
5. Cafe Panache | *Eclectic*
6. Cafe Matisse | *Eclectic*
7. River Palm Terrace | *Steak*
8. Scalini Fedeli | *Italian*
9. 410 Bank St. | *Caribbean/Creole*
10. Highlawn Pavilion | *American*
11. A Toute Heure | *American*
12. Bernards Inn | *American*
13. Pluckemin Inn | *American*
14. Adelphia | *American*
15. Fascino | *Italian*
16. 3 Forty Grill | *American*
17. Serenade | *French*
18. Cuban Pete's | *Cuban*
19. Don Pepe* | *Portuguese/Spanish*
20. Elements* | *American*
21. The Frog and the Peach* | *Amer.*
22. Osteria Giotto | *Italian*
23. Saddle River Inn | *Amer./Fr.*
24. Rat's | *French*
25. Arthur's Tavern | *Steak*
26. Fornos of Spain | *Spanish*
27. Lorena's* | *French*
28. The Manor | *American*
29. Old Man Rafferty's | *American*
30. Harold's NY Deli | *Jewish/Deli*
31. Carmine's | *Italian*
32. David Burke Fromagerie* | *Amer.*
33. Washington Inn* | *American*
34. Blue Point Grill | *Seafood*
35. McLoone's | *American*
36. Chef Vola's | *Italian*
37. Due Mari* | *Italian*
38. Bobby Flay Steak | *Steak*
39. It's Greek To Me | *Greek*
40. Stage Left* | *American*

MOST POPULAR CHAINS

1. Cheesecake Factory | *American*
2. Bonefish Grill | *Seafood*
3. Five Guys | *Burgers*
4. P.F. Chang's Bistro | *Chinese*
5. Ruth's Chris | *Steak*
6. Bobby's Burger Palace | *Burgers*
7. Chart House | *Seafood*
8. The Capital Grille | *Steak*
9. Legal Sea Foods | *Seafood*
10. Benihana | *Japanese*

Many of the above restaurants are among New Jersey's most expensive, but if popularity were calibrated to price, a number of other restaurants would surely join their ranks. To illustrate this, we have added seven lists comprising 49 Best Buys on page 15.

---

* Indicates a tie with restaurant above; excludes places with low votes, unless otherwise indicated; Top Food excludes dessert-only places.

Top Food

28
Nicholas | *American*
Lorena's | *French*

27
CulinAriane | *American*
DeLorenzo's Pies | *Pizza*
Shumi | *Japanese*
Steve & Cookie's | *American*
Chef's Table | *French*
Scalini Fedeli | *Italian*
Drew's Bayshore | *American*
Chef Vola's | *Italian*

26
Amada | *Spanish*
Le Rendez-Vous | *French*
Belford Bistro | *American*
Serenade | *French*
Cafe Panache | *Eclectic*

Peter Shields Inn | *American*
Old Homestead | *Steak*
Saddle River Inn | *Amer./French*
Cafe Matisse | *Eclectic*
Blue Bottle Cafe | *American*
Chez Catherine | *French*
La Riviera Gastronomia | *Italian*
Sono Sushi | *Japanese*
Washington Inn* | *American*
Peacock Inn | *Amer.*
Black Duck Sunset | *Eclectic*
Whispers | *American*
Zeppoli | *Italian*
Sagami | *Japanese*
Latour | *French*

Top Decor

27
Rat's
Ninety Acres at Natirar
Nicholas
Peter Shields Inn
Highlawn Pavilion

26
Amada
Peacock Inn
Buddakan

25
Stone House at Stirling Ridge
Washington Inn
Azure by Allegretti
Avenue
Bernards Inn

Cafe Matisse
Ram's Head Inn
Serenade
The Gables
Union Park Dining Room
American Cut
Son Cubano
Zylo
Saddle River Inn
Ebbitt Room
Bobby Flay Steak
Old Homestead

Top Service

28
Nicholas

26
Amada
Lorena's
Peacock Inn
Cafe Matisse

25
Washington Inn
Peter Shields Inn
CulinAriane
Serenade
Ram's Head Inn
Saddle River Inn
Scalini Fedeli
Il Capriccio

Chez Catherine
Whispers
A Toute Heure
Stage Left
Ebbitt Room
Latour
Steve & Cookie's
Bernards Inn
Chef Vola's
Chef's Table
Cafe Panache
Old Homestead*

TOPS BY CUISINE

AMERICAN

- 28 Nicholas
- 27 CulinAriane
- Steve & Cookie's
- Drew's Bayshore
- 26 Belford Bistro
- Peter Shields Inn
- Saddle River Inn
- Blue Bottle Cafe
- Washington Inn
- Peacock Inn

BURGERS

- 23 Pop Shop
- 22 Hiram's Roadstand
- White Manna
- Five Guys
- 21 Rutt's Hut

CHINESE

- 24 West Lake Seafood
- Hunan Taste
- 23 Tina Louise
- Chengdu 46
- Elements Asia

COFFEE SHOP/DINER

- 25 Rolling Pin Cafe
- 23 Small World Coffee
- 22 Mustache Bill's
- 21 Skylark
- Mastoris

CUBAN

- 25 Cucharamama
- Casual Habana Cafe
- La Isla
- 24 Zafra
- 23 Mi Bandera

ECLECTIC

- 26 Cafe Panache
- Cafe Matisse
- Black Duck/Sunset
- 25 Oliver a Bistro
- The Gables

FRENCH

- 28 Lorena's
- 27 Chef's Table
- 26 Le Rendez-Vous
- Serenade
- Saddle River Inn

GREEK

- 25 Varka
- Limani
- 24 Taverna Mykonos
- Stamna
- 23 Pithari Taverna

INDIAN

- 25 IndeBlue
- 23 Brick Lane Curry House
- Karma Kafe
- Palace of Asia
- Namaskaar

ITALIAN

- 27 Scalini Fedeli
- Chef Vola's
- 26 La Riviera Gastronomia
- Zeppoli
- Fascino
- Due Mari
- Brian's
- 25 Tre Famiglia
- Lu Nello
- Via 45

JAPANESE

- 27 Shumi
- 26 Sono Sushi
- Sagami
- 25 Sakura Bana
- Fuji Japanese

MEDITERRANEAN

- 24 Vine
- The Fig Tree
- Moonstruck
- Hamilton's
- Satis

MEXICAN

- 25 Taqueria Downtown
- 24 La Esperanza
- 23 El Azteca
- El Mesón Café
- Tortuga's Cocina

MIDDLE EASTERN

- 24 Dayi'nin Yeri
- Silk Road
- 22 Istanbul/Patisserie
- Norma's
- Beyti Kebab

PAN-LATIN/ SOUTH AMERICAN

- **25** Cucharamama
- **24** Zafra
- Costanera
- Sabor
- **23** Patria

PIZZA

- **27** DeLorenzo's Pies
- **25** Carluccio's Coal Fired Pizza
- DeLorenzo's Pizza
- Trattoria La Sorrentina
- Nomad Pizza

SEAFOOD

- **26** Due Mari
- **25** Varka
- Fin
- Dock's Oyster House
- Limani

SPANISH/PORTUGUESE

- **26** Amada
- **25** Fernandes Steakhouse II
- **24** Sol-Mar
- Casa Vasca
- Tapas de España

STEAKHOUSES

- **26** Old Homestead
- **25** Strip House
- Bobby Flay Steak
- Fernandes Steakhouse II
- Roots Steak

THAI

- **24** Origin
- Thai Kitchen
- Siri's
- Thai Thai
- **23** Bangkok Garden

TOPS BY SPECIAL FEATURE

BREAKFAST

- **25** Tisha's Fine Dining
- La Isla
- Hobby's Deli
- **24** Blue Morel
- Zafra

BRUNCH

- **26** Peacock Inn
- **25** Taqueria Downtown
- Elements
- Rat's
- Amanda's

CHILD-FRIENDLY

- **27** Steve & Cookie's
- **26** Sono Sushi
- Black Duck/Sunset
- Sagami
- **25** Dock's Oyster

HOTEL DINING

- **26** Amada (Revel)
- Old Homestead (Borgata)
- Peacock Inn
- Whispers (Hewitt Wellington)
- Union Park (Hotel Macomber)

OFFBEAT

- **27** Chef Vola's
- **25** Rolling Pin Cafe
- **24** Satis
- Upstairs
- **23** Homestead Inn

OUTDOOR DINING

- **25** Rat's
- The Gables
- **23** Maritime Parc
- **22** Sirena Ristorante
- Chart House

PEOPLE-WATCHING

- **26** Peacock Inn
- Zeppoli
- **25** Bernards Inn
- Lu Nello
- Buddakan

POWER SCENES

- **27** Scalini Fedeli
- **26** Serenade
- Old Homestead
- Saddle River Inn
- Chez Catherine

QUICK BITES

- **27** DeLorenzo's Pies
- **25** Rolling Pin Cafe
- Taqueria Downtown
- DeLorenzo's Pizza
- Hobby's Deli

QUIET CONVERSATION

- **27** Chef's Table
- **26** Peter Shields Inn
- Saddle River Inn
- Cafe Matisse
- Chez Catherine

SINGLES SCENES

25 Buddakan
Cucharamama
Cenzino
24 Luke Palladino
Shipwreck Grill

TRENDY

28 Lorena's
27 Shumi
Steve & Cookie's
Drew's Bay Shore
26 Amada

VIEWS

25 Ama Ristorante
23 Maritime Parc
Fleming's Steakhouse
22 Avenue
Zylo

WINNING WINE LISTS

28 Nicholas
27 Scalini Fedeli
26 Serenade
Restaurant Latour▽
Washington Inn

TOPS BY OCCASION

Some best bets in a range of prices and cuisines for these occasions.

ANNIVERSARY DINNER

28 Nicholas
26 Washington Inn
Peacock Inn
25 Ryland Inn
David Burke Fromagerie

BIRTHDAYS

28 Nicholas
26 Peacock Inn
25 Ryland Inn
Rat's
Agricola

BRIDAL & BABY SHOWERS

26 Union Park Dining Room
25 Rat's
Eno Terra
24 Hamilton's Grill
River Winds

BRUNCH WITH FRIENDS

25 Taqueria Downtown
Elements
24 Robin's Nest
22 Avenue

FIRST DATE

28 Nicholas
25 Buddakan
Ryland Inn
24 Raven & the Peach
22 Avenue

GRADUATION (MONTCLAIR)

26 Fascino
25 Lu Nello
23 Rare The Steak House

Corso 98
_| Bellissimo's

GRADUATION (NEW BRUNSWICK)

26 Due Mari
25 Stage Left
The Frog and the Peach
21 Panico's
20 Christopher's

GRADUATION (PRINCETON)

26 Peacock Inn
22 La Mezzaluna
Mediterra
Witherspoon Grill
_| Agricola

MOTHER'S DAY

26 Peacock Inn
25 Rat's
The Gables
David Burke Fromagerie
24 Brothers Moon

REHEARSAL DINNERS

25 Ram's Head Inn
Rat's
Eno Terra
24 Hamilton's Grill
_| Agricola

WEDDING RECEPTIONS

25 Ram's Head Inn
Ryland Inn
Rat's
The Gables
22 Molly Pitcher Inn

TOPS BY LOCATION

ATLANTIC CITY

27 Chef Vola's
26 Amada
   Old Homestead
25 Buddakan
   Il Mulino

CAPE MAY

26 Peter Shields Inn
   Washington Inn
   Union Park Dining Room
   Ebbitt Room
25 Tisha's Fine Dining

CHERRY HILL

25 The Capital Grille
24 Seasons 52
   The Kibitz Room
   William Douglas Steakhouse
   Caffe Aldo Lamberti

COLLINGSWOOD

26 Zeppoli
   Sagami
25 IndeBlue
   Bistro di Marino
   Sapori

HOBOKEN

25 Cucharamama
   La Isla
   Amanda's
24 Augustino's
   Dining Rm./Anthony David's

JERSEY CITY

25 Taqueria Downtown
24 Satis
23 Maritime Parc
   Porto Leggero
   Nha Trang Place

LAMBERTVILLE

26 Brian's
24 Hamilton's Grill Room
   Manon
23 Tortuga's Cocina
22 DeAnna's

MONTCLAIR

27 CulinAriane
26 Fascino
25 Osteria Giotto
24 Fin Raw Bar & Kitchen
   Blu

MORRISTOWN

25 Roots Steakhouse
24 Blue Morel
   Origin
   Sebastian's The Steakhouse
   La Campagna

NEWARK

25 Fernandes Steakhouse II
   Hobby's Deli
24 Sol-Mar
   Casa Vasca
   Seabra's Marisqueira

NEW BRUNSWICK

26 Due Mari
25 Stage Left
   The Frog and the Peach
24 Catherine Lombardi
   Steakhouse 85

PRINCETON

26 Peacock Inn
25 Blue Point Grill
   Elements
   Ruth's Chris

RED BANK

28 Nicholas
25 Via45
23 Char Steak House
   Dish
22 Juanito's

RIDGEWOOD

26 Latour
25 Sakura Bana
   Cafe' 37
24 Village Green
23 Brick Lane Curry House

SOMERVILLE

27 Shumi
24 Origin
   Da Filippo's
22 Martino's
   Wasabi Asian Plates

SUMMIT

25 Roots Steakhouse
23 Fiorino
   Taka Sushi
   La Focaccia
22 Huntley Taverne

TOPS BY DESTINATION

A selection of the best bets in a range of prices and cuisines near these points of interest.

ASBURY PARK BOARDWALK

21	Cubacán
	Pop's Garage
20	Langosta Lounge
19	McLoone's

BRIDGEWATER COMMONS MALL

24	Thai Kitchen
22	Verve
21	Cheesecake Factory
20	McCormick/Schmick's
19	California Pizza Kitchen

GARDEN STATE PLAZA

25	Capital Grille
23	Chakra
21	Zinburger
	Legal Sea Foods

LIBERTY STATE PARK

24	Satis
23	Maritime Parc
22	Light Horse Tavern
20	Liberty House
	Amelia's Bistro

MCCARTER THEATER (PRINCETON)

22	La Mezzaluna
	Mediterra
	Witherspoon Grill
┘	Agricola
	Mistral

NEWARK MUSEUM

23	Spanish Pavillion
21	Rio Rodizio
20	Nico
┘	Elbow Room

PAPER MILL PLAYHOUSE (MILLBURN)

28	Lorena's
24	Verjus
23	Basilico
21	Cara Mia
20	La Pergola

PNC ARTS CENTER (HOLMDEL)

27	Drew's Bayshore
24	Copper Canyon
23	Anna's Italian Kitchen
22	Trinity
19	It's Greek to Me

PRUDENTIAL CENTER (NEWARK)

25	Hobby's Deli
24	Je's∇
23	Fornos of Spain
	Dinosaur BBQ
19	Brick City Bar & Grill

SEASIDE PIER

23	Red's Lobster Pot
22	Sirena
	Lobster House
20	Windansea

SHORT HILLS MALL

27	Scalini Fedeli
26	Serenade
21	Cheesecake Factory
	Legal Sea Foods
20	Benihana

SOPAC (SOUTH ORANGE)

28	Lorena's
24	Highlawn Pavilion
	La Primavera Trattoria∇
21	Neelam
┘	Sam Mickail's CUT

THEATER DISTRICT (NEW BRUNSWICK)

25	Stage Left
24	Catherine Lombardi
23	Clydz
	Daryl
22	Makeda

WELLMONT THEATER (MONTCLAIR)

26	Fascino
24	Fin Raw Bar & Kitchen
	Costanera
23	Aozora
22	Salute Brick Oven Bistro

Best Buys

Top-rated restaurants $25 and under

1 DeLorenzo's Pies | *Pizza*
2 Rolling Pin Cafe | *American*
3 Taqueria Downtown | *Mexican*
4 Carluccio's Pizza | *Pizza*
5 DeLorenzo's Pizza | *Pizza*
6 Casual Habana Cafe | *Cuban*
7 La Isla | *Cuban*
8 Hobby's Deli | *Deli*
9 White House | *Sandwiches*
10 Nomad Pizza | *Pizza*

11 The Kibitz Room | *Deli*
12 Osteria Procaccini | *Pizza*
13 La Esperanza | *Mexican*
14 Pete & Elda's | *Pizza*
15 Dayi'nin Yeci | *Turkish*
16 Megu Sushi | *Japanese*
17 Thai Thai | *Thai*
18 Smitty's Clam Bar | *Seafood*
19 El Azteca | *Mexican*
20 Grimaldi's | *Pizza*

BY CITY

CHERRY HILL
24 The Kibitz Room
   Megu Sushi
23 Bobby Chez
   Bistro at Cherry Hill
22 Norma's

HACKENSACK
25 Casual Habana Cafe
22 Brooklyn's Brick-Oven Pizza
   White Manna
   Five Guys
21 Lotus Cafe

HOBOKEN
25 La Isla
23 Grimaldi's
22 Sri Thai
21 Napoli's
20 Benny Tudino's

JERSEY CITY
25 Taqueria Downtown
23 Nha Trang Place
22 Rumba's Cafe
   Five Guys
21 Amiya

JERSEY SHORE
25 Carluccio's Pizza
   White House
24 Pete & Elda's
   Megu Sushi
23 Smitty's Clam Bar

RIDGEWOOD
22 A Mano
   Brooklyn's Brick-Oven Pizza
19 Country Pancake House
   It's Greek to Me

RESTAURANT DIRECTORY

	FOOD	DECOR	SERVICE	COST

Aamantran ⓜ *Indian* — 21 | 17 | 20 | $25

Toms River | Victoria Plaza | 1594 Rte. 9 S. (Sunset Ave.) | 732-341-5424
A "large menu" of "tasty" tandoori and curry dishes draws locals to this "consistent" Toms River Indian, where a lunch buffet and BYO make for an affordable meal; some say its strip-mall digs "need a face-lift", but "friendly" servers "who don't rush you" and a Bollywood soundtrack compensate.

Aby's *Mexican* — 20 | 16 | 20 | $20

Matawan | 32 Main St. (High St.) | 732-583-9119
There's "something for everyone" on the "varied" menu of "spicy", "authentic" Mexican eats at this "casual" Matawan "neighborhood spot"; "reasonable" prices and BYO are pluses, and a live guitarist on Saturday nights boosts the "friendly" vibe; P.S. the Decor score may not reflect its recent move to new digs.

Acacia ⓜ *American* — 22 | 21 | 21 | $46

Lawrenceville | 2637 Main St. (bet. Craven Ln. & Phillips Ave.) | 609-895-9885 | www.acacianj.com
"Still a class act", this "noteworthy" Lawrenceville "mainstay" has been dishing out "well-prepared" "creative American cuisine" on Main Street for more than 20 years; though some think the "pretty" space might "need a lift" and others gripe about "inconsistent" eats and pricey tabs, fans laud the "pleasant staff" and "welcoming ambiance" – plus, BYO "can save you a few bucks."

🆕 Acanto Ristorante ⓜ *Italian* — - | - | - | E

Tenafly | 88 Piermont Rd. (N. Mahan St.) | 201-399-7171 | www.ristoranteacanto.com
A seasonally inspired menu of Italian cuisine with French and Greek influences is the thing at this upscale Tenafly spot where the simple but sophisticated decor – white tablecloths, leather seating, warm woods – keeps the focus on the chef's rotation of fresh pastas, Med favorites and housemade desserts; a glowing bar and cozy dining solarium add to the appeal.

Acquaviva delle Fonti ⓜ *Italian* — 20 | 21 | 20 | $48

Westfield | 115 Elm St. (Broad St.) | 908-301-0700 | www.acquaviva-dellefonti.com
A "good local place for special occasions", this "upscale" Italian in Westfield offers "nicely done" cuisine in a "lovely space" with a "stunning patio" that's "especially nice in summer"; service gets a muted response, and some think the "pricey" fare "plays second fiddle to the wonderful setting."

Adara 🅢ⓜ *Eclectic* — 19 | 20 | 22 | $68

Montclair | 77 Walnut St. (bet. Greenwood Ave. & Grove St.) | 973-783-0462 | www.restaurantadara.com
A "culinary adventure" into molecular gastronomy, this BYO, tasting menu–only Eclectic in Montclair is "intriguing and innovative" to some, more about "appearance than taste" to others; earth-toned walls and dark-wood floors make for a "warm and cozy setting" and

the staff is "friendly and attentive", but be warned, this "truly unique experience" is "expensive."

Adega Grill *Portuguese/Spanish*

| 21 | 20 | 20 | $39 |

Newark | 130-132 Ferry St. (bet. Madison & Monroe Sts.) | 973-589-8830 | www.adegagrill.com

"Plentiful" portions of Portuguese and Spanish classics – from "always fresh" seafood dishes and "proper steaks" to "excellent sangria" – draw fans to this "convivial", well-priced spot in Newark, an Ironbound "favorite" with bar, dining room and lounge options; a large fireplace and grapevine murals create a "cozy", wine-cellar (*adega*) feel, and the "gracious" staff adds to the "old-world ambiance."

Adelphia Restaurant & Lounge ● *American*

| 21 | 21 | 21 | $26 |

Deptford | 1750 Clements Bridge Rd. (Westville Almonesson Rd.) | 856-845-8200 | www.adelphiarestaurant.com

A "huge", "diversified" menu ensures there's "something for everyone" at this Deptford American, an "upscale diner" that also does time as an event space and dance lounge (with an LED-lit floor); the main room has a "banquet-hall" kind of "beauty" that manages to feel "comfortable", and fans appreciate "courteous" service almost as much as the "family-friendly" prices.

NEW Agricola *American*

| - | - | - | E |

Princeton | 11 Witherspoon St. (bet. Nassau & Spring Sts.) | 609-921-2798 | www.agricolaeatery.com

This long-awaited upscale American (set in the digs occupied by Lahiere's for over 90 years) brings the true meaning of farm-to-table to Princeton thanks to locally sourced ingredients grown and raised on its own Great Road Farm, just four miles away; wood beams, exposed-brick walls and industrial-chic lighting lend a contemporary rustic feel to the bi-level space, which also boasts an open kitchen and zinc-topped bar.

Ah' Pizz *Pizza*

| 20 | 18 | 19 | $24 |

Montclair | 7 N. Willow St. (bet. Bloomfield & Glenridge Aves.) | 973-783-9200 | www.ahpizz.com

A blisteringly hot, wood-burning oven turns out "true pizza *napoletana*" at this family-friendly Montclair BYO where "fresh ingredients", "plentiful" salads and "good" pastas put it "a cut above" the average joint; while some deem the service "spotty" and find the prices "a little expensive" for pies, others insist it's "worth the money for sure."

Ajihei Ⓜ *Japanese*

| 24 | 17 | 20 | $31 |

Princeton | 11 Chambers St. (bet. John St. & Lincoln Hwy.) | 609-252-1158

"Mouthwatering" sushi and "superbly fresh" sashimi await at chef Koji Kitamura's midpriced Japanese "paradise" in Princeton, provided you "can abide by all the rules" – think "rigid seating times", no parties larger than four and BYO only; the "unassuming" basement setting is "cozy" to some, just "small" to others, and "not super kid-friendly", but many find it "great for dates."

	FOOD	DECOR	SERVICE	COST

Akai Lounge *Japanese*
24 | 21 | 21 | $36

Englewood | 11 N. Dean St. (Palisade Ave.) | 201-541-0086 |
www.akailounge.com

For "modern sushi" served "nightclub-style", this "trendy" Englewood
Japanese convenient to the Bergen PAC lures finatics with a "broad
menu" of "fresh", "imaginative offerings" such as "creative rolls",
"good tuna pizza" and "the best lychee martini on this planet";
"young", "efficient" staffers preside over the "hip", but "comfortable",
plush-red digs, and while dinner tabs might be "on the higher end",
the "happy-hour prices" are "great."

Akbar *Indian*
21 | 19 | 19 | $25

Edison | 21 Cortlandt St. (Patrick Ave.) | 732-632-8822 |
www.akbarrestaurant.com

The "frequently replenished" lunch buffet and à la carte dinner
menu are packed with "classic", "reliable" subcontinental fare at
this affordable Edison Indian; service is "friendly" (if sometimes
"slow"), and the "comfortable", "upscale" setting makes it a "solid
spot for private parties."

Alchemist & Barrister ❶ *American*
18 | 18 | 18 | $35

Princeton | 28 Witherspoon St. (bet. Hulfish & Nassau St.) |
609-924-5555 | www.theaandb.com

Princeton locals head to this long-standing "go-to" for "reasonably
priced" American "standard bar food", plus more substantial entrees
and Sunday brunch; a "rustic" bar and "delightful" patio supplement
the traditional dining rooms, and though most "don't go for the decor", it's nonetheless a "cozy" place to "relax."

Al Dente ⊠ *Italian*
22 | 20 | 22 | $38

Piscataway | 1665 Stelton Rd. (Ethel Rd.) | 732-985-8220 |
www.aldenteristorante.com

A "warm, gracious" staff proffers pasta "like grandma's" and other
"fresh, tasty offerings" at this midpriced Piscataway Italian; with
murals, pillars and stained glass, the "wedding-hall decor" is "too
much" for some ("dine outdoors if possible"), though supporters
still find the experience "charming" enough for a "date" night.

Al Dente Italiana *Italian*
23 | 22 | 22 | $28

Moorestown | 1690 Nixon Dr. (Rte. 38) | 856-437-6593 |
www.aldenteitaliana.com

"Wonderful pasta dishes and pizzas" shine at this "reasonably
priced" Moorestown Italian, though regulars also "save room" for
the "luscious, cold wonder" of gelato in an "amazing variety of flavors"; BYO, an open kitchen and "attentive", "kid-friendly" service
boost the "lively", "neighborhood" vibe.

Aldo & Gianni ⊠ *Italian*
21 | 17 | 21 | $41

Montvale | A&P Shopping Ctr. | 108 Chestnut Ridge Rd. (Grand Ave.) |
201-391-6866 | www.aldoandgianni.com

"Even your Sicilian grandmother would approve" of the "classic" Italian
"home cooking" at this Montvale "standby"; some say it's "a little

pricey" for its "stodgy" strip-mall setting, but the "hospitable" staff maintains a "comfortable", "cozy" atmosphere.

Alice's Ⓜ *American*   20 | 18 | 18 | $38

Lake Hopatcong | 24 Nolans Point Park Rd. (Nolans Point Rd.) | 973-663-9600 | www.alicesrestaurantnj.com

The "ever-changing menu" spotlights "seasonal fruits and vegetables" at this midpriced Lake Hopatcong New American; while service can be "uneven", and the "casual", "noisy" digs might feel "more like a bar than a restaurant", thanks to the "lovely view" from the lakeside deck (especially "at sunset"), most still consider it a "great find."

A Little Bit of Cuba Dos *Cuban*   22 | 22 | 21 | $34

Freehold | 2 E. Main St. (South St.) | 732-577-8506 | www.alittlebitofcubados.com

A "great example" of "authentic" Cuban cuisine can be had at this "vibrant" Downtown Freehold hot spot with a "vacation feel"; even if some think the food "plays second bongo" to the "noisy" crowd and live tunes, service is "friendly", and fans say it makes for an affordable and "fun night out"; P.S. they'll make sangria if you BYO.

A Little Café ⓏⓂ *Eclectic*   23 | 20 | 23 | $30

Voorhees | Plaza Shoppes | 118 White Horse Rd. (bet. Burnt Mill Rd. & Lucas Ln.) | 856-784-3344 | www.alittlecafenj.com

For "consistently good" Eclectic eats with "unusual touches", chef Marianne Powell's seasonally changing menu "beats all expectations"; set in a Voorhees strip mall, the "cozy" and "cute" digs may be small, but the "portion sizes are not" – just add a "pleasant" staff, BYO and "fair" prices and you have a "real gem."

Allegro Seafood Grill *Portuguese*   23 | 22 | 21 | $32

Newark | 58 Kossuth St. (Niagara St.) | 973-344-4500 | www.allegroseafoodgrill.com

"Amazing portions" of traditional Portuguese fare mean you "get your money's worth" at this midpriced "local gem" in Newark; decorated with warm wood accents, the dining area is supplemented by a "great outside patio" for the warmer months.

Allen's Clam Bar Ⓜ *Seafood*   22 | 16 | 19 | $23

New Gretna | 5650 Rte. 9 (Maple Ave.) | 609-296-4106

"Fresh seafood" is the focus at this "always-packed", no-frills New Gretna clam house where the staff "really puts you at ease"; the BYO policy assists in keeping tabs "reasonable" – another reason it's a "family favorite."

Alstarz Bar and Grill ◗ *Eclectic*   18 | 20 | 18 | $26

Bordentown | 140 Rte. 130 S. (Rte. 206) | 609-291-0200 | www.alstarzbarandgrill.com

A "huge selection" of "casual" Eclectic pub grub makes this midpriced Bordentown sports bar fit "for groups with varying tastes"; though some say service is "so-so", expect an "upbeat", "friendly" atmosphere with "a ton of TVs" for "watching the game" and a "nice outdoor patio" for the warmer months.

	FOOD	DECOR	SERVICE	COST

Amada *Spanish* — 26 | 26 | 26 | $58

Atlantic City | REVEL | 500 Boardwalk (bet. Metropolitan & New Jersey Aves.) | 609-225-9900 | www.revelresorts.com

Jose Garces hits the jackpot in Atlantic City's Revel Resort where "amazing presentations" of his "sublime tapas" and "spectacular" ocean views shine in "elegant", "modern" surroundings; "extremely helpful" service completes the "excellent experience", which fans concede is "expensive", but "worth every dollar."

Amanda's *American* — 25 | 24 | 24 | $48

Hoboken | 908 Washington St. (bet. 9th & 10th Sts.) | 201-798-0101 | www.amandasrestaurant.com

"Classy is the key word" that captures this "upscale" Hoboken New American where a "thoughtful" wine list is matched with "creative" cuisine that "seduces you" amid the "genteel" surrounds of a "lovely" Victorian brownstone; the "romantic" vibe is a "dater's delight", but it's "not too stuffy to take your kids" for "special occasions" – either way, expect a "warm welcome" from the "attentive" staff.

A Mano *Pizza* — 22 | 20 | 20 | $24

Ridgewood | 24 Franklin Ave. (Chestnut St.) | 201-493-2000 | www.amanopizza.com

For "some of the best pizza this side of Naples", this "casual" Ridgewood pizzeria turns out Neapolitan pies "done the right way", blistered by wood-burning ovens (and certified as authentic), along with other "fresh" eats like "excellent panini" and "delicious" salads; some naysayers find the service "lacking" and the "decor a little cold", and while it "can be pricey" for 'za, the option to BYO can lighten tabs.

NEW Ama Ristorante Ⓜ *Italian* — 25 | 24 | 24 | $63

Sea Bright | Driftwood Cabana Club | 1485 Ocean Ave. (Imbrie Pl.) | 732-530-9760 | www.amaristorante.com

"Creative" takes on Tuscan cuisine are the forte of this upscale, oceanfront Italian in Sea Bright's Driftwood Cabana Club (relocated in 2012 from Atlantic Highlands), serving "NYC-quality" pastas and mussels "to dream of"; "attentive" service and "lovely" decor "evoking Italy" are all part of its appeal, as is the "breathtaking view."

Amarone *Italian* — 21 | 18 | 23 | $42

Teaneck | 63 Cedar Ln. (bet. Broad & Prince Sts.) | 201-833-1897 | www.amaroneristorante.net

The staff makes sure "you always feel welcome" at this Teaneck standby dishing up "well-prepared", "old-fashioned Italian fare" ("specials are often the thing to order"); it may be "a bit pricey" and some say the decor "needs a face-lift", but the "nice outdoor eating area" is a definite plus "in the right weather."

Amelia's Bistro *American* — 20 | 18 | 20 | $32

Jersey City | 187 Warren St. (bet. Essex & Morris Sts.) | 201-332-2200 | www.ameliasbistro.com

"Solid" New American eats (including a "wonderful" weekend brunch) and "friendly" service are highlights at this moderately priced Jersey City "neighborhood joint"; even if the "quaint" decor gets middling scores, it's a "great location for people-watching", and "outdoor seating is a big plus."

American Cut *Steak*
24 | 25 | 24 | $81

Atlantic City | REVEL | 500 Boardwalk (Metropolitan Ave.) | 609-225-9860 | www.americancutsteakhouse.com

Iron Chef Marc Forgione "does wonders" at this "beautiful", "special-occasion" steakhouse at Atlantic City's Revel Resort, where carnivore classics get a "welcome twist" by way of à la carte sauces and sides, plus seafood offerings such as chili lobster and hiramasa; "efficient" service is another plus, and if both the prices and the "noise level" trend high (with "Led Zeppelin playing in the background"), fans insist "you get your money's worth."

Amici Milano *Italian*
21 | 20 | 21 | $38

Trenton | 600 Chestnut Ave. (Roebling Ave.) | 609-396-6300 | www.amicimilano.com

"One of the last iconic Italian restaurants" in Chambersburg, aka "the Little Italy of Trenton", this neighborhood "favorite" dishes up "decent" traditional fare that "justifies repeat visits"; though some say the "decor needs updating", "reasonable" tabs and "friendly" service keep regulars "satisfied"; P.S. there's live piano music on Fridays and Saturdays.

Amiya *Indian*
21 | 21 | 19 | $25

Jersey City | Harborside Financial Ctr. | 160 Greene St. (bet. Pearl & 2nd Sts.) | 201-433-8000
Parsippany | 252 Rte. 46 W. (bet. Edwards & New Rds.) | 973-521-9100
www.amiyarestaurant.com

An "awesome" lunch buffet is the headliner at this "higher end" Indian duo in Jersey City and Parsippany, which also delivers "classier dinner options"; service that some describe as "hit-or-miss" doesn't deter devotees who praise the "relaxing yet stylish ambiance" and "reasonable prices."

Andiamo *Italian*
21 | 18 | 21 | $40

Haworth | 23 Hardenburgh Ave. (bet. Harrison St. & Knickerbocker Rd.) | 201-384-1551 | www.andiamorestaurant.net

A "friendly" crew ferries a menu that "runs the gamut from pizza to seafood" at this "dependable" (if slightly "pricey") neighborhood Italian in Haworth; "outdoor dining" on the deck supplements the "casual" dining room, and though the "bar scene" can be "noisy", it draws a "loyal crowd."

Andre's ⊠Ⓜ *American*
25 | 24 | 24 | $54

Newton | 188 Spring St. (bet. Adams & Jefferson Sts.) | 973-300-4192 | www.andresrestaurant.com

Chef-owner André de Waal "works at the art of food", pairing his "creative", seasonal American menu with "top-notch" wines at this "upscale" Newton "gem"; "folksy but professional" service matches the "intimate" setting that strikes "the right balance between formal and casual"; P.S. open Wednesday–Saturday only.

	FOOD	DECOR	SERVICE	COST

Angelo's Fairmount Tavern *Italian* | 21 | 18 | 21 | $33 |

Atlantic City | 2300 Fairmount Ave. (Mississippi Ave.) |
609-344-2439 | www.angelosfairmounttavern.com
A "reasonably priced" "reprieve" from Atlantic City "casino food",
this "old-style family Italian" delivers "huge portions" of "terrific
red-sauce dishes" with "homemade wine" to wash it all down; despite the "slightly dated" decor, it has a "friendly", "neighborhood
feeling" that suits fans who've "been going for years" and are "prepared to wait" for an "authentic" experience that "still delivers."

Anna's Italian Kitchen Ⓜ *Italian* | 23 | 18 | 20 | $42 |

Middletown | Fountain Ridge Shopping Ctr. | 1686 Rte. 35 S.
(Magnolia Ln.) | 732-275-9142 | www.annasitaliankitchen.com
"Solid Italian food" and service with a "personal touch" draw fans to
Anna Perri's Middletown BYO; while some find it a "little pricey for
the atmosphere" in the "so-so" strip-mall location, loyalists say it
feels "like the heart of Italia."

Anna's Ristorante *Italian* | 20 | 19 | 20 | $36 |

Summit | 67 Union Pl. (bet. Beechwood Rd. & Maple St.) |
908-273-4448 | www.annasristorante.com
"Convenient to the Summit train station", this neighborhood haunt
promises a "varied menu" of "straightforward" Italian cooking at
moderate prices; wines are offered but BYO is also welcome, and
solid service adds to the casual, "family-friendly" atmosphere.

Anthony's Coal Fired Pizza *Pizza* | 21 | 18 | 20 | $21 |

Clifton | Clifton Promenade | 852 Rte. 3 (Bloomfield Ave.) | 973-471-2625
Ramsey | 984 Rte. 17 N. (Airmount Ave.) | 201-818-2625
Edison | 80 Parsonage Rd. (bet. Lafayette & Oakwood Aves.) |
732-744-1500
www.anthonyscoalfiredpizza.com
Thanks to the "unique taste" imparted by a coal oven, the "lip-
smackingly good, crispy-crust pizzas" make these "reasonably
priced" chain links a "welcome change from your standard pizzeria"; the "noisy", "casual" settings strike some as "cookie-cutter",
but most maintain there's a "friendly" atmosphere brightened
by "outgoing" staffers.

Antonia's by the Park *Italian* | 22 | 19 | 22 | $41 |

North Bergen | 9011 Palisade Ave. (Woodcliff Ave.) |
201-868-0750 | www.antoniasbythepark.com
For "quality Italian cuisine" (including a Sunday brunch buffet)
matched by "friendly" service, North Bergen locals head to this "dependable", somewhat "pricey" haunt near North Hudson Park; the
"large", "casual" dining room perks up with live music on Fridays
and Saturdays – fans report a "good time all around."

Anton's at the Swan Ⓜ *American* | 22 | 22 | 21 | $49 |

Lambertville | Swan Hotel | 43 S. Main St. (Swan St.) |
609-397-1960 | www.antons-at-the-swan.com
With a "cozy" bar, "intimate" patio and "quiet", "old-fashioned" dining room, this upscale Lambertville American is a "romantic" setting

for tucking into "well-prepared" dishes that spotlight "farm-fresh" ingredients; it's a "bit pricey", but "cordial", "laid-back" service adds to the generally "pleasant experience."

Aoyama *Asian*
23 | 20 | 21 | $34

Martinsville | 1982 Washington Valley Rd. (Chimney Rock Rd.) | 732-271-2558

Aoyama Mendham *Asian*

Mendham | 84 E. Main St. (bet. Dean Rd. & Heritage Manor Dr.) | 973-543-9700

Aoyama Wyckoff *Asian*

Wyckoff | Boulder Run Shopping Ctr. | 319 Franklin Tpke. (bet. Godwin Ave. & Main St.) | 201-847-9900
www.aoyamaNJ.com

"Interesting" sushi rolls are a highlight on the "diverse menu" at this midpriced Asian trio where BYO bolsters the "value"; "pleasant", "fairly attentive" service is another plus, though the decor gets mixed marks, which is why "takeout is a staple" for many locals.

Aozora *French/Japanese*
23 | 19 | 19 | $42

Montclair | 407 Bloomfield Ave. (bet. Glenridge Ave. & Willow St.) | 973-233-9400 | www.aozorafusion.com

While the rolls "almost look too good to eat", there's "more than just sushi" on the "creative", "upscale" menu at this French-Japanese BYO in Montclair; though some grouse the "spare, simple" space is "not nearly equal to the food", and service can be "slow", supporters still "succumb and enjoy" a "well-prepared meal."

Arthur's Steakhouse & Pub *Steak*
21 | 18 | 20 | $32

North Brunswick | 644 Georges Rd. (bet. 4th Ave. & Milltown Rd.) | 732-828-1117 | www.arthurssteakhouse.org

"It's nothing fancy, just tasty, homey food" note "neighborhood car-nivores" about this "family-friendly" North Brunswick steakhouse; though the "casual", "kitschy" "pub atmosphere" gets middling scores, most reason you "can't beat it for the price."

Arthur's Tavern *Steak*
20 | 16 | 19 | $32

Morris Plains | 700 Speedwell Ave. (Franklin Pl.) | 973-455-9705 | www.arthurstavern.com

"Serious eaters" who "don't need fancy" tuck into "huge", "mouth-watering" steaks "so beautiful your date will be jealous" at this "family-friendly, no-frills" steakhouse in Morris Plains; the "long waits" and a "throwback" atmosphere ("complete with Tiffany lamps" and "red-checkered tablecloths") aren't for everyone, though most can't resist the "bang for your buck."

Arturo's ⓜ *Italian*
23 | 20 | 21 | $51

Midland Park | 41 Central Ave. (Greenwood Ave.) | 201-444-2466
Insiders admit it isn't easy "deciding what to order" from the "never-ending menu" and "extensive" rundown of daily specials at this "old-fashioned", "high-end" Southern Italian in Midland Park; the "efficient" staff maintains a "consistent" experience, though it's al-ways an extra "treat" when there's live music in the bar on weekends.

Arturo's *Pizza*

24 | 17 | 20 | $27

Maplewood | 180 Maplewood Ave. (Baker St.) | 973-378-5800 |
www.arturosnj.com

"Top-notch ingredients" from local farms embellish the "superb"
thin-crust pizzas that make chef-owner Dan Richer's Maplewood BYO
"deservedly popular"; the "bustling", "cramped quarters" can cause
"long waits" when the "crowds come out", but the servers "aim to
please" and most maintain the "well-priced" eats "make up for it."

Arugula *Italian*

23 | 20 | 21 | $34

Sewell | 373 Egg Harbor Rd. (bet. Bentley Dr. & County Rd. 651) |
856-589-0475 | www.arugularestaurant.net

"Fresh, seasonal" ingredients and homemade pastas drive the midpriced menu at this "fine" Sewell Italian BYO, where modern twists
on classic dishes produce "appetizing" results; servers are "accommodating", and though reservations can be "hard to get", fans say
it's "worth it."

Assaggini di Roma *Italian*

▽ 24 | 15 | 21 | $43

Newark | 134 Clifford St. (bet. Adams & Van Buren Sts.) | 973-466-3344

A "deceiving" storefront facade hides this Italian "charmer" in
Newark's Ironbound district, where "old-world" cuisine is highlighted
by "great" homemade sausages; service is "attentive", and if the space
isn't much to shout about, music on weekends keeps things "lively."

A Taste of Mexico *Mexican*

20 | 17 | 20 | $22

Princeton | 180 Nassau St. (bet. Moore St. & Vandeventer Ave.) |
609-924-0500
Princeton | Princeton Shopping Ctr. | 301 N. Harrison St.
(bet. Clearview Ave. & Terhune Rd.) | 609-252-1575

This "low-key" BYO Mexican duo gives Princetonians two options for
"simple", "tasty" "south-of-the-border" grub – a "hole-in-the-wall"
"tucked away" in a shopping center and a "small" but "great find" on
Nassau Street, both with warm-weather outdoor seating; a "friendly
staff" lends a "family feel", and low tabs complete the picture.

A Tavola Ⓜ *Italian*

21 | 17 | 20 | $32

Old Bridge | Deep Run Shopping Ctr. | 3314 Rte. 9 S. (Ferry Rd.) |
732-607-1120

Offering "dependable" Italian eats and a "family-atmosphere", this
"small" BYO in an Old Bridge strip mall is "great for a casual night
out"; though critics say there's "not much atmosphere", the service
is "friendly" and "prices are ok" – in sum, a "good local place."

Athenian Garden Ⓜ *Greek*

22 | 16 | 21 | $27

Galloway Township | 619 S. New York Rd. (Holly Brook Rd.) |
609-748-1818 | www.athenian-garden.com

"You get the feeling they're cooking just for you" at this "out-of-
the-way" Galloway Greek serving "well-prepared" "standard"
fare, including "plenty of fish", kebabs and vegetarian options;
"reasonable prices" and BYO add appeal for "family dinners" "without breaking the bank."

	FOOD	DECOR	SERVICE	COST

Atlantic Grill *Seafood* | 21 | 21 | 21 | $51 |

Atlantic City | Caesars Atlantic City Hotel & Casino | 2100 Pacific Ave.
(Arkansas Ave.) | 609-348-4411 | www.caesarsac.com
"Beautiful" boardwalk views are the daily catch at this big, "basic"
seafooder in Caesars Atlantic City, an outpost of a NYC chainlet;
while portions are "plentiful" and service "friendly", some find it
"overpriced" and say it's the "drinks" and the "sunset" that really
reel them in.

A Toute Heure ⬛Ⓜ *American* | 26 | 21 | 25 | $51 |

Cranford | 232 Centennial Ave. (Elm St.) | 908-276-6600 |
www.atouteheure.com
Offering "quintessential farm-to-table" dining in Cranford, this
"charming", "off-the-beaten-path" American (with sprinkles of Euro
flair) puts "food center stage" with an "inspired" seasonal menu and
"fantastic preparations" of "fresh, exciting" dishes; "top-notch service" and a BYO policy make "steep prices a little easier to swallow",
and while the "small dining room" gets "noisy and crowded" and "reservations are hard to get", for most, "it's easy to understand why."

Augustino's ⬛⊄ *Italian* | 24 | 19 | 22 | $49 |

Hoboken | 1104 Washington St. (bet. 11th & 12th Sts.) | 201-420-0104
"Consider yourself lucky to snag a table" at this "super-tiny" Hoboken
Italian, whose "delicious" "homestyle" fare and "rustic", "romantic"
vibe mean reservations are needed "well in advance"; sure, it can be
"cramped" and "loud", plus cash only, but the staff adds "spicy com-
mentary" to the meal, which makes many feel like "one of the family."

Avanti ⬛Ⓜ *Italian* | 21 | 20 | 22 | $38 |

Pennington | 23 W. Delaware Ave. (bet. Green & Main Sts.) |
609-737-7174 | www.avantipennington.com
"Comforting" Sicilian fare attracts a "loyal following" to this Italian
BYO in a "small", "charming" space in Downtown Pennington; "personable" service and moderate prices contribute to its reputation as
a "neighborhood gem."

Avenue *French* | 22 | 25 | 21 | $60 |

Long Branch | Pier Vill. | 23 Ocean Ave. (bet. Centennial Dr. &
Melrose Terr.) | 732-759-2900 | www.leclubavenue.com
"Can't-be-beat" views and a "spectacular setting" "right on the
beach" await the "dress-to-impress" crowd at this "trendy", "upscale" French brasserie in Long Branch's Pier Village touted for its
"fabulous food and cocktails"; "efficient, but aloof service" and
"costly" tabs are drawbacks, but considering it's one of the "most
happening" spots on the pier, most agree "you get what you pay for."

Avenue Bistro Pub *Eclectic* | 21 | 20 | 21 | $41 |

Verona | 558 Bloomfield Ave. (bet. Gould St. & Park Pl.) |
973-239-7444 | www.avenuebistropub.com
Chopped champion Michael Dilonno brings "consistently good"
bistro fare to this "interesting" Verona Eclectic, where an expansive
menu means you "can make a meal of the appetizers" alone; while

some find it a little "expensive", "good attitudes" prevail among the staff, and with outdoor seating next to a fire pit, fans say it's an "easy place to fall into."

Axelsson's Blue Claw *Seafood*

	23	24	21	$47

Cape May | 991 Ocean Dr. (Rte. 109) | 609-884-5878 |
www.blueclawrestaurant.com

Tucked in an "out-of-the-way" nook of Cape May, this midpriced seafooder draws fans with its "consistently" pleasing fare, "attentive" service and "comfortable" setting with a "great view of the back bays"; there's also a "cozy", "nautical-themed" bar for a predinner drink or half-price raw bar eats at happy hour.

Axia Taverna *Greek*

	23	22	22	$52

Tenafly | 18 Piermont Rd. (bet. Central Ave. & Riveredge Rd.) |
201-569-5999 | www.axiataverna.com

A "slightly modern twist" distinguishes the "upscale" Greek menu at this Tenafly "neighborhood find", where "fresh" fish is a "signature staple"; an "impressive" wine selection is displayed inside a glass case dividing the "clean, classy" space, which opens onto a "lovely" enclosed terrace, and a "welcoming" staff provides "typically" Mediterranean "hospitality."

Azúcar Ⓜ *Cuban*

	22	20	20	$37

Jersey City | 495 Washington Blvd. (bet. Newport Pkwy. & 6th St.) |
201-222-0090 | www.azucarcubancuisine.com

"Tasty", "filling" Cuban fare pairs well with "great" mojitos at this "hip" Jersey City hot spot, where both the "interesting" eats and the nightlife get a "little spicy"; the "lively" after-work bar scene becomes salsa-centric on weekends, and smokers deem the upstairs cigar lounge a "definite plus"; P.S. don't miss the sandwich made famous on *Throwdown! With Bobby Flay.*

Azure by Allegretti Ⓜ *Seafood*

	23	25	23	$70

Atlantic City | REVEL | 500 Boardwalk (bet. Metropolitan &
New Jersey Aves.) | 609-225-9870 | www.revelresorts.com

Chef Alain Allegretti "scores a lot of points" with his "consistently good preparations" of "fresh, light", Mediterranean-inspired fare at this "pricey" seafooder inside Atlantic City's Revel Resort; an "extensive" wine list, "on-point" service and "views of the ocean" from the "beautiful" dining room add to its appeal and make it "great for a date night."

Bacari Grill *Italian*

	21	21	21	$46

Washington Township | 800 Ridgewood Rd. (Pascack Rd.) |
201-358-6330 | www.bacarigrill.com

Hidden inside a bungalow in residential Washington Township, this "upscale" Italian offers an "imaginative" menu ("varied, tasty" antipasti) with "sometimes great" results; a "lovely", "modern but warm" setting suits "ladies-who-lunch", "first dates" and private parties, especially considering "innovative" cocktails and a "solid" Napa-centric wine list.

		FOOD	DECOR	SERVICE	COST

The Backyard ⊠Ⓜ *American*
24 | 23 | 23 | $43

Stone Harbor | 220 81st St. (2nd Ave.) | 609-368-2627 |
www.thebackyardrestaurant.com

With its "twinkling lights" and "California trellis", fans say the back-yard of this seasonal Stone Harbor American is "about as pretty a setting as you can come by" to enjoy "tasty" "modern" cuisine on a "nice summer evening"; the "small house" hosts indoor meals too, while service is "always good" and BYO "helps keep the tab down."

Bahrs Landing *Seafood*
19 | 18 | 20 | $39

Highlands | 2 Bay Ave. (Highland Ave.) | 732-872-1245 |
www.bahrslanding.com

Fresh fish "right off the boats" is the draw at this "typical" Shore seafood "joint", which has been "cranking out" "reliable" "dock 'n' dine" meals since 1917; while some find the "old-time menu" to be "uneven" and the "nautical" decor "dated", loyalists insist it's "a good value", even if you're mostly "paying for the view."

Baia *Italian*
19 | 21 | 20 | $39

Somers Point | 998 Bay Ave. (Goll Ave.) | 609-926-9611 |
www.baiarestaurant.com

A "delightful" view of Egg Harbor Bay lures summer diners to this Somers Point Italian, where the seafood-focused fare is overshadowed somewhat by the "exceptional" multilevel decks; "friendly bartenders", DJs and live reggae on Sundays keep things upbeat.

Bamboo Leaf Ⓜ *Thai/Vietnamese*
20 | 18 | 20 | $25

Bradley Beach | 724 Main St. (McCabe Ave.) | 732-774-1661
Howell | Howell Ctr. | 2450 Rte. 9 S. (bet. Farms Rd. & White St.) |
732-761-3939

"You can bring that favorite Riesling" to pair with "fresh, tasty" Thai-Vietnamese plates at these BYOs in Bradley Beach and Howell; if the bamboo decor doesn't impress many, "quick" service and "fair" prices bring in regulars "time and again."

Bangkok Garden *Thai*
23 | 16 | 20 | $28

Hackensack | 261 Main St. (bet. Camden & Salem Sts.) |
201-487-2620 | www.bangkokgarden-nj.com

You might "feel like bringing your passport" to this "authentic" Thai BYO in Hackensack where "spicy" curries, seafood and veggie-friendly dishes "can really sparkle"; though some lament "dated" decor, "charming" servers and "reasonable" prices keep fans coming back.

Bar Cara Ⓜ *Italian*
21 | 19 | 20 | $39

Bloomfield | 1099 Broad St. (bet. Watchung Ave. & Winding Ln.) |
973-893-3681 | www.bar-cara.com

"Higher-end" Italian cuisine "with a casual flair" lands at this Bloomfield spot via chef Ryan DePersio (of Fascino in Montclair), whose "interesting", "varied" menu includes thin-crust pizzas, pastas and other rustic eats; though it can seem a little "pricey", fans say "great" cocktails and an "energetic", "contemporary" vibe make it "well worth a visit."

	FOOD	DECOR	SERVICE	COST

Bareli's ☒ *Italian*
Secaucus | 219 Rte. 3 E. (bet. Plaza Ct. & Roosevelt Ave.) |
201-865-2766 | www.barelisrestaurant.com

23 | 22 | 23 | $59

A "classic white-tablecloth" Italian, this Secaucus "favorite" offers a "good" "old-school" menu and an "excellent" wine list suited to "business lunches"; accordingly, it's "expensive", but with "great" service from "tuxedoed waiters", "comfortable" armchairs and live piano music on weekends, many find it a "special place."

Barnacle Bill's ● *Burgers*
Rumson | 1 First St. (River Rd.) | 732-747-8396 |
www.barnaclebillsrumson.com

20 | 18 | 19 | $28

Despite a sizable seafood menu, it's the "huge", "excellent" burgers that many crave at this "casual" Rumson "sea shanty", though "heaven" can also be found in a "bucket of steamers and a beer"; many "miss the peanut" shells once strewn across the floor, but the "great riverside" vibe keeps 'em coming back, though "don't go hungry" as you're all but guaranteed a "long wait."

Barone's Tuscan Grille *Italian*
Moorestown | 280 Young Ave. (Centerton Rd.) | 856-234-7900

23 | 20 | 21 | $29

Villa Barone *Italian*
Collingswood | 753 Haddon Ave. (bet. Frazer & Washington Aves.) |
856-858-2999 | www.villabaronesite.com

"Huge" portions of "tasty", "affordable" Italian fare attract locals to these "casual" BYOs, serving thin-crust pizza, pasta and other standards; be prepared for "madhouse" weekend crowds, but a "warm" vibe and "friendly" service ensure their standing as "reliable favorites."

Basilico *Italian*
Millburn | 324 Millburn Ave. (bet. Main St. & Whittingham Terr.) |
973-379-7020 | www.basilicomillburn.com

23 | 21 | 22 | $47

"Sophisticated" Italian fare prepared with "just the right amount of flair" is "consistently good" at this "neighborhood find" in Downtown Millburn, popular with those attending the nearby Paper Mill Playhouse; the staff is "knowledgeable", and although some find it "noisy", others say the "lively", "lovely" atmosphere helps create a "NY dining experience" without the drive.

Basil T's *Italian*
Red Bank | 183 Riverside Ave. (Bodman Pl.) | 732-842-5990 |
www.basilt.com

21 | 20 | 21 | $39

Red Bank's "ever popular" brewpub is "full of happy customers" thanks to its "homey environment", plus a "lively bar scene", along with Italian "comfort food" and "excellent" homemade beers; "pleasant" service adds appeal, but many maintain it's "a bit overpriced."

NEW Bat Barry's *American*
Westwood | 170 Center Ave. (bet. Bergen St. & Westwood Ave.) |
201-666-2200 | www.batbarrys.com

– | – | – | M

A self-described seasonal bistro and tavern, this midpriced Westwood New American slings crowd-pleasing classics like French onion soup,

		FOOD	DECOR	SERVICE	COST

mussels, hanger steak and housemade desserts plus cocktails and a wine program that includes a selection of 20 bottles priced at $20; cafe chairs, exposed-brick walls and hardwood floors complete the cozy picture.

Baumgart's Café *American/Asian*　 18 | 16 | 18 | $26

Edgewater | City Pl. | 59 The Promenade (River Rd.) | 201-313-3889
Englewood | 45 E. Palisade Ave. (bet. Dean & Engle Sts.) | 201-569-6267
Livingston | Livingston Town Ctr. | 4175 Town Center Way
(Mt. Pleasant Ave.) | 973-422-0955
Ridgewood | 158 Franklin Ave. (bet. Cottage Pl. & Walnut St.) |
201-612-5688
www.baumgartscafe.com

"When you don't know what you want", fans tout these "cheap", "funky" "luncheonettes", where "Chinese diner" meets "Jewish deli" on the "large" menu of Pan-Asian and American fare; though many appreciate the "super-fast" staff, some are cool to "rushed" service, while others grouse about the "airport" noise levels and "overly bright lighting", but while it may be "nothing exceptional" to critics, "great" "homemade" ice cream, "dependability" and "reasonable" prices always "attract a local crowd."

Bazzarelli *Italian*　 20 | 15 | 18 | $33

Moonachie | 117 Moonachie Rd. (Joseph St.) | 201-641-4010 |
www.bazzarellirestaurant.com

A "good old standby", especially before Meadowlands events, this Moonachie Italian offers "consistent" "homestyle" dishes, with an emphasis on pizza and "red-sauce" pastas; though some report waiters can get "overwhelmed" (and diners too) in the "crowded, noisy" space, with such "affordable prices", a loyal "local" following feels it "never disappoints"; P.S. the Decor score may not reflect a post-Sandy restoration.

Belford Bistro *American*　 26 | 19 | 24 | $46

Belford | 870 Main St. (Lenison Ave.) | 732-495-8151 |
www.belfordbistro.com

At their "cozy" Belford "gem", chefs Kurt Bomberger and Crista Trovato have fans swooning over "creative", "excellent" American fare where the "knowledgeable staff seems to read minds"; "reservations are a must", for the "small" strip-mall space is usually "crowded", and while it's "a little pricey", "BYO makes it a relative bargain."

Bell & Whistle 🆇🆋 *American/Southern*　 20 | 22 | 20 | $38

Hopewell | 9 E. Broad St. (Greenwood Ave.) | 609-466-7800 |
www.bell-whistle.com

Part "casual diner", part "grown-up gourmet", this midpriced Hopewell American (named for a nearby church and firehouse) offers "fresh, contemporary" takes on gumbo and other Southern comforts; though some feel the chefs are still "working on the rhythm", most "love" the "gorgeous" stone-walled interior (and outdoor patio when the room is too "loud"), and while "some local wines are available", you can also BYO.

	FOOD	DECOR	SERVICE	COST

NEW Bellissimo's Ⓜ *Italian* — | — | — | E

Little Falls | 1 Newark Pompton Tpke. (Muller Pl.) | 973-785-4225 |
www.bellissimos-nj.com

After selling the space in 2007, the original owner is back at the
helm of this revived Little Falls Italian boasting an extensive menu
that also includes 25 daily specials; the tuxedoed staff and large,
luxe digs – think mahogany ceiling, tufted leather banquettes, glass
wine walls and a gas fireplace – suit the somewhat upscale tabs.

Bell's Mansion *American* — 20 | 20 | 19 | $33

Stanhope | 11 Main St. (bet. High St. & Rte. 183) | 973-426-9977 |
www.bellsmansion.com

Housed in a "historic" 19th-century mansion in Stanhope, this
"homey" midpriced American offers "creative", Polish-inflected fare
along with an extensive martini list; while critics decry "inconsistent"
fare and "so-so" decor and service, others enjoy a "cool breeze"
and "great view" from the patio while keeping an eye out for the
reputed resident "ghosts."

Belmont Tavern ⊅ *Italian* — 22 | 13 | 18 | $42
(aka Stretches)

Belleville | 12 Bloomfield Ave. (bet. Belmont Ave. & Heckel St.) |
973-759-9609

Don't let the "gritty" '60s "tavern" decor fool you – this "old-school",
"truly local" Belleville Italian serves up "great, traditional" dishes,
including chicken savoy worth "pushing your mama out of the way"
for; some declare the servers the "crankiest anywhere" and the wine
selection is "red or white", but many feel this "visit to another time"
is well "worth the trip."

Benihana *Japanese* — 20 | 20 | 21 | $35

Short Hills | 840 Morris Tpke. (South Terr.) | 973-467-9550
Edison | 60 Parsonage Rd. (bet. Mason St. & Oakwood Ave.) |
732-744-0660
Pennsauken | 5255 Marlton Pike (McClellan Ave.) |
856-665-6320
www.benihana.com

"Noisy" "fun" is served tableside at these "family-friendly" Japanese,
where "entertaining" chefs showcase "flashy" "knife skills" in the
service of "tasty" teppanyaki meats and seafood; sure, some find it
a little "silly", and the "shared table" concept "tired", but fans say
"nothing beats dinner and a show at these prices", especially for
"big groups" and "birthday parties."

Benito's Trattoria Ⓜ *Italian* — 23 | 20 | 22 | $39

Chester | 44 Main St. (bet. Perry & Warren Sts.) | 908-879-1887 |
www.benitostrattoria.com

"Tucked away" on a quaint street in Chester, this "good all-around"
Italian offers "traditional" Northern fare and "friendly" service; if
some find the space "noisy" at times, others say it's "great" for a
"date", especially with "a stroll" in the "cute" town afterwards, and
BYO helps "keep the tab low."

	FOOD	DECOR	SERVICE	COST

Benny Tudino's ●🍴 *Pizza* | 20 | 13 | 16 | $12 |

Hoboken | 622 Washington St. (bet. 6th & 7th Sts.) | 201-792-4132
"Gargantuan" slices of "delicious" pizza "requiring two plates" each
are the hallmark of this Hoboken "mainstay"; few would deny "zero
atmosphere" and "pretty rude" service, but at such "good prices",
it's still a "go-to", and besides, you can always "take the big pieces
home"; P.S. cash only.

The Bent Spoon *Ice Cream* | 27 | 18 | 22 | $8 |

Princeton | 35 Palmer Sq. W. (Hulfish St.) | 609-924-2368 |
www.thebentspoon.net
There's a "line out the door" "for good reason" at this Princeton ice
creamery offering "wildly imaginative" frozen treats created from
the "highest quality" local and organic ingredients (though some
think it's "all about the cupcakes"); seating is "limited" and some
gripe about "small portions" that "cost an arm and a leg", relatively
speaking, but most agree "it's worth a visit."

Bernards Inn *American* | 25 | 25 | 25 | $67 |

Bernardsville | The Bernards Inn | 27 Mine Brook Rd. (Quimby Ln.) |
908-766-0002 | www.bernardsinn.com
Set in a "charming" Bernardsville inn, this "elegant" New American
exudes "old-money" "sophistication" – from the "excellent" seasonal
menu to the "extensive" wine list to the "professional" service; for
those who find the dining room "stuffy" (or strictly for "special occasions"), the library bar offers an "informal" alternative, with a lighter
menu and prices that will still allow you to "send your kid to college."

Berta's Chateau *Italian* | 22 | 17 | 21 | $48 |

Wanaque | 7 Grove St. (Prospect St.) | 973-835-0992 |
www.bertaschateau.com
In business "forever" (since 1927, in fact), this Wanaque Italian "in
the middle of nowhere" is still "an old favorite" due to its "reliable"
"traditional" fare and "superb" Barolo-heavy wine list; if the "lovely
old mansion" feels a bit "outdated" to some, waiters who "know everyone" create a "family atmosphere" that keeps fans coming back.

Beyti Kebab *Turkish* | 22 | 14 | 19 | $28 |

Union City | 4105 Park Ave. (bet. 41st & 42nd Sts.) | 201-865-6281 |
www.beytigrill.com
"Tender, tasty" kebabs headline the "authentic" menu at this
"good-value" Union City Turkish that serves "simple", "fresh"
"Middle Eastern comfort food"; if there's little to love about the
"canteen" decor and occasional sound of a "buzz saw" from the on-
site butcher shop, live music and belly dancers provide a welcome
"treat" on Saturday nights.

Biagio's ● *Italian* | 20 | 19 | 19 | $35 |

Paramus | 299 Paramus Rd. (Dunkerhook Rd.) | 201-652-0201 |
www.biagios.com
"Good, hearty" standards attract a "local" crowd to this Paramus
Italian, where "attractive", if "outdated", decor reflects its dual

function as a banquet hall; although some find service "slow", a "friendly" vibe prevails, and its "reasonable value" is an added draw.

Bibi'z Restaurant & Lounge *Eclectic*   20 | 19 | 18 | $41

Westwood | 284 Center Ave. (bet. Irvington St. & Westwood Ave.) | 201-722-8600 | www.bibizlounge.com

The "fun" menu at this Westwood Eclectic runs the gamut from pasta to tacos to Korean sandwiches with "interesting", sometimes "very good", results, with an emphasis on grass-fed meats, sustainable seafood and organic dairy products; some appreciate the "easy going" vibe, even if it can mean "slow" service, but with "comfortable" seats and "talented" bartenders, no one's in much of a rush.

Biddy O'Malley's ● *American/Pub Food*   20 | 19 | 20 | $29

Northvale | 191 Paris Ave. (bet. Industrial Pkwy. & Walnut St.) | 201-564-7893 | www.biddyomalleys.com

"You won't leave hungry" from this "remote" Northvale pub, where "well-prepared" American bar grub can be an "enjoyable" accompaniment to "good libations" (but "stick to burgers" and fish 'n' chips for best results, fans say); the basic digs are "pleasant" enough – "if you can only find them."

Big Ed's BBQ *BBQ*   19 | 15 | 19 | $26

Matawan | 305 Rte. 34 (bet. Dock Rd. & Ellen Heath Dr.) | 732-583-2626 | www.bigedsbbq.com

"Beer and ribs, what more can you say?" about this Matawan "joint" that's known for its "bargain" all-you-can-eat plates of "more-than-passable" BBQ; service gets mixed reviews, but most agree the "pseudo-barn" quarters are "fun."

Big Fish
Seafood Bistro *Seafood*   20 | 19 | 19 | $36

Princeton | MarketFair | 3535 U.S. Rte. 1 (bet. Carnegie Center Blvd. & Farber Rd.) | 609-919-1179 | www.muer.com

True to its name, this Princeton mall seafooder offers an "expansive" midpriced menu of "good simple" fish in "huge portions"; the "funky", aquatic setting might get "too loud for conversation" and service can be "hit-or-miss", but sometimes the day's best catch is a "reasonably priced" drink during happy hour at the "jumping" bar.

Biggie's Clam Bar *American/Seafood*   20 | 17 | 19 | $28

Carlstadt | 430 Rte. 17 S. (bet. Broad St. & Division Ave.) | 201-933-4000 ●

Hoboken | 318 Madison St. (bet. 3rd & 4th Sts.) | 201-656-2161

Hoboken | 42 Newark St. (bet. Hudson & River Sts.) | 201-710-5520 ●

www.biggiesclambar.com

"Lawyers, truck drivers", "Hoboken's finest" and others crowd into these "casual", "old-school" clam/sports bars for seafood, burgers and "Italian-inspired" "pub food"; the setting is "nothing fancy" and can get "a bit noisy", especially during games, but with something "for everyone", and "great prices" to boot, many find them a "must-go"; P.S. the Carlstadt outpost attracts a Meadowlands fan base.

	FOOD	DECOR	SERVICE	COST

Big John's *Cheesesteaks* | 23 | 17 | 18 | $15 |

West Berlin | 185 Rte. 73 N. (bet. Fairview & Prospect Aves.) |
856-424-1186 | www.bigjohns.com

"Look past the decor and service" and head straight for the cheese-steak (which some tout as the "best outside of Philly") at this no-frills West Berlin sandwich shop; "reasonable" prices further appeal, and, hey, you "can't beat" the free pickle bar.

Bin 14 *Italian* | 23 | 23 | 21 | $42 |

Hoboken | 1314 Washington St. (bet. 13th & 14th Sts.) |
201-963-9463 | www.bin14.com

For those willing to "open their minds and palates", this "intimate" Hoboken wine bar can offer some culinary "fun" in the form of "inventive" Italian small plates paired with an "intriguing" selection of vinos; the "cozy" brick-walled room, which opens onto a "peaceful" backyard, makes for a "great date night" or "small group" gathering, and the only hitch is that tapas-driven "tabs can quickly soar."

Bistro at Cherry Hill *American* | 23 | 18 | 19 | $21 |

Cherry Hill | Cherry Hill Mall | 2000 Rte. 38 (Haddonfield Rd.) |
856-662-8621

Shoppers seeking "something different for lunch" retreat to this Cherry Hill Mall "oasis" occupying the former Woolworth's lunch counter, where "great" soups, sandwiches and other American bistro eats are whipped up in an open kitchen; if there's "not much atmosphere", that's to be expected for its "random" locale, and higher-than-food-court prices seem "reasonable" for such a "nice pit stop."

Bistro at Red Bank *Eclectic* | 21 | 19 | 21 | $38 |

Red Bank | 14 Broad St. (bet. Front & White Sts.) | 732-530-5553 |
www.thebistroatredbank.com

Catering to "lots of different tastes", this midpriced Red Bank Eclectic boasts a "broad", "interesting" menu spanning sushi, pizza, pasta and more, plus a NJ-based wine list (though BYO is also welcome); "accommodating" service enhances the "casual", exposed-brick setting, and if it can get "super-crowded" (and "a bit loud"), sidewalk seating in the warmer months promises "good people-watching."

Bistro di Marino Ⓜ *Italian* | 25 | 21 | 23 | $32 |

Collingswood | 492 Haddon Ave. (bet. Crestmont Terr. & Garfield Ave.) |
856-858-1700 | www.bistrodimarino.com

A Collingswood "favorite", this "go-to" bistro from chef Jimmy Marino offers "excellent" Italian fare, including a substantial menu of home-made gnocchi, served by a "friendly" staff; a "terrific" backyard garden lends a "European feel", with live jazz weekly, and BYO helps keep tabs "reasonable."

Bistro 55 ◐ *American* | 19 | 18 | 18 | $42 |

Rochelle Park | 55 Rte. 17 S. (bet. Becker & Grove Aves.) |
201-845-3737 | www.bistro-55.com

The "upbeat" menu at this Rochelle Park American bistro includes "some nice interpretations of pub favorites", but for some, the selection of "hard-to-find" craft beers is the main draw; a few cite "ordinary" dark-wood decor and sometimes "slow" service, but fans don't seem to mind.

Bistro Olé Ⓜ Portuguese/Spanish — 22 | 20 | 21 | $41

Asbury Park | 230 Main St. (Mattison Ave.) | 732-897-0048 | www.bistroole.com

The "unpretentious, satisfying" Portuguese-Spanish fare is "perfect for a date night" at this upscale, "energetic" Asbury Park eatery where the "ebullient owner" might "come over to chat", and there's "great people-watching" at the outdoor tables; BYO is a "big advantage for keeping the price down" (for the "must-have" sangria, "add your wine" to a "starter pitcher of fruits"), but since there's a "no-reservations" policy, "be prepared to wait."

Blackbird Dining Establishment Ⓜ French/Italian — ▽ 24 | 22 | 23 | $43

Collingswood | 714 Haddon Ave. (bet. Collings & Irvin Aves.) | 856-854-3444 | www.blackbirdnj.com

A "contemporary" French-Italian menu that incorporates Asian influences might be "adventurous for South Jersey", but diners deem Alex Capasso's Collingswood BYO an "excellent" player on the suburban Philly scene; with its "slightly hip", "modern" space and "polished" service, it's got a "bit of attitude" that seems to be working.

Black Duck on Sunset Eclectic — 26 | 21 | 24 | $46

West Cape May | 1 Sunset Blvd. (B'way) | 609-898-0100 | www.blackduckonsunset.com

Because it's "off the beaten path" in a "quaint old house", this West Cape May Eclectic is something of a "sleeper", but fans swoon over its "excellent", "creative" seafood-focused menu, with shout-outs for the "perfect" namesake duck; servers "aim to please", and with BYO and an early-bird prix fixe menu, it's also a "good value."

Black-Eyed Susans Café Ⓜ⇗ American — 24 | 19 | 22 | $49

Harvey Cedars | 7801 Long Beach Blvd. (78th St.) | 609-494-4990 | www.blackeyedsusanscafe.com

A "refreshing change for LBI", this BYO "gem" in Harvey Cedars from husband-and-wife team Christopher Sanchez and Ashley Pellagrino offers "expertly prepared", "local" American fare that's "interesting but not silly", served by a "friendly" staff in an "inviting", "quintessential beach" setting; it's cash-only and, some grouse, "hard on the wallet", but most "come away smiling" from this "homey, sweet place."

Black Forest Inn Continental/German — 24 | 22 | 22 | $37

Stanhope | 249 Rte. 206 N. (bet. Brookwood Rd. & Stonegate Ln.) | 973-347-3344 | www.blackforestinn.com

A taste of "old world Germany" can be found at this midpriced Stanhope Continental, where sauerbraten and schnitzel are "fit for a king" – albeit one who may have "cholesterol" issues; the "cozy" dark-wood "château" setting invokes "a step back in time" (specifically, "1970"), and "great" service from dirndl-clad waitresses rounds out the "authentic" journey.

	FOOD	DECOR	SERVICE	COST

Black Horse Diner ❷ *Diner*
Mount Ephraim | 152 N. Black Horse Pike (George St.) |
856-742-8989 | www.blackhorsediner.com

20 | 18 | 20 | $17

Those who "love diner food" are partial to this "comfortable" Mount Ephraim outpost for "good" grub "served hot" and "friendly", "swift" service; while some say it's "nothing exciting", the prices are "reasonable", and its 24/7 timetable means pancakes 'round the clock.

Black Horse Tavern Ⓜ *American*
Mendham | 1 W. Main St. (Mountain Ave.) | 973-543-7300 |
www.blackhorsenj.com

19 | 19 | 19 | $37

An "old standby" in "sleepy" Mendham, this 18th-century inn still "packs them in" for "consistent" American "comfort food" in a "classy" "Colonial" setting; while the offerings can seem "expensive" and service "uneven" to some, there's no denying the "quaint, country" surrounds afford a "pleasant respite", especially for the "after-church", "polo-collared" crowd; P.S. the adjacent pub can be a "fun", more casual option.

Black Trumpet *American*
Spring Lake | Grand Victorian Hotel | 1505 Ocean Ave. (bet. Madison & Newark Aves.) | 732-449-4700 | www.theblacktrumpet.com

22 | 21 | 21 | $53

In a "lovely setting" overlooking the ocean at the Grand Victorian Hotel in Spring Lake, this "charming" New American plates "elegant fare" and delivers it with "efficient" service; whether you're in the "intimate" interior or you "score a table on the porch", be sure to "bring the credit card."

Black Whale *Seafood*
Beach Haven | 100 N. Pennsylvania Ave. (bet. Centre St. & Dock Rd.) |
609-492-0025

22 | 19 | 21 | $32

"Fresh seafood is the emphasis" at this "friendly", moderately priced Beach Haven piscatorium; the "small bar area can be crowded" and "noisy", but since the "drinks are always flowing", there's usually a "festive crowd to hang out with."

Bloomfield Steak & Seafood House Ⓜ *Seafood/Steak*
Bloomfield | 409 Franklin St. (bet. Fremont & Montgomery Sts.) |
973-680-4500

21 | 18 | 22 | $38

A onetime rest stop for George Washington, this Bloomfield steakhouse occupies a 17th-century home, where "tasty" filets and seafood are its modern-day appeal; even if some find the interior "dark and cramped", diners appreciate an "aim-to-please" attitude among the staff, and in nice weather the outdoor patio makes a "great setting" to watch for Redcoats.

Blu Ⓜ *American*
Montclair | 554 Bloomfield Ave. (bet. Park St. & Valley Rd.) |
973-509-2202 | www.restaurantblu.com

24 | 18 | 21 | $48

It's "always a culinary experience" for fans of this "trendy" Montclair New American BYO, where a "constantly changing", "creative" menu encourages small-plate sampling; while critics say the "meager" decor "lacks warmth" (but sadly not "noise"), and service can trend "haughty", fans feel the "innovative" eats – even if "rather expensive" – "make up for it."

Blue Bottle Cafe 🗷 Ⓜ American

FOOD	DECOR	SERVICE	COST
26	20	23	$46

Hopewell | 101 E. Broad St. (Elm St.) | 609-333-1710 |
www.thebluebottlecafe.com

A "real gem" in the Princeton area, this Hopewell BYO draws "serious foodies" with its "excellent" New American fare served with "artistic" flair – plus "standout" desserts; it's "pricey but worth it", with "polished, unpretentious" service, and if it looks a bit like a "double-wide trailer" on the outside (and a "country cafe" within), that's hardly an issue when the food is such a "star"; P.S. reservations are a "must."

Blue Claw Crab Eatery Seafood

FOOD	DECOR	SERVICE	COST
24	16	20	$36

Burlington | 4494 Burlington Pike (bet. Campus Dr. & Salem Rd.) |
609-387-3700 | www.crabeatery.com

Its "bare-bones" decor might be a "total turnoff" to some, but "crab lovers" insist this Burlington seafood "shack" is the "real deal", with "perfectly cooked and seasoned" fish at "reasonable" rates (especially with BYO); just make sure to "get there early" because "waiting is de rigueur."

Blue Danube Ⓜ E European

FOOD	DECOR	SERVICE	COST
▽ 23	19	20	$33

Trenton | 538 Adeline St. (Elm St.) | 609-393-6133 |
www.bluedanuberestaurant.net

Pierogiphiles get their "Hungarian fix" (Polish, Romanian and German too) at this "cozy" Trenton hideaway, where stuffed cabbage and other "hearty" "country food" sure does "bring back memories"; although few are wowed by the "old-world" decor, the "personable" staff makes it a "family affair", and "good prices" keep the "many regulars" coming back.

🆕 Blue Fig Café Mediterranean

FOOD	DECOR	SERVICE	COST
-	-	-	M

Moorestown | 200 Young Ave. (bet. Centerton Rd. & E. Main St.) |
856-638-5186 | www.bluefigcafe.net

For a taste of the Mediterranean in Moorestown, this reasonably priced BYO storefront serves up classic favorites like assorted meze and kebabs, falafel, shawarma and housemade baklava plus a fresh juice bar; seating options include an outdoor patio while a color block wall anchors the modern but casual interior sporting framed photos of Beirut and artfully displayed Middle Eastern knickknacks.

Blue Fish Grill Ⓜ Seafood

FOOD	DECOR	SERVICE	COST
23	17	20	$25

Flemington | 50 Mine St. (Stangl Rd.) | 908-237-4528 |
www.thebluefishgrill.com

Fish tacos are a fan "favorite" at this "casual" "family" seafooder in Flemington, where "quality" ocean fare is served up at "unbelievably reasonable" prices (aided by BYO); there's an outdoor patio for warm-weather dines, and few seem to mind that there's "no atmosphere" inside, judging by "ridiculous waits."

Blue Morel *American* | 24 | 22 | 23 | $62 |
(fka Copeland)
Morristown | The Westin Governor Morris | 2 Whippany Rd.
(Lindsley Dr.) | 973-451-2619 | www.bluemorel.com
Set inside Morristown's Westin Governor Morris, this "high-end"
"modern" American might "save you a trip to NYC" with its "perfectly
prepared" dishes and "impressive" raw seafood choices; there's also
a "vibrant bar scene" fueled by "inventive cocktails", and "gracious"
service, but "be warned" – the experience "does not come cheap."

Blue Pig Tavern *American* | 21 | 21 | 20 | $40 |
Cape May | Congress Hall Hotel | 251 Beach Ave. (bet. Congress &
Perry Sts.) | 609-884-8421 | www.congresshall.com
"Enjoy the breeze" on the "cute" patio during the summertime, or
cozy up to the "romantic fireplace" in the colder months at this
"casual" American at Cape May's circa-1816 Congress Hall Hotel,
serving "generous" portions of pub fare featuring locally sourced
ingredients from the owners' nearby farm; if some find the service
merely "acceptable", insiders say prices are "reasonable" for an area
where "it can be hard to find a midpriced meal."

Blue Point Grill *Seafood* | 25 | 19 | 22 | $43 |
Princeton | 258 Nassau St. (Pine St.) | 609-921-1211 |
www.bluepointgrill.com
"Ultra fresh" seafood that's "simply prepared" and "cooked to perfection" draws crowds to this midpriced Princeton BYO, where the
day's catch comes from the owner's market next door; "friendly"
service is another plus, but the downside is that it's "loud, loud,
loud", so sidewalk seating "is best" when available, and regulars
suggest making reservations "to avoid those long waits."

Blue Rooster Bakery & Cafe Ⓜ *American* | 22 | 21 | 20 | $25 |
Cranbury | 17 N. Main St. (Scott Ave.) | 609-235-7539 |
www.blueroosterbakery.com
"Freshly baked" bread, scones and other "delicious" breakfast fare are
the draw of this "charming" cafe set in a Victorian house in Cranbury;
it also serves "interesting" American lunch fare and a "limited" weekend dinner menu (with BYO), and a front porch adds to its appeal.

Blue2O *Seafood* | 22 | 21 | 22 | $36 |
Cherry Hill | 1906 Marlton Pike W. (Haddonfield Rd.) |
856-662-0297 | www.blue2oseafoodgrill.com
"Quality" fish is served off the grill by a "professional" staff at this
"dependable seafooder" in Cherry Hill; the spacious, "modern"
room has booth seating, and while it "can be a little pricey", "great"
weekday dinner specials at the bar can be a "value."

Bobby Chez Ⓜ *Seafood* | 23 | 17 | 20 | $24 |
Margate | 8007 Ventnor Ave. (bet. Frontenac & Gladstone Aves.) |
609-487-1922
Cherry Hill | Tuscany Mktpl. | 1990 Rte. 70 E. (bet. Birchwood Park Dr. S. &
Old Orchard Rd.) | 856-751-7575

(continued)

(continued)

Bobby Chez

Collingswood | 33 W. Collings Ave. (Atlantic Ave.) | 856-869-8000
Mount Laurel | Centerton Sq. | 32 Centerton Rd. (Marter Ave.) |
856-234-4146
Sewell | 100 Hurffville Crosskeys Rd. (Glassboro Cross Keys Rd.) |
856-262-1001
www.bobbychezcrabcakes.com

"Amazing" "no-filler" crab cakes draw diners in droves to these
"relaxed" South Jersey "take-out joints", where signature treats like
lobster mashed potatoes might be "worth ruining your diet for";
"friendly" service helps compensate for "plain decor", and many
find the grab-and-go eats a "nice alternative to long waits" at the
usual summer haunts.

Bobby Flay Steak ⓜ *Steak*

25 | 25 | 24 | $69

Atlantic City | Borgata Hotel Casino & Spa | 1 Borgata Way
(Renaissance Point Blvd.) | 609-317-1000 | www.bobbyflaysteak.com

Bobby Flay "nails it" with "inventive takes on standard steakhouse
items" at his "top-notch" "carnivore's paradise" in AC's Borgata
Hotel; granted, the David Rockwell–designed dining room can get
"noisy" and tabs are "expensive", but service is "excellent" and most
agree "you get what you pay for."

Bobby's Burger Palace *Burgers*

21 | 17 | 18 | $16

Paramus | Bergen Town Ctr. | 610 Bergen Town Ctr. (Spring Valley Ave.) |
201-368-7001
Eatontown | Monmouth Mall Shopping Ctr. | 188 Rte. 35 (Rte. 36) |
732-544-0200
NEW Freehold | Freehold Raceway Mall | 3710 Rte. 9
(Cardigan Bay Ln.) | 732-677-7944
NEW Princeton | MarketFair | 3535 Rte. 1 (Meadow Rd.) |
609-919-0182
Cherry Hill | Cherry Hill Mall | 2000 Rte. 38 (Haddonfield Rd.) |
856-382-7462
www.bobbysburgerpalace.com

Iron Chef Bobby Flay's "creative burger joint" serves up "high-quality
meat, cooked the way you want it", with "crazy toppings" ("get it
crunchified with potato chips"), complemented by "addictive" fries
and "thick" milkshakes "to die for"; the "downside is the wait", and
many are "put out" by the communal seating, but others insist the
"affordable" eats are "worth it."

Bombay Bistro ⓜ *Indian*
(fka Dabbawalla)

21 | 20 | 20 | $27

Summit | 427 Springfield Ave. (bet. Maple St. & Woodland Ave.) |
908-918-0330 | www.thebombaybistro.net

"You can eat healthy" at this Summit BYO (fka Dabbawalla), which
"puts a modern spin on Indian food", with dishes such as a stuffed
lamb burger, as well as "fine traditional dishes", at moderate prices;
some feel the new incarnation is "more inviting" than before, and
while the service may not impress, many tout it as a "refreshing
change of pace in the area."

	FOOD	DECOR	SERVICE	COST

Bonefish Grill *Seafood*
21 | 20 | 21 | $34

Paramus | Crowne Plaza | 601 From Rd. (Ring Rd.) | 201-261-2355
East Brunswick | 335 State Rte. 18 (N. Amherst St.) | 732-390-0838
Green Brook | 215 Rte. 22 E. (bet. Highland St. & Lund Ln.) | 732-926-8060
Iselin | 625 US Hwy. 1 S. (Cheryl Dr.) | 732-634-7695
Pine Brook | 28 Rte. 46 (Hook Mountain Rd.) | 973-227-2443
Brick | 179 Van Zile Rd. (Rte. 70) | 732-785-2725
Middleton | 447 Rte. 35 (Chapel Hill Rd.) | 732-530-4284
Egg Harbor Township | 3121 Fire Rd. (Tilton Rd.) | 609-646-2828
Deptford | 1709 Deptford Center Rd. (Almonessen Rd.) | 856-848-6261
Marlton | 500 Rte. 73 S. (bet. Baker Blvd. & Lincoln Dr.) | 856-396-3122
www.bonefishgrill.com
Additional locations throughout New Jersey

Devotees of this "reliable" seafood sibling in the Outback family insist it's "a cut above" its chain identity, citing the "fresh, flavorful" fare (the Bang Bang Shrimp is "bangin'!") and "innovative" specials served up by a "friendly" staff; usually "jammed with happy diners", it can get "noisy", and some find it "a little pricey" too, but most agree it's "worth the cost."

Boulevard Five 72 *American*
23 | 22 | 22 | $56

Kenilworth | 572 Kenilworth Blvd. (24th St.) | 908-709-1200 | www.boulevardfive72.net

Offering an "extensive" wine list and "imaginative, well-prepared" cuisine (including prix fixe menus and Sunday brunch), this Kenilworth New American matches "expensive" tabs with a "lovely" setting that's "great for celebrations or just a nice night out"; fans say "everything is solid about this spot", including "attentive" service, making it a "top-notch restaurant for an upscale occasion."

Braddock's Ⓜ *American*
24 | 23 | 24 | $38

Medford | 39 S. Main St. (Coates St.) | 609-654-1604 | www.braddocks.com

A "pleasant" staff dishes up "tried-and-true" American fare and some "tasty, unusual dishes" at this Medford venue set in a "historic" circa-1844 house; even if it's a bit "pricey" to some, fans say the "lovely", Colonial-style surrounds are a "pleasant" place to "slow down and enjoy how life was and how it should be."

Brandl Ⓜ *American*
24 | 19 | 20 | $55

Belmar | 703 Belmar Plaza (8th Ave.) | 732-280-7501 | www.brandlrestaurant.com

Chef Chris Brandl's "creative" seafood offerings continue to impress fans at this "relaxed" Belmar BYO American with signature dishes such as crab cakes and 'lazy lobster'; while some are unimpressed by the strip-mall setting and think the service "could use some fine tuning", others feel like they've "traveled to NYC" for a "fine" dine (albeit with prices to match).

	FOOD	DECOR	SERVICE	COST

Brasilia Grill *Brazilian*

| 21 | 19 | 20 | $33 |

Newark | 97-99 Monroe St. (bet. Ferry & Lafayette Sts.) |
973-589-8682 | www.brasiliagrill.net ●

Though there are plenty of "Brazilian comfort foods" on the menu, the "fabulous" meats in the all-you-can-eat rodizio are the main "attraction" at this Newark churrascaria whose prices make it a "decent deal"; adorned with palm trees and colorful murals, the open space is brightened by a "friendly" crew mixing up "must-try" caipirinhas.

Brass Rail *American*

| 19 | 19 | 19 | $36 |

Hoboken | 135 Washington St. (2nd St.) | 201-659-7074 |
www.thebrassrailnj.com

"Decent" service and a "varied menu" of "tasty" American and Continental dishes make this a "dependable" Hoboken haunt "for happy hour or a date", though it's also a "good brunch option" on weekends; if the "vibrant bar scene" on the ground floor gets "noisy", you'll find a "classier, quieter" atmosphere upstairs, plus "outdoor seating in warmer weather."

Brennen's Steakhouse ● *Steak*

| 22 | 19 | 22 | $48 |

Neptune City | 62 W. Sylvania Ave. (Wall St.) | 732-774-5040

Fans are "always satisfied" by the "juicy" steaks served by a "pleasant" staff at this steakhouse "sleeper" in Neptune City; the atmosphere is "classy" in the "pub-type setting", where a "delightful" piano player performs Wednesdays–Sundays, and while the experience doesn't come cheap, many agree it's "well worth" the cost.

Brian's Ⓜ *French/Italian*

| 26 | 21 | 24 | $40 |

Lambertville | 9 Kline's Ct. (bet. Bridge & Ferry Sts.) | 609-460-4148 |
www.brianslambertville.com

"Loyal followers" "can't get enough" of chef-owner Brian Held's "mouthwatering" menu selections at this "bistro-style" Lambertville French-Italian; while the "tiny dining room" is usually "packed", service is "helpful" and BYO keeps tabs "manageable"; P.S. the "bargain" dinner prix fixe offers "great bang for the buck."

Brick City Bar & Grill ● *Pub Food*

| 19 | 19 | 18 | $31 |

Newark | 35 Edison Pl. (bet. Broad & Mulberry Sts.) | 973-596-0004 |
www.brickcitybar.com

"Big burger platters" and other beer-friendly pub grub come at moderate prices at this "huge" upscale sports bar "right across the street" from Newark's Prudential Center; most agree the location is "convenient for a bite before an event", though some advise you "leave plenty of time" because "service can be spotty."

Brick Lane Curry House *Indian*

| 23 | 18 | 20 | $30 |

Ridgewood | 34 Franklin Ave. (Chestnut St.) | 201-670-7311
Upper Montclair | 540 Valley Rd. (Bellevue Ave.) | 973-509-2100
www.bricklanecurryhouse.com

"Every mouthful is a joy" swoon fans of the "flavorful, fiery curries" at these midpriced Indian chain links in Ridgewood and Upper Montclair, where you can "pick your level of spiciness" (but "be careful if you're bold enough to order the phaal"); "pleasant" service and BYO perk up the "simple" settings, and they're "great for takeout as well."

Brickwall Tavern ❶ *Pub Food*   20 | 19 | 18 | $26

Asbury Park | 522 Cookman Ave. (Emory St.) | 732-774-1264 | www.brickwalltavern.com

The "boozy, noisy" atmosphere trumps the "good", if "not memorable", pub grub at this "popular" Asbury Park "watering hole"-cum-sports bar that also pours a "great selection of craft beers"; placards bearing "funny quotes" deck out the digs, where weekend dance parties and reasonable tabs make it "a great time out."

Brioso *Italian*   23 | 19 | 20 | $41

Marlboro | Willow Pointe Shopping Ctr. | 184 Rte. 9 (Sandburg Dr.) | 732-617-1700 | www.briosoristorante.com

Marlboro locals head to this "little gem in a strip mall" on Route 9 for "top-notch" Italian cuisine (including specials that "never disappoint") delivered by a "pleasant" crew; when it gets "busy", the "noisy atmosphere and crowded conditions" can be a "downside" for some, but at least BYO eases slightly pricey tabs.

Brio Tuscan Grille *Italian*   21 | 21 | 20 | $30

NEW Wayne | Willowbrook Mall | 1400 Willowbrook Mall (Willowbrook Blvd.) | 973-256-0001
NEW Freehold | Freehold Raceway Mall | 3710 Rte. 9 (Winners Circle) | 732-683-1045
Cherry Hill | Towne Place at Garden State Park | 901 Haddonfield Rd. (bet. Garden Park Blvd. & Marlton Pike) | 856-910-8166
Marlton | The Promenade at Sagemore | 500 Rte. 73 S. (bet. Brick Rd. & Marlton Pkwy.) | 856-983-0277
www.brioitalian.com

Dishing up "tasty", "consistent" Italian offerings in a "pleasant", slightly upscale atmosphere, these links of a "favorite chain" lure fans "for dates, company meetings" or "happy hour"; "reasonable prices" and "helpful" service are further highlights, and if you can snag a terrace seat "on a nice afternoon", "you won't be sorry."

The British Chip Shop *British*   ▽ 24 | 22 | 23 | $21

Haddonfield | 146 Kings Hwy. E. (Haddon Ave.) | 856-354-0204 | www.thebritishchipshop.com

"Crispy" fish 'n' chips stand out at this affordable Haddonfield BYO, but there's plenty of other "real British" fare to please Anglophiles ("mushy peas, anyone?"), including a "full English breakfast" on Sundays; a "pleasant atmosphere" benefits from an "enthusiastic" staff, and if you bring some "Smithwicks", you might just think you've taken a "quick trip across the pond."

Brooklyn's Coal-Burning Brick-Oven Pizzeria ⊟ *Pizza*   22 | 15 | 18 | $19

Edgewater | Edgewater Commons Shopping Ctr. | 443 River Rd. (Old River Rd.) | 201-945-9096
Hackensack | 161 Hackensack Ave. (Devoe Pl.) | 201-342-2727

(continued)

(continued)

Brooklyn's Coal-Burning Brick-Oven Pizzeria

Ridgewood | 15 Oak St (Ridgewood Ave.) | 201-493-7600

With "fresh mozzarella, fresh sauce" and "plentiful, tasty" toppings, the "crunchy, coal-fired pies" are "hard to beat" on "this side of the Lincoln Tunnel" swear purists of these "casual" Bergen County pizzerias; despite "no ambiance", "spotty" service and "cash-only", "no-slices" policies, they're usually "mobbed"; P.S. Hackensack offers beer and wine, while Edgewater and Ridgewood are BYO.

NEW Brother Jimmy's BBQ ● *American* — | — | — | M

New Brunswick | 5 Easton Ave. (Little Albany St.) | 732-249-7427 | www.brotherjimmys.com

This NYC-based BBQ chainlet comes to New Brunswick bringing with it stick-to-your-ribs ribs, wings and Southern sides; super-sized suds and 'concoctions' wash down the grub while decent prices jibe with the kitschy, honky-tonk digs.

Brothers Moon Ⓜ *American* 24 | 20 | 22 | $41

Hopewell | 7 W. Broad St. (Greenwood Ave.) | 609-333-1330 | www.brothersmoon.com

Fans flock to this "charming little bistro" on Hopewell's main street for chef-owner Will Mooney's "first-rate" New American menu, featuring "creative preparations of locally sourced products"; while the "low-key" setting gets mixed marks, "friendly" service ups the "dining pleasure" and BYO helps keep costs down.

Bruno's Restaurant & Pizza *Italian* 21 | 17 | 22 | $20

Haddonfield | 509 Hopkins Rd. (Jess Ave.) | 856-428-9505

Thanks to the "great pizzas" and "delicious" Italian fare dished up in "huge portions" at this Haddonfield haunt, regulars usually "end up with a meal for tomorrow" too; "welcoming" service adds to the "family atmosphere" in the "intimate", basic digs, and with "a liquor store right next door", handy BYO keeps tabs "reasonable."

Bruschetta Ⓢ *Italian* 20 | 20 | 21 | $40

Fairfield | 292 Passaic Ave. (Pier Ln.) | 973-227-6164 | www.bruschettarestaurantonline.com

"A favorite of locals", this white-tablecloth Fairfield "standby" turns out "traditional Italian fare" that's "well prepared and pleasantly served"; a "nice bar area" with nightly live piano music makes the experience "a little more upscale for a nice night out."

Bucu *Bakery/Burgers* 19 | 17 | 17 | $15

Paramus | 35 Plaza | 65 Rte. 4 W. (bet. Farview Ave. & Spring Valley Rd.) | 347-470-2828 | www.eatbucu.com

While the menu at this Paramus burger joint/bakery is packed with "tasty" hamburgers, "to-die-for" fries and "an assortment of other sandwiches that won't break the bank", devotees declare the "desserts make it special" ("always leave room" for the "homemade cupcakes"); a "helpful" staff keeps up the pace in counter-serve digs.

	FOOD	DECOR	SERVICE	COST

Buddakan *Asian*
`25` `26` `24` `$55`

Atlantic City | The Pier Shops at Caesars | 1 Atlantic Ocean
(Arkansas Ave.) | 609-674-0100 | www.buddakanac.com
"As good as the original in Philly" and its NYC sib, this "high-end
Stephen Starr creation" in the Pier at Caesars combines "interesting",
"well-presented" Pan-Asian fare with "delightful" service that's fit
for a "special occasion"; add in "beautiful", "modern" decor, with an
enormous gilded Buddha overlooking the dramatic communal tables,
and it's "like dining on a Hollywood set."

NEW Burgerwood *Burgers*
`-` `-` `-` `M`

Englewood | 24 N. Van Brunt St. (Palisade Ave.) | 201-871-8600 |
www.burgerwoodnj.com
This Englewood haven specializes in the eponymous hamburgers
(including turkey, veggie and grilled chicken cutlets) plus affordable crowd-pleasers such as nachos, pizza and shakes; photos of
movie starlets and a mural of legendary entertainers deck the exposed brick and subway-tiled walls, and there's also a full bar.

Busch's Seafood Ⓜ *Seafood*
▽ `21` `15` `18` `$42`

Sea Isle City | 8700 Anna Phillips Ln. (87th St.) | 609-263-8626 |
www.buschsseafood.com
A Sea Isle "institution" since 1882, this "typical old-time" seafooder is known for its "excellent" she-crab soup (served Sunday
and Tuesday) and other fin fare, though some feel it's "nothing
to write home about"; while some think the no-frills decor "could
be more welcoming", that doesn't stop loyalists from making
"fond memories" here.

BV Tuscany Ⓜ *Italian*
`24` `20` `24` `$42`

Teaneck | 368 Cedar Ln. (Palisade Ave.) | 201-287-0404 |
www.bvtuscany.com
Thanks to an "attentive" staff delivering a "diverse" menu of "classic"
Tuscan dishes at this "lovely" Teaneck Italian, it's no wonder locals
"rave about what a great find it is"; somewhat "expensive" prices are
matched by a "well-appointed, intimate" setting that's a "favorite"
for "special occasions."

Café Azzurro *Italian*
`22` `20` `21` `$43`

Peapack | 141 Main St. (bet. Todd & Willow Aves.) | 908-470-1470 |
www.cafeazzurronj.com
"A step-up from the usual red-sauce" offerings, this "casual" Peapack
BYO offers "dependable" Northern Italian cooking at a "fair price";
"pleasant", "capable" service helps compensate for occasional "long
waits", and beyond the "pretty" dining room, there's a "charming
outdoor patio" that's "wonderful in warmer weather."

Cafe Bello *Italian*
`23` `20` `21` `$38`

Bayonne | 1044 Avenue C (50th St.) | 201-437-7538 |
www.cafebellobayonne.com
Devotees say you "can't go wrong" with the "consistent" Italian menu
(and "spot-on" specials) at this Bayonne neighborhood "gem"; "well-

decorated", with Tuscan-inspired touches, it may appear "upscale" for the area, but prices are "moderate" and many feel "like family" here.

Cafe Emilia *Italian*
20 | 19 | 21 | $46

Bridgewater | 705 Rte. 202 N. (Charlotte Dr.) | 908-429-1410 | www.cafeemilia.com

"Homey, down-to-earth" cooking is the draw at this Bridgewater Italian, even if tabs are "expensive"; decorated in muted colors and Tuscan-inspired murals, the "small interior" can get "loud" and "crowded" (expect to see "a lot of regulars"), but an "attentive" staff ensures you "are treated well."

Cafe Graziella *Italian*
22 | 18 | 20 | $35

Hillsborough | Cost Cutters Shopping Ctr. | 390 Rte. 206 (Andria Ave.) | 908-281-0700 | www.cafegraziella.com

"Tasty", "classic" Italian dishes for "reasonable" prices make this "friendly" BYO a real "find" in Hillsborough; despite its "unlikely" strip-mall setting and rustic decor that strikes some as "dated", insiders insist "everything else takes a back seat to the food."

Cafe Loren Ⓜ *American*
▽ 25 | 22 | 24 | $48

Avalon | 2288 Dune Dr. (23rd St.) | 609-967-8228 | www.cafeloren.com

This "wonderful", "upscale" BYO has been an Avalon "find" for 30-plus years thanks to its "creative, fresh" New American cuisine served in a "cozy", "casual" dining room; out-of-town fans "wait all year to go there on vacation" because it's only open seasonally.

Cafe Madison ⊠Ⓜ *American*
23 | 24 | 23 | $45

Riverside | 33 Lafayette St. (Madison St.) | 856-764-4444 | www.cafemadison.com

With "impressive architecture" and "industrial-chic decor", this "high-end" Riverside American will make you "feel like you're in NYC"; the "amiable" staff "really tries to win you over" while serving "fresh, tasty cuisine", and though it might be "a bit pricey for regular visits", it's "perfect for that special night"; P.S. frequent live entertainment is another highlight.

Cafe Matisse Ⓜ *Eclectic*
26 | 25 | 26 | $73

Rutherford | 167 Park Ave. (bet. Highland Cross & Park Pl.) | 201-935-2995 | www.cafematisse.com

"Demanding foodies" revel in the "complex flavors" of "beautifully presented" Eclectic tasting menus at this "classy" Rutherford "jewel box", where the "passionate" staff "describes each dish with detail" and makes guests "feel special"; some cringe at the "NY prices", but loyalists declare it a "masterful meal deserving of its namesake"; P.S. the attached wine shop makes BYO a breeze.

Cafe Metro *Eclectic*
21 | 17 | 20 | $26

Denville | 60 Diamond Spring Rd. (bet. 1st & 2nd Aves.) | 973-625-1055 | www.thecafemetro.com

With "a lot of vegetarian dishes" on the Eclectic menu, this Denville "neighborhood gem" is a "paradise" for "healthy eaters"; the "relaxed", exposed-brick surrounds "feel like a Manhattan loft", and though it serves wines, optional BYO can "make it a bargain."

Cafe Panache *Eclectic*
| 26 | 24 | 25 | $59 |

Ramsey | 130 E. Main St. (bet. Island Ave. & Spruce St.) | 201-934-0030 | www.cafepanachenj.com

A "go-to place for special occasions", this Ramsey Eclectic delivers "artful presentations" of "inventive", "seasonal" fare in an "elegant setting" that's "always packed"; while it's undoubtedly "high-end", BYO "helps keep the price down", and "attentive", "professional" service caps an all-around "delightful evening."

NEW Café 37 Ⓜ *American*
| 25 | 21 | 21 | $46 |

Ridgewood | 37 S. Broad St. (bet. Hudson & Passaic Sts.) | 201-857-0437 | www.cafe-37.com

Chef-owner Cesar Sotomayor's "careful presentations" of "mouthwatering" New American cuisine shine at this "charming" Ridgewood BYO; "warm, eager" service and a "soothing" modern setting add up to a "gem of a spot" and a "great new addition to the local scene."

Cafe 2825 Ⓜ *Italian*
| 24 | 21 | 23 | $47 |

Atlantic City | 2825 Atlantic Ave. (Brighton Ave.) | 609-344-6913 | www.cafe2825.com

Those seeking an "alternative to the casino joints" don't go wrong at this "high-end" Atlantic City Italian where "consistently good" fare and a staff that "makes you feel at home" ensure a "relaxing" dine; it's small, with only a dozen tables alongside a "beautiful bar", but fans say it's just right for "taking out someone special."

Caffe Aldo Lamberti *Italian/Seafood*
| 24 | 23 | 23 | $44 |

Cherry Hill | 2011 Marlton Pike W. (bet. Grove St. & Washington Ave.) | 856-663-1741 | www.caffelamberti.com

"Great seafood, Italian-style" makes for a "wow experience" at this "top-shelf, special-occasion" spot, the Cherry Hill flagship of a regional restaurant group; the "attractive", contemporary digs and "courteous" service from a staff that "likes to spoil you" help justify somewhat "pricey" tabs.

Calandra's Mediterranean Grill *Mediterranean*
| 21 | 20 | 21 | $37 |

Fairfield | The Hampton Inn & Suites | 118 Rte. 46 E. (Lehigh Dr.) | 973-575-6500 | www.calandras.net

Regulars "always look forward" to the "fabulous bread" (from sibling Calandra's Bakery) at this "family"-friendly Med in Fairfield's Hampton Inn; "reasonable" tabs and "pleasant" service complement the "casual", Tuscan-inspired setting with seasonal patio seating.

California Pizza Kitchen *Pizza*
| 19 | 17 | 18 | $21 |

Paramus | Garden State Plaza | 1 Garden State Plaza (Roosevelt Ave.) | 201-587-0005

Short Hills | The Mall at Short Hills | 1200 Morris Tpke. (Service Rd.) | 973-379-3700

(continued)

(continued)

California Pizza Kitchen

Wayne | Willowbrook Mall | 1400 Willowbrook Mall (Rte. 46) |
973-837-9501

Bridgewater | Bridgewater Commons | 400 Commons Way
(Prince Rodgers Ave.) | 908-566-1225

Cherry Hill | Cherry Hill Mall | 2000 Rte. 38 (Mall Dr.) | 856-910-8121
www.cpk.com

"Interesting pizza combos", "hearty salads" and "many other tasty
choices" appeal to "the whole family" at this "reliable" national 'za
chain; fans who make it "a regular stop" say the "friendly" service and
"affordable" tabs mitigate the sometimes "crowded", "noisy" scene.

The Capital Grille *Steak*

25 | 24 | 24 | $64

Paramus | Garden State Plaza | 1 Garden State Plaza
(Garden State Plaza Pkwy.) | 201-845-7040

Cherry Hill | Cherry Hill Mall | 2000 Rte. 38 (Mall Dr.) |
856-665-5252

www.thecapitalgrille.com

Providing a "high-end" experience "from stem to stern", these chain
steakhouses in Paramus and Cherry Hill serve "consistently great"
chops, matched by an "impressive" wine list and "well-trained" staff –
all in "upscale" "men's club" surrounds that belie their mall locales;
sure, a "Brinks truck" would come in handy here, but fans deem the
price "digestible" for a "romantic evening", "power lunch" or those
times when you just need to "feel like a senator."

Capriccio Ⓜ *Italian*

24 | 23 | 23 | $55

Atlantic City | Resorts Casino & Hotel | 1133 Boardwalk
(Danny Thomas Blvd.) | 609-340-6789 | www.resortsac.com

Fans say dinner's "always delicious" at this "classy" Resorts Casino
Italian in Atlantic City, but it's the "great-value" Sunday brunch buffet
(which includes champagne) that's "not to be missed"; the bar offers tapas, plus live piano weekends, and, yes, there's an ocean view.

Cara Mia *Italian*

21 | 19 | 21 | $41

Millburn | 194 Essex St. (bet. Lackawanna Pl. & Main St.) |
973-379-8989 | www.caramiamillburn.com

"When you have guests or want a meal before a show" at the nearby
Paper Mill Playhouse, this "welcoming", family-run Millburn Italian
fits the bill with "well-presented", "classic" fare in an "energetic",
exposed-brick setting; BYO is "a big plus" for keeping tabs "easy on
the wallet", and there's even a liquor store next door.

Carluccio's
Coal Fired Pizza *Pizza*

25 | 21 | 24 | $18

Northfield | 1200 New Rd. (Tilton Rd.) | 609-641-4011 |
www.carlucciocoalfiredpizza.com

"Inventive toppings" stand out on the "fantastic variety" of "outstanding" coal-fired pizzas at this BYO Northfield "gem", which also
dishes "fab pastas" and "amazing calzones"; a bright, open dining
room and "great" service add appeal – no wonder fans find it a "nice
addition to the area."

	FOOD	DECOR	SERVICE	COST

Carmine's *Italian*

22 | 21 | 22 | $41

Atlantic City | Quarter at the Tropicana | 2801 Pacific Ave. (Iowa Ave.) | 609-572-9300 | www.carminesnyc.com

"Bring your appetite and friends", because "enormous, family-sized portions" of "satisfying red-sauce fare" mean "sharing is a must" at this AC Italian, "a twin sister to the NYC venue"; most don't mind the "noise levels" and somewhat "touristy" vibe, especially given the "pleasant" service and "good value" overall.

Carpaccio *Italian*

21 | 20 | 22 | $31

Middlesex | 651 Bound Brook Rd. (2nd St.) | 732-968-3242 | www.carpaccioristorante.com

Expect the "friendly" staff to "take care of you" at this Middlesex Italian serving pasta, seafood, steaks and other "standard" offerings; perhaps the "pink '80s decor" has "seen better days", but the generally "comfortable" atmosphere and "reasonable" tabs satisfy most.

Casa Dante *Italian*

22 | 20 | 22 | $51

Jersey City | 737 Newark Ave. (John F. Kennedy Blvd.) | 201-795-2750 | www.casadante.com

"Professional", "old-world" service complements the "tasty", "traditional" Italian cuisine at this long-standing "Jersey City classic", a "throwback to yesteryear in every way except for the current prices"; if some sniff at the "cheese factor" of the surrounds, it remains "a place for celebrations" for a "mixed crowd of young and old", with "fantastic" weekly entertainment to keep things "lively."

Casa Giuseppe ⓩ *Italian*

23 | 20 | 23 | $47

Iselin | 487 Rte. 27 (Talmadge Ave.) | 732-283-9111 | www.casagiuseppe.com

A "bit of Tuscany" "hidden on Route 27", this Iselin "gem" offers "above-average" Italian fare "without pretentiousness" in a "home-dining" setting; semi-steep tabs are countered by "attentive" service.

Casa Maya *Mexican*

21 | 18 | 19 | $24

Gillette | 615 Meyersville Rd. (Gillette Rd.) | 908-580-0799
High Bridge | 1 Main St. (Bridge St.) | 908-638-4032
www.casamayamexican.com

"Large portions" of "well-spiced", "consistent" Sonoran-style Mexican food "draw crowds" to these "cozy", "family-oriented" pit stops in Gillette and High Bridge; if the "colorful" Southwestern decor is "over the top" for some, "inexpensive" tabs and BYO are definitely "a draw", so "don't forget your *cervezas.*"

Casa Vasca *Spanish*

24 | 18 | 21 | $35

Newark | 141 Elm St. (Prospect St.) | 973-465-1350 | www.casavascarestaurant.com

"Homey and authentic", this Ironbound Spanish "old-timer" "never disappoints", turning out "huge" portions of "consistently good" Basque dishes since 1976; a "friendly" staff that treats you "like you're family", "reasonable prices" and a "cozy" atmosphere help keep it "down to earth", and as a bonus, there's a free attended parking lot.

	FOOD	DECOR	SERVICE	COST

Casona ⓜ Cuban
22 | 19 | 20 | $33

Collingswood | 563 Haddon Ave. (Knight Ave.) | 856-854-5555 | www.mycasona.com

For "something different with Cuban flair", fans head to this converted, circa-1905 "big old house" in Collingswood for "delicious" paella, "to-die-for crab guacamole", "many gluten-free options" and other "totally unique" specialties, served by a "friendly" staff; a wraparound porch provides a popular alfresco perch, and many deem it a "go-to celebration destination", even though it's BYO.

Cassie's Italian
19 | 15 | 18 | $27

Englewood | 18 S. Dean St. (bet. Englewood & Palisade Aves.) | 201-541-6760 | www.cassiespizzeria.com

"Generous portions" of "solid" fare – think "fresh, flavorful" brick-oven pizzas, pastas and "salads for sharing" – draw families "with kids" to this "busy" Englewood Italian; while naysayers "can't stand the noise" and find the service "lackadaisical" and 'za prices "a bit hard to swallow", supporters shrug and say it's "always fun."

Casual Habana Cafe Cuban
25 | 20 | 22 | $24

Hackensack | 125 Main St. (bet. Atlantic & Mercer Sts.) | 201-880-9844 | www.casualhabanacafe.com

The "tremendous", "authentic" "Cuban flavors" at this "low-key" BYO "gem" in Hackensack will "tantalize your palate" say amigos who credit the "hands-on owner" with creating a "relaxing", "personal dining experience"; "large" portions, "small" prices and an "accommodating" staff make it "wonderful for groups", while "spacious seating and dim lighting" mean it's also a "great date place."

Cathay 22 Chinese
21 | 18 | 19 | $30

Springfield | 124 Rte. 22 (bet. Hillside & Stern Aves.) | 973-467-8688 | www.cathay22.com

Serving up "inventive", "fresh and tasty" Sichuan dishes since 1985, this "upscale", "sit-down" Chinese in Springfield is "a cut above" the "typical takeout"; a "relaxed" vibe and "relatively sophisticated" environs help make up for its "Route 22" address, and while a few wallet-watchers cite slightly "high" tabs, others insists it's "reasonably priced" and tout its lunch menu as an "especially good value."

Catherine Lombardi ◑ Italian
24 | 24 | 24 | $57

New Brunswick | 3 Livingston Ave., 2nd fl. (George St.) | 732-296-9463 | www.catherinelombardi.com

Offering a "wonderful interpretation of traditional Italian dishes", this "high-end" second-floor sibling of New Brunswick's Stage Left "raises the bar" on "Sunday dinner at grandma's house" with "generous portions" of "homey" favorites paired with an "incredible" selection of handcrafted cocktails and an "extensive" wine list; there's a "lively bar", the "view over the square is tops" and two fireplaces "add cheer and warmth" to the "cozy" red dining room – "professional" service ensures that it's "always a pleasure."

	FOOD	DECOR	SERVICE	COST

NEW Central Kitchen *American*
- | - | - | M

Englewood Cliffs | 717 E. Palisade Ave. (Sylvan Ave.) | 201-503-0104 |
www.centralkitchennj.com

Handcrafted comfort classics get the seasonal, local treatment
at this Englewood Cliffs American where homey favorites, many
with an Italian accent, are served for weekend brunch, lunch and
dinner; prices are moderate and the newly renovated corner spot
is chic and modern with dark woods, a sleek marble bar and
warm-weather outdoor seating.

Cenzino ●🅑 *Italian*
25 | 21 | 25 | $55

Oakland | 589 Ramapo Valley Rd. (bet. Navajo Way & Thunderbird Dr.) |
201-337-6693 | www.cenzinos.com

"Fine dining at its best" is how *amici* describe this "top-flight"
"regional" Italian in Oakland, where the "engaging owner" is "always present" and the "traditional" black tie–wearing staffers
provide the "royal treatment"; the atmosphere is "comfortable"
and "cozy", and tipplers appreciate the "decent" wine list and
"generous drinks" at the bar, and though it's "expensive", many
deem it "a can't-miss dinner destination."

Chakra ●🅑 *American/Eclectic*
23 | 24 | 22 | $56

Paramus | 144 Rte. 4 (Arcadian Way) | 201-556-1530 |
www.chakrarestaurant.com

"A place to see and be seen", this "posh spot" is an "expensive"
"oasis" in Paramus serving "inventive" but "delicious" Eclectic–New
American eats and "fantastic drinks" to a "hopping" "under-40
crowd" out for a "romantic night", "special occasion" or dipping
into the "singles scene"; the "friendly" service is "attentive" and the
"dramatic", "exotic" decor combines Asian teak pieces with a wall of
water and "comfy booths."

Chambers Walk Cafe 🅑 *American*
22 | 20 | 21 | $36

Lawrenceville | 2667 Main St. (bet. Gordon & Phillips Aves.) |
609-896-5995 | www.chamberswalk.com

"Reliable", "well-prepared" American chow draws Lawrenceville locals to this "reasonably priced", "casual" BYO where "good" salads,
soups and sandwiches, attract the lunch crowd, and evenings mean
a "wonderful eclectic menu" of bistro-style apps and entrees; Friday
and Saturday brings live entertainment, and with a "friendly, inviting" vibe and "cozy" digs, "you feel at home."

Chand Palace *Indian*
22 | 18 | 19 | $19

Parsippany | 257 Littleton Rd. (Parsippany Rd.) | 973-334-5444 |
www.chandpalace.com
Piscataway | Piscataway Town Ctr. | 1296 Centennial Ave.
(Washington Ave.) | 732-465-1474 |
www.chandpalacerestaurant.com

A "great variety" of "tasty", "authentic" vegetarian Indian eats (prepared "from mild to spicy") awaits at these "very affordable" BYO
Piscataway and Parsippany siblings where the "amazing buffets" include "dozens of choices" and carnivores concede they "don't miss

the meat"; while there's "not much decor to speak of" and some find the service to be "so-so", boosters consider it a "steal" for the prices.

Chao Phaya *Thai* | 22 | 15 | 17 | $22 |

Somerset | Somerset Vill. | 900 Easton Ave. (Foxwood Dr.) | 732-249-0110
Somerville | 9 Davenport St. (bet. Hunterdon & Main Sts.) | 908-231-0655
www.chaophayathaicuisine.com

Dishing up "exceptional", "authentic" Thai tastes, these "accommo-dating" BYO Somerset and Somerville siblings adjust the "degree of spice" to "your personal preference"; while some complain that ser-vice can be "spotty" and the "simple" digs have "no atmosphere", "noise is not a problem" and even better, the "consistently good" eats are "a bargain."

Charley's Ocean Grill *American* | 19 | 20 | 19 | $34 |

Long Branch | 29 Avenel Blvd. (Marion Pl.) | 732-222-4499 |
www.charleysoceangrill.com

"Great views" of the ocean from double-decker verandas draw din-ers to this "comfortable" Long Beach American seafooder and "local watering hole"; though the "casual fare" rates "average" to most, and some miss the "quaint appeal" of its pre-renovation days, many appreciate the "accommodating staff" and "decent prices."

Charlie's ●≠ *American* | 21 | 17 | 19 | $28 |

Somers Point | 800 Shore Rd. (New Jersey Ave.) | 609-927-3663 |
www.charliesbar.com

Dishing up "legendary wings" and other American pub staples, plus affordable surf 'n' turf dinners, this "longtime" Somers Point watering hole is "where the locals go"; "generally crowded" and "loud", it's a lively place to "hang out with friends" and "watch a sporting event" on one of the flat-screen TVs; P.S. cash only.

Charrito's *Mexican* | 22 | 20 | 19 | $27 |

Hoboken | 1024 Washington St. (bet. 10th & 11th Sts.) | 201-659-2800
Hoboken | 121 Washington St. (bet. 1st & 2nd Sts.) | 201-418-8600

El Charro *Mexican*

Weehawken | 974 JFK Blvd. E. (47th St.) | 201-330-1130
www.loscharritos.com

There are "lots of options" on the menu of this BYO Mex trio serving "big portions" of "fresh, tasty" and "reasonably priced" fare, includ-ing "tableside guacamole"; the views of NYC are "unbeatable" at El Charro, and while some complain of "unpleasant" noise levels in the otherwise "charming" digs, outdoor seating at the Hoboken twins offers some respite.

Char Steak House *Steak* | 23 | 24 | 22 | $64 |

Raritan | 777 Rte. 202 N. (Quick Ave.) | 908-707-1777
NEW Red Bank | 33 Broad St. (Mechanic St.) | 732-450-2427
www.charsteakhouse.com

At this "trendy" Raritan steakhouse (with a Red Bank sibling that opened post-Survey), "well-versed" staffers serve up "outstanding" dry-aged cuts, "unbelievable" seafood and "to-die-for" desserts to "beautiful people" and "corporate" types; the "exciting decor" fills multiple dining rooms and a "great" bar, while the outdoor patio transports you to "someplace far more exotic than central Jersey", and though it's "pricey", most think it's "totally worth it."

Chart House *Seafood* 22 | 24 | 22 | $53

Weehawken | Lincoln Harbor | Pier D/T (Harbor Blvd.) | 201-348-6628
Atlantic City | Golden Nugget Hotel & Casino | Brigantine Blvd. & Huron Ave. | 609-340-5030 **Ⓜ**
www.chart-house.com

With a "world-class" vista of the Manhattan skyline from its Weehawken branch and marina views from the AC Golden Nugget locale, this "surf 'n' turf" "institution" has a "romantic", "special occasion" feel to enhance its "varied menu" of "good, fresh" seafood (and "don't miss the molten lava" dessert); some find it "touristy" and "pricey", and say you're "paying for the views", but fans deem the "total package" a "memorable experience."

Chateau of Spain *Spanish* 22 | 18 | 22 | $35

Newark | 11 Franklin St. (bet. Broad & Mulberry Sts.) | 973-624-3346 | www.chateauofspain.com

Amigos are "satisfied every time" by the "good-size portions" of "solid" Spanish fare at this Ironbound stalwart not far from the Prudential Center; "friendly" service and moderate prices help make up for "difficult" parking.

Cheesecake Factory ● *American* 21 | 21 | 20 | $28

Hackensack | Shops at Riverside | 197 Riverside Sq. (Hackensack Ave.) | 201-488-0330
Short Hills | Short Hills Mall | 1200 Morris Tpke. (John F. Kennedy Blvd.) | 973-921-0930
Wayne | Willowbrook Mall | 1700 Willowbrook Blvd. (Rte. 46) | 973-890-1400
Bridgewater | Bridgewater Commons | 400 Commons Way (Rte. 206) | 908-252-0399
Edison | Menlo Park Mall | 455 Menlo Park Dr. (Rte. 1) | 732-494-7000
Freehold | Freehold Raceway Mall | 3710 Rte. 9 (Raceway Mall Dr.) | 732-462-6544
Cherry Hill | Marketplace at Garden State Park | 931 Haddonfield Rd. (bet. Garden Park Blvd. & Marlton Pike) | 856-665-7550
www.thecheesecakefactory.com

There are "no surprises" at this "wildly popular" American chain, just "steady" food "turned up a notch" and served in "button-bursting portions" from a menu the size of *"War and Peace"*; though critics cite "long waits" and find the "decibels as high as the calorie count", many more call it a "fail-safe" choice where "you know what you're getting" and it's "always good."

Chef Jon's *Chinese* 20 | 14 | 17 | $23

Whippany | Pine Plaza Shopping Ctr. | 831 Rte. 10 (Mt. Pleasant Ave.) | 973-585-6258 | www.chefjons.com

"Though it's in a strip mall, it's not strip-mall Chinese" say fans of the "creative" "Shanghai-focused" fare whipped up at this "rare find" in Whippany; while the decor is deemed "typical", thoughts on service

	FOOD	DECOR	SERVICE	COST

range from "friendly" to "a little rough", but the "authentic" eats are "good enough" so that "you probably won't care"; P.S. it's BYO.

Chef Mike's ABG Ⓜ American/Seafood
(fka Atlantic Bar & Grill)

| 22 | 21 | 22 | $48 |

South Seaside Park | 10 Central Ave. (24th Ave.) | 732-854-1588 | www.atlanticbarandgrillnj.com

"Beautiful oceanfront views" through floor-to-ceiling windows enhance the "tasty", if "pricey", seafood and American fare at this South Seaside Park spot, and those who felt it went "downhill" after the departure of chef Mike Jurusz may be heartened by his return in 2013 (which may not be reflected in the Food score); the dining room is "warm and inviting" but can get "crowded" – so get there early because the "place fills up fast."

Chef's Table Ⓢ Ⓜ French

| 27 | 20 | 25 | $57 |

Franklin Lakes | Franklin Square Shopping Ctr. | 754 Franklin Ave. (Palis Ave.) | 201-891-6644 | www.tctnj.com

It's "like being in Paris" (by way of a Franklin Lakes strip mall) at this "fabulous" French BYO bistro, a "tour de force" starring "first-rate" chef Claude Baills and his "superb", "hearty" "classics"; Madame Baills guides the "excellent service", and since the "charming" place is "small", "reservations are a must" (and "hard to get") – still, "dedicated regulars" declare it "marvelous for special occasions."

Chef Vola's Ⓜ⤸ Italian

| 27 | 16 | 25 | $52 |

Atlantic City | 111 S. Albion Pl. (Pacific Ave.) | 609-345-2022 | www.chefvolas.com

"Those in the know" "plan well in advance" to score a "tough reservation" at this "off-the-beaten-trail" Atlantic City BYO where a "congenial" staff serves "excellent, authentic" Italian "home cooking" amid an "old-school" atmosphere that "feels like a secret club"; "don't expect fancy" in the "noisy" basement space (you'll be "jammed in like sardines"), but do bring cash to cover the "expensive" tabs for an all-around "delicious experience."

Chelsea Prime Steak

| 24 | 24 | 22 | $67 |

Atlantic City | Chelsea Hotel | 111 S. Chelsea Ave., 5th fl. (Pacific Ave.) | 609-428-4545 | www.thechelsea-ac.com

The steaks are "excellent" and the "old supper-club vibe" "romantic" (think "tiered seating", black-and-white decor) at this meatery in AC's boutique Chelsea Hotel; factor in "breathtaking views" of the Atlantic and "polished" service, and it's understandable why fans find it "simply a beautiful place to spend an evening."

Chengdu 46 Ⓜ Chinese

| 23 | 19 | 21 | $41 |

Clifton | 1105 Rte. 46 E. (Conklin Dr.) | 973-777-8855 | www.chengdu46.com

Serving "top-notch", "upscale" Chinese for 30 years, this Clifton "classic" may be "a little on the pricey side", but the "beautifully presented" "authentic" Sichuan fare "always lives up to expectations"; though the strip-mall locale is "a bit nondescript" and some think the menu and the decor are "getting a little long in the tooth", the staff still "greets you with a smile."

Chez Catherine 🌫️Ⓜ️ *French* | 26 | 23 | 25 | $69 |

Westfield | Best Western Westfield Inn | 431 North Ave. W. (bet. Broad & Prospect Sts.) | 908-654-4011 | www.chezcatherine.com

"Close to perfect" is how aficionados assess this "fantastic" French cafe adjacent to the Best Western Westfield Inn; lunch has à la carte options, but dinner is strictly prix fixe, and while opinions on the "formal" setting range from "elegant" to "tired", most agree the service is "outstanding" and the "food is inspiring" – even if "special-occasion" prices have some wondering, "are they based on the euro?"; P.S. jackets are recommended.

Chicken or the Egg *American* | 21 | 18 | 20 | $18 |

Beach Haven | 207 N. Bay Ave. (bet. 2nd & 3rd Sts.) | 609-492-3695 | www.492fowl.com

A "fun atmosphere" and "creative" menu items, including what some call the "best wings on earth", have fans clucking about this seasonally opened, "family-oriented" Beach Haven American that's a "staple on LBI"; "decent prices" and "quick, friendly" service are further reasons there are "lines are out the door for breakfast, lunch and dinner."

Chickie's & Pete's ❶ *Pub Food* | 21 | 20 | 21 | $23 |

Bordentown | 183 Rte. 130 (Ward Ave.) | 609-298-9182

Chickie's & Pete's Cafe ❶ *Pub Food*

Egg Harbor Township | 6055 Black Horse Pike (English Creek Ave.) | 609-272-1930
www.chickiesandpetes.com

The "crab fries are addictive" at these "loud" sports-bar chain links rife with "big-screen TVs" and pub-grub "staples" such as "pizza, wings, cheesesteak" and an "excellent tap beer selection"; the "casual" vibe ("silverware and plates aren't something they believe in") plus "good prices" and a "friendly" staff add up to a "fun place to spend an evening."

Chimney Rock Inn *American* | 19 | 16 | 19 | $23 |

Bound Brook | 800 N. Thompson Ave. (Chimney Rock Rd.) | 732-469-4600

Gillette | 342 Valley Rd. (Russell Ave.) | 908-580-1100
www.chimneyrockinn.com

"Tasty and filling" pub-grub standards, "great" thin-crust pizzas, "friendly" service and "good prices" bring groups and families to this "casual" New American duo in Bound Brook and Gillette; with fans cheering their teams on TV and Little Leaguers "haunting the place", the "popular" spots are "noisy" and "busy" on game days, and some think the tavernlike digs need "a makeover", but many regard them as "dependable local joints."

Chinese Mirch *Asian* | 19 | 18 | 20 | $22 |

NEW Edgewater | The Marketplace at Edgewater | 725 River Rd. (Russell Ave.) | 201-941-3069

(continued)

(continued)

Chinese Mirch

North Brunswick | 2800 Rte. 27 (Thomas Ave.) | 732-951-8424 | Ⓜ
www.chinesemirch.com

Well-priced "Chinese with an Indian flair" – think "exotic dishes" like crispy Sichuan lamb, chicken lollipop and fried okra – is served by a "helpful" staff at these "friendly" BYO siblings in Edgewater and North Brunswick (outposts of the NYC original); while some say the "quality is mixed", others applaud the "good selection" and "balanced flavors."

The Chophouse *Seafood/Steak*

24 | 24 | 24 | $47

Gibbsboro | 4 S. Lakeview Dr. (Clementon Rd.) | 856-566-7300 |
www.thechophouse.us

The "romantic" setting of this Gibbsboro chophouse, with its "delightful" view of Silver Lake and firepit-equipped deck, makes for a "special night out" over "great" steaks and "very good" seafood specials served by a "friendly" staff; though some find it "exceptionally noisy", and others deem it "too expensive", most say they'd gladly "go back soon", wallet willing.

Christie's Italian
Seafood Grill *Italian*

23 | 18 | 21 | $38

Howell | Howell Ctr. | 2420 Rte. 9 S. (White St.) | 732-780-8310 |
www.christiesrestaurant.us

An "extensive menu" of "wonderful" Italian eats (including "fresh" seafood and "tasty" pastas) and "big portions" define this "consistent", "classy" BYO in Howell; "don't be dissuaded" by the strip-mall locale urge devotees, who insist "it's nice inside" thanks to a recent redo, and "polite" service takes some of the sting out of somewhat "pricey" tabs.

Christopher's *American*

20 | 21 | 19 | $44

New Brunswick | Heldrich Hotel | 101 Livingston Ave. (bet. George & New Sts.) | 732-214-2200 | www.theheldrich.com

Tucked in New Brunswick's Heldrich Hotel, in the middle of the city's theater district, this "high-end" New American is a "nice addition to the local food scene" thanks to "good-quality" food and "great drinks"; while some find it "overpriced" and think "service could be improved", admirers appreciate the mod, "fancy" atmosphere.

Cinders Wood
Fire Grill ● *Eclectic*

20 | 21 | 18 | $34

Mine Hill | 319 Rte. 46 (bet. Iron Mountain Rd. & Wharton Ave.) |
973-928-7000 | www.cinderswoodfiregrill.com

"Share with others" so you can "try a lot" of the "interesting tapas offerings" advise aficionados of this Mine Hill steakhouse/small-plates specialist where the specials are "innovative", entrees include steaks, sushi, chicken and seafood and the wine list is "excellent"; some think given the "expensive" tabs, the "portions leave a lot to be desired", while others insist you "get more than your money's worth" – either way, the "atmosphere is awesome" in the rustic-chic setting.

Cinnamon *Indian*

21 | 16 | 20 | $23

Morris Plains | 2920 Rte. 10 W. (bet. Parks & Powder Mill Rds.) |
973-734-0040 | www.cinnamonindianrestaurant.com

"Great for carnivores and veggies" alike, this "local" BYO Indian churns out a "more diverse menu than the usual", including "multiple can't-resist dishes" and a daily "high-quality" lunch buffet (and dinner on Sundays) some call "the best deal around"; set in a Morris Plains strip mall, the large space may not impress, but the "accommodating" staff is "helpful and friendly" to both "rookies" and regulars alike.

Classic Quiche *Eclectic*

23 | 18 | 20 | $20

Teaneck | 333 Queen Anne Rd. (bet. Degraw Ave. & Fort Lee Rd.) |
201-692-0150 | www.classicquiche.com

"A mecca for quiche-lovers", this "casual" BYO Eclectic in Teaneck also offers "well-made" sandwiches, "lovely soups" and "surprisingly good" "light dinners" in a "simple setup"; the "charming outdoor area" is a "warm-weather delight", and there's occasional live music.

Clementine's Café ☒ *Creole*

23 | 21 | 21 | $46

Avon-by-the-Sea | 306 Main St. (bet. Garfield & Lincoln Aves.) |
732-988-7979 | www.clementinesavon.com

"Creative" Creole dishes and other "New Orleans–style" offerings are found at this Avon BYO that has two seatings per weekend eve; some "love" the "cutesy" decor boasting "different decorations for each season", while others find it a bit "off", but either way, there's no denying it's "interesting"; P.S. reservations highly recommended.

Clydz ◐ *American*

23 | 20 | 22 | $46

New Brunswick | 55 Paterson St. (bet. Joyce Kilmer Ave. & Spring St.) |
732-846-6521 | www.clydz.com

"Wild palates" are up for the "exotic" eats – think venison, antelope and python – served by a "well-educated staff" at this New Brunswick American where the "diverse" menu also includes "memorable" options for the less adventurous, plus "legendary" martinis that are themselves "worth the trip"; the "quaint", subterranean "speakeasy setting" boasts a "busy", "loud" bar, and while prices are "a bit high", "for a special night", fans deem it a "gem in the area."

The Coastline ◐ *American*

20 | 19 | 20 | $24

Cherry Hill | 1240 Brace Rd. (bet. Bortons Mill Rd. & Munn Ave.) |
856-795-1773 | www.coastlinenj.com

An "expansive" salad bar headlines the "decent" "diner-like" fare at this affordable Cherry Hill American, an "upbeat" spot frequented as much for its "busy bar scene" with live music and DJs; the setting is "comfortable" enough, and servers "friendly", while a "tasty" Sunday brunch buffet draws fans with ample "variety" at a low price.

Columbia Inn Ⓜ *Italian*

21 | 16 | 20 | $33

Montville | 29 Main Rd. (Morris Ave.) | 973-263-1300 |
www.thecolumbiainn.com

Pizza "famous for its very thin, crispy crust" and other "tasty" "standard Italian fare" make this "family-oriented" Montville trattoria a "local favorite"; set in a 19th-century building, the decor is "starting to look dreary" to some, and others feel the menu could use a "spruce-up" as well, but the "friendly", "casual" atmosphere and reasonable prices make it a "go-to" for many.

Conte's *Pizza*

23	14	19	$20

Princeton | 339 Witherspoon St. (Guyot Ave.) | 609-921-8041 | www.contespizzaandbar.com

For "divine" thin-crust pizza, fans "travel for miles" to this "cavernous" Princeton "institution" where it's "busy, noisy" and "there's always a line" – but it's all "worth it"; the "tired", "old-school decor" means there's "not much atmosphere", and while some find the service "slow", with "a full-service bar and a game on the tube", "what else can you ask for?"

Continental *Eclectic*

23	22	22	$37

Atlantic City | Pier Shops at Caesars | 1 Atlantic Ocean (Arkansas Ave.) | 609-674-8300 | www.continentalac.com

Everything comes with a "twist" at Stephen Starr's "nuevo retro" Eclectic at Atlantic City's Pier Shops at Caesars, from "inventive" tapas bites (cheesesteak eggrolls, Korean tacos) to "fun" martinis ("Tang in an alcoholic drink" = "genius"); diners dig the "*Jetsons*-like atmosphere" with seating both inside and on a faux-outdoor patio with fire pit, and considering the shared-plate eating style, tabs are "reasonable."

Copper Canyon *Southwestern*

24	22	21	$55

Atlantic Highlands | Blue Bay Inn | 51 First Ave. (bet. Bay & Center Aves.) | 732-291-8444 | www.thecoppercanyon.com

"De-lish" Southwestern chow, including lots of "tapaslike dishes", is the calling card of this "beautiful" spot inside Atlantic Highlands' Blue Bay Inn, where the fare can be paired with "awesome" margaritas concocted from an "extensive tequila selection" and served by an "attentive" staff; cognoscenti caution that noise levels can be "painful" and tabs do "climb", but many deem it "worth the trip" nonetheless.

Coriander: An Indian Bistro *Indian*

▽ 24	23	23	$25

Voorhees | Ritz Shopping Ctr. | 910 Haddonfield Berlin Rd. (bet. Voorhees Dr. & White Horse Rd.) | 856-566-4546 | www.coriandernj.com

"Incredibly detailed and delicate dishes" at this Voorhees BYO Indian are a "treat to the palate", boasting "amazing flavors" and just "the right amount of heat"; set in the Ritz Shopping Center, the "colorful, bright and beautiful" digs have an "upscale quality" (though the prices do not), and when you add "stellar" service, you have the ingredients for a "marvelous experience."

Corso 98 *Italian*

23	20	23	$45

Montclair | 98 Walnut Street (bet. Depot Sq. & Frink St.) | 973-746-0789 | www.corso98.com

This "top-notch" Montclair Italian "treats you like family", offering "creative", "homestyle" dinners served with "obvious pride" by "personable owners" and a "friendly" staff; exposed brick and low lighting lend a "nice atmosphere", and while wine and beer are available, BYO is welcome.

Costanera ⓜ *Peruvian*

24	20	22	$40

Montclair | 511 Bloomfield Ave. (bet. Fullerton Ave. & Park St.) | 973-337-8289 | www.costaneranj.com

Presenting a "sophisticated twist" on Peruvian specialties, this "lovely" Montclair BYO serves an "intriguing menu" of "exciting", "well-presented" dishes like "wonderful" grilled fish and "to-die-for" ceviche; "prices are great for the quality" and the "knowledgeable" staff is "happy to make suggestions", but weekend dinners can get a little "noisy" and "crowded", so some recommend a late lunch for a "leisurely", "delightful time."

Country Pancake House ⑦ *American*

19	13	17	$17

Ridgewood | 140 E. Ridgewood Ave. (Walnut St.) | 201-444-8395 | www.countrypancakehouse.net

You can "share a pancake with the entire neighborhood" at this American BYO in Ridgewood where the portions of "homestyle" cheap eats are as "ginormous" "as the menu is long"; though some find the service "spotty" and the "small", "nondescript" digs are usually "crowded" ("be prepared to wait"), since "you get two meals for the price of one", most think "it's worth it" – just remember to bring an "empty stomach" and cash since credit cards aren't accepted.

Court Street Restaurant & Bar *Continental*

21	20	21	$36

Hoboken | 61 Sixth St. (Court St.) | 201-795-4515 | www.courtstreet.com

Hobokenites say this "reliable" "neighborhood" Continental is "always a pleasure", thanks to a "huge menu" with "something for everyone" and an "extensive" wine list; add "friendly" service, reasonable prices, a "hang"-worthy mahogany bar and "nice ambiance" and you know why "everyone leaves happy."

Crab House *Seafood*

19	20	17	$39

Edgewater | 541 River Rd. (bet. Archer St. & Promenade) | 201-840-9311 | www.crabhouseseafood.com

"Fabulous" Hudson River and New York City views lure fans to this Edgewater outpost of a midpriced Floridian seafood chain slinging an "awesome array" of fin fare; no surprise, the decor is "nautical", and while some find the eats "hit-or-miss" and think the service "could be more attentive", given the "amazing location" and "long" happy hours, you might not notice.

Crab Trap *Seafood*

24	20	22	$35

Somers Point | 2 Broadway (Landing Ln.) | 609-927-7377 | www.thecrabtrap.com

Expect "pleasant" service and "fresh" fin fare at this "always-tasty" seafooder in Somers Point that's "been the same" "relaxed place" for more than 40 years; it's "always crowded", with especially "long waits in summertime", but the bar out back with "spectacular views" of Great Egg Harbor makes seating delays more "palatable."

| | FOOD | DECOR | SERVICE | COST |

Cranbury Inn *American*
18 | 20 | 19 | $36

Cranbury | 21 S. Main St. (bet. Evans Dr. & Station Rd.) |
609-655-5595 | www.thecranburyinn.com

Housed in a "quaint" Revolutionary War–era inn that's "rich in history", this Cranbury tavern offers "mostly satisfactory" Traditional American fare, like "turkey dinner with all the trimmings"; some say a menu that "doesn't change much" and sometimes "slow" service detract from its "lovely setting" and evident "potential."

Crown Palace *Chinese*
20 | 18 | 19 | $28

Marlboro | 8 N. Main St. (School Rd.) | 732-780-8882
Middletown | 1283 Rte. 35 (Green Oak Blvd.) | 732-615-9888
www.crownpalacerestaurant.com

"Consistent", "tasty" food, "and lots of it", draws a regular crowd to this bustling pair of "neighborhood" Chinese in Marlboro and Middletown, especially on weekends for "great fun" dim sum; some find the "flamboyant" digs complete with tropical fish tanks a bit "dated" and service "inconsistent", but fans deem it a "good value."

Cubacán *Cuban*
22 | 23 | 20 | $43

Asbury Park | 800 Ocean Ave. (Asbury Ave.) | 732-774-3007 |
www.cubacan.net

For "*deliciosas*" tapas, Asbury Park denizens head to this boardwalk Cuban, where "eclectic Latin fusion" dishes are "fairly priced" and "served up with flair" by a "solid" staff; the vibe is "funky hip island", and some describe the decibels as "slightly louder than a jackhammer" when it gets hopping – still, it "hits the spot after a day at the beach."

Cuba Libre *Cuban*
21 | 22 | 22 | $40

Atlantic City | Quarter at the Tropicana | 2801 Pacific Ave. (Iowa Ave.) |
609-348-6700 | www.cubalibrerestaurant.com

A "great change of pace from the standard AC fare", this "friendly", midpriced Cuban inside the Tropicana promises "authentic" eats (including weekend brunch) in a "lovely" setting that feels "like you've stepped into the streets of Cuba"; "loud music" lures partygoers onto the dance floor Friday and Saturday nights, while "incredible mojitos" and other "top-shelf cocktails" further fuel the "Latin vibe."

Cuban Pete's *Cuban*
20 | 21 | 19 | $29

Montclair | 428 Bloomfield Ave. (bet. Fullerton Ave. & Seymour St.) |
973-746-1100 | www.cubanpetesrestaurant.com

It's always a "party" at this "happening" Montclair hot spot that serves up "hearty" "reasonably priced" Cuban fare, and "plenty of it", in a "funky" "tropical" setting; BYO wine and they'll mix sangria in many flavors, and while some grouse about "deafening din", "cramped" seating and "rushed" service, others report a "fun time."

Cubanu ● *Cuban*
20 | 20 | 19 | $34

Rahway | 1467 Main St. (Lewis St.) | 732-499-7100 |
www.cubanu.com

"Plentiful" portions of "tasty" Cuban fare attract "locals" to this midpriced Rahway lounge, where "genuine" mojitos bring some spice to the meal, as do DJs, live music and dancing; if service gets mixed marks ("great" vs. "inattentive"), fans say the overall vibe is "friendly" and might just make you "feel like you're in Cuba."

Cubby's BBQ *BBQ*   20 | 14 | 17 | $22

Hackensack | 249 S. River St. (bet. Water St. & Wysocki Pl.) | 201-488-9389 | www.cubbysbarbeque.com

"Large slabs" of "tender", "messy" ribs at "decent" prices are the reason this Hackensack BBQ has been a "local hangout for years"; the "basic" serve-yourself space might encourage takeout, but check out the photos hanging on the walls – owner Bobby Egan was famously "once a conduit to North Korea."

Cucharamama Ⓜ *S American*   25 | 22 | 22 | $46

Hoboken | 233 Clinton St. (3rd St.) | 201-420-1700 | www.cucharamama.com

"Creatively delicious" cuisine, including "great" breads from a wood-burning oven, offers an "education in South American" cooking from chef and food historian Maricel Presilla at this "destination-worthy" Hoboken Pan-Latin, a sibling of nearby Zafra; although some find the digs "tight", "attentive" service, an "eclectic" vibe and "lively" cocktails help make "every meal a good time."

Cucina Calandra *Italian*   21 | 19 | 20 | $32

Fairfield | Best Western Fairfield Executive Inn | 216-234 Rte. 46 E. (Horseneck Rd.) | 973-575-7720 | www.cucinacalandra.com

"Solid" Italian "classics" are the centerpiece of this "family-friendly" spot in the Best Western Fairfield, where fans rave about "delicious" signature bread (and you can take a free loaf home); prices are "reasonable", especially at happy hour, and, if the "cavernous" "Italian-village" setting can seem "a little overdone", there's a "lovely" outdoor patio for warm evening dines.

CulinAriane Ⓩ Ⓜ *American*   27 | 22 | 25 | $59

Montclair | 33 Walnut St. (Pine St.) | 973-744-0533 | www.culinariane.com

"Great things happen" in the kitchen of *Top Chef* contestant Ariane Duarte, whose "lovingly prepared" dishes make this Montclair American BYO a "local gem"; with service that's "beyond gracious", plus an "intimate" space and limited hours (Wednesdays–Saturdays), it's no surprise that reservations are "tough" to get, but even with "NYC prices", converts say this "true standout" "should be on everyone's list."

Da Filippo's Ⓩ *Italian/Seafood*   24 | 18 | 22 | $40

Somerville | 132 E. Main St. (bet. Hamilton & Meadow Sts.) | 908-218-0110 | www.dafilippos.com

Seafood's the "specialty" at this "off-the-beaten-path" Somerville Italian, where Sicilian classics are "cooked with care"; BYO keeps tabs "reasonable", and if the vibe's somewhere between "warm, country home" and "private club", that's due to "personalized service" from chef-owner Filippo Russo, who occasionally "gets out of the kitchen to play the piano."

	FOOD	DECOR	SERVICE	COST

Dai-Kichi *Japanese* | 23 | 17 | 20 | $34

Upper Montclair | 608 Valley Rd. (bet. Bellevue & Lorraine Aves.) | 973-744-2954 | www.daikichimontclair.net

A "local favorite" for "reliably good" Japanese in Upper Montclair, this "casual" midpriced sushi house offers "fresh, nicely prepared" fish and "creative specials"; though quarters might be "tight", servers will make it a "quick" meal; P.S. there's also a "cool" bar upstairs.

Danny's ❶ *Steak* | 22 | 18 | 21 | $45

Red Bank | 11 Bridge Ave. (bet. Front & Monmouth Sts.) | 732-741-6900 | www.dannyssteakhouse.com

"Friendly" owner Danny Murphy makes "everyone feel welcome" at his "reliable" "upscale" Red Bank steak-and-sushi shop; though some dismiss it as "nothing special", others deem it "good for pre-theater" dining, and the bar scene is "always packed."

Dante's Ristorante *Italian* | 20 | 18 | 21 | $39

Mendham | 100 E. Main St. (bet. Cold Hill & Dean Rds.) | 973-543-5401 | www.dantenj.com

A "longtime standby", this Mendham Italian BYO executes an "impressive range" of "dependable" dishes, from homemade pastas to pizza, at "fair" prices; the "dark" space "needs a makeover" some say, but a "friendly" staff contributes to an overall "warm" vibe.

Daryl *American* | 23 | 23 | 22 | $50
(fka Daryl Wine Bar)

New Brunswick | Heldrich Hotel | 302 George St. (New St.) | 732-253-7780 | www.darylrestaurant.com

With its "creative" menu and "contemporary styling", this New American wine bar (now helmed by chef Zod Arifai of Montclair's Blu and Next Door) is a "change of pace" for New Brunswick according to fans; "extensive" vinos by the glass come in several sizes to encourage pairing, and though tabs trend "expensive", "unobtrusive" service and a "chic", "modern" setting make it suitable for a "date" night.

Da's Kitchen *Thai* | ▽ 25 | 21 | 23 | $26

Hopewell | 21 E. Broad Street (Seminary Ave.) | 609-466-8424 | www.daskitchenhopewell.com

"Delicious" "well-spiced" Thai cuisine draws diners to this storefront BYO in Hopewell, where "personable" chef Da Detoro creates "authentic" flavors at varying degrees of "heat" according to diners' fortitude; prices are affordable, and the "small, pleasant" space offers sidewalk seating during good weather.

Da Soli Ⓜ *Italian* | ▽ 25 | 22 | 20 | $39

Haddonfield | Shops at 116 | 116 Kings Hwy. E. (Tanner St.) | 856-429-2399 | www.dasolirestaurant.com

With its "well-prepared", "rustic" Northern Italian cuisine, headlined by handmade pastas, fans say this midpriced Haddonfield BYO in the Shoppes at 116 is a "welcome addition" to the area; service rates "attentive", and the space has "simple" Tuscan brick-floored decor with two-level seating.

Dauphin Grille ⓜ *American*   22 | 21 | 19 | $50
Asbury Park | Berkeley Hotel | 1401 Ocean Ave. (6th Ave.) | 732-774-3474 | www.dauphingrille.com

With "ingredients deftly handled by the kitchen", the "farm-to-fork" American fare pairs well with the "nice wine selection" at this pricey but "no-pretentions" venue inside Asbury Park's "cozy" Berkeley Hotel; frequent live jazz "sets the atmosphere" in the "comfortable", traditional space, and "wonderful alfresco dining" is a bonus.

Davia ⌿ *Italian*   22 | 18 | 22 | $37
Fair Lawn | 6-09 Fair Lawn Ave. (bet. River Rd. & 6th St.) | 201-797-6767 | www.daviarest.com

"Huge portions" mean there's "always something to take home" from this "inventive" Fair Lawn Italian, where a "homey" atmosphere and "warm" staff make it a "local" "favorite"; plus, fans say the four-course early-bird special might just be the "best in the state"; P.S. cash only.

David Burke Fromagerie ⓜ *American*   25 | 24 | 24 | $70
Rumson | 26 Ridge Rd. (Ave. of 2 Rivers) | 732-842-8088 | www.fromagerierestaurant.com

It's "art on a plate" rave fans who "keep coming back" for chef David Burke's "well-executed" American "innovations" at this Rumson "fine-dining" destination; with "heads-up" service and a "handsome, roomy" setting, there's "a lot to like here", and though tabs are "pricey", you "can't beat the value" on the "popular" Tuesday burger night; P.S. there's frequent live music too.

Dayi'nin Yeri *Turkish*   24 | 14 | 20 | $24
Cliffside Park | 333 Palisade Ave. (Cliff St.) | 201-840-1770 | www.dayininyerinj.com

Though this Cliffside Park BYO is known for its Turkish pizza, fans also tout its range of "delicious" dishes, including kebabs, "great fresh fish" and "fantastic" desserts; there's little love for the "small", "noisy" space, but "friendly" service and "good" prices help make it "worth a trip" for many.

DeAnna's ⊠ⓜ *Italian*   22 | 22 | 19 | $38
Lambertville | 54 N. Franklin St. (Coryell St.) | 609-397-8957 | www.deannasrestaurant.com

"Fresh" homemade pasta is the centerpiece of the "quality" Italian fare served up at this erstwhile bar in Lambertville, where a "party atmosphere" still prevails amid the "wild decor" and "vivacious" crowd; the staff is "friendly" though some say "service can be slow" and "pricey" for what it is – still, prix fixe specials midweek offer affordable alternatives, and courtyard seating is an all-summer draw.

Delicious Heights *American*   19 | 20 | 19 | $33
Berkeley Heights | 428 Springfield Ave. (Lone Pine Dr.) | 908-464-3287 ◑
Bedminster | 285 U.S. 202 (Somerville Rd.) | 908-234-1596 | www.deliciousheights.com

There's "something for everyone" on the "huge" menu of American "comfort" "staples" at these "upscale taverns" in Berkeley Heights and

Bedminster, even if some deem them merely "fair" and say service "leaves a bit to be desired"; it's the "lively bars", with their "large beer selection" and "lots of TVs" that seem to draw "crowds", although daytime specials can make them "handy" for lunch as well.

DeLorenzo's Pizza ⧄Ⓜ *Pizza* | 25 | 16 | 20 | $18 |

Hamilton Township | 147 Sloan Ave. (Alexander Ave.) | 609-393-2952 | www.delospizza.com

"If you're lucky enough to get a seat" at this Hamilton Township pizza stalwart, fans say you'll be treated to some "mighty good" "tomato pie" with "uniquely crisp crust" and "fresh, delicious toppings"; "good prices" and a BYO policy are pluses, and the new, no-frills setting offers booth seating, which suits those who are just here for a slice of "the legend."

DeLorenzo's Tomato Pies Ⓜ *Pizza* | 27 | 20 | 22 | $19 |

Robbinsville | Washington Town Ctr. | 2350 Rte. 33 (Robbinsville Edinburg Rd.) | 609-341-8480 | www.delorenzostomatopies.com

Though now in Robbinsville, this 66-year-old Trenton-born "classic" (operated by one branch of a famous 'za clan) still attracts legions of fans thanks to its "absolutely delicious" pizza with crust that's "perfectly charred", and salads that are "no slouch either"; you can still "expect long waits" in the new digs, which are a "dressed up" version of the old, and while it's BYO, insiders advise "birch beer goes best with the pie."

Delta's ●Ⓜ *Southern* | 22 | 21 | 20 | $40 |

New Brunswick | 19 Dennis St. (bet. Albany & Richmond Sts.) | 732-249-1551 | www.deltasrestaurant.com

"Authentic" soul food is the focus of this midpriced New Brunswick Southerner, which serves up crawfish, yams and "smothered everything" in a "cool, jazzy" brick-walled setting; down-home "hospitality" and live music weekends complete the scene, making it "nice" for "date night" or "after-work drinks."

Depot Market Cafe ⧄⇗ *American* | ▽ 24 | 16 | 22 | $15 |

Cape May | 409 Elmira St. (bet. Broad & Lafayette Sts.) | 609-884-8030

"Grab a quick, delicious bite" at this Cape May American, a "treasure" that "all the locals know about", serving "generous" portions of salads, sandwiches and burgers; it's "nothing fancy" – "you don't go for the decor" – meaning fans frequently get "takeout on the way to the beach"; P.S. cash only.

𝗡𝗘𝗪 Despaña *Spanish* | - | - | - | M |

Princeton | 235A Nassau St. (Chestnut St.) | 609-921-2992 | www.despanaprinceton.com

Pintxos, tapas, cheese, charcuterie and more are on offer at this Princeton BYO sibling of the boutique retailer-cum-Spanish cafe in NYC's SoHo; it offers self-service lunches and full-service dinners in a two-story, industrial-chic space, with a food market on the ground floor and two dining rooms on the second floor, plus a rooftop terrace and a sangria mixing bar.

Dimora *Italian*

23 | 19 | 20 | $59

Norwood | 100 Piermont Rd. (bet. Briarwood & Pierson Aves.) | 201-750-5000 | www.dimoraristorante.com

"Classic" Italian dishes draw a "lively" crowd of "regulars" to this Norwood "special-occasion" spot, where "fresh, tasty" seafood and homemade pasta are standouts; while it can be a "mob scene" on weekends, with "overwhelming" noise, "accommodating" waiters help maintain a "sophisticated" vibe, and though "expensive", fans insist it "never disappoints."

Dim Sum Dynasty *Chinese*

20 | 16 | 18 | $28

Ridgewood | 75 Franklin Ave. (bet. Chestnut & Oak Sts.) | 201-652-0686 | www.dimsumdynastynj.com

The dim sum at this "reliable" Ridgewood Cantonese "can be quite good" say regulars, who tout the "nice selection" served from carts on weekends; service can be "slow" (especially "on the weekend") and the "old-school" decor may not impress many, but for fans it "hits the spot", and BYO helps keep it affordable.

Dinallo's ◗ *Italian*

21 | 19 | 22 | $40

River Edge | 259 Johnson Ave. (New Jersey 4) | 201-342-1233 | www.dinallosrestaurant.com

"Time stopped" at this River Edge "oasis", where "old-timers" gather for midpriced "meatballs and gravy" and red-sauce Italian classics; "tight" seating makes it "cozy" (or "crowded", depending on your viewpoint), but the "nice" staff helps diners feel "at home", while a "bustling" bar reminds them that they're not.

The Dining Room at Anthony David's *Italian*

24 | 21 | 22 | $44

Hoboken | 953 Bloomfield St. (10th St.) | 201-222-8359 | www.anthonydavids.com

Chef-owner Anthony Pino takes an "innovative" approach to Northern Italian cuisine "without being pretentious" at this popular Hoboken BYO, set in a "romantic" room behind his gourmet market, where there's "more casual" seating; although the "cozy" setting seems "cramped" to some, and a no-reservations policy on weekends can generate "crazy waits", fans tout the "great team" and "consistent" brunch seven days a week.

Dino & Harry's *Steak*

24 | 22 | 23 | $65

Hoboken | 163 14th St. (Garden St.) | 201-659-6202 | www.dinoandharrys.com

"Awesome" chops are the reason this Hoboken "classic" steakhouse is "always packed" – that and the "grown-up", "meet-and-greet" atmosphere inside the former 19th-century saloon (an *On the Waterfront* location); an "old-fashioned" wine selection, live piano music and "friendly", "longtime" servers help it live up to the "Manhattan prices."

	FOOD	DECOR	SERVICE	COST

Dino's *Italian* 21 | 20 | 22 | $39

Harrington Park | 12 Tappan Rd. (Schraalenburgh Rd.) | 201-767-4245 | www.dinoshp.com

"Innovative", "well-prepared" takes on classic Italian dishes draw diners to this "serene" Harrington Park house, where a "warm" welcome is part of the appeal; a "nice" wine list and "fair" prices contribute to an all-around "good experience"; P.S. it's closed Tuesdays.

Dinosaur Bar-B-Que *BBQ* 23 | 19 | 19 | $33

Newark | 224 Market St. (bet. Broad & Mulberry Sts.) | 862-214-6100 | www.dinosaurbarbque.com

"Lip-smacking good" BBQ draws a Pru Center crowd and other downtowners to this Newark outpost of a NY-based clan; "civilized portions" come at "good prices", and if the space is often "jammed", that's because so many find it a "welcome addition" to the area's "renaissance."

Di Palma Brothers M *Italian* 23 | 19 | 20 | $33

North Bergen | 8728 John F. Kennedy Blvd. W. (bet. 87th & 88th Sts.) | 201-868-3005 | www.dipalmabrothers.com

"Do some antiquing" while you dine at this "old-style" North Bergen BYO, which purveys "humongous" family-style portions of "authentic" Italian fare alongside vintage furniture and curios; if the feeling of being "at Nonna's house" doesn't agree with all, others enjoy an "after-dinner browse", and moderate prices add to its overall appeal.

Dish M *American* 23 | 17 | 21 | $41

Red Bank | 13 White St. (Broad St.) | 732-345-7070 | www.dishredbank.com

"Imaginative" takes on "comfort food" are the hallmark of this Downtown Red Bank American, which emphasizes "fresh", "seasonal" and locally sourced ingredients; seating can be "cramped" in the "tiny" storefront, and many bemoan a "cacophony of noise", as well as an "inexperienced" staff, but BYO and prix fixe menus can make for a well-priced outing.

Diving Horse S M *Seafood* ▽ 25 | 22 | 23 | $54

Avalon | 2109 Dune Dr. (21st St.) | 609-368-5000 | www.thedivinghorseavalon.com

Between the "nice variety" of "creative, well-prepared" seafood specialties and bright, "big-city atmosphere" that includes rustic wood details and an appealing patio, this "high-class" Avalon BYO is "not your typical Shore restaurant"; "polished" service helps justify steep tabs, and BYO also "keeps down the cost."

NEW **Diwani** *Indian* - | - | - | M

Ridgewood | 47 E. Ridgewood Ave. (bet. Chestnut & Oak Sts.) | 201-445-6060 | www.diwaninj.com

Traditional Indian fare heats up this casual Ridgewood BYO (the former home of Mela) where meat and veggie curries, naan and tandoori specials are served amid deep red walls, with Bollywood films playing on a large flat-screen TV.

	FOOD	DECOR	SERVICE	COST

D'Jeet? *American*
21 | 17 | 18 | $30

Red Bank | 637 Broad St. (White St.) | 732-224-8887 |
www.djeetcatering.com

"A must-stop when visiting The Grove", this Red Bank American boasts "fresh, healthy choices" that "change with the seasons", including sandwiches, salads and "delish" pastas; moderate prices are a plus, and while the space is "comfortable", insiders find it "preferable" to relax "outside in good weather."

Dock's Oyster House *Seafood*
25 | 21 | 24 | $54

Atlantic City | 2405 Atlantic Ave. (Georgia Ave.) | 609-345-0092 |
www.docksoysterhouse.com

A "venerable establishment" since 1897, this "pricey" AC seafooder scores high with "outstanding", "classic" fin fare served by an "on-point" staff in a simple room so "tight" that you might "rub elbows" with your neighbors; nightly piano music, plus a wine list and mixed drink selection, "keep the place abuzz", though some find it merely "noisy" – still, for most it's a "memorable" experience.

The Doc's Place Ⓜ *American*
20 | 19 | 21 | $37

Somers Point | 646 Bay Ave. (Medical Center Way) |
609-926-0404 | www.thedocsplace.com

"You can sit alongside beautiful boats and look out at the bay" from the deck of this New American located at the Harbour Cove Marina in Somers Point, where a "friendly" staff serves up "reasonably priced" fare and "generously sized drinks"; although a few find "nothing special" about it, it's a "popular place", so "make a reservation well in advance in season."

Domenico's Ⓜ *Italian*
23 | 19 | 21 | $39

Ventnor | 5223 Ventnor Ave. (Little Rock Ave.) | 609-822-1300 |
www.domenicosattheshore.com

For a "sure meal", *amici* tout this BYO Italian in Ventnor, where "wonderful" eats come at "reasonable" prices; the owner and staff are "accommodating", but the "small, intimate" storefront space "books up quick", so reservations are recommended.

Dong Bang Grill ❶ *Korean*
20 | 18 | 19 | $37

Fort Lee | 1616 Palisade Ave. (Angioletti Pl.) | 201-242-4485 |
www.dongbanggrill.com

"Tasty" BBQ short ribs and other grilled meats are the specialty of this "authentic", midpriced Fort Lee Korean, although vegetarians and sushi-lovers will find plenty here too; while the service and the spacious interior with in-table grills may not impress, fans insist it's "one of the better ones" in town.

Don Pepe *Portuguese/Spanish*
22 | 18 | 21 | $40

Newark | 844 McCarter Hwy. (Cherry St.) | 973-623-4662 |
www.donpeperestaurant.com
Pine Brook | 18 Old Bloomfield Ave. (Changebridge Rd.) |
973-882-6757 | www.donpepeii.com

"Go with a group" to these "classic" Iberians in Newark and Pine Brook, where lobsters "the size of small boats" and other seafood dishes are meant "to be shared" (and paired with "great sangria"); though the "old-style" "Spanish" decor may seem "tired" to some, "friendly service" and "excellent prices" win the day.

Don Pepe's Steakhouse *Steak*

22 | 18 | 21 | $45

Pine Brook | 58 Rte. 46 W. (Van Winkle Rd.) | 973-808-5533 | www.donpepesteakhouse.com

Prime chops "prepared nicely" attract diners to this Pine Brook Iberian steakhouse, where "huge" portions of meats and seafood, backed by an extensive Spanish wine list, offer "great value"; service is "friendly", and despite grumbles about "outdated" decor and "loud, boisterous" groups, most deem it "worth a visit."

Dos Caminos Ⓜ *Mexican*

22 | 21 | 21 | $44

Atlantic City | Harrah's Resort Atlantic City | 777 Harrah's Blvd. (Renaissance Point Blvd.) | 609-441-5747 | www.doscaminos.com

Guacamole "freshly made" tableside is a fan favorite at the Harrah's Atlantic City outpost of this NYC-based chain (part of the BR Guest group) offering "standard" Mexican fare suitable for pre-"pool party" snacking; a "great view of the bay", substantial margarita menu and "friendly" service all contribute to the "great atmosphere."

Dream Cuisine Cafe Ⓢ Ⓜ *French*

∇ 26 | 20 | 23 | $44

Cherry Hill | Tuscany Mktpl. | 1990 Marlton Pike E. (Old Orchard Rd.) | 856-751-2800 | www.dreamcuisinecafe.net

The "exceptional French cooking" at this high-end BYO brings a "touch of France to a Cherry Hill shopping center"; though many think the "unassuming" storefront space "does not match the quality of the cuisine", most are willing to overlook it for a "culinary adventure" that "does not disappoint."

Drew's Bayshore Bistro *American*

27 | 18 | 23 | $47

Keyport | 25 Church St. (Front St.) | 732-739-9219 | www.bayshorebistro.com

Chef Andrew Araneo's "truly amazing" Cajun-accented New American cuisine "exceeds expectations" at his BYO "gem" in Keyport, where many of the dishes come with a "kick" and are probably "not for dieters"; "fair" prices and "pleasant" service are more reasons why diners agree it's "well worth the visit"; P.S. a post-Sandy move to its current location is not reflected in the Decor score.

Dublin Square ● *Irish/Pub Food*

18 | 21 | 20 | $26

Bordentown | 167 Rte. 130 (Ward Ave.) | 609-298-7100
Cherry Hill | 482 E. Evesham Rd. (Short Hills Dr.) | 856-520-8312
www.dublinsquarepubs.com

A "lively" crowd meets up for "traditional" Irish grub and a "good selection of brews" at these pubs sporting "old-world" "flair" in Bordentown and Cherry Hill; though some knock the eats as "overpriced" and "fair at best", most are happy to take a seat at the "handsome bar" and soak up the "great energy."

	FOOD	DECOR	SERVICE	COST

NEW Due M _Italian_ | - | - | - | E

Ridgewood | 18 E. Ridgewood Ave. (S. Broad St.) | 201-857-3232 |
www.dueridgewood.com

Housemade pastas and mozzarella and meats from a wood-fired grill
anchor the menu of Italian cuisine at this upscale BYO newcomer in
Ridgewood from chef-owner Chris Tarta; located on a corner near
the train station, the small space has a simple, contemporary look
and a bistro-like ambiance.

Due Mari _Italian_ | 26 | 24 | 24 | $57

New Brunswick | 78 Albany St. (Neilson St.) | 732-296-1600 |
www.duemarinj.com

The vibe is "classy" and "metropolitan" at this "elegant" New
Brunswick Italian from consulting chef Michael White and the
Altamarea Group, where an "innovative" menu features "beautiful" seafood and "exceptional" pastas, which are "impeccably"
served by a "helpful" staff; while it's "certainly not cheap", the
overall "outstanding experience" makes it a "good choice" for
a "special occasion."

E & V M⊅ _Italian_ | 24 | 17 | 22 | $31

Paterson | 320 Chamberlain Ave. (Colonial Ave.) | 973-942-8080 |
www.evrestaurant.com

"Mouthwatering" "red-sauce" Italian "goodness" comes in "generous portions" at this "friendly" Paterson "diamond in the rough"; it's
cash-only, but "affordable", so "be prepared" for "big crowds" and
"long waits", and "just ignore the decor" counsel cognoscenti.

Ebbitt Room ⑤M _American_ | 26 | 25 | 25 | $63

Cape May | Virginia Hotel | 25 Jackson St. (bet. Beach Ave. &
Carpenter Ln.) | 609-884-5700 | www.virginiahotel.com

A "wow from start to finish", this "haute" New American in Cape
May's "classic" Virginia Hotel offers "superb", "creative" dishes
sourced from the restaurant's own local farm, plus "attentive, formal" service; the Victorian-era house features an expansive front
porch for cocktails and an "elegant" dining room, making it a "destination" for a "romantic", "memorable" meal.

Eccola _Italian_ | 22 | 19 | 20 | $40

Parsippany | 1082 Rte. 46 W. (Beverwyck Rd.) | 973-334-8211 |
www.eccolarestaurantnj.com

"Dependable", "delicious" cooking is the calling card of this "cozy"
Parsippany Italian, a "surprise in a typical strip mall"; the tile-floored
space "can get quite loud", but "accommodating" service and "reasonable" prices still keep it "drawing crowds" "after all these years."

Edward's Steakhouse ⑤ _Steak_ | 21 | 21 | 21 | $63

Jersey City | 239 Marin Blvd. (bet. 14th St. & Portner Pl.) |
201-761-0000 | www.edwardssteakhouse.com

After a seven-months hiatus courtesy of Sandy, this "hidden gem" of
a steakhouse in Jersey City is back on track after a complete renovation (which may not be reflected in the Decor score), with the

kitchen moving to the second floor and the dining room to the ground floor of its circa-1870s brownstone; though it's "expensive", everything's "well done" here, and the servers, who all returned, "remember you and your preferences."

Efe's Mediterranean Grill ● *Mediterranean*

| 21 | 16 | 18 | $21 |

New Brunswick | 32 Easton Ave. (Somerset St.) | 732-249-4100
Princeton | 235 Nassau St. (Olden St.) | 609-683-1220
www.efesgrill.com

Supporters are "never disappointed" by the "solid" Mediterranean meze and "terrific" grilled fare on offer at this New Brunswick and Princeton BYO duo; opinions split on service ("friendly" vs. "spotty") and "decor is, eh", but it's "inexpensive" and there's always takeout.

Egan & Sons ● *Irish*

| 20 | 21 | 19 | $32 |

Montclair | 118 Walnut St. (bet. Forest & Frink Sts.) | 973-744-1413 | www.egannsons.com
West Orange | 104 Harrison Ave. (bet. Cherry & Main Sts.) | 973-736-3355 | www.eganswestorange.com

An "energetic" crowd "kicks back" at these midpriced Montclair and West Orange "hangouts" where the "typical" Irish pub fare is "surprisingly good", and the house microbrews are "above par"; service strikes some as "rude", and others prefer to "go early for the quiet", warning that the "noise can raise the dead some nights."

El Azteca *Mexican*

| 23 | 17 | 22 | $16 |

Mount Laurel | Ramblewood Shopping Ctr. | 1155 Rte. 73 N. (Ramblewood Pkwy.) | 856-914-9302 | www.elaztecanj.com

Fans predict "you will not be disappointed" with the "consistently delicious", "authentic" food at this "relaxed" Mount Laurel Mexican; there's "not a lot of ambiance", but service is "friendly", prices are "awesome" and to top things off you can BYOT ("bring your own tequila for margaritas").

NEW Elbow Room Newark *American*

| - | - | - | I |

Newark | 41 Halsey St. (Bleeker St.) | 973-642-2300 | www.elbowroombrooklyn.com

Brooklyn's haute mac 'n' cheese chainlet comes to Newark offering a grown-up twist on an American comfort classic – think chicken tinga, Jamaican jerk and lobster with lemongrass along with the cheddar-slicked original, all served in paper containers; wallet-friendly prices jibe with the neo-rustic digs where wainscoted walls, wood floors and school-house chairs hearken to a simpler time.

El Cid *Spanish*

| 22 | 18 | 20 | $45 |

Paramus | 205 Paramus Rd. (bet. Century Rd. Ext. & Starling Ct.) | 201-843-0123

"No one leaves hungry" from this Paramus Spanish serving "mammoth" helpings of "flavorful" fare, including "Fred Flintstone–size" prime ribs, backed by "awesome" sangria and served by an "efficient" staff; the "ginormous portions" and "noisy" ambiance make it suitable for "coming with a group", and while some find it "a little expensive", many report a "fun outing" nonetheless.

	FOOD	DECOR	SERVICE	COST

Elements *American* — 25 | 24 | 24 | $68

Princeton | 163 Bayard Ln. (bet. Birch & Leigh Aves.) |
609-924-0078 | www.elementsprinceton.com
Fans attest it's a "revelation" to dine on culinary "magician" Scott
Anderson's "innovative, unforgettable" New American tasting
menu featuring local, sustainable ingredients at this "foodie destination" in Princeton; add "amazing" cocktails, "attentive yet unobtrusive" service and an "elegant", "contemporary" room, and most
agree there's "little not to love about this place" – except maybe
the "NY prices."

Elements Asia *Asian* — 23 | 21 | 21 | $30

Lawrenceville | Village Commons | 4110 Quakerbridge Rd.
(bet. Avalon Way & Run Dr.) | 609-275-4988 | www.elementsasia.com
A welcome "surprise" in a strip mall, this "reliable" Lawrenceville
BYO has a "great way" with sushi rolls, as well as a variety of other
"well-prepared" Asian fusion fare; "friendly" service, "appealing",
"modern" decor and "pleasant" prices are further reasons most are
"never disappointed" here.

Elements Cafe M *American* — ▽ 23 | 19 | 21 | $38

Haddon Heights | 517 Station Ave. (bet. Atlantic Ave. & U.S. 30) |
856-546-8840 | www.elementscafe.com
At this New American BYO in Haddon Heights, chef Fred Kellerman
"loves what he does and you can tell" by his "innovative" small plates,
which have "continued to evolve" for a decade; it's a bit of a local "secret", but "remarkable" deals like the $15 Sunset Dinner (Tuesdays-
Thursdays) are why those in the know keep "coming back."

NEW Elena Wu Restaurant & Sushi Bar *Asian* — - | - | - | M

Voorhees | Voorhees Town Ctr. | 12106 Town Center Blvd. (Echelon Rd.) |
856-375-2289 | www.elenawurestaurant.com
Longtime area restaurateur Elena Wu returns with this Asian BYO in
the Voorhees Town Center where Chinese favorites (some with a
French accent) keep company with Thai dishes and an extensive selection of sushi; white tablecloths, chandeliers and a granite sushi
bar lend an elegant feel while prices are reasonable.

El Mesón Café *Mexican* — 23 | 17 | 21 | $26

Freehold | 40 W. Main St. (Throckmorton St.) | 732-308-9494
Amigos regard this "popular" Freehold Mexican BYO-cum-market a
"cut above the competition" for its "satisfying" portions of "authentic" south-of-the-border standards; expect "courteous" service and
a wait for a table indoors and outside, where there's "great people-
watching" in warm weather.

El Tule M *Mexican/Peruvian* — ▽ 25 | 16 | 22 | $31

Lambertville | 49 N. Main St. (bet. Coryell & York Sts.) |
609-773-0007 | www.eltulerestaurant.com
At this colorful Lambertville BYO, both "excellent" Peruvian fare and
"wonderful" Mexican dishes share the menu; a "sweet" staff that

	FOOD	DECOR	SERVICE	COST

"takes the time to explain" the menu and "reasonable" prices also make it "worth a visit", but the dining area is "small", so weekend reservations are recommended.

Elysian Café *French*

23	23	22	$36

Hoboken | 1001 Washington St. (10th St.) | 201-798-5898 | www.elysiancafe.com

Set in a "painstakingly restored" 1895 saloon, this "charming" Hoboken bistro serves a "satisfying" menu of "well-priced" French favorites; with "friendly" servers who "know their stuff", a "relaxing", "inspired" interior and "pleasant" outdoor seating that's prime for Washington Street people-watching, it's no surprise that it's "always busy."

Eno Terra *Italian*

25	24	23	$55

Kingston | 4484 Rte. 27 (Old Lincold Hwy.) | 609-497-1777 | www.enoterra.com

"Excellent farm-to-table options" are the focus of this Kingston Italian where "outstanding" food is served by a "beyond attentive" staff in "attractive" surroundings; some find the location "tough to get to", while others grouse about "pricey" tabs and "small" portions, but many "cannot say enough good things" about the experience, and deem it "worth every penny."

Eppes Essen *Deli*

19	13	16	$24

Livingston | 105 E. Mt. Pleasant Ave. (bet. Glendale Ave. & Greenwood Ct.) | 973-994-1120 | www.eppesessen.com

The "delicious", "artery-clogging" sandwiches are "piled high" at this "solid" Jewish deli in Livingston, where pastrami and corned beef are the headliners, alongside knishes and stuffed derma; the quarters may be diner-style, and critics kvetch about "slow" service, but supporters swear it's a trip to the "Lower East Side without the commute."

NEW Escape ⓑ *Southern*

-	-	-	E

Montclair | 345 Bloomfield Ave. (bet. Gates Ave. & Willow St.) | 973-744-0712 | www.escapemontclair.com

At this upscale BYO newcomer on Montclair's Bloomfield Avenue, chef-owner Bryan Gregg (ex Ho-Ho-Kus Inn) and chef de cuisine George Mandakas create Lowcountry Southern cuisine with ingredients from Jersey farms, served à la carte as well as on a four-course tasting menu (and a three-course vegetarian version); exposed brick, farming tools and photographs grace the simple storefront space.

Espo's *Italian*

22	16	20	$29

Raritan | 10 Second St. (bet. Anderson & Thompson Sts.) | 908-685-9552

"Red-sauce" pasta and "plenty of it" means you "always walk out with leftovers" from this Raritan Italian, which has been serving "good peasant food" since 1974; the space is "dimly lit" with "tight" seating, and it's cash only, but the overall "comfy" "character" wins out, and most consider it a "great value."

	FOOD	DECOR	SERVICE	COST

Esty Street *American*
25 | 23 | 24 | $63

Park Ridge | 86 Spring Valley Rd. (Spring Valley Rd.) |
201-307-1515 | www.estystreet.com

The "sophisticated" setting at this Park Ridge American – evoking a private club, with dark paneling and a library bar – is ideal for "special occasions", as is the "superb", "innovative" menu and "extensive" wine list, and "polished" service; the "tremendous attention to detail" makes for an "outstanding" experience that's "worth" the "high price."

Etc. Steakhouse *Kosher/Steak*
▽ 25 | 23 | 23 | $53

Teaneck | 1409 Palisade Ave. (State St.) | 201-357-5677 |
www.etcsteakhouse.com

"There is always something new" at this "gourmet" kosher steakhouse in Teaneck, where "amazing" chops are locally sourced, "cooked to perfection" and accompanied by seasonal vegetables; despite high prices, the "small" storefront space and "great" service have a "relaxing" effect on fans; P.S. BYO, as long as it is kosher and mevushal, and it's closed Friday and Saturday.

Europa South Ⓜ *Portuguese/Spanish*
23 | 18 | 21 | $46

Point Pleasant Beach | 521 Arnold Ave. (Richmond Ave.) |
732-295-1500 | www.europasouth.com

"Excellent" paella and other "fresh, well-made" Iberian "favorites" pair well with "to-die-for" sangria and some "unusual" wines at this Point Pleasant Beach haunt; sure, it's "a little pricey", and the exposed-brick and dark-wood decor may be "nothing special", but "courteous" service and frequent live music and dancing add an appealing "touch of Europe."

🆕 Europe
- | - | - | M

Café & Grill *Turkish*

Tenafly | 1 Highwood Ave. (Piermont Rd.) | 201-569-4444 |
www.europecafegrill.com

Rustic tile floors, dark woods, exposed brick and an open kitchen set the welcoming tone at this Tenafly Turkish storefront serving well-known dishes such as hummus, shepherd salad and kebabs along with a selection of brick-oven pides (a cousin to the pizza) and other grilled specialties; a $12 prix fixe lunch sweetens already reasonable prices, but don't forget to pick up a bottle of your favorite vino – it's BYO.

The Famous &
Original King of Pizza *Pizza*
22 | 17 | 17 | $13

Berlin | 3 S. Whitehourse Pike (Berlin Cross Keys Rd.) |
856-753-8797 ◑
Cherry Hill | 2300 Rte. 70 (Cornell Ave.) | 856-665-4824
www.thefamouskingofpizza.com

"Save the toll" to Philly and get your "great hot pies" in South Jersey say fans of these family-run Cherry Hill and Berlin pizzerias; they also serve hoagies, salads and other "quick-meal" fare in serviceable digs, with affordable prices (and BYO) to boot.

	FOOD	DECOR	SERVICE	COST

Far East Taste   *Chinese/Thai*

| 23 | 12 | 20 | $20 |

Eatontown | 19 Main St. (Lewis St.) | 732-389-9866 |
www.fareasttaste.com

"Blink, and you'll miss" this Chinese/Thai BYO "hole-in-the-wall"
in Eatontown, where the "generous" portions of "tasty" grub are a
"great value"; there's "not much atmosphere" inside, making takeout a good option.

Farnsworth House ◑ *Continental*

| 21 | 21 | 22 | $38 |

Bordentown | 135 Farnsworth Ave. (bet. Church St. & Miles Ave.) |
609-291-9232 | www.thefarnsworthhouse.com

A "reliable" mainstay in "charming, historical" Bordentown, this
midpriced Continental offers a wide range of "well-presented"
dishes, from steaks to pasta, served in "classic" decor; for a lighter
dine, the "fun" downstairs bar offers a "nice variety" of craft beers
and a more casual menu.

Fascino ⊠ *Italian*

| 26 | 22 | 24 | $54 |

Montclair | 331 Bloomfield Ave. (bet. Gates Ave. & Willow St.) |
973-233-0350 | www.fascinorestaurant.com

A "win from start to finish", this "upscale" Montclair Italian from ris-
ing star Ryan DePersio is a "consistent" "favorite" for its "elegant",
"innovative" interpretations of "traditional" dishes (and his mom's
"alluring" desserts); the "comfortable" setting "permits quiet conversation", while service is "gracious", and though it's "expensive",
a BYO policy and an "out-of-this-world" tasting menu can make it
seem like "a steal."

Federici's ⊘ *Pizza*

| 22 | 16 | 20 | $22 |

Freehold | 14 E. Main St. (bet. Center & South Sts.) | 732-462-1312 |
www.federicis.com

"Head straight for the pizza" say fans of this family-run Freehold
Italian, a popular "standby" where thin-crust pie is a local favorite;
some say you'll need to "look past" the "plain", "tired" decor, and
maybe "grab an outdoor table", but it's "reasonably priced", and,
hey, a "sometime Springsteen haunt."

Fedora Café Ⓜ *Eclectic*

| 22 | 20 | 20 | $22 |

Lawrenceville | 2633 Main St. (bet. Craven Ln. & Phillips Ave.) |
609-895-0844 | www.fedoracafe.webs.com

Everything's "eclectic" at this "funky" Lawrenceville "hangout" –
from the "interesting" menu of sandwiches and "comfort food" to
the mismatched furniture; the service leaves little impression and
some find the decor "tired", but few can resist the "decadent" desserts, and most agree it's a "good value."

Fernandes Steakhouse II *Portuguese/Spanish*

| 25 | 22 | 23 | $44 |

Newark | 152-158 Fleming Ave. (Chapel St.) | 973-589-4344 |
www.fernandessteakhouse.com

"Rodizio is the way to go" at this popular Iberian steakhouse in
Newark's Ironbound, where the skewered meats are "done right", as

are "outstanding" chops and seafood (backed by "tasty" sangria); if the location's "a bit rough" and the space "noisy", well, the "tons of food" at "excellent prices" wins out ("no one leaves hungry or poor").

Ferry House *American/French*　　22 | 19 | 22 | $52

Princeton | 32 Witherspoon St. (Spring St.) | 609-924-2488 | www.theferryhouse.com

The "innovative" cuisine and "fine-dining" feel of this French-American BYO make for a "romantic night out" in Downtown Princeton, even if a few say it has "slipped" a bit in recent years; some decry "dated" decor, and service gets mixed marks ("attentive" vs. "poor"), but for loyalists, who don't mind the "expensive" tabs, it remains a "special-occasion" "favorite."

Fiddleheads Ⓜ *American*　　22 | 18 | 22 | $35

Jamesburg | 27 E. Railroad Ave. (bet. Church St. & Pergola Ave.) | 732-521-0878 | www.fiddleheadsjamesburg.com

"Innovative selections", including daily empanadas and the occasional wild game, make this "quaint" New American a "lucky find" in "sleepy" Jamesburg; a "welcoming" staff creates a "warm" "neighborhood" vibe that helps many overlook decor that some say "needs an update", and BYO makes it all that much more "affordable."

15 Fox Place *Italian*　　22 | 21 | 23 | $56

Jersey City | 15 Fox Pl. (bet. Giles & West Side Aves.) | 201-333-1476 | www.womcatering.com

"Make room for the feast you will encounter" advise fans of the multi-course, "old-school" Italian "home cooking" served prix fixe – only in the Jersey City house once occupied by the chef-owners – an "intimate" and "unique" setting with different rooms (and a patio), each with its own decor and capacity; while it's "pricey", it's a "treat" for couples, groups and "small family parties" (plus you're sure to "take home a doggy bag") – just remember reservations are a must and it's BYO.

55 Main Ⓢ *American*　　22 | 19 | 21 | $37

Flemington | 55 Main St. (bet. Capner & Court Sts.) | 908-284-1551 | www.55main.com

"Inventive dishes presented beautifully" make this "dependable" New American bistro from chef Jonas Gold "worth the trip" to Downtown Flemington; despite decor some find "lacking", the vibe is "friendly and low-key" and a "BYO policy helps keep the tabs down" – in sum, a "fine choice."

The Fig Tree *American*　　24 | 23 | 23 | $61

Hoboken | 306-308 Park Ave. (bet. 3rd & 4th Sts.) | 201-420-0444 | www.thefigtreehoboken.com

The "sophistication" of this New American newcomer "tucked away on a quiet street" comes as something of a "surprise" to Hobokenites, who find its "fine-dining" fare an "excellent addition" to the scene; if the prices "seem out of step with the neighborhood", a prix fixe menu makes it more "affordable", so aficionados advise just "take your sweetie" and imagine you're "in the West Village."

Filomena Cucina Italiana *Italian*

24 | 21 | 22 | $29

Clementon | 1380 Blackwood Clementon Rd. (bet. Cherrywood Dr. & Little Gloucester Rd.) | 856-784-6166 | www.filomenascucina.com

Amici are "always pleased" by the "terrific" homemade pastas and other classic dishes at this midpriced Clementon Italian, which offers live entertainment several nights a week in the "casual", rustic space; service is "consistent" and the prices are "reasonable", especially on the lighter-fare bar menu.

Filomena Cucina Rustica *Italian*

23 | 23 | 23 | $34

West Berlin | 13 Berlin Cross Keys Rd. (White Horse Pike) | 856-753-3540 | www.filomenasberlin.com

Fans return "over and over" to this West Berlin Italian for "consistently" "good-quality" traditional dishes, including Mama Filomena's signature potato gnocchi; some find the "beautiful" space suited to "romantic dinners", while others arrive early for the weekday prix fixe dinners (three courses for $22).

Filomena Lakeview *Italian*

24 | 24 | 23 | $36

Deptford | 1738 Cooper St. (bet. Almonesson Rd. & Martanna Ave.) | 856-228-4235 | www.filomenalakeview.com

A local "favorite" for a "special night out", this midpriced Deptford Italian offers "delicious" Abruzzian cuisine, including signature hand-rolled gnocchi, in a "beautiful" fireplace-studded former inn; "great" service adds to the appeal, and a "cute" bar with occasional live music offers a more upbeat dine.

Fin Ⓜ *Seafood*

25 | 24 | 24 | $51

Atlantic City | Tropicana Casino & Resort | 2831 Boardwalk (Iowa Ave.) | 800-345-8767 | www.tropicana.net

The "sophisticated" menu showcases "super-fresh seafood, prepared simply", plus "fantastic" prime steaks at this "comfortable" fine-dining spot inside AC's Tropicana Hotel; though the "lively" setting can get "loud", soothing ocean views and a beachy color scheme make it "feel like summer", and given the accommodating service, fans say it's "worth every penny."

Fin Raw Bar & Kitchen *Seafood*

24 | 21 | 21 | $46

Montclair | 183 Glen Ridge Ave. (bet. Forest & Williow Sts.) | 973-744-0068 | www.finrawbarandkitchen.com

With its "awesome" oyster selection and "creatively prepared" fish, this Montclair seafooder has become a "welcome addition" to the city's dining scene; distressed wood and exposed beams stand out in the "pretty" rustic space, which can get "crazy noisy", so insiders advise "come early" to beat the crowds, and while some cite "spotty" service as a drawback, BYO "is always a plus."

Fiorino Ⓩ *Italian*

23 | 22 | 21 | $50

Summit | 38 Maple St. (bet. Springfield Ave. & Union Pl.) | 908-277-1900 | www.fiorinoristorante.com

"Lovingly prepared" Tuscan fare lures "trust-funders" to this "swanky" Summit Italian, where an "excellent wine list" and "professional" service can make for a "romantic", "unhurried" dine; whether it's drinks at the "old-school" bar or a meal in the dining room with colorful murals, fans find it a "great night out" – "until the bill arrives."

Fire & Oak *American*
20 | 21 | 19 | $40

Jersey City | Westin Jersey City Newport Hotel | 479 Washington Blvd. (6th St.) | 201-610-9610
Montvale | Courtyard by Marriott | 100 Chestnut Ridge Rd. (Upper Saddle River Rd.) | 201-307-1100
www.fireandoak.com

A "lively" lounge scene is the main draw at these hotel "hot spots" in Montvale and Jersey City, where the "sleek", "modern" settings morph into "pickup city" on weekends; though a "broad" New American menu – sushi, truffle fries – offers "something for everyone", some find the fare "inconsistent" and service "spotty", but for many the pair works well for "business lunches" or those nights when you just want to "forget you drive a minivan."

Firefly American Bistro *American*
22 | 20 | 20 | $45

Manasquan | Inn on Main Hotel | 152 Main St. (bet. Parker & Taylor Ave.) | 732-223-0152 | www.fireflymanasquan.com

"Imaginative" "high-end comfort food" made from local ingredients is the forte of this American "conveniently located" in Manasquan's Inn on Main; a "comfortable" interior with a fireplace and an outdoor patio compensate for what some describe as "erratic" service, and BYO helps curb costs.

Fish *Seafood*
22 | 23 | 21 | $50

Asbury Park | The Post Bldg. | 601 Mattison Ave. (Emory St.) | 732-455-8181 | www.fishasburypark.com

Admirers tout the "creative, fresh" fin fare at this Asbury Park seafooder, housed inside a "great old bank" building featuring "high ceilings" and an option to dine inside the vault; a "friendly, capable" staff tends the "lively" scene, and though some report it's "a bit pricey", they maintain it's "absolutely worth it."

Five Guys *Burgers*
22 | 16 | 19 | $12

Hackensack | Home Depot Shopping Ctr. | 450 Hackensack Ave. (Commerce Way) | 201-343-5489
Jersey City | 286 Washington St. (bet. Columbus Dr. & Pearl St.) | 201-433-6700
Millburn | Millburn Mall | 2933 Vauxhall Rd. (bet. Milburn Ave. & Valley St.) | 908-688-8877
Edison | Wick Shopping Plaza | 561 Rte. 1 S. (Queenfield Ave.) | 732-985-5977
Parsippany | 804 Rte. 46 (bet. Beverwyck & Edwards Rds.) | 973-335-5454
Watchung | Blue Star Shopping Ctr. | 1701 Rte. 22 (bet. New Providence & Terrill Rds.) | 908-490-0370
Brick | Habitat Plaza | 588 Rte. 70 (Cedar Bridge Ave.) | 732-262-4040
Toms River | Orchard Shopping Plaza | 1311 Rte. 37 W. (bet. Bimini Dr. & St. Catherine Blvd.) | 732-349-3600

(continued)

(continued)

Five Guys

Mount Ephraim | Audubon Crossing Shopping Ctr. | 130 Black Horse Pike (Nicholas Rd.) | 856-672-0442
Voorhees | Eagle Plaza Shopping Ctr. | 700 Haddonfield Berlin Rd. (White Horse Rd.) | 856-783-5588
www.fiveguys.com
Additional locations throughout New Jersey

This popular chain is "not for your diet", thanks to its "yummy", "fresh" burgers, "huge" portions of "killer" fries and "plentiful" free peanuts, dished out by a "friendly" counter staff; the decor is strictly "no-frills", but fans don't mind since it's "fast, fun" and "filling."

Fleming's Prime Steakhouse & Wine Bar *Steak*

23 | 22 | 22 | $60

Edgewater | City Pl. | 90 The Promenade (River Rd.) | 201-313-9463
Marlton | 500 Rte. 73 S. (bet. Brick Rd. & Marlton Pkwy.) | 856-988-1351
www.flemingssteakhouse.com

For "city dining in the suburbs", chop fans choose these "upscale" chain steakhouses, where "good beef is matched with good bottles" (including 100 wines by the glass) and served by an "accommodating" staff; "dimly lit", with "wood paneling" and "comfortable seats", they offer a "classic" setting for "special occasions", and while "you pay dearly" for the experience, early birds can catch a few "bargains" at the bar; P.S. Edgewater offers "beautiful" Manhattan views.

Flirt Sushi Lounge *Japanese*

22 | 21 | 20 | $39

Allendale | 140 W. Allendale Ave. (Myrtle Ave.) | 201-825-9004 | www.flirtsushi.com

"Pleasantly different" sushi combos "titillate" more than taste buds at this "hip" Allendale BYO, where items with "provocative" names, "dim lighting" and "sexy music" create a "club-type" vibe; though "friendly", servers can be "slow", and prices trend "high", those longing for a Latin Lover (roll) find it a "great place to bring a date."

Fontana di Trevi Ⓜ *Italian*

22 | 19 | 21 | $41

Leonia | 248 Fort Lee Rd. (bet. Broad Ave. & Oak Tree Pl.) | 201-242-9040 | www.fontanaditrevirestaurant.com

Successor to the Manhattan haunt that inspired Billy Joel's 'Scenes from an Italian Restaurant', this "intimate" Leonia Italian serves "consistently good" midpriced fare, highlighted by tableside Caesars and housemade desserts; it can get "loud" in the "simple" storefront space, and be prepared to "wait" on weekends – and these days you'll have to BYO bottle of red, bottle of white.

Fornelletto Ⓢ Ⓜ *Italian*

23 | 24 | 24 | $56

Atlantic City | Borgata Hotel Casino & Spa | 1 Borgata Way (Renaissance Point Blvd.) | 609-317-1000 | www.theborgata.com

Chef Stephen Kalt purveys Italian fare "done right" at this upscale-casual eatery inside AC's Borgata Hotel; the "fabulous" wine list pairs nicely with the wine-cellar decor and the service is "attentive" and "knowledgeable", still, some find it "hard to justify" the high tabs, which seem "priced for high rollers."

	FOOD	DECOR	SERVICE	COST

Fornos of Spain *Spanish* | 23 | 20 | 22 | $44 |

Newark | 47 Ferry St. (Union St.) | 973-589-4767 |
www.fornosrestaurant.com

"Come hungry" to this Ironbound "stalwart" dishing out "heaping
plates" of "delicious" paella and other "old-world" Spanish fare, plus
"great" sangria; the sprawling 250-seater "packs them in", so brace
for some "bustle" and "noise", but servers have things "well con-
trolled", and with "so much food for your buck", there's no wonder
it's a Down Neck "favorite."

410 Bank Street *Caribbean/Creole* | 25 | 21 | 23 | $52 |

Cape May | 410 Bank St. (Lafayette St.) | 609-884-2127 |
www.410bankstreet.com

For most, the "vibrant" Caribbean-Creole cooking of chef Henry Sing
Cheng served by an "attentive" team in a "quaint" Victorian setting
keeps this "Cape May winner" a "must-go-to" "year after year";
sure, tabs are "pricey" and waits can be "lo-ong" even with reservations ("a must"), but loyalists declare it's "worth it"; P.S. diners can
BYO or choose from the NJ wines offered.

Franco's Metro *Italian* | 22 | 16 | 19 | $30 |

Fort Lee | Plaza West | 1475 Bergen Blvd. (bet. Lester St. & Oakdene Ave.) |
201-461-6651 | www.francosmetro.com

A "neighborhood" standby for 40 years, this Fort Lee Italian offers a
"large" menu of "flavorful", "no-pretense" dishes and brick-oven
pizzas (as well as the traditional kind); if the strip-mall setting fails
to impress, the more "casual" pizzeria is "great for takeout", and
prices are moderate, especially with early-bird specials.

Frankie Fed's Ⓜ *Italian* | 22 | 15 | 22 | $23 |

Freehold Township | 831 Rte. 33 E. (Kozloski Rd.) | 732-294-1333 |
www.frankiefeds.com

"You don't leave hungry" thanks to the "generous" portions at this
Freehold BYO serving "amazing thin-crust" pies and other Italian
fare (though some say "stick to the pizza"); "bargain" prices and a
"friendly" staff keep it "always busy."

Frenchtown Inn Ⓜ *Eclectic/French* | 22 | 23 | 22 | $49 |

Frenchtown | 7 Bridge St. (Front St.) | 908-996-3300 |
www.frenchtowninn.com

Set in a "charming" "old inn" on the banks of the Delaware River,
this Frenchtown French-Eclectic offers a variety of "quaint" dining
experiences – from formal to tavern style – in its four rooms and outdoor porch; some think the fare varies too (from "sublime" to "standard"), and it can be "expensive", but those who like to "step back
in time" feel it's "well worth the trip."

Frescos *Italian/Mediterranean* | 23 | 21 | 22 | $43 |

Cape May | 412 Bank St. (bet. Broad & Lafayette Sts.) |
609-884-0366 | www.frescoscapemay.com

"Fresh, inspired" Med-Italian cuisine, including "plenty of seafood
options", distinguishes this pricey Cape May stalwart (sibling of

410 Bank) set in a "colorful Victorian cottage"; "helpful" service ensures a "well-paced" meal, and while "local wines" are on the menu, BYO is also welcomed; P.S. regulars say it "tends to be crowded, so reservations are a must."

Fresco Steak & Seafood Grill *Seafood/Steak*

23 | 22 | 22 | $41

Milltown | Heritage Shopping Plaza | 210 Ryders Ln. (Tices Ln.) | 732-246-7616 | www.restaurantfresco.com

"Huge" portions of "consistently" "tasty" steaks and seafood are "reasonably priced" at this Milltown "neighborhood" "favorite", an "unexpected" find in a small shopping plaza; no surprise that it's "packed" on weekends then, but a "great-deal" prix fixe also makes it a weekday draw, while its BYO policy also helps "keep the bill down."

The Frog and the Peach *American*

25 | 23 | 24 | $59

New Brunswick | 29 Dennis St. (Richmond St.) | 732-846-3216 | www.frogandpeach.com

A "trendsetter" in New Brunswick for 30 years, this "gourmet" American helmed by Bruce Lefebvre offers "creative" seasonal cuisine that fans consider a "real must for the foodie in you", with "wines to match", plus "knowledgeable" service in a "charming", diverse space (the garden room is "jungle dining at its finest); it's "quite pricey", and some fret that it's grown "pretentious", but many deem it "worth every penny" for a "special night out."

Fuji Japanese Restaurant Ⓜ *Japanese*

25 | 22 | 22 | $35

Haddonfield | Shops at 116 | 116 Kings Hwy. E. (Chestnut St.) | 856-354-8200 | www.fujirestaurant.com

Matt Ito's Haddonfield Japanese is "still at the top" say his fans, thanks to "wonderfully prepared" sushi and cooked fare, as well as an "excellent" omakase tasting menu; "authentic" decor, solid service and "moderate" tabs add up to an all-around "first-class" experience.

Full Moon Café *Eclectic*

20 | 18 | 18 | $22

Lambertville | 23 Bridge St. (Klines Ct.) | 609-397-1096 | www.cafefullmoon.com

Lambertville locals like this "upbeat" cafe for "yummy" ,"simple" breakfasts and lunches – and once a month (yes, on the full moon) dinner; the space is "small", and some say service might "go downhill a bit" when it's crowded, but with modest prices and such a "friendly" vibe – aided by a rotating collection of art – many find it "worth a visit."

The Gables Restaurant *Eclectic*

25 | 25 | 23 | $64

Beach Haven | Gables Inn | 212 Centre St. (bet. Bay & Beach Aves.) | 609-492-3553 | www.gableslbi.com

An "interesting seasonal menu" pairs with "delightful" wine selections at this "superb" fine-dining Eclectic in Beach Haven, where the "elegant" Victorian B&B setting (including a "magical" patio) makes it a "romantic destination"; "high" prices are matched by "personal service" that ensures a "pleasurable evening" fit for a "special occasion."

	FOOD	DECOR	SERVICE	COST

Gaetano's *Cheesesteaks*
▽ 21 | 15 | 20 | $12

Berlin | 437 Rte. 73 N. (bet. Commerce Ln. & D'Angelo Dr.) | 856-753-1919 | www.gaetanosberlin.com

Thanks to the "excellent cheesesteaks", "over-stuffed sandwiches" and "yummy" pizzas at this long-standing Berlin pit stop, "you will not leave hungry"; cheap prices add allure, but given the compact, no-frills setting, regulars "recommend it for takeout."

Gallagher's Steak House *Steak*
23 | 22 | 22 | $57

Atlantic City | Resorts Casino & Hotel | 1133 Boardwalk (New Jersey Tpke.) | 609-340-6555 | www.gallaghersresorts.com

"All the essentials" can be found at this Resorts AC link of a NY steak-house chain – "tender", "mouthwatering" beef and sides in portions "big enough for two", served "quickly and efficiently" in a "relaxing" setting; it's "expensive", but fans "highly recommend" it nonetheless.

Gam Mee Ok ●🅼🅼 *Korean*
▽ 22 | 18 | 20 | $22

Fort Lee | 485 Main St. (Edwin Ave.) | 201-242-1333 | www.gammeeok.com

A "hot bowl" of seolleongtang (ox bone soup) really "hits the spot" and pairs well with kimchi at this Fort Lee Korean, which originated on Manhattan's 32nd Street; with moderate prices in a simply decorated space – plus 24/7 hours – it's a clear "comfort-food" destination.

Garlic Rose Bistro *Eclectic*
20 | 17 | 20 | $37

Cranford | 28 North Ave. W. (bet. Eastman St. & Union Ave.) | 908-276-5749
Madison | 41 Main St. (bet. Green Village Rd. & Waverly Pl.) | 973-822-1178
www.garlicrose.com

"Vampires beware", it's "all garlic everything" at these Eclectic bistros, where the namesake ingredient can be found throughout the "comfort-food" menu – even the ice cream – usually in "just the right amount"; the "old-school" digs are "cozy" and prices are moderate, making the duo "favorite" "standbys", as long as you "take your mouthwash"; P.S. the Madison location is BYO.

Gennaro's 🅼 *Italian*
▽ 21 | 18 | 21 | $39

Princeton | 47 State Rd. (bet. Cherry Hill & Jefferson Rds.) | 609-497-2774 | www.gennaros-princeton.com

A "solid" lineup of old world classics, studded with some "interesting" specials, recommend this Princeton Italian set in a small strip mall; "accommodating" servers create an "at home" vibe, and BYO can "make it an excellent buy."

NEW G Grab & Go 🅂 *Sandwiches*
- | - | - | I

Edison | 260 Talmadge Rd. (bet. Ethel & New Durham Rds.) | 732-662-5055 | www.g-grabandgo.com

Classic Italian sandwiches get a gourmet makeover at this 20-seat Edison eatery from *Top Chef* contestant Mike Isabella, a Jersey native with DC cred (Graffiato, Bandolero); breakfast burritos meet cheesesteaks, chicken parm and more on the daytime-only menu, and the bites top out at $11.

	FOOD	DECOR	SERVICE	COST

GG's Restaurant *American*
▽ 23 | 21 | 22 | $42

Mount Laurel | DoubleTree Guest Suites Mount Laurel |
515 Fellowship Rd. (Rte. 73) | 856-222-0335 |
www.ggsrestaurant.com

Diners are pleasantly "surprised" to discover such a "high-level"
midpriced New American inside the Mount Laurel DoubleTree
Suites; the "serene" atmosphere is augmented by live piano music
Tuesdays–Saturdays, and fans say there's a "very nice" staff.

Girasole *Italian*
23 | 22 | 22 | $53

Atlantic City | Ocean Club Condos | 3108 Pacific Ave. (bet. Chelsea &
Montpelier Aves.) | 609-345-5554 | www.girasoleac.com

Dishing up "downright delicious" cuisine (including homemade pastas, brick-oven pizzas and raw dishes) in an "attractive", Versace-
furnished setting, this "expensive" Southern Italian "gem" a block
off the boardwalk almost "makes you forget you're in hectic Atlantic
City"; the "romantic" atmosphere and "polished" service further
make it a "favorite for special occasions."

Girasole *Italian*
24 | 20 | 23 | $40

Bound Brook | 502 W. Union Ave. (bet. Tea St. & Thompson Ave.) |
732-469-1080 | www.girasoleboundbrook.com

It's "hard to get reservations" at this Bound Brook "jewel", thanks to
"high-quality" "traditional" Italian cuisine prepared with "creative"
touches; though some fault the "tight", "noisy" space, a "warm",
"personal" atmosphere prevails, and servers are "attentive" without
"rushing you", while BYO helps keep prices in check.

NEW Giulia's Kitchen Ⓜ *American*
- | - | - | M

Cliffside Park | 696 Anderson Ave. (Grant Ave.) | 201-945-1680 |
www.giuliaskitchen.com

Contemporary American comfort food has Italian leanings at this
Cliffside Park newcomer, where the seasonal menu relies heavily on local ingredients, and homemade sorbets provide a grand finale; pen-
dant lamps made from mason jars and other upcycled elements adorn
the simple space, and moderate tabs are a pleasant epilogue.

Giumarello's Ⓜ *Italian*
25 | 22 | 23 | $48

Westmont | 329 Haddon Ave. (bet. Maple & Marne Aves.) |
856-858-9400 | www.giumarellos.com

A "longtime fixture" in the Haddon Township area, this Northern
Italian "consistently" impresses with its "old-world" cuisine (and
signature mussels) and able service; while it can get a "little
pricey", its "huge" bar boasts a "good happy hour" (with occasional live music), and a "quiet dinner" is also an option, especially
for a "special occasion."

Giuseppe Restaurant *Italian*
24 | 23 | 23 | $46

North Haledon | High Mountain Plaza | 5 Sicomac Rd. (High Mountain Rd.) |
973-423-4006 | www.giusepperestaurant.com

There's "no chicken parmigiana allowed" at this high-end contemporary Italian tucked away in a North Haledon strip mall, where Roman

chef-owner Giuseppe Staiano adds his "innovative" touch to "authentic" dishes; with a "small", "homey" dining room and "friendly" waiters, diners find it a "cozy choice", though some may opt to linger at the "large, active" bar.

Gladstone Tavern _American_

| 21 | 20 | 20 | $43 |

Gladstone | 273 Main St. (Pottersville Rd.) | 908-234-9055 | www.gladstonetavern.com

The statue of a steed on the "pretty" historic building's front porch lets you know you're in horse country at this "classic" but "easygoing" Gladstone American where the "seasonal" "comfort food" is "solid" and the "upscale bar" is a "fun scene", albeit "noisy"; a fireplace and a "beautiful patio" add to the "charm", and while some think it's a "bit pricey", many appreciate the "convivial atmosphere."

GoodFellas 🗷 _Italian_

| 23 | 21 | 22 | $45 |

Garfield | 661 Midland Ave. (Plauderville Ave.) | 973-478-4000 | www.goodfellasnj.com

"Don't fuhggedaboutit" advise devotees of this Garfield Italian run by "wonderful people", offering "superb" presentations of "well-done" classics; a "quaint bar", warm woods, soft lighting and "fabulous background music" create an "outstanding atmosphere" – it's "well worth the bill."

Good Karma Cafe 🗷 _Vegetarian_

| 22 | 15 | 20 | $20 |

Red Bank | 17 E. Front St. (Wharf Ave.) | 732-450-8344 | www.goodkarmacafenj.com

"Even nonvegans enjoy" the "imaginative", "delicious" dishes served by the "warm, friendly" staff at this "moderately priced" Red Bank vegetarian; the "small", simply decorated dining room is "often packed", meaning "takeout is always a good option."

Grain House _American_

| 20 | 20 | 21 | $41 |

Basking Ridge | Olde Mill Inn | 225 Rte. 202 (Maple Ave.) | 908-221-1150 | www.oldemillinn.com

Set in the historic Olde Mill Inn, this Basking Ridge American "takes you back to 1700s horse country" and delivers "copious portions" of "solid" "comfort food"; a "not-outrageously expensive" Sunday brunch buffet and "popular" pub room across the hall draw crowds, and while some find the Colonial digs a bit "tired", fireplaces and beamed ceilings still lend an "old-world charm."

Grand Cafe 🗷 _French_

| 23 | 23 | 24 | $67 |

Morristown | 42 Washington St. (bet. Court St. & Schuyler Pl.) | 973-540-9444 | www.thegrandcafe.com

"An elegant delight" is how fans characterize this "appropriately named" "formal" French in Morristown offering "classic" Gallic fare and "professional" service; "quiet" and "intimate", it's "lovely for an occasion", even if it's "a bit pricey", and while some demur at the "dated" digs and somewhat "blue-haired" clientele, dining on the "beautiful" warm-weather patio allows you to "pretend you're 20 and in Paris."

	FOOD	DECOR	SERVICE	COST

Grand Lux Cafe *Eclectic* — 20 | 20 | 19 | $30

Paramus | Westfield Garden State Plaza | 1 Garden St. Plaza
(Garden State Plaza Pkwy.) | 201-909-0399
NEW **Cherry Hill** | Cherry Hill Mall | 2000 Rte. 38 (Haddonfield Rd.) |
856-486-7232
www.grandluxcafe.com

With "portions as gigantic as the menu is long", it's "impossible not
to find something you like" at these "glitzy", "upscale" Cheesecake
Factory cousins in Cherry Hill and Paramus, where the "solid", reasonably priced Eclectic eats are "not bad for a mall"; they're "always
busy" and service can be "spotty", but for many the "desserts are
the draw" – just "make sure to save room."

NEW **Grange** Ⓜ *American* — - | - | - | E

Westwood | 31 Westwood Ave. (bet. B'way & Center Ave.) |
201-497-3788 | www.grangewestwood.com

Chef Christine Nunn (of the late Picnic in Fair Lawn) helms this
Westwood newcomer, which offers a seasonal menu of traditional
American comforts with a slight French twist; the brick-walled, exposed beamed space is intimate, so reservations are a good idea, as
is a bottle of your best wine, since it's BYO.

Grato *Italian* — 22 | 23 | 21 | $44

Morris Plains | 2230 Rte. 10 W. (Tabor Rd.) | 973-267-4006 |
www.gratorestaurant.com

"*Perfetto*" declare *amici* about this "upscale" but "casual" Morris
Plains Italian (younger sibling of the neighboring Tabor Road Tavern)
where the "varied menu" ranges from "traditional classics" to "seasonal variations" and the "interesting" drinks are "wonderful"; while it
can get noisy, fireplaces, "beautiful light fixtures" and "cozy seating"
still make for a "romantic atmosphere" and service is "attentive" –
most deem it a "lovely choice."

Greek Taverna *Greek* — 21 | 18 | 19 | $33

Edgewater | City Pl. | 55 The Promenade (River Rd.) | 201-945-8998
Glen Rock | Glen Rock Mall | 175 Rock Rd. (Doremus Ave.) |
201-857-4528
Montclair | 292 Bloomfield Ave. (Gates Ave.) | 973-746-2280
www.greektavernausa.com

"You won't leave hungry" from this "casual", "friendly" threesome
serving "huge portions" of "tried-and-true" "authentic" Greek eats
at "reasonable prices"; the "large", rustic Mediterranean-themed
spaces "can get quite loud" and there's "sometimes a wait" – just
remember that Glen Rock has a full-service bar, while Montclair and
Edgewater are BYO.

Grimaldi's *Pizza* — 23 | 17 | 19 | $21

Hoboken | 133 Clinton St. (2nd St.) | 201-792-0800
Hoboken | 411 Washington St. (bet. 4th & 5th Sts.) | 201-792-0010
www.grimaldis.com

"Honoring the quality and legacy" of its original location, "Brooklyn
comes to NJ" in the form of "can't-beat" thin-crust, brick-oven pizza

some deem "the best" in Hoboken; while this duo is "a little less casual" and a bit more "expensive" than a by-the-slice joint, the atmosphere is still "inviting" and the staff is "friendly" – it's "so worth it."

	FOOD	DECOR	SERVICE	COST

Grissini *Italian*

22	20	19	$57

Englewood Cliffs | 484 Sylvan Ave. (Dillingham Pl.) |
201-568-3535 | www.grissinirestaurant.com

"Fancy cars, lots of gold jewelry" and the chance to "bump into the *The Real Housewives of New Jersey*" is what you get at this "long-standing" "upscale" Italian "high up on Englewood Cliffs – with prices to match"; since it can get "noisy", those in the know "sit in the back room", and while some grouse that the servers "play favorites" with "regulars", it remains a popular "place to be seen."

Grub Hut *BBQ/Mexican*

21	14	18	$28

Manville | 307 N. Main St. (Knopf St.) | 908-203-8003 |
www.grubhutbbq.com

"Enormous portions" of "outstanding" BBQ ribs and "interesting Mexican dishes", all served "under the same roof", lure fans to this "cheap", "no-frills" BYO in Manville – a "fun dive" that's "not pretty but is pretty good"; the staff is "friendly", and even with "no atmosphere", the "tiny place fills up fast", so admirers advise "get there early."

Guru Palace *Indian*
(fka Rupee Room)

19	19	18	$24

North Brunswick | 2215 Hwy. 1 S. (bet. Commerce Blvd. & Elizabeth St.) |
732-398-9022 | www.gurupalacerestaurant.com

The eats may be "standard" but the vibe is "unique" at this BYO Indian in a North Brunswick strip mall where the "out-of-this-world" decor includes walls of waterfalls, continuously changing colored lights and chairs that look like "chromosomes"; hungry shoppers appreciate the "fine" lunch buffet, and while thoughts on service range from "friendly" to just "ok", most agree the tabs are "reasonable."

Halcyon Seafood Brasserie Ⓜ *Seafood*

22	24	20	$48

Montclair | 114 Walnut St. (bet. Forest & Frink Sts.) |
973-744-4450 | www.halcyonbrasserie.com

"Fresh fish", "creative dishes", "tasty cocktails" and a "cool" upstairs lounge lure locals to this "delicious" Montclair seafooder, the "pricey" "white-tablecloth sister" of Egan's next door; though the large half-moon bar and lots of marble make for "noisy" conditions that contradict its name, "good energy" and "great atmosphere" are further reasons many "love this place."

Hamburgao ❶ *Brazilian*

21	15	18	$15

Kearny | 282 Kearny Ave. (bet. Bergen & Garfield Aves.) |
201-991-1771
Newark | 288 Lafayette St. (Adams St.) | 973-465-1776

For a "great twist on a hamburger", "locals love" the "delish" Brazilian sandwiches filled with "everything under the sun" at this "lively", "open-at-all-hours" BYO duo where the "tasty", hearty eats (including "incredible" fries and desserts) draw crowds for lunch and "late-night snacks"; the super-casual digs match the cheap prices.

	FOOD	DECOR	SERVICE	COST

Hamilton & Ward *Steak*
▽ 24 | 22 | 22 | $67

Paterson | 101 Ward St. (bet. Clark & Main Sts.) | 973-345-8444 |
www.hamiltonandward.com

"Large, well-marbled" dry-aged steaks backed by more than 400
wines are the draw at this "beautiful" Paterson steakhouse decked
with a curving marble bar, luxe leather banquettes and wood paneling; service is "courteous" (although a few find it "lackluster"), and
while the "high-quality" victuals are "pricey", most think they're
"worth the money" – especially for a "special occasion."

Hamilton's Grill Room *Mediterranean*
24 | 23 | 23 | $50

Lambertville | 8 Coryell St. (bet. Lambert Ln. & Union St.) |
609-397-4343 | www.hamiltonsgrillroom.com

A "pleasure" for 25 years, Jim Hamilton's "charming" "hidden"
Lambertville BYO "never disappoints" with its seasonally "changing
menu" of "consistently inventive" Mediterranean dishes served in a
"beautiful setting" on the Delaware River; "varied rooms" make up
the "cozy, welcoming" interior – add a "well-informed and attentive
staff" and warm weather alfresco dining, and though pricey, devotees deem it a "destination."

Hanami *Chinese/Japanese*
18 | 16 | 18 | $30

Cresskill | 41 Union Ave. (Allen St.) | 201-567-8508
Westwood | 301 Center Ave. (bet. Irvington St. & Westwood Ave.) |
201-666-8508
www.hanamirestaurant.com

An "adequate selection" of "mildly Asian", if "bland", eats means this
Chinese-Japanese BYO duo in Cresskill and Westwood has "something for everyone", from "great fusion" to the "usuals"; critics pan
the "one-size-fits-all" "flavors" and find it "pricey" for what it is, but
service is "friendly" and lunchtime bento boxes are a "deal."

Harold's
New York Deli *Jewish/Deli*
22 | 15 | 19 | $27

Edison | 3050 Woodbridge Ave. (May St.) | 732-661-9100 |
www.haroldsfamousdeli.com

"Oy vey" cry menschen over the "monster"-size helpings at this
"old-fashioned" Jewish deli in Edison serving "foot-tall" sammies
that "feed a small army", pancakes as big as a "hubcap" and more,
served "with just the right touch of attitude"; given the "massive
portions", prices are "reasonable", though the "diner-style" digs
offer "no atmosphere", and some sniff "quantity does not equal
quality" – still, many recommend the "unique" experience, as long
as you "bring your appetite."

Harry's Lobster House *Seafood*
22 | 15 | 20 | $48

Sea Bright | 1124 Ocean Ave. (New St.) | 732-842-0205 |
www.harryslobsterhouse.com

Fans love the "surprisingly good" fin fare at this "old-school" Sea
Bright seafooder with fireplace dining and a full bar; though service is just "ok", the prices are palatable, all adding up to an
"enjoyable dining experience."

	FOOD	DECOR	SERVICE	COST

Harry's Oyster Bar *Seafood*   22 | 20 | 19 | $40

Atlantic City | Bally's Atlantic City Hotel & Casino | 1900 Pacific Ave. (Ohio Ave.) | 609-431-0092 | www.harrysoysterbar.com

"Fresh fish, well prepared", a "great raw bar" and "lots of beer" are the highlights of this "upscale beach bar"-cum-seafood and sports hang that "looks out over the ocean" from its digs in AC's Bally's Hotel; "moderate" prices make up for the "spotty", if "friendly", service.

Harvest Bistro Ⓜ *American/French*   21 | 22 | 20 | $53

Closter | 252 Schraalenburgh Rd. (bet. Durie Ave. & Old Hook Rd.) | 201-750-9966 | www.harvestbistro.com

"Cozy, rustic" and "sophisticated", this Closter "gem" serves "creative", but "substantial", "seasonal" Franco-American fare in a "posh" setting with a wood-burning fireplace where you'll "feel like you're in an Aspen cabin"; things get "lively" when the "bar comes alive at night", and while some find the service "uneven", many recommend it for a "special night" – just be sure to "bring lots of money."

Harvest Moon Inn Ⓜ *American*   23 | 22 | 22 | $46

Ringoes | 1039 Old York Rd. (bet. Larison & Sandra Rds.) | 908-806-6020 | www.harvestmooninn.com

The "above-average", "creative" American fare matches the "comfortable", "homey" Federal-style building and "lovely" "country setting" of this upscale "old standby" in Ringoes; service is "attentive" and the "formal" (but not "stuffy") dining room is an "excellent choice" for "special occasions", while the "rustic" tavern section offers "outstanding handcrafted beers" and a less expensive but still "top-notch" casual menu – either way it "draws a good crowd."

Harvey Cedars Shellfish Co. ⊅ *Seafood*   20 | 15 | 17 | $33

Beach Haven | 506 Centre St. (Pennsylvania Ave.) | 609-492-2459
Harvey Cedars | 7904 Long Beach Blvd. (bet. 79th & 80th Sts.) | 609-494-7112
www.harveycedarsshellfishco.com

"Really fresh" seafood draws crowds to this seasonal BYO duo, an "LBI institution"; it's a "zoo on weekends", and a few think the fare's "gone downhill", but many find them "great at the end of a beach day."

Hat Tavern *American*   20 | 18 | 21 | $31

Summit | Grand Summit Hotel | 570 Springfield Ave. (bet. Blackburn Rd. & Tulip St.) | 908-273-7656 | www.hattavern.com

"Hidden" in the Grand Summit Hotel, this "warm and jolly" Traditional American is a well-priced "sleeper" in Summit, offering "great burgers", a "fun variety of small plates" and an "interesting list of beers"; dark-wood paneling, a long marble bar and cushy leather seating make for a pubby feel, though the low ceiling, live music and concrete floor can make it "noisy" – still, patrons plead "don't let the secret out."

Helmers' *German*   20 | 17 | 18 | $33

Hoboken | 1036 Washington St. (11th St.) | 201-963-3333 |
www.helmersrestaurant.com

Aficionados advise "stick with the specialties" at this circa-1936 Hoboken "classic" dishing out "large portions" of German *essen* like sliced steak, sauerbraten and "sausages of various types", plus a "good selection of beer"; the wood-paneled tavern is "cozy" and "prices are fair", and while some think its "time has come and gone", others deem it a "perfect place for spring or the Oktoberfest."

Highlawn Pavilion *American*

24 | 27 | 25 | $64

West Orange | Eagle Rock Reservation | 1 Crest Dr. (Eagle Rock Ave.) | 973-731-3463 | www.highlawn.com

"On a clear night" "you can see Manhattan forever" from a perch at this upscale New American "destination" in West Orange, a "high-class place" that's "perfect for a romantic evening" or "special occasion"; service is "impeccable", and while some say the "food doesn't quite match the awesome view", others deem it "top-notch", plus there's a "lovely" outdoor bar – so "bring your checkbook."

High Street Grill *American*

▽ 24 | 23 | 23 | $35

Mount Holly | 64 High St. (bet. Commerce St. & Rancocas Rd.) | 609-265-9199 | www.highstreetgrill.net

An "impressive craft beer and wine selection" and "perfect portions" of solid New American fare are the main draws at this "cozy" "hidden gem" in Mount Holly; the "dimly lit" two-story space is "warm and inviting" and the staff is "friendly", and even if some call tabs "a little on the high side", it attracts a diverse local crowd, from families to couples to "power brokers holding court."

Hiram's Roadstand *Hot Dogs*

22 | 13 | 18 | $17

Fort Lee | 1345 Palisade Ave. (Harmon Ave.) | 201-592-9602

"Leave your attitude at home and enjoy" the "delicious" deep-fried hot dogs and "juicy" burgers at this "old-time road stand", a "guilty pleasure" in Fort Lee since 1932; while the digs may be "dingy" and the service "a bit rough", it's "as authentic as they come."

Hobby's Delicatessen *Deli*

25 | 14 | 21 | $20

Newark | 32 Branford Pl. (Halsey St.) | 973-623-0410 | www.hobbysdeli.com

Deli devotees say this circa-1962 Newark "institution" near the Prudential Center is "not to be missed", citing "excellent" Jewish "comfort food", including sandwiches "piled high" with "real-deal" pastrami and corned beef, and "must"-try brisket; it's open for breakfast and lunch (and dinner before Devils' home games) and the staff is "friendly and helpful", while the "old-fashioned" digs are "terrific or divey depending on your POV."

Ho-Ho-Kus
Inn & Tavern *American*

21 | 23 | 21 | $50

Ho-Ho-Kus | 1 E. Franklin Tpke. (Sheridan Ave.) | 201-445-4115 | www.hohokusinn.com

The "elegant surroundings" of this "classy" historic 18th-century inn in Ho-Ho-Kus help set the tone for a seasonal Traditional American menu paired with an "excellent wine list" (or you can BYO); while some sniff "service is spotty" and find it "pricey" for the portions, with five dining rooms, plus a "lovely" outdoor area and more "casual" tavern, many tout it as a "pleasant choice" for a "quiet", "romantic dinner", Sunday brunch or "special occasion."

Hollywood Cafe ● *American*
22 | 20 | 21 | $18

Woodbury Heights | 904 Mantua Pike (Elm Ave.) | 856-251-0011 | www.thehollywoodcafeandsportsbar.com

A "huge menu" with "something for everyone" and a vintage Corvette on display headline this Woodbury Heights eatery serving "large portions" of Americana that's "a step above typical diner food"; the "big" space, which includes a "full sports bar", can get "loud", but "reasonable" prices, "friendly" service and a "fun" atmosphere add up to a "good time" for most.

Holsten's ● *American*
19 | 17 | 19 | $18

Bloomfield | 1063 Broad St. (Watchung Ave.) | 973-338-7091 | www.holstens.com

"The quintessential ice cream parlor" is how boosters describe this "no-frills" American "classic" in Bloomfield (site of *The Sopranos*' finale), where "scrumptious confections and shakes", plus "tasty" sandwiches and burgers, draw everyone from "blue-haired matrons" to "tattooed heavy metal types"; while some say the "old-fashioned decor" could use "updating", "for a nostalgia fix", many deem it a "must-try in the neighborhood."

Homestead Inn *Italian*
23 | 18 | 22 | $59

Trenton | 800 Kuser Rd. (bet. Barbara Dr. & Nottinghill Ln.) | 609-890-9851

"No menus", "no frills" and "no surprises" define this "venerable" "old-school" Italian in Trenton serving up "consistently delicious pastas", steaks and chops to "locals and regulars" since 1939; it's pricey, and some liken it to "eating in someone's basement", but "if they know you, you're treated like a king", and while the "quality never changes" one thing has – "credit cards are now accepted."

Hotel Tides Ⓜ *American*
∇ 22 | 22 | 22 | $50

Asbury Park | 408 Seventh Ave. (bet. Grand & Park Aves.) | 732-897-7744 | www.hoteltides.com

"Hidden" away in a "modern" boutique hotel in Asbury Park, this "eclectic" New American offers "painstakingly prepared" dishes with a seafood focus; the vibe in the tin-tiled room is "subdued" and "trendy", with "welcoming" servers, and if some find the fare a "bit pricey", fans say this "find" is "worth it."

Hotoke ●Ⓩ *Asian*
20 | 23 | 19 | $37

New Brunswick | 350 George St. (bet. Bayard & Paterson Sts.) | 732-246-8999 | www.hotokerestaurant.com

It "feels like Manhattan – in a good way" at this "urban-chic" New Brunswick Pan-Asian, a "huge", "dark and loungey" bi-level space where under the watchful eye of a jumbo Buddha, "excellent signature drinks" wash down "unique sushi combinations" and a "cool bar scene" brings out an "older college crowd" later in the evening; some gripe over "hit-or-miss" eats and "pricey", "small portions", but with weeknight happy-hour specials and weekend DJs, it "totally works" for many others.

Hummus Elite *Mediterranean*
21 | 16 | 18 | $21

Englewood | 39 E. Palisade Ave. (bet. Dean & Engle Sts.) | 201-569-5600 | www.hummuselite.com

This "small storefront" BYO in Englewood churns out a "wonderful variety" of "fresh and delicious" hummus and other "authentic" kosher Med eats, served by a "friendly" staff; tabs are as low-key as the simple, "tiny" setting, but keep in mind in observance of the Sabbath, it's closed Saturdays.

Hunan Chinese Room *Chinese*
22 | 19 | 20 | $27

Morris Plains | 255 Speedwell Ave. (bet. Gregory & Hanover Ave.) | 973-285-1117

"High-quality Chinese classics" and "tasty", "creative" specialties are "served with efficiency" at this "wonderful transformation of a former diner" in Morris Plains; add a full bar, lunch specials and reasonable prices and it's no wonder why they've been in business since 1982.

Hunan Taste *Chinese*
24 | 23 | 22 | $32

Denville | 67 Bloomfield Ave. (Main St.) | 973-625-2782 | www.hunantaste.com

Sinophiles "program the GPS and get to Denville", home of this "top-notch" "fancy Chinese" they consider "the best" in the area thanks to a "huge menu" of "excellent" Hunan, Mandarin and Sichuan specialties plus "exotic" drinks all served by a "warm, friendly" staff; the "over-the-top", "pagoda"-like space is "big enough to be its own Chinatown", and while the glam comes at prices some find "steep", many consider it worth" the "splurge."

Hunkar Restaurant Ⓜ *Turkish*
▽ 25 | 21 | 23 | $29

Carlstadt | 319 Hackensack St. (Small St.) | 201-507-0606 | www.hunkarrestaurant.net

A "long list of outstanding dishes" lures fans to this "authentic" Turkish BYO in Carlstadt, which "looks unprepossessing from the outside" but turns out "some of the area's best" "home cooking" "this side of Istanbul" according to aficionados; prices are moderate and the staff is "friendly and helpful" – add a back patio with Manhattan views and it's just "wonderful."

Huntley Taverne *American*
22 | 24 | 22 | $49

Summit | 3 Morris Ave. (Springfield Ave.) | 908-273-3166 | www.thehuntleytaverne.com

"Always convivial", this Summit American is a "constant favorite" of locals for its "delicious" "locally sourced fare", "amazing desserts" and "extensive wine list" presented by a "friendly staff" in a "rustic yet trendy" "ski-lodge-type" space with "high" beamed ceilings, "roaring" fireplaces and a "beautiful patio"; the "lively bar" is "packed" with both "singles and couples" resulting in "high energy" (read: "noise"), but most agree the vibe "matches the high prices."

	FOOD	DECOR	SERVICE	COST

Ibby's Falafel *Mideastern*
20 | **13** | **17** | **$13**

NEW **Edgewater** | 10 Hilliard Ave. (McCurry Ln.) | 201-941-8801
Jersey City | 303 Grove St. (Wayne St.) | 201-432-2400 ◗
Freehold | 4 W. Main St. (South St.) | 732-409-1234 ⊟
www.ibbysfalafels.com

"Quality" falafel, "fresh" hummus and other "tasty", "quick bites" are "a great value for your money" at these "busy" Middle Eastern joints; some say "you aren't going there for the service" or the "casual", "hole-in-the-wall" settings, and regulars concur that they're more about "takeout" anyway.

Iberia ◗ *Portuguese/Spanish*
22 | **18** | **21** | **$37**

Newark | 63-69 Ferry St. (Prospect St.) | 973-344-5611
Newark | 80-84 Ferry St. (bet. Congress & Prospect Sts.) | 973-344-7603 Ⓜ
www.iberiarestaurants.com

"Be sure to come hungry" (but "pace yourself") if you're up for the "challenge" of "all-you-can-eat rodizio" ferried by a "courteous" crew at these "loud, casual" Iberian siblings in Newark; some say the decor "could use a face-lift", but given the "heaping" portions of "tasty" food, most agree the "price is right."

I Gemelli Ristorante *Italian*
▽ **25** | **17** | **25** | **$40**

South Hackensack | 268 Huyler St. (bet. Dinallo & Hoffman Sts.) | 201-487-4220 | www.igemelliristorante.com

For "well-prepared", "old-fashioned" Italian fare, "regulars" fill this South Hackensack BYO where the eats might not be "innovative", but everything tastes "homemade"; service is "spectacular", and while it's not cheap and the location is a "little out of the way", *amici* insist it's "worth the trip" and "the price."

Ikko *Japanese*
25 | **21** | **23** | **$30**

Brick | Brick Plaza | 107 Brick Plaza (Chambers Bridge Rd.) | 732-477-6077 | www.ikkosteakhouse.com

"First-rate sushi" and other "authentic" Japanese fare draw locals to this "excellent" midpriced Brick BYO, where hibachi chefs are "entertaining" and servers treat diners like "old friends"; though some find the decor "lackluster", most agree the "food makes up for it."

Il Capriccio ⊠ *Italian*
25 | **24** | **25** | **$61**

Whippany | 633 Rte. 10 (Parsippany Rd.) | 973-884-9175 | www.ilcapriccio.com

"For special occasions or high-level business", fans tout this "upscale" Whippany Italian offering "sophisticated, well-prepared" cuisine and a wine list that's "a dream come true – if you have deep pockets" – served by an "accommodating", "meticulous" staff; the atmosphere is "formal" in the "high-end" setting, which is enlivened by "live piano music" Wednesdays–Saturdays.

Il Fiore *Italian*
24 | **19** | **21** | **$33**

Collingswood | 693-695 Haddon Ave. (Collings Ave.) | 856-833-0808

Regulars say the "outstanding" eats are "worth the wait to get a table" at this "reliable" Collingswood Italian; even if it can get "crowded and noisy" (seating's so tight that "surrounding tables can join your conversation"), service "excels" and BYO boosts the "bang for the buck."

Il Michelangelo *Italian*
21 | 20 | 20 | $45

Boonton | 91 Elcock Ave. (bet. Highwood Terr. & McCaffrey Ln.) | 973-316-1111 | www.ilmichelangelo.com

Boonton locals tuck into "wonderful" pastas and "delicious" seafood at this welcoming Italian housed inside a 19th-century stagecoach inn; although a few feel it's become "inconsistent", front-porch seating and an upstairs lounge complement the white-tablecloth dining room, which also frequently hosts "great wine-and-food-pairing events."

Il Mondo Vecchio ⊠ *Italian*
25 | 20 | 21 | $51

Madison | 72 Main St. (bet. Central & Greenwood Aves.) | 973-301-0024 | www.ilmondovecchio.com

The "superb" Italian fare explains why this high-end Madison BYO is such "a tough reservation"; some suggest it "suffers from its popularity", as opinions are mixed on the service ("professional" vs. "snippy"), and tables in the "intimate" space are "so close you barely have room to swallow" – still, loyalists point out that it's "more reasonably priced than its sister restaurant", Scalini Fedeli.

Il Mulino *Italian*
25 | 22 | 24 | $73

Atlantic City | Trump Taj Mahal | 1000 Boardwalk (Virginia Ave.) | 609-449-6006 | www.ilmulino.com

"Top-notch" cuisine wins high praise at this "exclusive" Trump Taj Mahal outpost of the famed NYC Italian, where the "lovely", "formal" decor matches "white-glove" service from a staff that "aims to please"; most justify the "pricey" tabs for a "special-occasion" dining experience that's "not to be missed."

Il Villaggio ⊠ *Italian/Seafood*
24 | 21 | 23 | $49

Carlstadt | 651 Rte. 17 N. (Berry Ave.) | 201-935-7733 | www.ilvillaggio.com

The Italian seafood is a "pricey but worthwhile" "treat" report regulars of this "long-standing local favorite" in Carlstadt; "high-end" service also make it a popular "place to go for that special night out", even if the "upscale" surrounds are a "bit over the top" for some.

IndeBlue *Indian*
25 | 21 | 23 | $31

Collingswood | 619 Collings Ave. (White Horse Pike) | 856-854-4633 | www.indebluerestaurant.com

"Each dish is better than the last" swoon fans of chef-owner Rakesh Ramola's "excellent" Indian fare at this "trendy" "neighborhood gem" in Collingswood; even if some say it's "more expensive than the usual" options, BYO and "personable" service are pluses.

India on the Hudson *Indian*
20 | 17 | 18 | $29

Hoboken | 1210 Washington St. (bet. 12th & 13th Sts.) | 201-222-0101 | www.indiaonthehudson.com

"Better-than-average" Indian cuisine at moderate prices brings Hoboken locals to this casual, compact spot; a "fresh", simple setting with exposed-brick walls completes the picture.

	FOOD	DECOR	SERVICE	COST

NEW Indiya M *Indian* — — — M

Collingswood | 612 Haddon Ave. (bet. Garfield & Zane Aves.) | 856-858-0020 | www.indiyarestaurant.com

Chef Vipul Bhasin brings his flair for contemporary Pan-Indian cuisine to Collingswood's Restaurant Row at this BYO newcomer, offering plenty of vegetarian options alongside tandoori meats and fish; yellow walls and cobalt banquettes enliven the compact storefront, and moderate prices become even more so during a daily lunch buffet.

Inlet Café *Seafood* 20 | 18 | 20 | $37

Highlands | 3 Cornwall St. (Shrewsbury Ave.) | 732-872-9764 | www.inletcafe.com

A "peaceful view" of Sandy Hook Bay recommends this seasonal Highlands seafooder, a "casual", "lively" hang with a dine-on deck; the midpriced menu is "not fancy", and some find it "more expensive than expected", but it's hard to knock as a "pleasant spot" to "watch the boats go by"; P.S. post-Sandy renovations are not reflected in the Decor score.

Inn at Millrace Pond Restaurant *American/Continental* 22 | 24 | 22 | $44

Hope | Inn at Millrace Pond | 313 Johnsonburg Rd. (Milbrook Rd.) | 908-459-4884 | www.innatmillracepond.com

With its "intimate, romantic" main dining room and rustic downstairs bar boasting a "huge fireplace", this "quaint" American-Continental set in an 18th-century Hope gristmill is a popular "place to go for an upscale dinner"; welcoming service adds to the "pleasant atmosphere"; P.S. wallet-watchers recommend the tavern menu as a more "reasonably priced" option.

Inn at Sugar Hill Restaurant Ⓢ M *American* 20 | 21 | 21 | $35

Mays Landing | Inn at Sugar Hill | 5704 Mays Landing-Somers Point Rd. (Old River Rd.) | 609-625-2226 | www.innatsugarhill.com

Sweet indeed are the fireplace-equipped Victorian dining rooms at this "romantic" Mays Landing inn, which also boasts "awesome" veranda views of the Great Egg Harbor River; "friendly" service is another plus, and while some feel the kitchen's Traditional American fare "needs an upgrade", most agree the "lovely setting" is ideal for a "date."

Inn of the Hawke Restaurant *American* 18 | 20 | 19 | $29

Lambertville | Inn of the Hawke | 74 S. Union St. (bet. Union & Wilson Sts.) | 609-397-9555 | www.innofthehawke.com

Though the "menu changes regularly", expect "upscale pub food" with "farm-fresh ingredients" and a "wide choice of beer" at this midpriced Lambertville American set in a 19th-century mansion; solid service and a "comfortable" setting, with "cozy" indoor seating and (during warmer months) outdoor dining in the "sweet little garden" out back, also help make it a popular "local hangout."

Irish Pub & Inn ●⊅ *Pub Food*

FOOD	DECOR	SERVICE	COST
21	21	21	$21

Atlantic City | 164 St. James Pl. (Pacific Ave.) | 609-344-9063 |
www.theirishpub.com

"Lots of locals" head to this "boisterous" 24/7 Atlantic City "institution" for "typical" pub grub and "cold beer" served by a "friendly" staff in "hole-in-the-wall" digs that would be at home "in Ireland"; while some gripe that it's "cash-only", the "awesome prices" make it an "affordable" option "after a long night in the casinos."

Iron Hill Brewery & Restaurant *American/Pub Food*

FOOD	DECOR	SERVICE	COST
22	22	21	$28

Maple Shade | 124 E. Kings Hwy. (Lenola Rd.) | 856-273-0300
NEW Voorhees | Voorhees Town Ctr. | 13107 Town Center Blvd.
(Burnt Mill Rd.) | 856-545-9009
www.ironhillbrewery.com

Regulars "love the changing beer menu" and "delightful" comfort food ferried by a "helpful" crew at this brewpub duo where "prices are reasonable for the portions and the quality"; it's "kid-friendly", and the setting is "accommodating for big parties", plus there's a "great bar area for watching the game."

Isabella's American Bistro Ⓜ *American*

FOOD	DECOR	SERVICE	COST
19	18	20	$36

Westfield | 39 Elm St. (bet. Broad St. & North Ave.) | 908-233-8830
There's "lots of comfort food" on the "well-rounded", moderately priced American menu at this "cute" Westfield BYO; with high ceilings and casual decor, the small space is "normally packed", but the "competent" staff keeps up the pace.

Istanbul Restaurant & Patisserie *Turkish*

FOOD	DECOR	SERVICE	COST
22	19	20	$25

North Brunswick | 1000 Aaron Rd. (Rte. 1) | 732-940-1122 |
www.theistanbulrestaurant.com

"Delectable" kebabs and other "delicious options" make this North Brunswick Turkish an "interesting change of pace"; while the "casual" setting "doesn't look promising from the outside" to some, "helpful" service enhances the experience, and BYO helps keep tabs affordable.

It's Greek To Me *Greek*

FOOD	DECOR	SERVICE	COST
19	16	18	$24

Clifton | Promenade Shops at Clifton | 852 Rte. 3 W. (bet. Bloomfield & Passaic Aves.) | 973-594-1777
Englewood | 36 E. Palisade Ave. (bet. Dean St. & Grand Ave.) |
201-568-0440
Fort Lee | 1611 Palisade Ave. (Angioletti St.) | 201-947-2050
Hoboken | 538 Washington St. (6th St.) | 201-216-1888
Jersey City | 194 Newark Ave. (Jersey Ave.) | 201-222-0844
Ridgewood | 21 E. Ridgewood Ave. (bet. Broad & Chestnut Sts.) |
201-612-2600
Westwood | 487 Broadway (bet. Irvington St. & Westwood Ave.) |
201-722-3511
Holmdel | 2128 Rte. 35 (Laurel Ave.) | 732-275-0036
Long Branch | Pier Vill. | 44 Centennial Dr. (Chelsea Ave.) | 732-571-0222
www.itsgreektome.com

"Casual, simple" Greek "classics" come in "huge portions" at these "nothing-fancy" chain links that are "fine for convenience"; some say the service can be "uneven", but it's "kid-friendly" and prices are "affordable" (especially with BYO at all locations except Long Branch).

Ivy Inn *American*

| 21 | 23 | 22 | $44 |

Hasbrouck Heights | 268 Terrace Ave. (bet. Kipp Ave. & Washington Pl.) | 201-393-7699 | www.ivyinn.com

An "attentive" staff delivers "consistent" Traditional American and Continental fare (including a "lovely" Sunday brunch and a "fab" early dining menu) at this Hasbrouck Heights "jewel" set in a circa-1870s stagecoach inn; most say it's "worth the cash" for "special occasions", with a "cozy, romantic" setting, where frequent live piano is a "nice touch."

Izakaya *Japanese*

| 23 | 24 | 23 | $52 |

Atlantic City | Borgata Hotel Casino & Spa | 1 Borgata Way (Renaissance Point Blvd.) | 609-317-1000 | www.theborgata.com

With its modern lounge setting and "funky" music, Michael Schulson's Japanese in the AC Borgata Hotel can be a "great place to start your night", especially when the "upscale" eats – "creative" sushi rolls and robatayaki – are made "small" to accompany cocktails; prices are casino-typical "high", but Monday night specials are an affordable option.

Jack Baker's *American/Seafood*

| 20 | 20 | 20 | $34 |

Point Pleasant Beach | 101 Channel Dr. (Boston Ave.) | 732-892-9100 | www.wharfsidenj.com

Baker's Water Street

Toms River | 4 Robbins Pkwy. (Water St.) | 732-240-4800 | www.bakerswaterstreet.com ●

Jack Baker's Lobster Shanty *American/Seafood*

Point Pleasant Beach | 81-83 Channel Dr. (Boston Ave.) | 732-899-6700 | www.pointpleasantlobstershanty.com

"Stunning" water views distinguish this midpriced coastal trio, which offers dockside dining and "decent" eats to the summer "crowds" (and are open year-round); the Point Pleasant pair are "old-time favorites" for "consistent seafood" and "shore decor" (with Lobster Shanty fully renovated post-Sandy), while Toms River serves "better-than-average pub fare" and hosts a "lively see-and-be-seen scene."

Jack's Café *American/Eclectic*

| 22 | 14 | 19 | $25 |

Westwood | 325 Broadway (bet. Jefferson & Westwood Aves.) | 201-666-0400 | www.jackscafenj.com

Fans are "always eager to see the daily specials" at this "friendly" Westwood BYO serving "creative" American-Eclectic eats; while the "small" space is often "crowded" and some say the decor "could use an upgrade", the "food more than makes up for it", and it's "fairly priced" to boot.

J&K Steakhouse *Steak*

| 22 | 19 | 22 | $47 |

NEW **Montclair** | 44 South Park (bet. Church St. & The Crescent) | 973-746-7800

(continued)

(continued)

J&K Steakhouse

Morristown | 56 South St. (Community Pl.) | 973-998-8061
www.jandksteakhouse.com

Prime dry-aged beef is the "main draw", but the menu also includes seafood and vegetarian selections at this chophouse duo where a "bargain" prix fixe option and BYO ("a rare find with a steakhouse") help temper otherwise steep tabs; the decor may be "nothing too fancy", but a "responsive" staff maintains a "warm" atmosphere.

Janice *American/Italian*   21 | 17 | 19 | $37

Ho-Ho-Kus | 23 Sheridan Ave. (bet. Orvil Ct. & Warren Ave.) |
201-445-2666 | www.janiceabistro.com

"Delicious" American breakfast and lunch fare and "yummy Italian cuisine by night" lure locals to this Ho-Ho-Kus "hole-in-the-wall" that "gets full quickly"; given the "diner"-like digs, a few feel tabs are "a bit high for what it is", and service gets mixed marks, but at least BYO is "always a nice treat."

Java Moon *American*   23 | 19 | 21 | $21

Jackson | 1022 Anderson Rd. (County Rd. 537) | 732-928-3633 |
www.javamooncafe.com

"A favorite lunch place" for visitors to Jackson's nearby shopping outlets, this "pleasant" pit stop slings a "great array of sandwiches" and other "fresh, delicious" American eats; the "quaint log cabin" setting can get "crowded", but "huge portions" and BYO keep things affordable.

JBJ Soul Kitchen Ⓜ ⊅ *American*   ▽ 21 | 17 | 21 | I

Red Bank | 207 Monmouth St. (bet. Bridge & Shrewsbury Aves.) |
732-842-0900 | www.jbjsoulkitchen.org

A "great concept" in "charitable" community dining, this regional American kitchen run by the Jon Bon Jovi Soul Foundation is strictly "pay what you can" ($10 is suggested or you can volunteer time instead) for a three-course meal made from local ingredients; though diners may have to "sit with other people", the "happy crowd" doesn't mind, especially if "Jon himself" is in the house; P.S. open Thursdays–Sundays and "no alcohol served or allowed."

Je's Ⓜ *Southern*   ▽ 24 | 18 | 23 | $25

Newark | 34 William St. (Halsey St.) | 973-623-8848

"Bring your appetite" for some "good ol' Southern cooking" (including "fabulous" daily specials) served by a "friendly" staff at this low-key Newark vet; moderate prices are a plus, and "decor isn't important" to fans, who deem it "a down-home experience not to be missed."

Jimmy Buff's *Hot Dogs*   20 | 13 | 17 | $12

Kenilworth | 506 Blvd. (bet. 20th & 21st Sts.) | 908-276-2833
West Orange | 60 Washington St. (Columbia St.) | 973-325-9897 ⊅
www.jimmybuff.com

Even if it's just "for special occasions when your cholesterol readings are low", fans aver "sometimes you just need to indulge" in a "one-of-a-kind" Italian hot dog with "all the trimmings" at this "tradition" in Kenilworth and West Orange; the "kitschy", counter-serve settings are "definitely no-frills", but service is "hospitable" and budget-friendly prices are a plus; P.S. cash only in West Orange.

Jimmy's *Italian*

23 | 17 | 21 | $45

Asbury Park | 1405 Asbury Ave. (bet. Drummond & Prospect Aves.) | 732-774-5051 | www.jimmysitalianrestaurant.com

Regulars insist you "can't go wrong" with the "tasty" red-sauce fare at this "old-school" Italian in Asbury Park; though some find the decor "tired" and the tabs "a little pricey", the "seasoned" staff ensures a "reliable" experience that makes it a "popular" local "standby."

Joe Pesce *Italian/Seafood*

▽ 25 | 21 | 23 | $45

Collingswood | 833 Haddon Ave. (Fern Ave.) | 856-833-9888 | www.joepescerestaurant.com

Some of the "best seafood in the area" stands out on the menu of "fresh, homemade, very Italian" eats at this "pricey" Collingswood BYO; meanwhile, the staff "makes you feel welcome" amid a "cozy" space decked out in a white-and-blue nautical theme.

Joe's Peking Duck House Ⓜ❥ *Chinese*

23 | 16 | 20 | $24

Marlton | Marlton Crossing Shopping Ctr. | 145 Rte. 73 S. (Old Marlton Pike) | 856-985-1551 | www.joespekingduckhouse.com

"Exceptional" noodle soups, "fab" Peking duck, "wonderful" week-end dim sum and other "consistent", "authentic" dishes make this cash-only spot in Marlton a "great find" for those who "don't want to go to the big cities" for Chinese; the casual, strip-mall setting doesn't earn raves, but service is solid and BYO keeps tabs in check.

Jose's Mexican Cantina *Mexican*

20 | 18 | 19 | $24

New Providence | 24 South St. (bet. Gales Dr. & Springfield Ave.) | 908-464-4360
Warren | Quail Run Ctr. | 125 Washington Valley Rd. (Quail Run) | 732-563-0480
www.josescantina.com

Mexican cooking that's "a cut above" "continues to draw regulars" at this "neighborhood favorite" duo in New Providence and Warren; done up in "funky" decor, the "tight quarters" might "get crowded easily", but service is "efficient", prices are cheap and BYO's a "bonus."

Jo-Sho Ⓩ *Japanese*

▽ 25 | 17 | 20 | $37

Somerset | 120 Cedar Grove Ln. (New Brunswick Rd.) | 732-469-8969

"Fantastic" sushi and other "authentic", midpriced Japanese dishes shine at this "mom-and-pop" strip-mall spot in Somerset; somewhat "tired" decor and mixed marks for service don't deter loyalists who "focus on the food" and find themselves "in heaven with the quality."

Juanito's *Mexican*

22 | 18 | 20 | $25

Howell | 3930 Rte. 9 S. (Aldrich Rd.) | 732-370-1717 | www.juanitos2howell.com
Red Bank | 159 Monmouth St. (West St.) | 732-747-9118 | www.juanitosredbank.com

"Delish" guacamole "prepared at your table", "authentic burritos and other Mexican favorites" are dished up in "hearty" portions at these "friendly" BYOs in Howell and Red Bank; while the "traditional decor" may not impress, fans find the "price point quite pleasing."

Justin's Ristorante Ⓜ *Italian* | 22 | 17 | 22 | $32 |

Hawthorne | 234 Lafayette Ave. (bet. Llewellyn & South Aves.) | 973-423-4345 | www.justinsristorante.com
Wood-Ridge | 269 Hackensack St. (bet. Marlboro & Windsor Rds.) | 201-933-4276 | www.justinsristoranteii.com

The "no-surprises", "basic" Italian cooking at these Hawthorne and Wood Ridge BYOs promises "value for your money" – especially the "bargain" early-bird prix fixe; though some feel the decor could be "updated", regulars say there's "just a relaxed feeling about the place", with a staff that "makes everyone feel welcome."

Just Restaurant *American* | ▽ 24 | 22 | 23 | $62 |

Old Bridge | 2280 Rte. 9 S. (bet. Fairway Ln. & Jake Brown Rd.) | 732-707-4800 | www.justrestaurantnj.com

Old Bridge insiders say the "interesting" menu and "great cocktails" are "just right" at this "upscale" New American "go-to" in an "unexpected location" on Route 9; while some describe the experience as "heaven", "pricey" tabs will "bring you back to earth", but at least the staff does "a great job at creating a VIP vibe."

Kailash Ⓜ *Indian* | 21 | 17 | 21 | $28 |

Ridgewood | 22 Oak St. (bet. Franklin & Ridgewood Aves.) | 201-251-9694 | www.kailashindiancuisine.com

A "varied" menu of Indian specialties plus an "excellent" buffet with plenty of "fresh, hot replacements" keep Ridgewood locals coming back to this midpriced BYO; "courteous" service and a "calming" vibe in the red-hued dining room round out the experience.

Kanji *Japanese* | 24 | 22 | 20 | $34 |

Tinton Falls | 980 Shrewsbury Ave. (Rte. 35) | 732-544-1600 | www.kanjisteakhouse.com

Fans are "never disappointed" by the "fresh", "unique" sushi at chef-owner Roger Yang's "crowded" Japanese in Tinton Falls; the show at the teppanyaki grill lends a "fun", "family-friendly" appeal, while BYO keeps the costs moderate; P.S. there's a liquor store nearby too.

Karma Kafe *Indian* | 23 | 19 | 20 | $28 |

Hoboken | 77 Jefferson St. (bet. 5th & 6th Sts.) | 201-610-0900 | www.karmakafe.com

Known for its "simple, tasty" lunch buffet, this "little gem" in Hoboken pairs "ample portions" of "flavorful" Indian fare with "creative" cocktails delivered by a "polite" staff; "reasonable" prices match the "unpretentious" setting, and if the somewhat "cramped" space gets "crowded", "additional outdoor seating" is a plus.

Kaya's Kitchen Ⓜ *Vegetarian* | ▽ 25 | 21 | 22 | $21 |

Belmar | 1000 Main St. (10th Ave.) | 732-280-1141 | www.kayaskitchenbelmar.com

Even "carnivores get a craving" for the "creative" vegan and vegetarian eats that "utilize flavors from around the globe" at this affordable Belmar BYO; "live music on some nights" enhances the "cozy" vibe, while the "friendly" crew "makes you feel welcome."

KC Prime *Steak* | 22 | 21 | 21 | $44 |

Lawrenceville | 4160 Quakerbridge Rd. (Grovers Mill Rd.) | 609-275-5418 | www.kcprimerestaurant.com

Those seeking "meat and plenty of it" head to this Lawrenceville steakhouse near the Quaker Bridge Mall for "surprisingly good" chops and other "dead-on staples" ("fish, vino"); fans tout "friendly", "efficient" service and a "warm" atmosphere (though some find the environs a little "dark"), and if dinner can be "pricey" for everyday dining, the "fabulous" brunch buffet is a "great value" at $19.

Kevin's Thyme ⊠ *American* | 25 | 16 | 21 | $37 |

Ho-Ho-Kus | 614 N. Maple Ave. (bet. Brookside Ave. & 1st St.) | 201-445-6400 | www.kevinsthyme.com

A "first-class" kitchen dishes out "delicious", "innovative" New American cuisine at this "tiny" Ho-Ho-Kus storefront BYO popular with "ladies who lunch" and many others who dinner (Thursdays–Saturdays only); though it's "cramped", a "fun" outdoor patio opens in warm months, and prices are "reasonable."

Khun Thai *Thai* | 22 | 18 | 18 | $33 |

Short Hills | 504 Millburn Ave. (Short Hills Ave.) | 973-258-0586 | www.khunthairestaurant.com

A Short Hills "fixture", this "casual" Thai offers a "vast" menu of "well-prepared", "spicy" curries, soups and noodles in a modern, split-level space; though some say service can be "haphazard", prix fixe "deals" and a BYO policy are happy upsides.

Khyber Grill *Indian* | 21 | 19 | 20 | M |

South Plainfield | 684 Oak Tree Ave. (bet. Case Dr. & Park Ave.) | 908-226-5544 | www.khybergrillusa.com

"Variations" on "classic" North Indian fare are the specialty of this "friendly" South Plainfield BYO, where "awesome naan" accompanies tandooris and curries; though the strip-mall space doesn't appeal to everyone, fans hightail it to the lunch buffet, where there's a "variety" to sample at an "amazing price."

Kibitz Room *Deli* | 24 | 15 | 17 | $18 |

Cherry Hill | Shoppes at Holly Ravine | 100 Springdale Rd. (Evesham Rd.) | 856-428-7878 | www.kibitzroom.com

"Bring a forklift" to this "classic" Jewish deli in Cherry Hill, where "two can share" one of its "huge" sandwiches, and the pickle bar is a "don't-miss"; the "cafeteria decor" and "corny counter banter" may not impress, and some kvetch "it's the prices that'll give you heartburn", but most agree the nosh is the "real deal."

Kiku *Japanese* | 21 | 22 | 21 | $42 |

Alpine | 5-9 Rte. 9 W. (Ruckman Rd.) | 201-767-6322
Paramus | 365 Rte. 17 (Midland Ave.) | 201-265-7200

With "knives flying" and "onion volcanoes" erupting, it's a carnivores' "Disneyland" at these Japanese steakhouses in Alpine and

| | FOOD | DECOR | SERVICE | COST |

Paramus, where "entertaining" chefs grill up "tasty" meats tableside to the delight of "grandkids" and others; sure, the "sleek" spaces might get "noisy", especially when they're "celebration" central, and some find them "expensive", but most are just focused on the "great show."

Kimchi Hana Korean-Japanese Restaurant *Japanese/Korean*
| 23 | 18 | 19 | $27 |

South Plainfield | Middlesex Mall | 6101 Hadley Rd. (Stelton Rd.) | 908-755-0777

Though it's "far from Flushing", this South Plainfield Korean-Japanese offers "authentic" table-grilled BBQ with "lots of cool sides", plus sushi; opinions of the service range from "efficient" to "ok", and some caution the no-frills dining room is overpowered by the braziers' "smoky aroma" ("be prepared to wash your clothes"), but affordable pricing and BYO augment its appeal.

Kinara *Indian*
| 21 | 18 | 20 | $31 |

Edgewater | 880 River Rd. (bet. Garden Pl. & Hilliard Ave.) | 201-313-0555 | www.kinararestaurant.com

A "solid" lineup of "classic" Indian dishes, with a few Chinese-fusion options, attracts diners to this "pleasant" Edgewater BYO; although the strip-mall setting "isn't inspiring" to most, a "friendly environment" prevails, and moderate prices, especially for the lunch buffet, also make it "worth seeking out."

Kinchley's Tavern ●♨ *Pizza*
| 22 | 14 | 18 | $20 |

Ramsey | 586 N. Franklin Tpke. (Orchard St.) | 201-934-7777

"Incredible" pizza with "crackerlike" crust is the reason locals crowd into this "old-school" Ramsey tavern, even if some find the rest of the menu just "so-so"; diehards deem the "perfectly crispy" pies are "worth putting up with" a "cramped" setting and sometimes "rushed" service; P.S. "low prices" but cash only.

Klein's *Seafood*
| 23 | 19 | 20 | $40 |

Belmar | 708 River Rd. (Main St.) | 732-681-1177 | www.kleinsfish.com

"Simply prepared", "fresh" seafood and "delicious sushi" are delivered by a "pleasant" staff at this "popular" Belmar "staple"; "reasonable" prices are another plus, and for fans, dining "out on the deck overlooking the river" and "watching the fishing boats come and go" is what "the NJ Shore is all about."

Knife & Fork Inn ● *American*
| 24 | 23 | 24 | $54 |

Atlantic City | 29 S. Albany Ave. (Pacific Ave.) | 609-344-1133 | www.knifeandforkinn.com

This "wonderful" 1912 American "landmark" in an "oddly elegant building" may be an AC "institution", but its "menu has kept pace with the times", featuring "outstanding" "steaks and chops" along with "always fresh" seafood; an "excellent wine selection" and "efficient, friendly" service help ease the sting of "pricey" tabs.

Komegashi *Japanese*
| 23 | 20 | 21 | $33 |

Jersey City | 103 Montgomery St. (Warren St.) | 201-433-4567

(continued)

Komegashi

Jersey City | 99 Town Square Pl. (bet. River Dr. & Washington Blvd.) | 201-533-8888
www.komegashi.com

"Very good" sushi attracts diners to this Japanese duo in Jersey City, where "interesting" maki rolls pair well with "potent" cocktails; "attentive" service and "fair" prices add to their appeal, and the "fantastic view" of Manhattan at the Newport Marina location provides the wow factor.

Konbu Ⓜ *Japanese*

23 | 18 | 22 | $31

Manalapan | Design Ctr. | 345 Rte. 9 S. (Center Dr.) | 732-462-6886
The chef is not afraid to "experiment" at this Manalapan Japanese BYO, where "innovative" sushi rolls made with the "freshest" fish are fan "favorites"; even if some say the "quiet" decor is "looking a bit frayed around the edges", service gets good marks, and insiders advise going "during the week" to avoid the crowds.

Krave Café Ⓩ *American*

25 | 23 | 24 | $41

Newton | 102 Sparta Ave. (bet. Lincoln Pl. & Orchard St.) | 973-383-2600 | www.kravecaterers.com
The "excellent" "creative" cuisine at this Newton New American is a "nice surprise" for the rural dining scene; "enthusiastic" servers and an "upbeat" setting give fans a "sweet sense of being home", and midrange prices are aided by a BYO option – "the food deserves your better bottles" advise oenophiles.

Krogh's ◑ *American*

21 | 20 | 21 | $28

Sparta | 23 White Deer Plaza (bet. Wallkill Rd. & Winona Pkwy.) | 973-729-8428 | www.kroghs.com
The "standard pub fare" at this Sparta tavern on Lake Mohawk may be perfectly "fine", but it's the "amazing" homebrews on tap that draw folks in – that and the "enchanting", "fairy-tale" setting; "friendly" service and "average" prices suit the scene, and there's extra "fun" on weekends with live music.

Kubel's *Seafood*

19 | 17 | 20 | $29

Barnegat Light | Bayview Ave. (7th St.) | 609-494-8592
Long Beach Township | 8200 Long Beach Blvd. (81st St.) | 609-494-4731 | www.kubels2.com ◑
Dishing up "decent portions" of "basic" American "comfort food", "from burgers and cheesesteaks" to "solid seafood" platters, these "institutions" in Barnegat Light and Long Beach Township are "where the locals go" to "relax over drinks"; if the "noisy", "old-school bar" ambiance is only "ok", "at least the servers are happy to help", and "great happy-hour specials" keep tabs affordable.

Kuzina by Sofia *Greek*

22 | 17 | 21 | $26

Cherry Hill | Sawmill Vill. | 404 Rte. 70 W. (Sawmill Rd.) | 856-429-1061 | www.kuzinabysofia.com
"The mezes alone" are worth a visit to this Cherry Hill Greek BYO, which "makes its strip-mall setting shine" with "reasonably priced",

"authentic, tasty" dishes; diners report adequate service (but with some cries of "not friendly"), and if it's "not a place for quiet conversation", that's because it's "always packed."

Kyma Greek Cuisine *Greek/Seafood*   ▽ 23 | 21 | 21 | $33

Somerville | 24 E. Main St. (bet. Bridge & Warren Sts.) | 908-864-4730 | www.kymacuisine.com

True to its name, which means 'wave', this midpriced Somerville Greek BYO offers "very good" seafood-focused fare alongside traditional dishes, like "spanakopita to die for"; an "upbeat" modern vibe and "great hospitality" from the staff are further reasons it's a "fave spot" of many.

Labrador Lounge *Eclectic*   21 | 16 | 20 | $43

Normandy Beach | 3581 Rte. 35 N. (Peterson Ln.) | 732-830-5770 | www.labradorlounge.com

A "diversified" menu of "tasty, creative" Eclectic fare is served by an "accommodating" staff at this "hippie" Normandy Beach BYO from Marilyn Schlossbach (Dauphin Grille, Langosta Lounge, Pop's Garage, etc.); the vibe is "laid-back" and "personal" in the "beachy" setting, and many consider it one of the "best for outdoor dining."

La Campagna *Italian*   24 | 19 | 21 | $45

Morristown | 5 Elm St. (South St.) | 973-644-4943 | www.lacampagnaristorante.com

A "consistently good" menu of "well-prepared" classics draws crowds to this "old-school" Italian BYO in Morristown, where service that's "not pretentious" and "fair" prices add to the appeal; "tight seating" means diners are "packed" in "cheek-by-jowl", especially on weekends, but for some, "hearing your neighbor's conversation" is part of the "charm."

La Cipollina Ⓜ *Italian*   21 | 21 | 21 | $42

Freehold | 16 W. Main St. (South St.) | 732-308-3830 | www.lacipollina.com

The "*delizioso*" traditional fare is "not run-of-the-mill" report regulars of this "established Italian eatery" in Freehold; a BYO option eases slightly "expensive" tabs, and the "friendly", tuxedoed staff maintains an "elegant", old-fashioned atmosphere.

La Couronne Ⓢ *Italian*   23 | 19 | 22 | $40

Montclair | 23 Watchung Plaza (bet. Fairfield St. & Watchung Ave.) | 973-744-2090

"A true taste of Italy" can be found at this "reliable neighborhood" BYO in Montclair, where "great" thin-crust pizzas are among the "well-prepared" midpriced standards; if the white-tablecloth decor fails to impress, at least "reasonably quiet dining" is possible here, and "friendly" service is part of the draw.

La Dolce Vita *Italian/Seafood*   22 | 19 | 21 | $41

Belmar | 400 Ocean Ave. (4th Ave.) | 732-749-3177 | www.ladolcevitabelmar.com

"Steps from the ocean" in Belmar, this "scenic" Italian offers "generous portions" of "authentic", "well-prepared" pastas and seafood dishes; "tight seating" is alleviated in summer by an outdoor patio, and for those "tempted to leave the beach early", the late afternoon prix fixe can be a "good value"; P.S. a full bar is now available.

La Esperanza *Mexican* 24 | 22 | 23 | $23

Lindenwold | 40 E. Gibbsboro Rd. (bet. Cooper Ave. & White Horse Pike) | 856-782-7114 | www.mexicanhope.com

Fans of this family-run "gem" praise the "authentic", "homestyle" Mexican eats, served in a brightly colored Lindenwold house; add "delicious" margaritas, a "great" tequila selection, "friendly" service and "reasonable" prices, and "what else do you need?"

Lafayette House *American* 22 | 21 | 22 | $32

Lafayette | Old Lafayette Vill. (bet. Morris Farm Rd. & New Jersey 94) | 973-579-3100 | www.thelafayettehouse.com

A "favorite" stop after a "visit to Olde Lafayette Village", this mid-priced American offers an "enjoyable" meat-and-potatoes meal in a "fancy" "barn" setting, complemented by "one-of-the-family" service; though some find it "dated", most agree on the "great" Sunday brunch buffet, and a tavern menu offers a more affordable option.

La Focaccia *Italian* 23 | 20 | 22 | $46

Summit | 523 Morris Ave. (Aubrey St.) | 908-277-4006 | www.lafocaccianj.com

"Fresh flavors" and a "varied" menu "keep it interesting" at this "sophisticated" Italian BYO set in a Summit storefront; while "noise" can be a "challenge", and regulars say prepare for a "wait" (even "with reservations"), the "lovely" space and servers who are "happy to accommodate" help make it "worth a trip."

La Fontana Coast *Italian* ▽ 23 | 21 | 21 | $41

Sea Isle City | 5000 Landis Ave. (50th St.) | 609-486-6088 | www.lafontanacoast.com

With its "nicely executed" Italian menu, including homemade pastas and desserts, fans are not surprised this seasonal Sea Isle City BYO is usually "filled with regulars"; the Mediterranean villa–inspired space exudes an "old-world charm", though it can get "noisy", but prices are moderate and there's an "outdoor patio" for summer evening dines.

La Griglia ⌧ *Italian/Seafood* 23 | 19 | 22 | $51

Kenilworth | 740 Kenilworth Blvd. (26th St.) | 908-241-0031 | www.lagriglia.com

A "varied" menu of "well-turned-out" seafood-centric fare makes this "special-night" Italian "well worth a trip to sleepy Kenilworth" ; white tablecloths and modern lighting create a "warm" atmosphere, though it's a bit of a "tight squeeze" that can get "noisy", and while "pricey", it'll spare you the "travel to Manhattan."

La Isla *Cuban* 25 | 15 | 20 | $23

Hoboken | 104 Washington St. (bet. 1st & 2nd Sts.) | 201-659-8197 | www.laislarestaurant.com

You might "swear your Cuban grandma's in the kitchen" at this "tiny" Hoboken BYO, where everything from papa rellena to French toast (which was featured on *Throwdown! With Bobby Flay*) is "authentic" and "delicious", and comes at "great prices"; "prompt" service is an added bonus, and while few warm to the space that resembles a "Caribbean diner" with "limited seating", aficionados insist "this place is the real deal."

L'Allegria *Italian*

| 23 | 21 | 22 | $53 |

Madison | 11 Prospect St. (bet. Lincoln Pl. & Main St.) | 973-377-6808 | www.lallegria.com

A "longtime Madison standby", this "reliable" Italian offers "well-executed", "authentic" fare backed by a "great" wine list and served by a solid staff; the "intimate" setting has an "elegant Roman" feel, and while the tabs can get high, many consider it "worth the expense" for a "special evening."

Lambertville Station *American*

| 20 | 21 | 20 | $36 |

Lambertville | Inn at Lambertville Station | 11 Bridge St. (Klines Ct.) | 609-397-8300 | www.lambertvillestation.com

Housed in an old rail depot on the Delaware and Raritan Canal, this "charming" Lambertville American is a "reliable stop" for a "satisfying" meal or to "grab a drink" after shopping; it may be something of a "tourist destination", but few deny the appeal of warm weather "trackside dining", the "really cool" cellar wine bar or the overall "beautiful setting."

La Mezzaluna *Italian*

| 22 | 20 | 21 | $42 |

Princeton | 25 Witherspoon St. (bet. Lincoln Hwy. & Spring St.) | 609-688-8515 | www.lamezzaluna.com

Fans of this "nice" Italian BYO in Downtown Princeton extol its "fresh, creative" dishes, "deft" service and a "welcoming" ambiance in the "vibrant" dining room; though some find it a tad "pricey", others insist it's "worth the price."

Landmark Americana
Tap & Grill ❷ *American/Pub Food*

| 22 | 21 | 19 | $23 |

Glassboro | 1 Mullica Hill Rd. (Main St.) | 856-863-6600 | www.landmarkamericana.com

A "local hangout" for Rowan University students, this Glassboro pub serves "better-than-expected" bar food (including "all-you-can-eat" wings on Saturdays) alongside "amazing" drink specials; service doesn't leave much of an impression, but prices are modest, and with lots of big screens, it's "the ultimate spot" to watch a game.

Langosta Lounge *Eclectic*

| 20 | 19 | 19 | $38 |

Asbury Park | Asbury Park Boardwalk | 1000 Ocean Ave. (bet. 2nd & 3rd Aves.) | 732-455-3275 | www.langostalounge.com

A "cool, quirky" offering from the 'Kitschens' empire of Marilyn Schlossbach, this "festive" Eclectic on the Asbury Park boardwalk offers around-the-world-in-a-day "vacation cuisine" that's often "delicious" (if occasionally "puzzling" to some); and if a few note the "friendly" servers sometimes "seem to be grooving too much on the vibe", just grab a "mojito or two" and you might be too.

La Pastaria *Italian*

21 | 18 | 19 | $32

Summit | 327 Springfield Ave. (bet. Summit & Waldron Aves.) | 908-522-9088

Red Bank | 30 Linden Pl. (Hudson Ave.) | 732-224-8699

www.lapastaria.com

"Reliable" sums up these midpriced BYO trattorias in Red Bank and Summit, offering an "inventive" menu of "fresh", "beautifully" prepared Italian fare; sure, they can get "a little too noisy", and some say service can be "hit-or-miss", but "generous portions" and "decent" prices make them "worth the trip" and "sometimes the wait."

La Pergola *Italian*

20 | 21 | 21 | $48

Millburn | 120 Essex St. (Lackawanna Pl.) | 973-376-6838 | www.lapergolanj.com

An "extensive" menu of "enjoyable" classics "pleases" patrons of this Millburn Italian, but it may be "quiet sophistication" that is the primary draw, given its proximity to the Paper Mill Playhouse; the "cavernous" space with large windows is "comfortable", while service overall is "strong", and "NYC" prices are aided by BYO.

La Primavera Trattoria Ⓜ *Italian*

▽ 24 | 22 | 24 | $43

West Orange | 500 Pleasant Valley Way (Eagle Rock Ave.) | 973-669-0966

"Don't overlook this quiet gem" say fans of this West Orange strip-mall trattoria, a sibling of the Wilshire Grand's Primavera; "reliable" midpriced Italian dishes ("fish especially shines"), "great" service and a "cozy" ambiance make this a local "favorite."

La Riviera Gastronomia Ⓜ⇆ *Italian*

26 | 16 | 22 | $31

Clifton | 429 Piaget Ave. (bet. Delaware & Montgomery Sts.) | 973-772-9099

"Don't let the discreet exterior fool you" say fans of this Clifton storefront BYO, where the Calabretta family serves up "incredible" "homestyle" Italian dishes "cooked with love", including housemade pastas, "appetizers that sparkle" and salad dressing that alone is "worth the trip" for some; sure, there's "no decor", no reservations and no credit cards, but fans aren't complaining, especially when the staff "makes you feel like family" and "the bill won't raid your wallet."

ⓃⒺⓌ La Sera Ⓜ *Italian*

- | - | - | M

Wyckoff | 393 Franklin Ave. (bet. Everett & Wyckoff Aves.) | 201-485-8793 | www.laserarestaurant.com

Restaurateur Vincent Padula (of Oakland's Cenzino) has opened this midpriced Italian in Wyckoff in homage to his mother, Serafina; son Marc oversees the kitchen, turning out a menu that includes traditional dishes as well as a smattering of American offerings, which are served in a space that's a bit more upscale than that of its elder sibling.

Las Palmas ☾ *Cuban*

▽ 24 | 20 | 21 | $24

West New York | 6153 Bergenline Ave. (bet. 61st & 62nd Sts.) | 201-861-1400 | www.laspalmasrestaurantnj.com

When West New Yorkers want "to forget the work day", this eatery and nightclub does the trick, serving "tasty", "real Cuban" cuisine and sangria in a "laid-back" atmosphere; the place heats up on weekends with "excellent" live music and "dancing", and the "large portions" and modest prices make it a "great value."

La Spiaggia *Italian*
23 | 20 | 23 | $48

Ship Bottom | 357 W. Eighth St. (bet. Barnegat Ave. & Shore Rd.) | 609-494-4343 | www.laspiaggialbi.com

"Fresh ingredients" shine in the "well-prepared" Northern Italian cuisine at this higher-end Ship Bottom BYO from the Stragapede brothers; while the room may be "kind of dark", the staff's "attitude is always bright" and the atmosphere is "pleasant."

La Strada *Italian*
23 | 20 | 22 | $38

Randolph | 1105 Rte. 10 E. (bet. Irish Spring Rd. & Morris Tpke.) | 973-584-4607 | www.lastradarestaurant.com

"Delicious" "classics" are the hallmark of this "family-run" Randolph Italian that's "been in business for a long time" thanks to "dependable" fare, "friendly" service and moderate prices; the "quiet", "white-napkin" setting makes it a popular destination for "holidays" and "special nights out"; P.S. though it serves wine, BYO is permitted.

La Tapatia *Mexican*
▽ 24 | 16 | 18 | $20

Asbury Park | 707 Main St. (bet. Asbury & Sewall Aves.) | 732-776-7826

"Eat where the locals" do, this "reasonably priced" Asbury Park Mexican cantina where a "friendly" staff delivers "grande" portions of "delicious", "authentic" *comida,* including a range of tacos and tamales, at "reasonable" prices; a "friendly" staff oversees the "bustling" dining room and full bar.

Latour Ⓜ *French*
26 | 22 | 25 | $60

Ridgewood | 6 E. Ridgewood Ave. (Broad St.) | 201-445-5056 | www.latourridgewood.com

Chef Michael Latour has been creating "showstopping" French cuisine for more than a decade at this Ridgewood storefront BYO, aided by a "courteous" staff; fans find the Gallic "country" setting "lovely", albeit "cramped", and while a few wish the "pricey" menu "would change more often", most assert it's "well worth the cost", especially considering the "bargain" prix fixe dinner offered four nights a week.

Latz's by the Bay Ⓜ *American*
21 | 20 | 22 | $41

Somers Point | 801 Bay Ave. (New Jersey Ave.) | 609-788-8838 | www.latzsbythebay.com

"Fresh" seafood is a highlight at this Somers Point BYO American, which also serves afternoon tea and Sunday brunch; the traditional setting boasts bayside views of "beautiful boats in the harbor" (hint: "ask for a window table").

The Laurel Ⓜ *American*
21 | 19 | 18 | $28

Maplewood | 175 Maplewood Ave. (bet. Baker St. & Highland Pl.) | 973-762-0050 | www.thelaurelnj.com

"Creative" American fare with "touches of international inspiration" is on offer at this "adorable" Maplewood spot from a father-daughter team; the storefront space is "tiny" to be sure, and some say service "doesn't match the quality of the cooking", but prices are moderate (with BYO), and so far, fans find it a "good place to meet for breakfast" (plus lunch and dinner) in the neighborhood.

La Vecchia Napoli Ⓜ Italian
`22` `19` `20` `$45`

Edgewater | 2 Hilliard Ave. (River Rd.) | 201-941-6799 | www.lavecchianapoli.com

"Good, old-fashioned" Italian dishes draw locals to this "cute" Edgewater "standby" where fans tout "well-prepared" veal and other specials, plus a "diverse" wine list; if the "intimate" space strikes some as "dated", sidewalk tables offer an alternative view, and moderately expensive tabs make it a "value."

Legal Sea Foods Seafood
`21` `19` `20` `$41`

Paramus | Garden State Plaza | 1 Garden State Plaza (Garden State Plaza Pkwy.) | 201-843-8483
Short Hills | The Mall at Short Hills | 1200 Morris Tpke. (John F. Kennedy Pkwy.) | 973-467-0089
www.legalseafoods.com

A "knowledgeable" staff assists with the "huge" menu of "consistently fresh, well-prepared" aquatic fare (including "out-of-this world" clam chowder) and a "lovely wine selection" at this "serious seafood place" in Paramus and Short Hills; it's "a bit pricey" for some, and there's "not much to look at" in the "crowded", "upmarket chain" surrounds – still, devotees declare it's "worth it" to "satisfy your craving."

Lemongrass Viet-Thai
Restaurant Thai/Vietnamese
`23` `19` `21` `$23`

Morris Plains | 1729 Rte. 10 E. (Headley Ave.) | 973-998-6303 | www.lemongrassnj.com

"Authentic pho" with "broth to die for" is a "hit" among the "fresh" Viet-Thai selections at this affordable BYO in an "offbeat" Morris Plains strip mall; with its "friendly", "knowledgeable" service and low-key "lounge feel", insiders say it's a "welcome change for the Route 10 dining scene."

Le Rendez-Vous Ⓜ French
`26` `19` `23` `$56`

Kenilworth | 520 Boulevard (21st St.) | 908-931-0888

The French cuisine is "nothing less than superb" at this "quaint" Kenilworth bistro, where chef-owner Philippe Lièvre presents a "constantly changing" seasonal menu, served by an "attentive" staff; oui, it can be "as cramped as the Paris Metro at rush hour", and "it's not cheap" either, but the cost is alleviated by BYO – and fans say "bring your best."

Levant Grille Mediterranean
`21` `22` `22` `$34`

Englewood | 34 E. Palisade Ave. (bet. Dean St. & Grand Ave.) | 201-503-1200 | www.levantgrille.com

"Fresh, delicious" Persian and Turkish specialties are delivered by "friendly" servers overseeing "your dining pleasure" at this "upscale" Englewood Mediterranean; the "nicely appointed" contemporary space and "reasonable" tabs (especially with BYO) make it a "nice change of pace."

Liberty House ⓜ *American*

20 | 23 | 20 | $50

Jersey City | Liberty State Park | 76 Audrey Zapp Dr. (Freedom Way) | 201-395-0300 | www.libertyhouserestaurant.com

"Spectacular views" of the Manhattan skyline plus an "outdoor garden area" for warm-weather dining headline the "gorgeous" setting at this upscale American in Jersey City's Liberty State Park; fans praise the "imaginative" fare while contrarians find it "nothing to brag about", especially for prices that are "over the top" – still, many consider it a "wonderful find" for "special occasions."

Library IV *Steak*

24 | 20 | 21 | $29

Williamstown | 1030 N. Black Horse Pike (bet. Brookdale Blvd. & Lake Ave.) | 856-728-8064 | www.libraryiv.com

Hand-cut steaks by the ounce are "cooked to perfection" swear loyalists of this "solid" Williamstown steakhouse, a "family favorite" that also offers seafood, a "great salad bar" and other American eats in a traditional setting with shelves of books in the dining room; "attentive" service and "value" pricing complete the picture.

Library III ◑ *Steak*

25 | 20 | 22 | $33

Egg Harbor Township | 6605 Black Horse Pike (Spruce Ave.) | 609-645-7655

Newly installed at an Egg Harbor golf course after 40 years in its former home, this midpriced steakhouse "favorite" is still serving "tender" cuts ordered directly from the kitchen, where they are "cooked to perfection" while diners sample the "ultrafresh" salads; the library theme continues in the new space, which also boasts a bar overlooking the links, and the same old team is "right on top of things."

Library II ◑ *Steak*

24 | 20 | 21 | $40

Voorhees | 306 Rte. 73 (Braddock Mill Rd.) | 856-424-0198 | www.librarytwo.com

"Top-quality steaks cut to order" and an "outstanding traditional salad bar" tempt fans of this long-running surf 'n' turf "fave" in Voorhees; the bookish setting is "too dark" and "noisy" for some, but most find it a "pleasant" experience with "friendly" service and moderate tabs.

⬛NEW Lidia's Cuban Kitchen *Cuban*

- | - | - | M

Cranford | 117 N. Union Ave. (bet. Alden St. & Springfield Ave.) | 908-272-8226 | www.lidiascubankitchen.com

Simple, authentic Cuban fare – from empanadas to lechon asada – arrives in Cranford via this midpriced family-run eatery, which also offers a small coda of Italian standards; the space is rustic and colorful, and if you BYO, they'll mix up some mojitos or sangria.

Light Horse Tavern *American*

22 | 22 | 20 | $40

Jersey City | 199 Washington St. (Morris St.) | 201-946-2028 | www.lighthorsetavern.com

A "charming oasis in Jersey City" with high ceilings, exposed-brick walls and seasonal patio seating, this "beautifully renovated"

American is a "local favorite" for its "upscale tavern food" and "decent beer selections"; even if it's "a bit pricey" and service can be "slow", regulars assure it's a "treat" – "if you're not in a rush."

Lilly's on the Canal Ⓜ *Eclectic*   20 | 20 | 19 | $37

Lambertville | 2 Canal St. (bet. Bridge & Coryell Sts.) | 609-397-6242 | www.lillysgourmet.com

The "rustic, canal-side" locale and "enjoyable" outdoor seating make this "friendly" Lambertville Eclectic a "delightful" stop "after a walk on the canal"; "gorgeous desserts" get a special mention, and there's optional BYO in addition to the selection of local wines available.

Limani Ⓜ *Greek*   25 | 19 | 23 | $42

Westfield | 235 North Ave. W. (Lenox Ave.) | 908-233-0052

Fans "get spoiled" after feasting on the "consistently wonderful" seafood "with a Mediterranean flair" at this Westfield Greek; "attentive" service and a "warm", "intimate" atmosphere help compensate for the "noise factor" (especially when it's "packed"), and BYO helps "keep prices within reason."

NEW Lisa's Mediterranean Kitchen *Mediterranean*   - | - | - | M

Ridgewood | 28 Oak St. (bet. Franklin & Ridgewood Aves.) | 201-251-8686 | www.lisasmediterraneancuisine.com

The former Lisa's Turkish Kitchen finds new life on Ridgewood's Oak Street, serving a Med menu in a gold-toned room with French doors that open onto a sidewalk cafe; what haven't changed are the moderate prices and the sister-owners' signature lamb dumplings and kebabs, served with bread baked on-site daily; P.S. it's BYO.

Lithos *Greek*   23 | 24 | 23 | $52

Livingston | 405 Eisenhower Pkwy. (bet. Dorsa & Eagle Rock Aves.) | 973-758-1111 | www.lithosgreekrestaurant.com

Insiders "rave" about the "expertly prepared" seafood and other "upscale" Greek fare at this "lovely" Livingston locale; the "elegant", contemporary decor and "attentive" service are accompanied by "special-occasion" prices, though the lunch prix fixe is a "bargain."

Little Food Cafe *Sandwiches*   ∇ 23 | 17 | 22 | $17

Bayonne | 330 Kennedy Blvd. (10th St.) | 201-436-6800 🌫
Pompton Plains | 585 Newark Pompton Tpke. (bet. Manor & Poplar Aves.) | 973-616-8600 🆂
www.thelittlefoodcafe.com

A "friendly, fast" crew delivers a "solid menu" at these "relaxed" sandwich specialists in Bayonne and Pompton Plains; "nothing-fancy" digs "get the job done", and BYO adds to the overall "value."

Little Tuna *Seafood*   22 | 20 | 21 | $32

Haddonfield | 141 Kings Hwy. E. (bet. Haddon Ave. & Mechanic St.) | 856-795-0888 | www.thelittletuna.com

As a "lunch spot for local professionals" or a "date-night" destination, this Haddonfield BYO seafooder caters to "fish lovers" with various preparations of "fresh tuna" and other fin fare that bring "a true bang of quality for your buck" (and you "can't beat the early-bird" three-course menu); solid service and "cozy", "quiet" digs round out an "enjoyable" experience.

LoBianco ⏢Ⓜ American
▽ 23 | 21 | 22 | $41

Margate | 20 S. Douglas Ave. (bet. Atlantic & Ventnor Aves.) | 609-350-6493 | www.restaurantlobianco.com

Fans issue "no complaints" about this Margate "favorite" run by husband-and-wife team Nicolas and Stephanie LoBianco, serving up a menu of all-American faves such as fish 'n' chips and some of the "best short ribs ever", plus "lots of good specials", in a 'beach-casual' setting; the BYO policy helps keep tabs reasonable; P.S. hours vary by season.

Lobster House Seafood
22 | 20 | 20 | $37

Cape May | Fisherman's Wharf | 906 Schellengers Landing Rd. (Rte. 109) | 609-884-8296 | www.thelobsterhouse.com

"Nothing beats sitting on the dock" at this Cape May "landmark", where "outrageously fresh" seafood is "not fancy" but "consistently good" and "reasonably priced"; though some think the "location trumps the food" and warn of "big waits" for a table, others tout it for its "many options", from cocktails on the nearby schooner-cum-cocktail lounge or the "gem" of an outdoor raw bar.

Locale Italian
21 | 22 | 22 | $52

Closter | 208 Piermont Rd. (Ruckman Rd.) | 201-750-3233 | www.locale208closter.com

The "roomy", white-tablecloth dining room and "delightful" patio make for a "tasteful" setting for a "well-prepared" meal at this up-scale Closter Italian where the "servers aim to please"; a few feel it's "overpriced", but most consider it "a pleasant surprise" in a "part of Bergen County starving for fine dining."

NEW Local Seasonal Kitchen ⏢Ⓜ American
- | - | - | E

Ramsey | 41 W. Main St. (New St.) | 201-962-9400 | www.localsk.com

True to its name, this Ramsey New American from Steven Santoro (NYC's Fresco and erstwhile La Côte Basque and Café des Artistes) offers a diverse menu inspired by the seasons and focused on local, sustainable ingredients; brick, earth tones and wooden tables create a warm setting that belies its strip-mall locale, as do urban prices, but the option to BYO (wine only) helps keep tabs in check.

Lola Latin Bistro Ⓜ Pan-Latin
21 | 19 | 19 | $33

Metuchen | 87 Central Ave. (bet. Middlesex Ave. & Park Sq.) | 732-548-5652 | www.lolalatinbistro.com

Wash down "delicious Latin fusion" fare with "wine from the liquor store next door" at this moderately priced Metuchen BYO; even if service elicits mixed opinions and the dining room can get "crowded", regulars report "it feels like you stumbled into a fun house party", especially if you find a "spot on the outside patio near the fire pit."

			FOOD	DECOR	SERVICE	COST

Lola's *Spanish*
22 | 19 | 20 | $38

Hoboken | 153 14th St. (Bloomfield St.) | 201-420-6062 |
www.lolas-tapas-wine-bar-hoboken.com
Loyalists find themselves "craving" the "interesting", "delicious" hot
and cold tapas selections (including numerous daily specials) at this
midpriced Spanish wine bar in Hoboken; service is accommodating
and the "intimate" space with an indoor fountain and wine-barrel tables has a "romantic" atmosphere.

Lorena's Ⓜ *French*
28 | 23 | 26 | $61

Maplewood | 168 Maplewood Ave. (bet. Baker St. & Depot Plaza) |
973-763-4460 | www.restaurantlorena.com
Chef-owner Humberto Campos Jr.'s "attention to detail" ensures "art-
istry in every dish" at this Maplewood "jewel" showcasing his "sublime" French cuisine in a "cozy", "romantic" setting; "exquisite" service
adds to a "gourmet experience" that's "special occasion"–worthy, with
tabs to match (but a BYO policy helps "keep total costs down").

Los Amigos *Mexican/Southwestern*
21 | 19 | 20 | $29

Atlantic City | 1926 Atlantic Ave. (bet. Michigan & Ohio Aves.) |
609-344-2293
West Berlin | 461 Rte. 73 N. (bet. Franklin Ave. & Lenz Ln.) |
856-767-5216 Ⓜ
www.losamigosrest.com
"Just have a margarita and forget about" your diet at these long-
running siblings in Atlantic City and West Berlin, where "solid"
Mexican-Southwestern eats are delivered by a "fast, friendly" crew;
if the colorful decor seems "outdated" to some, prices are reasonable, with happy-hour deals to boot.

Lotus Cafe *Chinese*
21 | 15 | 19 | $24

Hackensack | Hackensack Plaza | 450 Hackensack Ave.
(bet. Commerce Way & Rte. 4) | 201-488-7070 | www.lotuscafenj.com
"Not your run-of-the-mill Chinese", this "steadfast" Hackensack
BYO offers "something for everyone" (including "health-conscious
diners") with its "tasty, abundant" options; "tucked away in a shopping center", the setting is "nothing fancy", and service can be "un-
predictable", but it's usually "fast" and prices are "reasonable."

LouCás *Italian*
23 | 20 | 22 | $39

Edison | Colonial Village Shopping Ctr. | 9 Lincoln Hwy. (Parsonage Rd.) |
732-549-8580 | www.loucasrestaurant.com
"Seafood and pasta are the standouts" at this "bustling strip-mall
BYO" Italian in Edison, where "imaginative specials" supplement the
menu with "something for everyone"; "accommodating" service and
"handsome" decor help compensate for often loud, "crowded" conditions, though loyalists just "ignore the noise and enjoy the value."

Luca's Ristorante *Italian*
24 | 21 | 23 | $38

Somerset | 2019 Rte. 27 (bet. Allamano Way & Rolling Hills Dr.) |
732-297-7676 | www.lucasristorante.com
"A real find tucked away in a little strip mall", this "unassuming"
Somerset BYO dishes up "interesting Italian fare" with "creative

twists on classic preparations" at "fair" prices; "attentive, but not obtrusive" service and "cozy" decor add to the "charming experience."

Luciano's *Italian* 22 | 22 | 22 | $43

Rahway | 1579 Main St. (Monroe St.) | 732-815-1200 | www.lucianosristorante.com

With its "spacious", "white-tablecloth" dining room, "nice bar area" and fireplace, this Rahway Italian "feels more upscale" than the "reasonable" prices may reflect; serving up homemade pastas, sea-food dishes and other "solid", "old-style" fare, the "personable" staff is "helpful with the wine selection" too.

Lucky Bones Backwater Grille *American* 21 | 18 | 21 | $31

Cape May | 1200 Rte. 109 S. (Schellenger St.) | 609-884-2663 | www.luckybonesgrille.com

"Simple, fresh" and "tasty" sum up the fare at this "friendly" Cape May American, a "casual, come-as-you-are place" that's suited for the "whole family"; "amazing" thin-crust pizza, "ice-cold" beer and "affordable" prices help make up for "long waits", especially "during the summer months."

Luigi's *Italian* 22 | 19 | 22 | $36

East Hanover | Berkeley Plaza | 434 Ridgedale Ave. (McKinley Ave.) | 973-887-8408 | www.luigisrestaurant.info

The "attentive" staff "makes you feel at home" at this "busy" neighborhood Italian "gem" in East Hanover; even if the "casual" decor is "nothing to speak of", there's a "cozy", "kid-friendly" vibe, and the "huge portions" of "solid", "reliable" fare promise "great value for the money."

Luigi's Pizza Fresca *Italian/Pizza* 21 | 18 | 21 | $17

Burlington | 1700 Columbus Rd. (Neck Rd.) | 609-239-8888
Marlton | 529 Old Marlton Pike W. (Cropwell Rd.) | 856-810-8888
www.luigispizzafresca.com

The "friendly" staffers are "all smiles" at these "neighborhood piz-zerias" in Burlington and Marlton specializing in thin-crust pies with an array of creative toppings, plus sandwiches and pastas; even if the surrounds are no-frills, local delivery service and "competitive" prices help explain why it comes "recommended."

Luke Palladino *Italian* 24 | 22 | 24 | $52

Atlantic City | Harrah's Resort Atlantic City | 777 Harrah's Blvd. (Renaissance Point Blvd.) | 609-441-5576
Northfield | Plaza 9 Shopping Ctr. | 1333 New Rd. (Tilton Rd.) | 609-646-8189
www.lukepalladino.com

"Old-world peasant" meets "upscale" "foodie" at this pair of "imaginative" Italians, where "well-sourced" seasonal ingredients and homemade pastas anchor an "unpretentious" menu; open kitchens showcase chef Palladino and company at both the "intimate" "hole-in-the-wall" storefront in Northfield (which is BYO) and the Harrah's Atlantic City, and reservations are a "must."

	FOOD	DECOR	SERVICE	COST

Lu Nello ☒ *Italian*
25 | 23 | 24 | $68

Cedar Grove | 182 Stevens Ave. (Lindsley Rd.) | 973-837-1660 | www.lunello.com

"Expensive, but worth every penny", this "upscale" Italian in Cedar Grove is a "class act" offering a "wonderful menu of outstanding dishes", plus a "mind-boggling list of specials", served by a "knowledgeable" staff; an "excellent wine list", "romantic" atmosphere and "spacious, comfortable" environs help most get over the "credit-card shock" and contribute to a "top-notch" experience.

LuNello's Montville Inn *American/Italian*
21 | 21 | 19 | $45

Montville | 167 Rte. 202 (River Rd.) | 973-541-1234 | www.montvilleinn.com

"More appealing" with a "solid" "new menu slanted toward Italian fare", this upscale Montville Italo-American on the site of a pre-Revolutionary inn creates "well-prepared" dishes with produce from its own farm; a "caring" staff caters to guests in the "subdued" dining room, while the "bar scene" is a more "high-volume experience."

Madame Claude Cafe ☒⌐ *French*
∇ 22 | 17 | 18 | $34

Jersey City | 364½ Fourth St. (Brunswick St.) | 201-876-8800 | www.madameclaudecafe.com

"Well-prepared" Gallic standards are a relative "bargain" (especially with BYO) at this "tiny bistro with real French flavor" in Jersey City; the "funky" space is often "crowded, but in a clever way" that "transports" you, with "awesome" weekly live jazz to boot; P.S. cash only.

Mad Batter *American*
22 | 19 | 21 | $31

Cape May | Carroll Villa Hotel | 19 Jackson St. (bet. Carpenter Ln. & County Hwy. 604) | 609-884-5970 | www.madbatter.com

"Unusual twists" on French toast and other morning fare offer a "vacation from the breakfast doldrums" at this "quaint", "kitschy" Cape May American housed in a Victorian B&B; there's "tasty" lunch and dinner too, and though service gets mixed reviews ("perfect" to "poor"), regulars find the porch-front dining "heavenly."

Madeleine's Petit Paris ☒ *French*
24 | 21 | 24 | $53

Northvale | 416 Tappan Rd. (White Ave.) | 201-767-0063 | www.madeleinespetitparis.com

Amis insist the "superb" French cuisine is "worth every penny" at this "special-occasion" spot in Northvale; a few find the scene "a tad old-fashioned", but fans swoon you'll be "greeted with such warmth, your cares will disappear"; P.S. BYO Tuesday nights.

Main Street *American/Continental*
20 | 17 | 19 | $32

Kingston | 4581 Rte. 27 (Laurel Ave.) | 609-921-2778

Main Street Bistro & Bar *American/Continental*
Princeton | Princeton Shopping Ctr. | 301 N. Harrison St. (bet. Clearview Ave. & Terhune Rd.) | 609-921-2779 | www.mainstreetprinceton.com

A "helpful" staff delivers "simple, straightforward" American-Continental eats, including "tempting" seasonal specials, at this "dependable" Princeton bistro and its Kingston BYO sibling; both offer outdoor seating while the latter is also a gourmet bakery (open for breakfast and lunch only), and "reasonable" tabs help explain why they're "popular with locals."

Makeda *Ethiopian*
22 | 21 | 20 | $36

New Brunswick | 338 George St. (bet. Bayard St. & Livingston Ave.) | 732-545-5115 | www.makedas.com

"Convenient to New Brunswick's theaters", this midpriced Ethiopian offers a "wonderful selection" of "exotic , well-prepared" dishes; even if some say service is "mixed", the "rich, woody decor" makes for an "unexpectedly elegant" setting that "becomes a lounge" later in the evening, with live music Fridays and Saturdays.

Málaga's Restaurante *Spanish*
∇ 26 | 21 | 23 | $36

Hamilton | 511 Lalor St. (Hewitt Ave.) | 609-396-8878 | www.malagarestaurant.com

A "friendly, fun" staff dishes up "huge portions" of "delicious" Spanish cuisine that "hits the spot" at this midpriced Hamilton "classic"; insiders say the "open space" can get "crowded" on weekends (expect a full-on "party atmosphere" for the monthly flamenco performances), so it's best to go early and "relax with a pitcher of sangria" at this "diamond in the rough."

Manco & Manco Pizza *Pizza*
23 | 15 | 19 | $11

Ocean City | 758 Boardwalk (8th St.) | 609-398-0720 🏧 Ⓜ
Ocean City | 920 Boardwalk (9th St.) | 609-399-2548 ⊟
www.mancospizza.com

These "popular" Ocean City pie parlors have been Shore "staples" since the late 50s, serving up "classic boardwalk pizza" that many claim is "the bomb"; the scene is "delicious" too – fans say "there's nothing better" than a couple of slices at the counter "watching the people on the boardwalk" pass by.

Manon Ⓜ ⊟ *French*
24 | 20 | 22 | $48

Lambertville | 19 N. Union St. (bet. Bridge & Coryell Sts.) | 609-397-2596

For a "bit of Provence" in Lambertville, Francophiles tout this "charming bistro" offering "traditional French country" fare "prepared authentically"; *amis* advise "definitely make reservations" for a seat in the "tiny" space, and while some find it "pricey for a BYO", many say the "overall experience is worth it."

The Manor Ⓜ *American*
24 | 24 | 24 | $64

West Orange | 111 Prospect Ave. (Woodland Ave.) | 973-731-2360 | www.themanorrestaurant.com

A "bastion of civilized dining", this "special-occasion stalwart" in West Orange purveys "fancy" Traditional American cuisine alongside a "knockout" wine list in a "grand" manor house set amid 20 manicured acres; not surprisingly, it's a "wedding mill" on weekends, and some find the "old-world charm" merely "stuffy", not to mention "expensive", but devotees who like to "feel like a VIP" deem it "worth the extravagance"; P.S. jackets required.

	FOOD	DECOR	SERVICE	COST

Mantra *Indian*
21 | **21** | **20** | **$37**

Jersey City | 253 Washington St. (bet. Montgomery & York Sts.) | 201-333-8699
Paramus | 275 Rte. 4 W. (bet. Forest Ave. & Lakeview St.) | 201-342-8868 ◐
www.mantranj.com

The "creative kitchens" at these "upscale" siblings in Jersey City and Paramus send out "tasty" "nuevo" Indian cuisine that offers a "change from more common fare"; the "sleek", "modern" surroundings are "comfortable", while service gets mixed marks and tabs are "a little pricey", but regulars assure "you'll leave with a smile."

Marco & Pepe Ⓜ *American*
23 | **18** | **20** | **$38**

Jersey City | 289 Grove St. (Mercer St.) | 201-860-9688 | www.marcoandpepe.com

A "young, hip crowd" heads to this Jersey City New American for "unpretentious, tasty" eats at moderate prices, served by a "hipster" staff; "sunlight streaming in through the windows" lends an old-world bistro feel, and while some find the "noise levels" too high when it's "crowded", sidewalk seating's an option "in nice weather."

Margherita's Ⓜ *Italian*
21 | **18** | **19** | **$27**

Hoboken | 740 Washington St. (8th St.) | 201-222-2400 | www.margheritascafe.com

"Tasty pizzas" and other "hearty", "no-nonsense" Italian eats served in "huge portions" are "a great value for your money" at this Hoboken BYO; though there might be a "wait for a table" if it's "crowded" (especially "on weekends"), the "friendly" service and "casual" vibe suit a neighborhood crowd.

Maritime Parc Ⓜ *American/Seafood*
23 | **24** | **21** | **$56**

Jersey City | Liberty State Park | 84 Audrey Zapp Dr. (Freedom Way) | 201-413-0050 | www.maritimeparc.com

The "stunning views of the adjacent marina" and "magnificent" Manhattan skyline at this "romantic" New American in Jersey City's Liberty State Park "can't be beat" – especially when you can "enjoy the outdoor seating" in summer; it's "expensive", but the seafood-centric offerings are "well-prepared and fresh", and served by an "attentive" staff.

Market Roost Ⓜ *Eclectic*
▽ **23** | **18** | **19** | **$21**

Flemington | 65 Main St. (bet. Capner & Court Sts.) | 908-788-4949 | www.marketroost.com

Fans say it's a "treat" to swing by for "fresh" breakfast fare, "gourmet" lunch offerings (including "unique" sandwiches) and housemade desserts at this Flemington Eclectic; the casual space also features a design-centric gift shop, and BYO complements the modest prices.

Martini Beach *Eclectic*
22 | **22** | **22** | **$43**

Cape May | 429 Beach Ave. (bet. Decatur & Jackson Sts.) | 609-884-1925 | www.martinibeachcapemay.com

The "attentive" staff makes guests "feel at home" at this "comfortable" Cape May Eclectic with a "beautiful view of the ocean" and frequent live music throughout the summer; "creative martinis (natch)" and "wonderful" globe-trotting eats add up to an "enjoyable" "gourmet" experience.

Martino's ⓂCuBan   22 | 17 | 19 | $23

Somerville | 212 W. Main St. (Doughty Ave.) | 908-722-8602 | www.martinoscuba.com

"Yummy" Cuban eats dished up in "enormous portions", plus an "excellent" lunch buffet, are a "good value" at this "busy" Somerville BYO; the "hole-in-the-wall" setting gets middling scores, though "personable" staffers help make guests "feel at home", and while you may have to "wait awhile", fans insist it's "100% worth it."

Masina Trattoria Italiana ● Italian   20 | 19 | 20 | $37

Weehawken | Sheraton Lincoln Harbor | 500 Harbor Blvd. (19th St.) | 201-348-4444 | www.masinatrattoria.com

Though it's "tucked into a hotel" (Weehawken's Sheraton Lincoln Harbor), this "decent" midpriced Italian is "almost like a neighborhood restaurant" according to fans; while the service gets mixed reviews, the "casual" setting is boosted by "beautiful" waterfront views of the Manhattan skyline.

Mastoris ● Diner   21 | 18 | 21 | $24

Bordentown | 144 Rte. 130 (Rte. 206) | 609-298-4650 | www.mastoris.com

An "oversized NJ diner for oversized appetites", this "old-fashioned" Bordentown "mainstay" is noteworthy for its "huge menu, huge portions and reasonable prices", as well as "wonderful" complimentary cheese and cinnamon breads and "out-of-this-world" baked goods; while some find the "hearty" fare "just ok" and think service "could be faster" and the "massive" space "could use a face-lift", others insist "you won't leave hungry or disappointed."

Mattar's Bistro ● American   23 | 22 | 23 | $38

Allamuchy | 1115 Rte. 517 (Ridge Rd.) | 908-852-2300 | www.mattarsbistro.com

At this Allamuchy American, the "varied" menu of "delicious, beautifully presented" eats includes "lighter fare" like salads, small plates and sushi as well as "heartier" entrees such as steaks, seafood and pastas; "reasonable" tabs and a "friendly" vibe (there's "always a handshake and hello" from the owner) bring locals back "again and again", and weekly live music's another plus.

Matt's Red Rooster Grill Ⓜ American   26 | 24 | 24 | $48

Flemington | 22 Bloomfield Ave. (bet. Broad & Main Sts.) | 908-788-7050 | www.mattsredroostergrill.com

Chef-owner Matt McPherson "really knows his way around the grill" marvel fans of this "creative" (if somewhat "pricey") New American set in a "beautiful Victorian house" in Flemington; with a "quieter" upstairs dining room and the "theater" of an open kitchen downstairs, it has a "cheerful energy" enhanced by "professional" service – and BYO "makes it even more appealing."

	FOOD	DECOR	SERVICE	COST

Max's Seafood Café *Seafood* — ▽ 26 | 23 | 23 | $30

Gloucester | 34 N. Burlington St. (Hudson St.) | 856-456-9774 |
www.maxsseafoodcafe.com

An "accommodating" staff ferries "outstanding seafood" that's
"caught-that-day–fresh" and a "good selection" of craft beers at this
midpriced "neighborhood gem" in Gloucester; frequent live music is
another plus amid an "awesome" 19th-century space accented with
rich wood details and a handcrafted antique bar.

McCormick & Schmick's *Seafood* — 20 | 20 | 20 | $41

Hackensack | Shops at Riverside | 175 Riverside Sq. (Hackensack Ave.) |
201-968-9410
Bridgewater | Bridgewater Commons | 400 Commons Way
(Prince Rodgers Ave.) | 908-707-9996
Atlantic City | Harrah's Resort Atlantic City | 777 Harrah's Blvd.
(Reanaissanse Point Blvd.) | 609-441-5579
Cherry Hill | Garden State Park | 941 Haddonfield Rd. (Severn Ave.) |
856-317-1711
www.mccormickandschmicks.com

Popular for "business and pleasure", these "upscale" seafood chain
links offer a "daily changing" menu of "freshly caught" fare in a "relaxing" setting; a few find them too "cookie-cutter", but "pleasant"
service is a plus and "happy-hour specials" lure the after-work crowd.

McLoone's *American* — 19 | 21 | 18 | $41

West Orange | South Mountain Recreation Complex | 9 Cherry Ln.
(Northfield Ave.) | 862-252-7108 | www.mcloonesboathouse.com
Fords | 3 Lafayette Rd. (Ford Ave.) | 732-512-5025 | www.mcloones.com
Asbury Park | 1200 Ocean Ave. (bet. 4th & 5th Aves.) |
732-774-1400 | www.mcloones.com
Long Branch | 1 Ocean Ave. (Laird St.) | 732-923-1006 |
www.mcloones.com

Expect "hefty" tabs to "reflect the setting" at these American siblings
from restaurateur Tim McLoone, especially given the "beachfront
dining" at the Asbury Park and Long Branch locations; while it's hard
to argue with the "great atmosphere", some report that "service varies" and "wish the food lived up to the views."

Mediterra *Mediterranean* — 22 | 22 | 22 | $47

Princeton | 29 Hulfish St. (bet. John & Witherspoon Sts.) |
609-252-9680 | www.mediterrarestaurant.com

This "trendy" "Princeton favorite" from the Terra Momo gang draws
well-heeled locals to Palmer Square with "wonderfully flavorful"
seasonal Med fare, plus breads "to die for" and a "superb wine list",
served by an "attentive" staff; it's "expensive", and some grouse
about "noisy" acoustics in the rustic-chic interior, but the "charming
patio" offers a "lovely" alfresco alternative.

Meemah Ⓜ *Chinese/Malaysian* — 23 | 15 | 20 | $22

Edison | Colonial Village Shopping Ctr. | 9 Lincoln Hwy. (Parsonage Rd.) |
732-906-2223 | www.meemah.com

Dishing out "a great combination of Malaysian and Chinese", this
Edison strip-mall BYO has been a "reliable", "local favorite for years"

for its "fresh and vibrant flavors", as well as "satisfying", "tried-and-true" classics; though some think "it seems to have slipped some" and the "decor needs an update", with "reasonable prices" and a "caring" owner, fans insist it's "worth a try."

Megu Sushi *Japanese*

FOOD	DECOR	SERVICE	COST
24	19	21	$25

Ventnor City | 5214 Atlantic Ave. (S. Weymouth Ave.) | 609-289-8693
Cherry Hill | Tuscany Mktpl. | 1990 Marlton Pike E. (Old Orchard Rd.) | 856-489-6228
Moorestown | 300 Young Ave. (bet. Centerton Rd. & Main St.) | 856-780-6327
www.megusushi.com

The sushi savvy "keep coming back" to these "comfortable" Japanese siblings for what they insist is "the best in the region" thanks to "top grade, fresh fish" and a "variety" of cooked dishes; Sunday and Monday discounts make the already "reasonable" prices even sweeter, and while Cherry Hill also fires up the hibachi and the Ventnor City location opened post-Survey, all three locations are BYO.

Mehndi ●Ⓜ *Indian*

FOOD	DECOR	SERVICE	COST
23	23	21	$39

Morristown | 88 Headquarters Plaza | 3 Speedwell Ave. (Park Pl.) | 973-871-2323 | www.mehtanirestaurantgroup.com

It "feels like an Indian palace" at this "upscale" "gem" "tucked away" in Morristown's Headquarters Plaza, where the "exquisite" dishes from the subcontinent appeal to "adventurous and conservative palates" alike and the "exotic" cocktails are "amazing"; the staff is "helpful", and though some think it's "overpriced", the tab for the "excellent" lunch buffet is easier to swallow.

Mekong Grill Ⓜ *Vietnamese*

FOOD	DECOR	SERVICE	COST
20	16	19	$27

Ridgewood | 24 Chestnut St. (bet. Franklin & Ridgewood Aves.) | 201-445-0011 | www.mekonggrillrestaurant.com

"Well-prepared" Vietnamese "comfort food", including "yummy pho", makes this "reliable" Ridgewood BYO a "fantastic addition" to the local "dining scene"; the "cozy" simple storefront is decked with sleek woods and the staff is "friendly" – even better, it's a "good value."

Memphis Pig Out *BBQ*

FOOD	DECOR	SERVICE	COST
21	17	18	$33

Atlantic Highlands | 67 First Ave. (Center Ave.) | 732-291-5533 | www.memphispigout.com

"Fall-off-the-bone" ribs remain the draw at this midpriced paean to pork in Atlantic Highlands, where both plates and walls are "filled with pigs and whimsy"; service is "prompt", if "no frills", and some say the "dark", "down-home" digs are a "bit outdated", but others insist this "BBQ treat" is "worth a trip."

Merion Inn *American*

FOOD	DECOR	SERVICE	COST
22	23	22	$49

Cape May | 106 Decatur St. (Columbia Ave.) | 609-884-8363 | www.merioninn.com

A Cape May "icon", this upscale "classic American" is a "step back in time", offering "well-prepared" fare and "friendly" service to a "mature" clientele in a "Victorian" setting boasting a "huge antique bar"; live piano music "really adds to the overall atmosphere."

	FOOD	DECOR	SERVICE	COST

Mesob ⓜ Ethiopian
23 | **21** | **23** | **$31**

Montclair | 515 Bloomfield Ave. (bet. Fullerton Ave. & Park St.) | 973-655-9000 | www.mesobrestaurant.com

"Breathe in the wonderful spices and dig in" (with your hands or injera bread) at this "casual" Montclair Ethiopian, a "delectable" "destination" with "fair prices" and the "added bonus" of BYO; "warm lighting", exposed brick and colorful folk art create a "wonderful environment", and "helpful" servers explain the slightly "exotic" eats to the uninitiated – it's a "different experience from the everyday."

Mesón Madrid Spanish
20 | **16** | **18** | **$38**

Palisades Park | 343 Bergen Blvd. (Palisades Blvd.) | 201-947-1038 | www.mesonmadridrestaurant.com

"You won't leave hungry" from this "old standby" in Palisades Park serving up "big portions" of "consistently good" Spanish cuisine and "great sangria" for over 30 years; while some say the faux Iberian rustic decor "needs to be spruced up", prices are "decent", service is "pleasant" and it's "still drawing crowds" (especially on weekends).

Metro Diner ❶ American/Diner
20 | **19** | **20** | **$16**

Brooklawn | 100 Rte. 130 (Browning Rd.) | 856-456-3690 | www.metrodinernj.com

Brooklawn boosters boast breakfast is the "best" at this diner where you "can't beat" the "variety" of Americana, including "great" specials; "friendly servers", "good" prices and a "laid-back" vibe appeal to families and the spiffed-up decor helps to make it a "night-out place" too – either way, big portions mean you "always come home with leftovers."

Metro North Italian
19 | **20** | **19** | **$38**

Princeton | 378 Alexander St. (Lawrence Dr.) | 609-454-3121 | www.metronorthprinceton.com

"When you can't find your own kitchen", fans recommend this "reliable", "conveniently located" Princeton Italian (formerly home to the Rusty Scupper) serving a "varied" menu of "well-prepared", "moderately priced" fare; the atmosphere is "inviting" in the "roomy" upscale-rustic space where there's a "nice" outdoor patio and a "lively mature bar scene."

Metropolitan Cafe Eclectic
21 | **20** | **20** | **$42**

Freehold | 8 E. Main St. (South St.) | 732-780-9400 | www.metrocafenj.com

A little piece of "Manhattan in Freehold", this "expensive" Eclectic turns out "interesting", "Asian-influenced" plates in a spacious, contemporary setting; frequent live DJs and a "great martini menu" anchor the bar scene, and "pleasant" service is a plus.

Metuchen Inn American
23 | **23** | **22** | **$46**

Metuchen | 424 Middlesex Ave. (bet. Linden & Oak Aves.) | 732-494-6444 | www.themetucheninn.net

"Fancy, but fun", this "fine-dining" New American in Metuchen is a "perfect spot for a special occasion" thanks to a "creative menu", "outstanding wine selection" and "old-world-style" service; a post-fire renovation has "re-created" the "beautiful", "comfortable and airy decor" in the circa-1843 building with a "lively bar", and while it's "pricey", most think it's "well worth the trek" and the "money."

Mexican Food Factory *Mexican*   21 | 20 | 21 | $22
Marlton | 601 Rte. 70 W. (Cropwell Rd.) | 856-983-9222
"Huge portions" of "consistently good" Mexican grub, plus "classic margaritas" and microbrews all "delivered quickly" make this "fes-tive" Marlton cantina a "popular spot"; sporting rustic, dark-wood beams and booths, colorful walls and various Frida Kahlo prints, the "cool-looking" decor belies the name and the outdoor patio is a "nice" locale in warm weather – add reasonable prices and weekly live music and most agree it's "worth the trip."

Mia ⚡Ⓜ *Italian*   24 | 24 | 23 | $63
Atlantic City | Caesars Atlantic City Hotel & Casino | 2100 Pacific Ave. (Arkansas Ave.) | 609-441-2345 | www.miaac.com
With its Roman columns and "high, high, high" ceilings, this Italian in Atlantic City's Caesars makes a "classy, romantic" setting for a "special occasion", with "fab", "gourmet" pastas and seafood from chefs Georges Perrier and Chris Scarduzio; service is "professional", and though some find it "too expensive", a prix fixe menu several nights a week can be a better bet.

Mi Bandera *Cuban*   23 | 21 | 22 | $29
Union City | 518 32nd St. (bet. Central & Summit Aves.) | 201-348-2828
Serving up generous portions of "flavorful" Cuban fare – think churrasco and parrillada – washed down with "the best sangria", this midpriced Union City spot atop a supermarket of the same name has garnered a loyal following for close to 20 years; solid ser-vice and tropical-themed decor (colorful walls and table linens, palm tree tchotchkes and faux thatched-roof window treatments) help make it a "fun place to dine."

Midori *Japanese*   23 | 17 | 20 | $32
Denville | Denville Commons Mall | 3130 Rte. 10 W. (bet. Franklin & Hill Rds.) | 973-537-8588 | www.midorirestaurant.com
An "extensive menu of fun rolls", "very fresh" sushi and a variety of cooked Japanese dishes lures locals to this Denville strip-mall BYO; green tablecloths pay homage to the translation of its name while paper lanterns keep the lighting of the spacious digs low, and though prices for the "high-end" eats "aren't bashful", half-price Wednes-day sushi-bar lunches and online coupons appease wallet-watchers.

Mie Thai *Thai*   23 | 18 | 20 | $24
Woodbridge | 34 Main St. (bet. Berry & Pearl Sts.) | 732-596-9400 | www.miethai.com
"Freshly made" Thai fare that "hasn't been Americanized" is the draw at this Woodbridge BYO; "reasonable prices", "consistent" service and a "lovely" atmosphere complete the picture; P.S. cognoscenti caution "'mild' here means fire."

Mikado *Japanese*   22 | 19 | 20 | $32

Cherry Hill | 2320 Marlton Pike W. (bet. Cornell & Union Aves.) | 856-665-4411
Maple Shade | 468 S. Lenola Rd. (Rotary Way) | 856-638-1801
Marlton | Elmwood Shopping Ctr. | 793 Rte. 70 E. (Troth Rd.) | 856-797-8581
www.mikado-us.com

The "extensive selection" of "fresh" sushi, sashimi and maki, as well as cooked Japanese entrees, are as "tasty" as they are "visually pleasing" at this South Jersey trio; "attentive" servers deliver the "huge portions" "quickly" in the "serene" settings, and prices are "extra good"; P.S. the Cherry Hill locale is BYO and hibachi-free.

Mike's Seafood *Seafood*   21 | 16 | 18 | $28

Sea Isle City | 4222 Park Rd. (43rd Pl.) | 609-263-3458 | www.mikesseafood.com

Adjacent to a fish market and take-out joint, this no-frills, waterside Sea Isle City seafooder has a view of the harbor's fishing fleets from the dining area, where you can "sit outside at large picnic tables and feast" on the daily catch; while a few find it "a bit overpriced", that doesn't deter the "long lines" of fans who consider it a Shore "staple"; P.S. open from May to mid-October.

Milford Oyster House *Seafood*   25 | 23 | 24 | $48

Milford | 92 Rte. 519 (York St.) | 908-995-9411 | www.milfordoysterhouse.com

Fans deem this "superb" seafooder "worth the drive to Milford" for its "fresh", "first-rate" fin fare, "sophisticated wine list" and desserts "to die for"; it "feels like home" in the "cozy" renovated stone mill – whether in the dining room or "delightful" tavern – thanks to "welcoming" service from the "wonderful" host and "friendly" staff, and while it's "expensive", most report a "lovely time."

Mill at Spring Lake Heights Ⓜ *American*   20 | 22 | 19 | $44

Spring Lake Heights | 101 Old Mill Rd. (Ocean Rd.) | 732-449-1800 | www.themillnj.com

The "roomy", contemporary dining space boasts a "spectacular view of Old Mill Pond and surrounding nature" at this long-running Traditional American in Spring Lake Heights; while some gripe about "above-average prices" and "lackluster" service, for most the "beautiful location" and "quality" eats compensate, especially the "great selection" at Sunday brunch.

Miller's Ale House ◗ *Pub Food*   21 | 20 | 22 | $22

Mount Laurel | 554 Fellowship Rd. (Rte. 73) | 856-722-5690 | www.millersalehouse.com

A "fantastic" drinks menu (including more than 75 beers) and a "diverse" selection of "tasty" pub grub are the draw at this Mount Laurel link of the Floridian chain; myriad flat-screens in the "large", "roadhouse-style" digs make it "fun if you're a sports fan", and while it can get "crowded" and "loud", the "friendly" staff is "fast" and the "price is right."

	FOOD	DECOR	SERVICE	COST

Minado *Japanese*　　22 | 18 | 19 | $31

Little Ferry | 1 Valley Rd. (River St. Ext.) | 201-931-1522
Morris Plains | 2888 Rte. 10 W. (bet. Parks & Powder Mill Rds.) |
973-734-4900
www.minado.com

The "sushi is the star" at this "all-you-can-eat extravaganza" in
Little Ferry and Morris Plains, a Japanese "family-favorite" buffet chain offering an "extensive" "variety" of salads, hot entrees
and "to-die-for" desserts along with the "delicious", "very fresh"
seafood; a "friendly staff" keeps the "comfortable", cavernous
"food factory" "orderly" and prices are "reasonable" – if you "come
hungry, you'll leave satisfied."

Ming Ⓜ *Asian*　　22 | 22 | 21 | $35

Edison | Oak Tree Shopping Ctr. | 1655-185 Oak Tree Rd. (bet. Dayton Dr. &
Wood Aves.) | 732-549-5051 | www.mingrestaurants.com

Ming II Ⓢ *Asian*

Morristown | Hyatt Morristown at Headquarters Plaza | 3 Speedwell Ave.
(bet. Spring & Water Sts.) | 973-871-2323 | www.ming2morristown.com

From the folks behind Mehndi and Moghul, this "fancy" duo in
Morristown and Edison "delivers" an "exciting blend" of cuisines on
its "creative" Pan-Asian menu, with "portions resulting in tomorrow's
leftovers"; the "welcoming" staff makes "great" recommendations
amid the "exotic" surroundings, and while some find it a bit "pricey",
others insist the "journey is well worth it."

NEW Mistral *Eclectic*　　- | - | - | M

Princeton | 66 Witherspoon St. (Hulfish St.) | 609-688-8808 |
www.mistralprinceton.com

Like the eponymous Mediterranean wind, this Princeton Eclectic
newcomer from the acclaimed team behind Elements showcases
chef Scott Anderson's global small-plates cuisine that changes with
the seasons; the space has a spare Japanese serenity created by
blond woods, and with moderate prices, plus BYO, you could spend
a little or a lot, appetite depending.

MK Valencia ❶ *American/Italian*　　▽ 21 | 22 | 21 | $47

Ridgefield Park | 228 Main St. (Park St.) | 201-494-4830 |
www.mkvalenciarestaurant.com

"An exquisite reminder of Manhattan" in Ridgefield Park, this
"sophisticated", "ambitious" New American–Italian has become
a "lively" "destination" thanks to a "tasty", "distinctive menu"
that matches the "ultracontemporary" digs – including a swanky
dining room decked with sleek, private wine lockers – that belie
its storefront location in a "faded neighborhood"; "attentive" service
is another plus, and though it's "pricey", many find themselves
"yearning to return."

Mockingbird Cafe Ⓜ *American*　　22 | 17 | 18 | $27

Basking Ridge | 60 S. Finley Ave. (Henry St.) | 908-766-1106
Dishing out "delicious" "homemade" eats, this Basking Ridge
American is a "local go-to" for the "best breakfast", brunch, "cozy

lunch" and dinner, all at "reasonable prices"; while service gets mixed marks and disgruntled diners complain of "sold-out" dishes, "pleasant" outdoor seating is a consolation.

Moghul ⓜ Indian

21 | 19 | 19 | $29

Edison | Oak Tree Shopping Ctr. | 1655-195 Oak Tree Rd. (bet. Henry St. & Sugar Rd.) | 732-549-5050 | www.moghul.com

"Among the many" Indian spots in Edison, this longtime BYO from the Mehtani Restaurant Group "offers more variety than most", with its extensive array of "authentic" and "creative" subcontinental dishes; it's "packed on weekends" thanks to a "scrumptious" lunch buffet, and while critics complain of "inconsistent" quality, "spotty" service and "high" prices, defenders insist it's "fantastic" for takeout.

Mohawk House American

22 | 24 | 21 | $49

Sparta | 3 Sparta Jct. (Rte. 181) | 973-729-6464 | www.mohawkhouse.com

"Rustic charm" and a "unique" but "wonderful menu" of "seasonal" American fare served by a "helpful" staff draw devotees to this "high-class" establishment in Sparta; it offers "all the joys of a mountain resort lodge" with its vaulted ceilings, enormous fireplace and exposed-brick walls, and while some grumble over "stringent portions" and "expensive" tabs, others deem it a "nice treat."

Mojave Grille Southwestern

21 | 19 | 20 | $37

Westfield | 35 Elm St. (bet. Broad St. & North Ave.) | 908-233-7772 | www.mojavegrille.com

Offering an "adventure for the taste buds" for close to 20 years, this Westfield BYO is a "neighborhood favorite" boasting a "diverse" selection of "imaginative" and "classic" Southwestern fare with "a little spice"; service is "friendly" and "the price is right", and while some think the "menu needs updating" and the "simple setting" feels "cafeteria-esque", warm weather outdoor seating "is a bonus."

Molly Pitcher Inn Restaurant American

22 | 24 | 22 | $49

Red Bank | Molly Pitcher Inn | 88 Riverside Ave. (Front St.) | 732-747-2500 | www.themollypitcher.com

"Magnificent water views add to the experience" at this "elegant", "special-occasion" American along the Navesink River in Red Bank; though some say it "feels a little dated" and find the "semi-formal" atmosphere (jackets are required Friday–Sunday evenings) a "bit stuffy", the "well-executed" fare (including a "quality Sunday brunch") and solid service have earned it a "loyal following."

Mompou ⓈSpanish

22 | 22 | 21 | $32

Newark | 77 Ferry St. (bet. Congress & Prospect Sts.) | 973-578-8114 | www.mompoutapas.com

Serving up "terrific tapas", Spanish specialties and a "great selection" of wine, beer and cocktails, this Ironbound Iberian is "a delightful find in Newark"; exposed brick and stone walls, a rolled steel bar and industrial-chic lighting create a funky atmosphere and the outside garden is "lovely", and while small-plate tabs can "add up quickly", it's a "popular place" nonetheless.

	FOOD	DECOR	SERVICE	COST

Monsoon ⓜ *Indian*

▽ 25 | 21 | 21 | $25

Mount Laurel | 4180 Dearborn Circle (Rte. 38) | 856-234-0080 |
www.monsoonindian.com

"There's no threat of rain" at this "wonderful" Mount Laurel BYO
Indian where the "delicious" dishes can be "spiced accordingly" to
please "first-time tasters" and seasoned diners alike, and the popular lunch buffet "has something for everyone"; prices are "reasonable", service is "attentive" and the chic, modern space sports
sleek, subcontinental design touches.

Monster Sushi *Japanese*

20 | 17 | 17 | $35

Summit | 395 Springfield Ave. (Maple St.) | 908-598-1100 |
www.monstersushi.com

Sibling to the Manhattan originals, this "busy" Summit Japanese BYO
dishes out "generous portions" of "consistently good", "fresh" sushi;
some think the "novelty has faded", and knock the fare as "overpriced"
and service in "need of improvement", but the "fun", "large" setting
with monster movie posters appeals to "families with children."

MoonShine Modern Supper Club ❶ *American*

19 | 20 | 19 | $50

Millburn | 55 Main St. (Millburn Ave.) | 973-218-6042 |
www.moonshinesupperclub.com

"You'll feel like you're in TriBeCa" at this "hip" bi-level American in
Millburn (convenient to the Paper Mill Playhouse) serving a "varied"
seasonal menu of "pricey" "comfort food" paired with "interesting"
wines and beers plus "inventive cocktails" that "riff on its name"; the
"inviting" modern space offers multiple seating options, and while
some knock the staff as "untrained", others praise it as "friendly"
and "eager to please."

Moonstruck ⓜ *American/Mediterranean*

24 | 24 | 23 | $51

Asbury Park | 517 Lake Ave. (bet. Main St. & Ocean Ave.) |
732-988-0123 | www.moonstrucknj.com

Enthusiasts advise "don't miss" this American-Mediterranean "favorite" in a three-story Victorian house overlooking Wesley Lake in
Asbury Park, where "enjoyable" fare comes with "impeccable" service; the no-reservations policy makes for "long waits", but "great"
live piano music and "excellent" drinks from the first-floor bar makes
the delay a bit more "fun."

Morton's The Steakhouse *Steak*

25 | 23 | 24 | $67

Hackensack | Shops at Riverside | 1 Riverside Sq. (Hackensack Ave.) |
201-487-1303
Atlantic City | Caesars Atlantic City Hotel & Casino | 2100 Pacific Ave.
(Missouri Ave.) | 609-449-1044 ❶
www.mortons.com

A steakhouse "standard-bearer", these "big-ticket" chain links in AC
and Hackensack offer "excellently prepared" cuts of beef and "grand
sides" "served professionally" amid an "ambiance of wealth and
class"; some find them a bit "staid" and could do without the "high"
wine pricing, but overall they're considered among "the best."

	FOOD	DECOR	SERVICE	COST

Mr. Chu *Chinese*
21 | 16 | 18 | $24

East Hanover | 44 Rte. 10 W. (bet. Littell Rd. & Ridgedale Ave.) | 973-887-7555

The "authentic", "dependable" Chinese eats at this East Hanover BYO keep it "packed with locals" and families looking for "good portions" at "great prices"; "prompt" service means you "zip in and zip out" of the "unpretentious" "converted-diner" setting, where you can expect waits on weekends, but even so, fans insist it's "worth a drive."

Mud City Crab House *Seafood*
23 | 18 | 21 | $32

Manahawkin | 1185 E. Bay Ave. (Marsha Dr.) | 609-978-3660 | www.mudcitycrabhouse.com

For fans, this seasonal crab "shack" in Manahawkin close to LBI has become a "Shore tradition", thanks to "super crab cakes" and "always fresh" fin fare "served with a smile"; the "paper tablecloths add to the ambiance", and while just about all agree the no-reservations policy (and consequential "lo-ong" waits) can be a "pain", most feel it's "worth it"; P.S. it's BYO.

Mussel Bar by Robert Wiedmaier ●Ⓜ *Belgian*
▽ 24 | 22 | 22 | $38

Atlantic City | REVEL | 500 Boardwalk (Metropolitan Ave.) | 609-225-9851 | www.revelresorts.com

"Perfect for a night out" or a "quick, quality bite", this midpriced gastropub brings a "tasty" bit of Belgium to Atlantic City's Revel thanks to "creative mussel combinations", "mouthwatering burgers" and a beer list that "looks like the white pages"; "well-trained" staffers preside over the dark-wood digs featuring a bar studded with mollusk shells and lager-bottle light fixtures – add frequent live music and "great" desserts and wagers declare it "a winner."

Mustache Bill's Diner ⊅ *Diner*
22 | 16 | 21 | $17

Barnegat Light | Broadway & Eighth St. (8th St.) | 609-494-0155
Some of the "best pancakes around", an "extensive" omelet selection and other cheap diner grub keep this cash-only Barnegat Light BYO "packed from opening to close"; the "devoted" insist it's "worth the wait", and a staff with "the patience of saints" maintains the "family"-friendly vibe in the "'50s" setting; P.S. call ahead for hours.

Nagoya *Japanese*
24 | 19 | 23 | $30

Mahwah | Ramapo Ctr. | 1007 MacArthur Blvd. (Glasmere Rd.) | 201-818-9933 | www.nagoyacuisine.com

"Top-notch" sushi and a "warm, friendly" staff draw regulars "two or three times a week" to this Japanese "must-try" in Mahwah; a fish-filled stone waterfall and paper lanterns contribute to the "lovely atmosphere", and while it's "not cheap", "BYO helps keep the bill down."

Namaskaar Ⓜ *Indian*
23 | 19 | 21 | $29

Englewood | 120 Grand Ave. (bet. Englewood Ave. & Garrett Pl.) | 201-567-0061 | www.namaskaar.com

"Good for aficionados and novices" alike, this "authentic" Indian BYO in Englewood is a "hidden gem" offering "fantastic" fare, including a "don't-miss" lunch buffet; opinions on the digs are mixed ("cozy" vs. "drab"), but service is "gracious" and the menu is "well priced."

Nana's Deli *Deli*
23 | 14 | 19 | $22

Livingston | 127 S. Livingston Ave. (Wilson Terr.) | 973-740-1940 | www.nanasdeli.com

Regulars "rave" the "secret-recipe tuna" is the "best on the planet" and the salads are "sensational" at this Livingston deli stalwart offering "delicious Jewish-style dishes"; the owner is "friendly" and prices are "high", but what you're getting is "quality"; P.S. it's open for lunch-seating only, but the take-out counter is open until 6:30 PM.

Nanni Ristorante *Italian*
22 | 19 | 24 | $54

Rochelle Park | 53 W. Passaic St. (bet. Cedar Dr. & Rochelle Ave.) | 201-843-1250 | www.nanni.com

"Like stepping back 25 years", this "sophisticated" Rochelle Park Italian may be "old-fashioned" but "regulars" revel in the "well-prepared" dishes and "very good wine selection" served by an "attentive staff"; opinions on the space range from "beautiful" to "tired", and while prices are high, loyalists say it's "well worth the cost."

Napoli's Brick Oven Pizza *Pizza*
21 | 18 | 20 | $17

Hoboken | 1118 Washington St. (bet. 11th & 12th Sts.) | 201-216-0900 | www.napolishobokenpizza.com

"A step-up from the typical storefront joint" this local Hoboken BYO is considered a "hidden gem" by fans of its "great" "brick-oven pizza" crowned with "toppings better than most", plus "simple classic Italian fare" like pastas and heros; service is "quick" and "friendly" and while the digs are simple, "affordable" tabs appeal.

Nauvoo Grill Club *American*
19 | 23 | 19 | $43

Fair Haven | 121 Fair Haven Rd. (bet. River Rd. & Willow St.) | 732-747-8777 | www.nauvoogrillclub.com

With a "welcoming", "beautiful" Mission-style setting boasting four stone fireplaces, this "pricey" Fair Haven American oozes atmosphere; though some find the fare "average" and opinions on the service are mixed ("friendly" vs. "unengaged"), the burgers are deemed "quite good" and the "pours are generous" in the "cozy" bar.

Navesink Fishery Ⓜ *Seafood*
25 | 14 | 19 | $35

Navesink | A&P Shopping Ctr. | 1004 Rte. 36 S. (Sears Ave.) | 732-291-8017 | www.navesinkfishery.com

Sure, it's in a strip mall, but this "casual" BYO piscine purveyor boasts "top-notch" "fresh, fresh, fresh" seafood – no surprise since it's part of a fish market; prices are reasonable, and while service is "slow" and the "tired" decor may remind some of an "old aunt's dining room", finatics still "recommend it to anyone."

Neelam *Indian*
21 | 16 | 18 | $26

Berkeley Heights | 295 Springfield Ave. (bet. Kuntz & Snyder Ave.) | 908-665-2212
South Orange | 115 S. Orange Ave. (bet. Grove & Scotland Rd.) | 973-762-1100

(continued)

Neelam

Middletown | Village Mall | 1178 Rte. 35 S. (bet. New Monmouth Rd. & Penelope Ln.) | 732-671-8900 Ⓜ
www.neelamrestaurant.com

Locals say you'll find "better-than-decent Indian" at this "unpretentious" BYO trio where there are "no surprises" – just "reliable, if staid" eats; the "decor is tired" and "service is glacial", but at least the staff is "friendly" and the lunchtime "buffets are a fantastic bargain."

Nero's Grille *Steak*　　　　19 | 16 | 19 | $47

Livingston | 618 S. Livingston Ave. (Hobart Gap Rd.) | 973-994-1410 | www.neros.com

You'll "see everyone you know" at this "solid" but "pricey" steakhouse in Livingston, where "old-timers and regulars" tuck into the "wide variety" of chops, fish and salads plus Italian favorites like pastas and pizza; critics say the "country-club" setting could "use a makeover" and "service is spotty", but the baby-boomer bar scene is "bustling."

Next Door Ⓜ *American*　　　　22 | 16 | 20 | $35

Montclair | 556 Bloomfield Ave. (bet. Park St. & Valley Rd.) | 973-744-3600
A "changing menu" of "creative comfort food" – think "awesome burgers" and "great salads" – makes this "no-frills" Montclair BYO (sibling to neighboring Blu) "perfect" for a "quick bite" post- or "pre-movie", and it's "priced to take the kids"; an "intimate setting" means "close seating", but fans still find it an "enjoyable" "bargain."

Nha Trang Place *Vietnamese*　　　　23 | 12 | 17 | $18

Jersey City | 234 10th St. (bet. Erie St. & Jersey Ave.) | no phone
"It's all about the pho" at this "popular" Jersey City BYO where the rest of the "cheap", "authentic" Vietnamese victuals are also "delicious" – "you really can't go wrong"; sure, the "cafeterialike" space is "no frills" and the service is only "ok", but phonatics predict "if you're a food lover, you'll be pleased."

Nicholas ●Ⓜ *American*　　　　28 | 27 | 28 | $103

Red Bank | 160 Rte. 35 S. (bet. Cooper Blvd. & Frost Ave.) | 732-345-9977 | www.restaurantnicholas.com

Nicholas and Melissa Harary's "epitome" of "exquisite" fine New American dining in Red Bank is truly "second to none" – and once again voted the state's Most Popular restaurant and No. 1 for both Food and Service; the prix fixe–only menus of "flawlessly executed" seasonal fare are "presented beautifully" by a "top-notch" staff in a "modern" setting that's "upscale" yet "welcoming", and while the prices make it strictly a "special treat" for most, the "bar menu is a pretty good deal."

Nick's Pizzeria & Steak House *Italian/Pizza*　　23 | 19 | 21 | $13

Sicklerville | 579 Berlin Cross Keys Rd. (bet. Chews Landing Williamstown & Sicklerville Rds.) | 856-740-0707
Clayton | 4 N. Delsea Dr. (Clayton Ave.) | 856-881-3222
Glassboro | 644 Delsea Dr. (bet. Bristol & Delsea Manor Drs.) | 856-307-1100

(continued)

(continued)

Nick's Pizzeria & Steak House

Williamstown | 47 S. Main St. (Garwood Ave.) | 856-728-3322
www.nickspizzaonline.com

Serving up a "wide variety" of "delicious" pizza, subs, "huge salads" and more in a "nice family atmosphere", these BYO Italians have kept South Jersey satisfied with "large and filling" pies since 1976; whether you eat in, takeout or go for delivery, supporters say the staff is "great" and even better are the "very reasonable" prices.

Nico Kitchen & Bar ⊠ *Eclectic*   20 | 20 | 19 | $40

Newark | New Jersey Performing Arts Ctr. | 1 Center St. (Park Pl.) | 973-642-1226 | www.nicokitchenbar.com

Neo-Italian tapas are the focus of this Eclectic from Ryan DePersio (Bar Cara, Fascino), "conveniently" located inside Newark's NJPAC; the high-ceilinged space is "larger than you'd expect", and while some feel it's "still working out the kinks", with "slow" service that makes showgoers feel like a "captive audience", others insist it's "improved of late"; P.S. on performance nights, it's prix fixe only.

Nikko *Japanese*   24 | 18 | 21 | $37

Whippany | 881 Rte. 10 E. (Metro West Dr.) | 973-428-0787 | www.nikkonj.com

Sushi and sashimi are "delightfully fresh" at this "long-standing" Japanese "favorite" in Whippany, where "interesting rolls" come with "lots of fillings"; if the decor is less impressive, "gracious" service and moderate prices that feel like a "good value" compensate.

Ninety Acres at Natirar Ⓜ *American*   25 | 27 | 24 | $72

Peapack | 2 Main St. (bet. Olde Dutch Rd. & Ramago Way) | 908-901-9500 | www.ninetyacres.com

Follow the "long and winding road" to this "breathtaking", "palatial" Peapack estate, where the carriage house is now a culinary institute serving chef David C. Felton's "excellent", "inventive" New American cuisine sourced from an onsite farm, alongside an "extensive" wine list; fans tout kitchen-side seating (with a "fun" chef's-choice prix fixe) and a "fantastic" outdoor patio, and while tabs are "extravagant", most agree it's a "special place in every way."

Nomad Pizza Ⓜ⋻ *Pizza*   25 | 19 | 21 | $23

Hopewell | 10 E. Broad St. (bet. Blackwell & Greenwood Aves.) | 609-466-6623 | www.nomadpizzaco.com

With its thin crusts, "inventive" topping combos and "loving preparation", this cash-only Hopewell BYO is "totally rocking the pizza world" say piezani, who only wish the "quaint" place weren't so "impossible to get into"; the itinerant oven-equipped REO Speedwagon from which it gets its name is available for private events, but for those dining in-house, the digs are "small" with "family-style tables", and aficionados advise it's "not for the hipster-phobic."

Nori *Asian*   21 | 15 | 18 | $34

Caldwell | 406 Bloomfield Ave. (bet. Gould & Washburn Pls.) | 973-403-2400

(continued)

Nori

Montclair | 561 Bloomfield Ave. (Maple Pl.) | 973-655-8805
www.nori-sushi.com

Fans of these Japanese BYO siblings in Montclair and Caldwell say
they're "worth a trip" for sushi that's "fresh" and "well prepared", as
well as a few standout entrees; devotees are undeterred by decor
that some find "outdated."

Norma's *Mideastern*

| 22 | 15 | 21 | $24 |

Cherry Hill | Barclay Farms Shopping Ctr. | 995 Rte. 70 E. (Ronaldo Terr.) |
856-795-1373 | www.normasrestaurant.com

"Tasty", "traditional" Middle Eastern fare at "reasonable prices"
draws fans to Norma Bitar's BYO "neighborhood gem" in Cherry Hill;
service is "attentive" (if "not overly friendly"), and some think the
no-frills decor "could be updated", but things perk up on weekends
when belly dancing makes for a "fun night out."

NEW North End Bistro *American*

| – | – | – | I |

Princeton | 354 Nassau St. (Harrison St.) | 609-683-9700 |
www.northendprinceton.com

Many mac 'n' cheeses grace the comfort-food menu of this Princeton
American newcomer from the Procaccini brothers (of the eponymous
osterias), who take a straightforward approach to burgers, pastas
and tacos too; affordable prices, including a reasonable wine list
(plus a BYO option), match the casual fare and bistro setting, and
there's an outdoor patio for warm weather dining.

Novita Bistro & Lounge ● *Italian*

| 20 | 20 | 21 | $37 |

Metuchen | 25 New St. (Pearl St.) | 732-549-5306 |
www.novitanj.com

A "pleasant surprise" in Metuchen, this "neighborhood" trattoria offers "delicious" contemporary Italian dishes at "reasonable" prices,
with "friendly" service to boot; there's also a "dynamic" lounge, which
serves a more casual menu of panini and pizza, and features "enjoyable" live jazz Thursdays–Saturdays.

Nunzio Ristorante Rustico *Italian*

| 23 | 21 | 21 | $44 |

Collingswood | 706 Haddon Ave. (bet. Collings & Irvin Aves.) |
856-858-9840 | www.nunzios.net

Chef Nunzio Patruno brings his Mediterranean flair to this midpriced Collingswood BYO, where "tasty", "authentic" Italian dishes
are "served attractively" in a room evocative of a small-town piazza;
the "friendly" toque is "often visiting tables" in the "comfortable"
space, which some say is "noisy", and he also offers occasional
cooking classes for those who want to try this at home.

NEW Nuovo Trattoria *Italian*

| – | – | – | E |

Manalapan | 345 Rte. 9 (bet. Center Dr. & Town Pointe) |
732-308-9600 | www.nuovotrattoria.com

Homemade is the mantra at this upscale Manalapan Italian, where
pastas and sauces join brick-oven pizzas on the made-from-scratch
list and old-school classics get a modern touch; earth tones distin-

guish the simple space, and though it trends expensive, BYO may take some of the edge off.

Oceanos   *Seafood* | 24 | 22 | 23 | $51 |

Fair Lawn | 2-27 Saddle River Rd. (bet. B'way & Williams St.) | 201-796-0546 | www.oceanosrestaurant.com
The "Greek gods" might enjoy this Fair Lawn seafooder, where "consistently delicious" fish that "tastes like it was just caught" has a distinct Mediterranean twist; modern decor and "friendly" service provide an "unexpected corner of civility", and though it's on the "pricey" side, fans deem it "worth it", especially for a "special occasion"; P.S. alfresco aficionados advise "sitting on the patio is a must."

Octopus's Garden   *Seafood* | 23 | 23 | 22 | $37 |

West Creek | 771 S. Main St. (Mayetta Landing Rd.) | 609-597-8828 | www.theoctopussgardenfishhouse.com
Fans say it's "worth a trip off the island" to dine at this former LBIer, now in West Creek, serving "delicious", "well-prepared" seafood, backed by Jersey wines (or you can BYO); service is "dependable", while a "pleasant" atmosphere prevails in the "big, bustling" space, and fans find prices "more than reasonable for the quality."

Old Bay Restaurant ●⊠   *Cajun/Creole* | 20 | 20 | 19 | $31 |

New Brunswick | 61-63 Church St. (Neilson St.) | 732-246-3111 | www.oldbayrest.com
With its "party atmosphere" and "great beer selection", it's no wonder this New Brunswick Cajun-Creole is a "popular hangout for Rutgers students"; the "standard N'Awlins grub" is "nicely done" (if "faux", some sniff) and "reasonably priced", while live music keeps it "mobbed" on weekends – fans have "no complaints."

Old Homestead ⊠   *Steak* | 26 | 25 | 25 | $72 |

Atlantic City | Borgata Hotel Casino & Spa | 1 Borgata Way (Renaissance Point Blvd.) | 609-317-1000 | www.theoldhomesteadsteakhouse.com
"Stellar" steaks as "tender as can be" and a wine list "worth reading and coveting" draw "high rollers" to this "classic" "upscale" spin-off of the NYC original in AC's Borgata; the "Jersey-chic" space is "always busy", and sometimes "loud", but the servers are "polished professionals", and meat eaters insist it's "worth the visit" and the expense.

Old Man Rafferty's   *American* | 19 | 19 | 19 | $29 |

Hillsborough | 284 Rte. 206 (Lindstrom Dr.) | 908-904-9731
New Brunswick | Kilmer Sq. | 106 Albany St. (bet. George & Neilson Sts.) | 732-846-6153
Asbury Park | Steinbach Bldg. | 541 Cookman Ave. (Emory St.) | 732-774-1600
www.oldmanraffertys.com
There's "something for everyone" on the "huge" menu of "reliable", "hearty" Americana at these "pub-type" eateries, though "delicious" cakes and "creamy treats" might tempt you to "eat dessert first"; some say service "can be hit-or-miss", but with "fair prices" and a "fun", sometimes "madhouse", vibe, they're popular with "families" and "students."

	FOOD	DECOR	SERVICE	COST

Oliver a Bistro ⓜ *Eclectic* | 25 | 20 | 22 | $37 |

Bordentown | 218 Farnsworth Ave. (Church St.) | 609-298-7177 |
www.oliverabistro.com

Fans lament "the secret is out" about this "terrific" storefront BYO in
Downtown Bordentown, where "talented" chef Matthew McElmoyl
assembles "superior" "in-season" ingredients for his "outstanding"
Eclectic fare; the "quaint" space is either "delightfully small" or
"tight", depending on your view, but "pleasant" service adds to the
all-around "charming" vibe.

One 53 *American* | 24 | 21 | 23 | $49 |

Rocky Hill | 153 Washington St. (bet. Crescent & Princeton Aves.) |
609-924-1019 | www.one53nj.com

Seasonal "farm-fresh" ingredients stand out in the "consistently
well-prepared" dishes at this "hip" New American in Rocky Hill,
where the "bistro-esque" offerings include homemade pastas and
"simple grilled meats" (and "don't overlook the burger"); the "cozy"
space can feel "crowded", and some balk at "fine-dining" prices, but
most deem it an overall "class act" that's "worth the trip."

The Orange Squirrel ❶🅧 *American* | 21 | 16 | 20 | $54 |

Bloomfield | 412 Bloomfield Ave. (Orange St.) | 973-337-6421 |
www.theorangesquirrel.com

"Serious cooking" with a "creative edge" draws diners to this "com-
pletely unexpected" New American in a "run-down" section of
Bloomfield; despite "playful" decor, the "cramped" space seems
"more diner than dining" to some who find it hard to reconcile with
"expensive" tabs, but to fans the changing menu is "always memorable" and worth a whirl "when the wallet is heavy."

Origin *French/Thai* | 24 | 20 | 21 | $38 |

Basking Ridge | 25 Mountainview Blvd. (Martinsville Rd.) |
908-647-7781
Morristown | 10 South St. (S. Park Pl.) | 973-971-9933 ⓜ
Somerville | 25 Division St. (South St.) | 908-685-1344 ⓜ
www.originthai.com

"Inventive" Thai fare comes with a "French twist" at this BYO trio,
where diners take a "culinary adventure" with some "interesting"
stops along the way (wild boar, ostrich); while some complain of
"spotty" service and "high noise levels", others dig the "funky vibe"
and "eclectic", dimly lit surrounds and consider it "well worth it
for a treat."

Osteria Giotto *Italian* | 25 | 20 | 22 | $45 |

Montclair | 21 Midland Ave. (Portland Pl.) | 973-746-0111 |
www.osteria-giotto.com

"Terrific" Italian dishes "with a modern spin" are why aficionados
advise that you "call a month in advance" for reservations at this
"classy" Montclair BYO; some decry "packed" quarters that can be
"too noisy for comfort" and service that's "slipping a bit", but sidewalk tables provide a quieter dine and "oversized" portions make
tabs seem downright "reasonable."

	FOOD	DECOR	SERVICE	COST

Osteria Morini *Italian*
24 | 19 | 21 | $48

Bernardsville | 107 Morristown Rd. (Finley Ave.) | 908-221-0040 |
www.osteriamorini.com

"Divine" homemade pastas headline the modern Italian menu at
chef Michael White's Bernardsville osteria, an offshoot of his
SoHo original; the inauspicious strip-mall locale and "noisy" "bistro"
vibe don't deter an "upper-crusty" crowd that appreciates the
"buzz", as well as its "considerate" service and "robust" wine list.

Osteria Procaccini *Pizza*
24 | 19 | 21 | $24

Kingston | 4428 Rte. 27 (bet. Heathcote Rd. & Spruce Ln.) |
609-688-0007 Ⓜ
Pennington | 7 Tree Farm Rd. (Rte. 31) | 609-303-0625
www.osteriaprocaccini.com

The pizza has a "nice, thin crust" and "fresh, delicious" toppings
at this pair of affordable osterias; they're often "packed", so you
can "expect long waits", but fans insist they're "so worth it";
P.S. Pennington has a wine bar, while Kingston is BYO.

Oyster Creek Inn
Restaurant & Boat Bar Ⓜ *Seafood*
24 | 19 | 22 | $27

Leeds Point | 41 Oyster Creek Rd. (Moss Mill Rd.) | 609-652-8565 |
www.oystercreekinnnj.com

This "cute" Leeds Point seafooder may be "in the middle of nowhere",
but fans say it's "well worth" seeking out for "great" "unpretentious"
fare and "spectacular views" of the marshes; "reasonable prices"
make it "nice for families", and you can dock your boat.

Pad-Thai Authentic
Thai Cuisine *Thai*
22 | 17 | 18 | $22

Highland Park | 217 Raritan Ave. (bet. 2nd & 3rd Aves.) |
732-247-9636 | www.pad-thai.com

"Fiercely spicy", "tasty" Thai is on offer at this Highland Park storefront, where fans say the "authentic" eats go well with Siam-brewed
beers; the "'60s tiki" decor gets a lukewarm reception, and some
find the service "hit-or-miss", but at least it's "reasonably priced."

Pairings Palate + Plate Ⓜ *American*
23 | 21 | 22 | $51

Cranford | 1 South Ave. E. (Union Ave.) | 908-276-4026 |
www.pairingscranford.com

The "creative" New American fare at this "shiny" Cranford BYO
newcomer "mostly hits the mark" say fans; though the space is
"lovely", some diners find the "hard, stiff" chairs irksome, and
others note the bill can "really add up" – fortunately, a prix fixe on
Wednesdays and tapas on Thursdays are "true bargains."

Paisano's Restaurant Ⓢ *Italian*
22 | 20 | 21 | $38

Rutherford | 132 Park Ave. (bet. Donaldson Ave. & Franklin Pl.) |
201-935-5755 | www.paisanos.com

With its "old-style" fare and "pleasant" setting, it's no surprise this
Rutherford Italian is a "favorite gathering place" for locals; the main
room can get "noisy" on weekends, but there's a back patio for
summer dines, and the option to BYO "helps keep the price down."

	FOOD	DECOR	SERVICE	COST

Palace of Asia *Indian*
23 | 20 | 19 | $29

Lawrenceville | Village Square Shopping Ctr. | 540 Lawrence Square Blvd. S. (Quakerbridge Rd.) | 609-689-1500
Cherry Hill | Americas Best Value Inn | 2389 Rte. 70 W. (Donahue Ave.) | 856-773-1200
www.palace-of-asia.com

"A bit of love" goes into the "delicious" fare at this Indian duo in Cherry Hill and Lawrenceville, where the "phenomenal" lunch buffet might be "one of the region's best bargains"; service gets mixed reviews, but both offer "refined" surroundings.

Palazzo *Italian*
20 | 19 | 21 | $42

Montclair | 11 S. Fullerton Ave. (Bloomfield Ave.) | 973-746-6778 | www.palazzonj.com

"Like something out of a Rat Pack movie", this "neighborhood" Italian in Montclair serves up "reliably yummy" classic fare in an "old-school" setting, alongside a small wine selection (or BYO); live jazz on weekends "adds additional ambiance", and fans note that servers know the value of a "well-paced meal."

The Palm *Steak*
24 | 21 | 23 | $64

Atlantic City | Quarter at the Tropicana | 2801 Pacific Ave. (Iowa Ave.) | 609-344-7256 | www.thepalm.com

Fans say this "upbeat", upscale steakhouse chain link in the Tropicana "comes up aces" with steaks "like butter", "knowledgeable" service and a "great bar scene"; critics complain of "impersonal" service and "jackhammer-loud" acoustics from the "low ceiling", but others tout it as a worthwhile splurge "if you just won the jackpot."

Pamir *Afghan*
21 | 19 | 19 | $31

Morristown | 11 South St. (Dehart St.) | 973-605-1095 | www.pamirrestaurant.com

"Just the right mix of spices" livens up the "tasty" Afghan fare at this Morristown BYO, where "lovely" lamb entrees are a "must-order" according to fans; many find its new location near the town green "a step up", and occasional belly dancing makes it "even more attractive", as do "reasonable" prices – all in all, a "welcome change" for those seeking "something different."

Panico's *Italian*
21 | 20 | 22 | $51

New Brunswick | 103 Church St. (Neilson St.) | 732-545-6100 | www.panicosrestaurant.com

For a "pre-theater" meal or a "special occasion", this "old-school" New Brunswick Italian does the trick, thanks to "very good" fare, an "extensive" wine list and a "romantic" setting; some find it "tired-looking", plus "pricey" for the area, but prix fixe early-bird specials and live piano some nights help make it a "favorite" of many.

Park & Orchard *Eclectic*
22 | 17 | 20 | $41

East Rutherford | 240 Hackensack St. (bet. Orchard St. & Union Ave.) | 201-939-9292 | www.parkandorchard.com

"Funky" "nouveau cuisine" is "piled high" at this East Rutherford Eclectic, where vegetarians and the "health conscious" have "lots" of "inspired" options, but there's also "something for everyone" else, plus an "unsurpassed" wine list; "moderate" prices, "cordial" service and a "great" bar scene help many overlook the "noisy" setting with a "warehouse" feel.

	FOOD	DECOR	SERVICE	COST

Park Steakhouse *Seafood/Steak*

| 24 | 21 | 23 | $62 |

Park Ridge | 151 Kinderkamack Rd. (bet. Berthoud & Perry Sts.) | 201-930-1300 | www.theparksteakhouse.com

"Quality" steaks with "all the accoutrements" recommend this "quintessential local" steakhouse in Park Ridge, which also boasts "fine" seafood and "strong" drinks; some find it "overpriced" and in "need of remodeling", but "professional" service and a "warm ambiance" help make for a "special" experience.

Park West Tavern *American*

| 20 | 20 | 20 | $38 |

Ridgewood | 30 Oak St. (Ridgewood Ave.) | 201-445-5400 | www.parkwesttavern.com

"From burgers to haute cuisine", this Ridgewood New American (sibling of Park Steakhouse) dishes out a solid midpriced menu of "gastropub" fare in a "warm" "clubhouse" setting, but it's the "terrific" bar that's the "real gem"; though some complain of "inconsistent" service, many return, pointing out it's "nice to be able to get a cocktail" in a "BYO town."

NEW The Pass Ⓜ *French*

| - | - | - | E |

Rosemont | 88 Kingwood Stockton Rd. (Rosemont Ringoes Rd.) | 609-961-1887 | www.atthepass.com

Charcutier and chef Matthew Ridgway (PorcSalt) teams up with chef Paul Mitchell (ex Philly's Fountain) to create weekly changing three-course prix fixe menus of country French cuisine at this high-end Rosemont BYO; set in a picturesque Victorian building that used to be a general store, the rustic space also boasts a vintage deli counter selling artisanal charcuterie and other local gourmet goods; P.S. open for dinner Wednesdays–Saturdays.

Passariello's Pizzeria & Italian Eatery *Italian/Pizza*

| 22 | 18 | 20 | $16 |

Moorestown | 13 W. Main St. (bet. Church & Mill Sts.) | 856-840-0998
Voorhees | 111 Laurel Oak Rd. (White Horse Rd.) | 856-784-7272
www.passariellos.com

"Old favorites" for a "quick lunch", these BYO pizzerias in Moorestown and Voorhees serve up "reliable" pies and other Italian standards, all at "reasonable" prices; they're "self-serve" in "cafeteria-style" digs, which means many fans prefer to grab and go.

Patria Ⓜ *Pan-Latin*

| 23 | 23 | 21 | $43 |

Rahway | 169 W. Main St. (Elizabeth Ave.) | 732-943-7531 | www.patrianj.com

An "inventive" menu of Pan-Latin eats is the centerpiece of this "happening" Rahway lounge, helmed by chef Andrew DiCataldo from its former NYC incarnation; the "lively" space hosts "*música increíble*" and dancing on weekends, which is a "good time" that doubles as a workout for "burning off" the "delicious" tapas and sangria.

	FOOD	DECOR	SERVICE	COST

Patsy's *Italian*
22 | 18 | 22 | $38

Fairview | 332 Bergen Blvd. (bet. Cliff St. & Jersey Ave.) | 201-943-0627 | www.patsysristorante.com

"Delicious traditional" Italian fare like "momma" might make is on offer at this Fairview "old favorite"; some say it's "not much to look at", but that doesn't deter loyal locals who praise the "friendly" staff and insist it's a "must-go", *"capisce*?"

The Peacock Inn Restaurant *American*
26 | 26 | 26 | $72

Princeton | Peacock Inn | 20 Bayard Ln. (bet. Boudinot & Nassau Sts.) | 609-924-1707 | www.thepeacockinn.com

Everything is "top-notch" at this "elegant" Princetonian, from the "excellent" "farm-to-table" American cuisine by Nicholas alum Manuel Perez to the "lovely", "warm" setting in a "luxury" inn near campus; "impeccable" service completes the package, but given the cost, some go only when "someone else is paying."

Penang *Malaysian/Thai*
22 | 19 | 19 | $23

Lodi | 334 N. Main St. (Garibaldi Ave.) | 973-779-1128
East Hanover | 200 Rte. 10 W. (New Murray Rd.) | 973-887-6989 | www.penangnj.com
Princeton | Nassau Park Pavilion | 635 Nassau Park Blvd. (Quakerbridge Rd.) | 609-897-9088 | www.penangprinceton.com

Those in need of a "Pan-Asian spice fix" say these Malaysian-Thai siblings do the trick with their "tasty", "pretty authentic" dishes served "fast" and at "reasonable" prices; while the decor strikes some as "Zen" and others as simply "gloomy", and service can be "spotty", a "busy, fun" vibe wins the day, though a few prefer to "stick to take out"; P.S. East Hanover and Princeton are BYO.

Pete & Elda's ⬤ *Pizza*
24 | 16 | 20 | $22
(aka Carmen's Pizzeria)

Neptune City | 96 Woodland Ave. (Rte. 35) | 732-774-6010 | www.peteandeldas.com

Since 1957, "generations" of fans have been "coming back for more" of the "crispy", "light-as-air" thin-crust pies dished up by an "efficient" staff at this "casual", no-frills Neptune City pizzeria; though it can get "crowded" and "noisy" at peak times, a lively "bar scene" and late hours help make it a "Shore favorite."

Peter Shields Inn *American*
26 | 27 | 25 | $60

Cape May | 1301 Beach Ave. (Trenton Ave.) | 609-884-9090 | www.petershieldsinn.com

Set in a "gorgeous" 1907 beachfront manse, this Cape May American is a "real winner" thanks to the "amazing views", "elegant" digs and "superbly prepared" "classic" fare; "comfortable", "well-spaced seating" and "attentive service" help make for a "quiet retreat", and while tabs are "on the pricey side", a BYO option helps "hold down costs."

P.F. Chang's China Bistro *Chinese*
21 | 21 | 20 | $31

Hackensack | The Shops at Riverside | 390 Hackensack Ave. (Commerce Way) | 201-646-1565

(continued)

(continued)

P.F. Chang's China Bistro

West New York | 10 Port Imperial Blvd. (Riverbend) | 201-866-7790
Freehold | Freehold Raceway Mall | 3710 Rte. 9 (Winners Circle) |
732-308-1840
Atlantic City | The Quarter at the Tropicana | 2801 Pacific Ave.
(bet. Brighton & Iowa Aves.) | 609-348-4600
Princeton | Marketfair Mall | 3545 Rte. 1 (Meadow Rd.) | 609-799-5163
Marlton | The Promenade at Sagemore | 500 Rte. 73 S. (Marlton Pkwy.) |
856-396-0818
www.pfchangs.com

"Upscale Americanized Chinese" is the draw at these "consistently comforting" chain links where signature specialties like "wonderful" lettuce wraps plus gluten-free options and "trendy" cocktails are "served efficiently at a reasonable cost"; while some gripe about the "noise level", others think the "busy" vibe makes it "fun."

Phillips Seafood   *Seafood*   `21` `19` `21` `$39`

Atlantic City | Pier Shops at Caesars | 1 Atlantic Ocean (Arkansas Ave.) |
609-348-2273 | www.phillipsseafood.com

An "excellent" view and "tasty" seafood are the hallmarks of this "dependable" Atlantic City link in a Maryland chain where "crab dishes are the way to go" and the Pier One at Caesars locale is perfect for "people-watching"; prices are "reasonable", and for the lucky and unlucky alike, it's "a nice break from gambling."

Phily Diner   ● *Diner*   `20` `19` `19` `$17`

Runnemede | 31 S. Black Horse Pike (Plaza Pl.) | 856-939-4322 |
www.philydiner.com

It's "nothing fancy", but this "classic" '50s-retro diner in Runnemede slings "good", affordable grub in "decent" portions 24 hours a day; it's "shiny clean" and there's "never a long wait", but whether the attached sports bar is "fun" or just "rowdy" is for you to decide.

Pho Anh Dao   *Vietnamese*   `22` `13` `19` `$14`

Edison | 691 US Hwy. 1 (bet. East Side & Wooding Aves.) | 732-985-7977

"When the hankering hits", phonatics head to this Edison Vietnamese BYO for its "hot, flavorful" pho that comes out "fast"; the focus here is "not on the decor" of the strip-mall space, but for an "authentic", "value" meal, diners say you "can't really go wrong."

Piccola Italia   Ⓜ *Italian*   `25` `21` `23` `$52`

Ocean Township | 837 W. Park Ave. (Andorian Trail) | 732-493-3090

The "attention to detail" paid to the "creative" cuisine at this "upscale", "real-deal" Italian in Ocean makes it a "rare find"; though it's "hidden away" in a strip mall, the setting is "refined", and with "great" service and a sizable wine list, fans have "no need to travel to NYC."

Pic-Nic   *Portuguese/Spanish*   ▽ `24` `20` `23` `$26`

East Newark | 224 Grant Ave. (bet. Central & Sherman Aves.) |
973-481-3646 | www.picnicrestaurant.com

"Huge portions" of "highly reliable" Portuguese specialties are served "the old-fashioned way", backed by a "good wine selection", at this affordable East Newark Iberian; add in a "welcoming" staff and "quiet, romantic" setting (there's a domed ceiling painted like the sky), and fans say it's "well worth the trip."

Piero's ☒ Italian

22	20	22	$51

Union Beach | 1411 New Jersey 36 (bet. Patterson & Wesley Aves.) | 732-264-5222 | www.pierosrestaurant.com

"Solid" Italian "comfort food" with the occasional "continental twist" is the draw at this midpriced Union Beach "go-to"; some feel it could "use a makeover", but live music makes for a "good" (if "loud") time, and regulars return because "you feel like family here."

NEW Pig & Prince ●☒ American

20	23	18	$48

Montclair | Lackawanna Plaza | 1 Lackawanna Plaza (Bloomfield Ave.) | 973-233-1006 | www.pigandprince.com

Under the vaulted ceiling of a renovated train station (whose architect died on the Titanic), this "gorgeous" Montclair newcomer offers a "thoughtfully created" American menu of farm-to-table dishes with some "unexpected flavors"; while some say it still needs "fine tuning" and "price-to-portion ratios" raise a few eyebrows, overall, diners consider it a "wonderful" addition to the local scene, and the "full bar" is a plus in a mostly BYO town.

Pino's La Forchetta ● Italian

20	21	20	$43

Marlboro | 448 Rte. 9 N. (Clayton Rd.) | 732-972-6933 | www.famouspinos.com

A "piece of Brooklyn in Central Jersey", this Marlboro Italian boasts "above-average" standards at "fair-value" prices, including a three-course prix fixe; the bar heats up weekends (and gets "noisy" for some) with DJ's, dancing and live entertainment, and all in all, fans find it a "nice change of pace" for the area.

Pithari Taverna Greek

23	20	20	$32

Highland Park | 28 Woodbridge Ave. (Raritan Ave.) | 732-572-0616 | www.thepithari.com

Taverna Ouzo Greek

Monroe Township | 146 Applegarth Rd. (Old Church Rd.) | 609-426-9700

The "true meaning of opa" might be found at these "charming" Greek "bistros" in Highland Park and Monroe Township, serving "hefty" portions of "authentic" Greek fare, including "nicely pre-pared", "fresh" seafood; though a "tight squeeze" at times, the "small" blue-and-white "oases" host a "joyful" atmosphere, aided by "friendly" waiters and "reasonable" prices; P.S. Pithari is BYO.

PJ's Pancake House American

18	14	16	$19

Princeton | 154 Nassau St. (bet. Vandeventer Ave. & Witherspoon St.) | 609-924-1353 | www.pancakes.com

A "cult favorite", this "down-home" Princeton "institution" still at-tracts "long lines" of "town and gown" alike for its "signature" pan-cakes and other American "diner fare", although former fans lament the food's "gone downhill", "graffiti-scarred" tables are testament to "generations of students" who've sought "comfort food" here at "reasonable prices."

	FOOD	DECOR	SERVICE	COST

P.J. Whelihan's ● *Pub Food* | 21 | 20 | 20 | $21 |

Cherry Hill | 1854 Marlton Pike E. (bet. Graydon Ave. & Greentree Rd.) | 856-424-8844
Haddonfield | 700 Haddon Ave. (Ardmore Ave.) | 856-427-7888
Maple Shade | 396 S. Lenola Rd. (bet. New Jersey 38 & Old Kings Hwy.) | 856-234-2345
Medford Lakes | 61 Stokes Rd. (bet. Tabernacle Rd. & Trading Post Way) | 609-714-7900
Sewell | 425 Hurffville Crosskeys Rd. (Kings Way) | 856-582-7774
www.pjspub.com

"Hot 'n' honey wings" downed with "fun, cheap drinks" are the heart and soul of these South Jersey sports pubs, serving "basic", "affordable" American grub in an "upbeat" setting; if service can be "lacking" and the vibe "rowdy" and "loud" during games, fans shrug that's "what you'd expect."

Plantation *American* | 19 | 20 | 19 | $42 |

Harvey Cedars | 7908 Long Beach Blvd. (bet. 79th & 80th Sts.) | 609-494-8191 | www.plantationrestaurant.com

"Stick to the basics" and "you'll eat well" say insiders of this Harvey Cedars American where the "pretty", upscale surrounds have "year-round" appeal for "LBIers"; service gets mixed marks and tabs aren't cheap, but if you don't mind that it's "noisy", it can be "fun to eat at the bar", where you'll "save some money" on budget-friendly options.

Pluckemin Inn ⊠ *American* | 25 | 24 | 24 | $63 |

Bedminster | 359 Rte. 206 S. (Pluckemin Way) | 908-658-9292 | www.pluckemininn.com

"Far from the madding crowd", this "pretty country inn" in Bedminister is "special occasion"–worthy, serving "imaginative", "sophisticated" American fare in a restored farmhouse, where a three-story tower showcases an "astounding" wine list; though "casually elegant" is the presiding vibe, some prefer a "less formal" experience in the tavern or on an outdoor patio.

Ponzio's *Diner* | 20 | 18 | 20 | $21 |

Cherry Hill | 7 Rte. 70 W. (Kings Hwy.) | 856-428-4808 | www.ponzios.com

This Cherry Hill "institution" "knows how to feed the masses" – as well as "pols and sports stars" – with "stunning" portions of "reliable diner food" and a bakery that makes some "want dessert as an entree"; the "classic" setting is "clean", and while some think service "could be improved", few question its "staying power" as a local "standby."

Pop's Garage *Mexican* | 21 | 18 | 20 | $23 |

Asbury Park | Asbury Park Boardwalk | 1000 Ocean Ave. (2nd Ave.) | 732-455-3275
Shrewsbury | The Grove | 520 Broad St. (bet. Meadow Dr. & Patterson Ave.) | 732-530-7677
www.popsgaragenj.com

This "funky" taqueria in Shrewsbury from the Kitschens Group turns out "tasty", "exceptionally fresh" Mexican fare made with locally sourced and sustainable ingredients in "lively", beach-themed settings; despite gripes about "slow" service, many deem it a "fun place to go with a small group"; P.S. the Asbury Park location was tempo-rarily closed due to Sandy at press time.

Pop Shop *American*

23 | 21 | 22 | $17

Collingswood | 729 Haddon Ave. (Washington Ave.) | 856-869-0111 | www.thepopshopusa.com

Whether it's pancakes, burgers or a "gazillion types" of grilled cheese, this "cute", "retro" soda fountain in Collingswood has "something for everyone", including a "great vegetarian selection", on its American comfort-food menu; the "chaotic" "family" environment can either be "lots of fun" or a "delightful way to lose your hearing", but with such "reasonable" prices, fans say you "will not leave dissatisfied."

Porta ● *Pizza*

24 | 19 | 20 | $31

Asbury Park | 911 Kingsley St. (bet. 1st & 2nd Aves.) | 732-776-7661 | www.pizzaporta.com

"Awesome designer pizzas" and other "creative" "seasonal selec-tions" pack 'em in to this midpriced Asbury Park Italian; while some find the service "questionable", most say the "fun, eclectic" atmo-sphere is "worth the wait", with picnic-table seating, bocce ball, live jazz for Sunday brunch and late-night concerts and dance parties.

Portobello *Italian*

21 | 22 | 20 | $41

Oakland | 175 Ramapo Valley Rd. (Spruce St.) | 201-337-8990 | www.portobellonj.com

Set in a "huge", "beautiful" multilevel space that "makes you feel you've entered Tuscany", this Oakland Italian boasts a "wide vari-ety" of "very nicely executed" osteria-style fare; if some dislike the "catering-hall" vibe and find service "spotty", others tout "unbeliev-able" lunch specials that are a "great bargain."

Portofino Ristorante Ⓜ *Italian*

21 | 18 | 20 | $50

Tinton Falls | 720 Tinton Ave. (Water St.) | 732-542-6068 | www.portofino-ristorante.com

A "family-run Italian" in Tinton Falls, this "local" trattoria serves up "delicious homemade" eats and a "great wine list" in upscale-casual digs; the "views are pleasant", and cognoscenti counsel when black-vested waiters rattle off the roster of "special specials", be sure to ask for the prices – for they're probably "high."

Portofino's *Italian*

21 | 17 | 19 | $31

Morristown | 29 Mills St. (Early St.) | 973-540-0026 | www.portofinosrestaurant.com

For a "laid-back" meal at a "great value", fans of this Morristown Italian BYO say you cannot go wrong with its "solid" "red-sauce" dishes; if the "cozy" space "has little charm" for most and "basic" service fails to impress, a "nice" "local" vibe still wins the day.

Porto Leggero Ⓩ *Italian*

23 | 22 | 22 | $47

Jersey City | 5 Harborside Pl. (Pearl St.) | 201-434-3200 | www.portoleggero.net

Fans insist the "sophisticated" Italian cuisine "will not disappoint" at this "high-end" spot in Jersey City's Financial District co-owned by

Michael Cetrulo of Scalini Fedeli; "accommodating" servers work the "striking" space with soaring ceilings and brick walls, an "elegant" setting for an "intimate" dinner or "business" lunch, albeit at "expense-account" prices.

Portuguese Manor *Portuguese/Spanish* | 23 | 16 | 22 | $34 |

Perth Amboy | 310 Elm St. (bet. Fayette & Smith Sts.) | 732-826-2233 | www.portuguesemanorrestaurante.com

The staff is "eager to serve you" "huge portions" of "classic", "comforting" Iberian dishes at this "welcoming" Perth Amboy "institution"; though some suggest the decor "could use an update", others are content with "a few glasses of the incredible sangria" and "a dance after dinner"; P.S. there's live music and DJs on weekends.

Prickly Pear 🅱🅜 *American* | 22 | 19 | 22 | $37 |

Hackettstown | Main Street Plaza | 80-30 Main St. (Stiger St.) | 908-979-0003 | www.pricklypearrestaurant.com

"Creative", "consistently good" American fare is the forte of this midpriced Hackettstown BYO; although its strip-mall location is a drawback for some, "friendly" service is a plus, and a monthly "cooking school" offers fans a chance to DIY and is a "great value" to boot.

PrimoHoagies *Sandwiches* | 21 | 15 | 19 | $11 |

NEW **Marlboro** | Marlboro Plaza | 104 U.S. 9 (bet. Bartram & Newman Springs Rd.) | 732-696-8800

Avalon | 3252 Dune Dr. (bet. 32nd & 33rd Sts.) | 609-368-8600 🅢

Hammonton | 120 S. White Horse Pike (bet. B'way & Woodlawn Aves.) | 609-567-7466

Rio Grande | ShopRite Shopping Ctr. | 1500 Rte. 47 (5th St.) | 609-846-7532

Burlington | 611 W. Rte. 130 (Mott Ave.) | 609-747-0041

Cherry Hill | 826 Haddonfield Rd. (bet. Graham & Hollis Aves.) | 856-662-1010

Cinnaminson | Chestnut Hill Plaza | 2806 Rte. 130 N. (Taylors Ln.) | 856-303-9700

Mount Laurel | Larchmont Commons Shopping Ctr. | 3111 Rte. 38 W. (Ark Rd.) | 856-235-4200

Swedesboro | 120 Center Square Rd. (Oaks Dr.) | 856-241-1226

Voorhees | Eagle Plaza Shopping Ctr. | 700 Haddonfield Berlin Rd. (White Horse Rd.) | 856-782-7790

www.primohoagies.com

Additional locations throughout New Jersey

"Crusty on the outside and chewy on the inside", the rolls are what "make it all happen" at this Philly-based sandwich chain specializing in "classic hoagies" that are "packed" with "high-quality" meats and cheeses; though there's "not much in the way of decor", and a few complain prices are "high for what they give you", most consider it a "decent" pit stop.

The Pub *Steak* | 21 | 18 | 20 | $32 |

Pennsauken | 7600 Kaighns Ave. (Crescent Blvd.) | 856-665-6440 | www.thepubnj.com

There are "ample reasons" this "classic" Pennsauken chophouse "still packs them in" after 50-plus years – "reliable" steaks "cooked in an open hearth", a "well-stocked" salad bar and the sense of "stepping into a time machine", among them; the "cavernous" dining room can be "loud", and critics complain of "lackluster" service and "unimpressive" eats for the "price", but others "find comfort" in the feeling that "nothing has changed" here.

Puccini's Ⓜ *Italian* | 22 | 21 | 22 | $43 |

Jersey City | 1064 West Side Ave. (B'way) | 201-432-4111 | www.puccinisrestaurant.com

Those seeking a "quiet dinner" of "traditional" "fine" Italian fare appreciate this "old-school", "upscale" Jersey City stalwart; its "beautifully well-kept", "formal" space is popular for private functions, with "friendly" service and valet parking as added benefits; P.S. "dress nice" advise aficionados.

Queen Margherita
Trattoria Ⓩ *Italian* | 24 | 20 | 22 | $33 |

Nutley | 246 Washington Ave. (Grant Ave.) | 973-662-0007 | www.queenmargherita.com

"You're one of the family" at this Nutley BYO where "delicious" homemade pastas and wood-fired pizzas are served in a "cozy" "neighborhood" setting, with "wonderful" desserts from the adjoining bakery; "tight quarters" and "long lines" don't deter fans, who like the "moderate prices" and say a "warm welcome" from the owners also makes it a "c'mon-back place" for many.

The Quiet Man ◗ *Pub Food* | 23 | 20 | 22 | $28 |

Dover | 64 E. McFarlan St. (Hudson St.) | 973-366-6333 | www.quietmanpub.com

"Not your typical bar food", the fare at this "cozy" Irish pub in Dover includes "incredible" shepherd's pie and "quality" fish 'n' chips, among other "comforts"; a "friendly" staff welcomes "regulars" who congregate for "good beers" and live music on weekends, and all comes at the "right price."

Raimondo's ⓏⓂ *Italian* | 24 | 20 | 21 | $47 |

Ship Bottom | 1101 Long Beach Blvd. (11th St.) | no phone | www.raimondoslbi.com

"Terrific" Italian dishes make this Ship Bottom BYO a "must-try" for "fine dining" on LBI, especially for early-birders who appreciate the "great-value" prix fixe; service is just "ok", and in summer it can be "crowded" and "noisy", so locals wait for the "magic months when the tourists are gone."

Ram's
Head Inn Ⓜ *American* | 25 | 25 | 25 | $57 |

Galloway | 9 W. White Horse Pike (bet. Ash & Taylor Aves.) | 609-652-1700 | www.ramsheadinn.com

A "grande dame of South Jersey", this "simply elegant" Galloway American serves "first-class" "traditional" fare featuring produce sourced from its own nearby farm; boasting "charming" Colonial decor, the multiroom house is "formal" without "fussiness", with "excellent" service to match, making it a "romantic" venue for weddings.

| | FOOD | DECOR | SERVICE | COST |

Rare The Steak House *Steak*

| 23 | 20 | 22 | $59 |

Little Falls | 440 Main St. (Fairfield Ave.) | 973-256-6699 |
www.rarestk.com

A change of pace from the "big-name chains", this "small" suburban
steakhouse in Little Falls serves up "great" chops and seafood in a
"lovely" space with a "sound level perfect for conversation"; it's
pricey, as expected for the genre, but "attentive" waiters boost the
overall "positive experience."

Rat's ☑ *French*

| 25 | 27 | 24 | $61 |

Hamilton | Grounds for Sculpture | 16 Fairgrounds Rd. (Sculptors Way) |
609-584-7800 | www.ratsrestaurant.org

A "make-believe" "château" nestled in the "gorgeous" gardens
of a sculpture park – "what could be more charming?" posit
admirers of this "magical" Hamilton French, voted New Jersey's
No. 1 for Decor, where "enthusiastic" waiters serve "sublime"
cuisine in a "most civilized manner"; an outdoor patio is a good
spot to enjoy a "marvelous" Sunday brunch, and while it's "quite
expensive", many deem it "worth the price", especially if you "stroll
the grounds afterward."

Raven & the Peach *American*

| 24 | 24 | 24 | $62 |

Fair Haven | 740 River Rd. (bet. Church St. & Fair Haven Rd.) |
732-747-4666 | www.ravenandthepeach.net

The "atmosphere is abundant" at this "elegant", "romantic" New
American in Fair Haven serving "carefully prepared", "creative
selections" and an "excellent" wine list in a *Casablanca*-like setting
with low lighting, dark woods and potted palms; "pleasant" service
is another plus, and while it's "expensive", for many it's "a real treat"
on "special occasions."

Raymond's *American*

| 21 | 18 | 19 | $28 |

Montclair | 28 Church St. (bet. Fullerton Ave. & Park St.) |
973-744-9263 | www.raymondsnj.com
NEW Ridgewood | 11 Oak St. (Ridgewood Ave.) |
201-445-5125

"It's all about brunch" at this "upscale diner" in Montclair (and its new
sequel in Ridgewood), where "satisfying" "homestyle" American fare,
including "transformative" French toast, is served by an "upbeat"
crew in "retro" "bistro" surrounds with "snappy" black-and-white
tiles and "antique" seltzer bottles; it can get "noisy", but prices are
"fair", and if you don't want to "wait in line", lunch and dinner can be
less crowded; P.S. both are BYO.

Rebecca's ☑ *Cuban*

| 23 | 21 | 22 | $45 |

Edgewater | 236 Old River Rd. (Thompson Ln.) | 201-943-8808 |
www.rebeccascubanrestaurant.com

A "tiny" "treasure" tucked "under the cliffs", this Edgewater BYO offers "sophisticated", if "pricey", Cuban fare in a "charming" space
with a "nice" back garden; seating is "limited", so reservations are
essential, but "wear your *ropas nuevas*", sit by the patio fountain and
you might have a "great date."

	FOOD	DECOR	SERVICE	COST

Red ● *American*

| 21 | 22 | 20 | $51 |

Red Bank | 3 Broad St. (Front St.) | 732-741-3232 | www.rednj.com
A "young", "upscale" crowd congregates at this "cool", "modern" Red Bank American, where the "interesting" (to some, "wacky") menu has a "little bit of everything", from gnocchi to sushi; a "romantic" upstairs bar serves "inventive" cocktails, and "pricey" tabs are consistent with the "NY" vibe.

NEW Red Knot *American*

| - | - | - | M |

Kenilworth | Galloping Hill Golf Club | 3 Golf Dr. (Galloping Hill Rd.) | 908-686-1556 | www.gallopinghillgolfcourse.com
Set inside the new clubhouse at Kenilworth's Galloping Hill Golf Course, this gastropub offers a refined take on hearty classics, including BBQ, burgers and brick-oven pizza, with something for every budget; the room sports Craftsman-style decor and floor-to ceiling windows, and there's a seasonal patio overlooking the course.

Red's Lobster Pot *Seafood*

| 23 | 17 | 20 | $33 |

Point Pleasant Beach | 57 Inlet Dr. (B'way) | 732-295-6622 | www.redslobsterpot.com
Lobster and other ocean fare "tastes like it was just caught" – and often was – at this seasonal "shore shack" on the inlet at Point Pleasant Beach, where fishing boats pull right up to the dock; there's "not much elbow room" inside (and a "wait" on weekends), but deck seats offer a "great view", and BYO makes for an even more "reasonably priced" meal.

Redstone American Grill ● *American*

| 22 | 22 | 21 | $38 |

Marlton | The Promenade at Sagemore | 500 Rte. 73 S. (bet. Brick Rd. & Marlton Pkwy.) | 856-396-0332 | www.redstonegrill.com
For a "casual", "lively" meal after shopping at The Promenade at Sagemore, this Marlton American offers "consistently good" grill-centric fare in "pleasant" dark-wood decor; though some find it a tad "pricey" for the area, others say it's a "favorite" lunch spot, especially on the outdoor patio, and at night, it can be "happening" with a "noisy" bar scene and "great people-watching."

Remington's ☒ *American*

| 21 | 19 | 20 | $50 |

Manasquan | 142 Main St. (Parker Ave.) | 732-292-1300 | www.remingtonsnj.com
Reservations are "a must" at this Manasquan "'in' spot", where "interesting preparations" of seafood stand out on the menu of "fancy" New American fare; some find it "overpriced", especially given the "casual" barlike atmosphere, but as a "NY-style" option for the area, many feel it's "worth a try."

Renault Winery
Gourmet Restaurant ☒ *American*

| 23 | 23 | 24 | $43 |

Egg Harbor | Renault Winery Resort & Golf | 72 N. Bremen Ave. (Liebig Ave.) | 609-965-2111 | www.renaultwinery.com
Set in New Jersey's oldest vineyard, this Egg Harbor resort's American draws oenophiles with a six-course prix fixe dinner menu complete

with "wonderful pairings" and a "second-to-none" Sunday champagne brunch; the "friendly" staff and "beautiful view of the golf course" lend appeal, even if some chalk up the praise of the "expensive" eats to enthusiastic imbibing during pre-meal winery tour tastings; P.S. dinner served Friday and Saturday only.

Reservoir Tavern ● ☒ Ⓜ *Italian* | 23 | 13 | 18 | $26 |

Boonton | 92 Parsippany Blvd. (Intervale Rd.) | 973-334-0421 | www.therestavern.com

Prepare for a "ridiculously long wait" at this "old-school" Boonton Italian, but fans promise your patience will be "amply rewarded" with "terrific" brick-oven pizza and "homestyle" fare at "great prices"; ok, the "roadhouse" space looks "dated", it's "noisy" and service can be "hit-or-miss", but it's "always packed" nonetheless.

Restaurant Latour Ⓜ *American* | ▽ 26 | 26 | 26 | $104 |

Hamburg | Crystal Springs Resort | 1 Wild Turkey Way (Woodcott Dr.) | 973-827-0548 | www.crystalgolfresort.com

With its "outstanding" cuisine, featuring locally sourced meats and vegetables, and "superb" 9,000-label wine cellar, this Hamburg prix fixe–only American at the Crystal Springs Resort is considered a "world-class" player; "excellent" service in an "elegant" room over-looking the "breathtaking" hill country top off what some call an "ultimate dining experience" that's "well worth" the "very expensive" tabs.

Ridge Thai ☒ *Thai* | 21 | 17 | 19 | $29 |

Ridgewood | 50 Chestnut St. (bet. Franklin & Ridgewood Aves.) | 201-493-9929 | www.ridgethai.com

"Authentic Thai flavors" abound at this "reasonably priced" Ridgewood BYO, where "good simple" dishes mingle with "some innovative surprises", including a papaya salad "so spicy it bites back"; the digs are "tiny" and "cramped", but with such a "friendly" vibe, "it seems to work."

Rio Rodizio *Brazilian* | 21 | 20 | 20 | $40 |

Newark | 1034 McCarter Hwy. (Bridge St.) | 973-622-6221
Union | 2185 Rte. 22 W. (Chestnut St.) | 908-206-0060
www.riorodizio.com

A seemingly "endless supply of meat" draws diners to these mid-priced Brazilians in Newark and Union, where waiters deliver non-stop skewers, and a "tempting" salad bar includes hot dishes and sushi; some feel it's "quantity over quality", and the "clubby" vibe with "techno music blasting" can be distracting, but one thing's certain – "you won't go home hungry."

Risotto House *Italian* | 22 | 16 | 20 | $33 |

Rutherford | 88 Park Ave. (Franklin Pl.) | 201-438-5344 | www.therisottohouse.com

"The name says it all" (or does it?) at this Rutherford Italian BYO, where "smooth, creamy" risotto is the signature, but "other classic dishes" are also "consistently good"; the decor may be "plain" and "dark", but "nice" service and prices that "won't break your budget" help make it a "local favorite."

	FOOD	DECOR	SERVICE	COST

Ristorante Giorgia *Italian*

| 25 | 21 | 22 | $47 |

Rumson | 102 Avenue of 2 Rivers (bet. Black Point & Ridge Rds.) |
732-741-3880 | www.ristorantegiorgia.com

Family-owned and -run by a Calabrian native, this "authentic" upmarket BYO Italian in Rumson draws "locals" with "excellent" eats, including housemade pastas and other tip-of-the-Boot specialties; evoking a Tuscan farmhouse, the "small", "charming" digs can get "noisy", but the "attentive" staff helps make it a "true gem."

Ritz Seafood Ⓜ *Seafood*

| 24 | 17 | 21 | $37 |

Voorhees | Eagle Plaza Shopping Ctr. | 910 Haddonfield Berlin Rd. (bet. Voorhees Dr. & White Horse Rd.) | 856-566-6650 |
www.ritzseafood.com

A kitchen that "really knows how to treat fish" produces "imaginative", "delicious" dishes at this Voorhees seafooder, where Food Network–famous coconut cream pie is the grand finale and BYO aids already "reasonable" prices; loyalists warn that the "dreary" strip-mall digs are "very deceiving", insisting that it "rivals the best fine restaurants"; P.S. you "must call for reservations", especially for dining "after the movies" at the nearby Rave.

River Grille ❶ *American*

| - | - | - | I |

Chatham | 34 River Rd. (bet. Perrin St. & Watchung Ave.) |
973-701-1125 | www.chathamrivergrille.com

Chef Eric Moody brings his award-winning mac 'n' cheese and other elevated American pub fare to a former tavern in an industrial corner of Chatham; a U-shaped bar and a host of TVs share space with a small dining area, while prices pair with the laid-back atmosphere, and the place perks up regularly with open mike nights and live music.

River Palm Terrace *Steak*

| 25 | 21 | 23 | $65 |

Edgewater | 1416 River Rd. (Palisade Terr.) | 201-224-2013
Fair Lawn | 41-11 Rte. 4 (bet. Paramus Rd. & Saddle River Pathway) |
201-703-3500
Mahwah | 209 Ramapo Valley Rd. (Rtes. 202& 17 S.) | 201-529-1111
www.riverpalm.com

It's not just steaks that are "always great" at this "classy" chophouse trio – fans like the "always fresh" seafood and sides too (even "outstanding" sushi at Edgewater and Mahwah), and the bartenders "can really pour a drink"; sure, an "old boys' club" vibe presides, and some gripe about "preference for regulars", but even with "long waits" and "special-occasion" prices, they're deemed "well worth it."

River Winds ❶ *American*

| 24 | 24 | 23 | $36 |

West Deptford | 1075 Riverwinds Dr. (Avocet Ln.) | 856-579-7900 |
www.theriverwindsrestaurant.com

A "pleasant surprise" on the banks of the Delaware River, this mid-priced West Deptford American serves "ample" portions of "great" seafood-focused fare in a "lovely" "country-club" setting at the edge of the RiverWinds Golf Course; a "thriving" bar offers extensive happy-hour specials, and fans say it's a "delightful" place to sit and "gaze toward Philadelphia."

	FOOD	DECOR	SERVICE	COST

Roberto's Dolce Vita *Italian*
▽ 23 | 19 | 22 | $39

Beach Haven | 12907 Long Beach Blvd. (Indiana Ave.) |
609-492-1001

"Classy dining at the Shore" defines this midpriced "red-sauce" Italian BYO where "traditional" fare has a "seaside flair"; while some find the decor a "little dated", a "lovely atmosphere" prevails, and with a staff that "make you feel welcome", fans call it a "special night out."

Robin's Nest *American*
24 | 23 | 23 | $28

Mount Holly | 2 Washington St. (White St.) | 609-261-6149 |
www.robinsnestmountholly.com

Fans give their "compliments to the chef" at this "lovely" Mount Holly American set in a historic Victorian overlooking the Mill Race Waterway, where the "delectable menu" "makes decisions difficult" and desserts are "out of this world"; the "homey" digs are "comfortable", tabs are "reasonable" and service is solid – in sum, "delightful."

Robongi *Japanese*
22 | 17 | 20 | $31

Hoboken | 520 Washington St. (bet. 5th & 6th Sts.) | 201-222-8388
Weehawken | Port Imperial Ferry Terminal | 4800 Port Imperial Blvd.
(Regency Pl.) | 201-558-1818
www.robongi.com

"Fresh sushi", an "interesting menu with lots of choices" and "good prices" keep this "very cool" Japanese duo "packed" with families, couples on "date nights" and others who appreciate the "nightlife vibe"; Hoboken means "fish netting decor" and BYO while the Weehawken outpost pours "awesome sake", and both locations boast outdoor dining in warm weather.

Rob's Bistro Ⓜ *French*
22 | 15 | 21 | $43

Madison | 75 Main St. (bet. Central & Greenwood Aves.) |
973-377-0067 | www.robsbistro.com

This "intimate" BYO storefront in Madison boasts "wonderful", "inventive" French bistro fare by chef-owner Rob Ubhaus; the vibe blends "just the right touch of casual and friendly" in the "simple" setting, and when you add "reasonable prices", you have the makings of a "neighborhood gem."

Rocca Ⓜ *Italian*
23 | 19 | 22 | $39

Glen Rock | 203 Rock Rd. (bet. Glen Ave. & Main St.) | 201-670-4945 |
www.roccaitalianrestaurant.com

"Everything is done with care" at this "classy", "innovative" BYO Italian in Glen Rock where the "menu doesn't disappoint", thanks to "some real wow" dishes served by a "pleasant", "helpful" staff; some find it "a little pricey" and the decor "lacking", but for others it's a "solid" choice in the "Jersey suburbs"; P.S. the neighboring Market at Rocca offers items to-go.

Rocky Hill Inn Ⓜ *American*
19 | 18 | 20 | $32

Rocky Hill | 137 Washington St. (Princeton Ave.) | 609-683-8930 |
www.rockyhilltavern.com

For "updated classics", "a variety of interesting dishes" and "excellent craft beers", this "small-town take on a gastropub" in Rocky Hill is a "relaxing", "homey standby" set in a historic Colonial inn well-suited to its American menu; service is "charming" and prices are "reasonable" (especially in the more casual tavern), and while a few dismiss it as "unexceptional", others consider it a "pleasure."

Rod's Steak & Seafood Grille *Seafood/Steak*

`22` `23` `22` `$48`

Morristown | Madison Hotel | 1 Convent Rd. (bet. Madison Ave. & Old Turnpike Rd.) | 973-539-6666 | www.rodssteak.com

The "old-world feel" of this Morristown fine-dining "landmark" lures with its "varied menu" of surf 'n' turf, "fabulous drinks" and a "great wine list" all served in a "plush" Victorian setting decked with "beautiful dark woods" and seating options that include restored Pullman cars; the staff is "well trained" and prices reflect the "classy" environs, and though some think it tries to be "fancier than it is", most still call it a "treat."

Rolling Pin Cafe 🗷 *American/Sandwiches*

`25` `20` `22` `$18`

Westwood | 341 Broadway (Westwood Ave.) | 201-666-4660 | www.therollingpincafe.com

Considered "a shrine" by locals, this "friendly" American BYO in Westwood serves up breakfast, tea and what many say is "the best lunch around" – think "off-the-charts" soups, "fresh salads", "delicious sandwiches" and "killer scones"; walls lined with vintage rolling pins make for a "quaint environment", but the "tiny gem" gets "crowded" so "get there early" or plan to "wait patiently", because it is "worth the wait."

Rooney's Oceanfront *Seafood*

`21` `21` `21` `$48`

Long Branch | 100 Ocean Ave. N. (Cooper Ave.) | 732-870-1200 | www.rooneysocean.com

The seafood is "fresh" and "satisfying" at this Long Branch seasider, but it's the "beautiful" ocean view, along with a "great wine menu" and live classic rock Fridays, that make it "almost too popular"; some find it "pricey", but the "pleasant" brunch buffet can seem a "bargain."

Roots Steakhouse *Steak*

`25` `24` `24` `$65`

Summit | 401 Springfield Ave. (Maple St.) | 908-273-0027
Morristown | 40 W. Park Pl. (Market St.) | 973-326-1800
www.rootssteakhouse.com

"Bustling" and "big-fisted", this duo of "classic", "clubby" chophouses in Summit and Morristown "does all the important things well", from "killer" steaks and "fabulous" shellfish to a "world-class wine list and terrific cocktails"; prices are "NYC"-"steep", and while the "fortysomethings"-filled bar can seem "like a mosh pit at peak hours", the "professional" staff helps to make dinner a more "civilized experience."

RosaLuca's Italian Bistro *Italian*

▽ `24` `21` `23` `$42`

Asbury | 1114 Rte. 173 (bet. Mine & Stortz Rds.) | 908-238-0018 | www.rosalucas.com

Fans of this "off-the-beaten"-path Italian in Asbury tout "consistently great", "authentic" fare that includes produce from the owners' garden, served "with a personal touch" by an "attentive", "friendly" staff; the "cheery" dining room rounds out what most agree is a "thoroughly enjoyable" experience.

Rosa Mexicano *Mexican*
| 22 | 22 | 21 | $39 |

Hackensack | Shops at Riverside | 390 Hackensack Ave. (Rte. 4) | 201-489-9100 | www.rosamexicano.com

"Nobody does fresh guacamole and pomegranate margaritas better" than this "lively" Hackensack outpost of the "NY staple" dishing out a "diverse menu" of "classy" Mexicana "with a twist"; the modern, haute-cantina digs are "fabulous" and an outdoor patio lures mall-goers thirsty for a post-shopping cocktail, while "friendly", "attentive" service helps ease the "sticker shock."

Rosemary & Sage Ⓢ Ⓜ *American*
| 24 | 21 | 22 | $54 |

Riverdale | 26 Hamburg Tpke. (bet. Haycock & Morris Aves.) | 973-616-0606 | www.rosemaryandsage.com

"Tucked away" in "sleepy Riverdale", this "family-run", "old-time favorite" boasts an "ever-changing" New American dinner menu of "well-prepared", "imaginative" dishes and "interesting specials" served by a "friendly" staff in "comfortable" (if "close") quarters; it's not cheap, but the five-course prix fixe dinner is a "bargain" and the "wine list is affordable", and most deem it a "special place" that's "well worth the trip"; P.S. open Wednesdays–Sundays only.

Rosie's Trattoria *Italian*
| 22 | 20 | 20 | $38 |

Randolph | 1181 Sussex Tpke. (Brookside Rd.) | 973-895-3434 | www.rosiestrattoria.com

For "fresh, tasty" fare, this Randolph Italian may be "a little out of the way", but regulars insist it's "worth the ride" for "dependable" eats, a "great" outdoor deck and an "always lively" bar; service can be "spotty" and the "decor could use an upgrade", but "all in all" it's a "good local place."

Royal Warsaw ●Ⓜ *Polish*
| 23 | 20 | 22 | $31 |

Elmwood Park | 871 River Dr. (bet. Garden Dr. & Roosevelt Ave.) | 201-794-9277 | www.royalwarsaw.com

It's like going "back to the old country" at this Elmwood Park Polish, thanks to "delicious, hearty portions" of "soul-soothing" "favorites", "pierogi like Nana's" and "terrific selections" of vodkas and beer; prices are "reasonable" and the service is "pleasant" – it's "always a great experience."

Rumba Cubana *Cuban*
| 22 | 21 | 21 | $22 |

NEW **North Bergen** | 1807 45th St. (Tonnelle Ave.) | 201-553-9100

North Bergen | 7420 Broadway (75th St.) | 201-854-4000 www.rumbacubanarestaurant.com

Rumba's Cafe *Cuban*

Jersey City | 513 Central Ave. (North St.) | 201-216-9655 | www.rumbascafe.com

"Like being on a cruise ship in the Caribbean", this "crowded, fun and inexpensive" Cuban trio in North Bergen and JC serves up *"excelente comida"*, "delish" sangria and "terrific" mojitos and margaritas in a "warm, family atmosphere"; service is "good" (speaking Spanish enhances the experience), and the brightly colored decor lends a tropical feel – it's "a great find."

Ruth's Chris Steak House *Steak*
25 | 23 | 24 | $64

Weehawken | Lincoln Harbor | 1000 Harbor Blvd. (19th St.) | 201-863-5100

Parsippany | Hilton Parsippany | 1 Hilton Ct. (Campus Dr.) | 973-889-1400

Atlantic City | The Walk | 2020 Atlantic Ave. (bet. Arkansas & Michigan Aves.) | 609-344-5833

Princeton | Princeton Forrestal Vill. | 2 Village Blvd. (College Rd.) | 609-452-0041

www.ruthschris.com

Carnivores love these chain chophouses for "tender", "fail-safe" steaks on signature "sizzling plates", and there's plenty for seafood lovers too (e.g. "spectacular" crab cakes); the ambiance is "classy", service is "attentive" and, sure, an "expense account" would help, but loyalists deem the experience "worth every cent."

Rutt's Hut ♇ *Hot Dogs*
21 | 13 | 18 | $12

Clifton | 417 River Rd. (bet. Delawanna Ave. & Peekay Dr.) | 973-779-8615

"Hallowed ground for frankophiles", this "fantastic old-school dive" is a "cheap," "cash-only" Clifton "institution" slinging "can't-beat rippers" (deep-fried hot dogs) along with "down-home" fries, burgers, "kick-ass" onion rings and cold brews for 85 years; while options include a bar and dining area, with "lackadaisical" service and a "never-left-the-1950s atmosphere", many get their order "travelin'" (to-go, don't you know).

The Ryland Inn *American*
25 | 24 | 24 | $80

Whitehouse | 115 Old Hwy. 28 (bet. Clark Ln. & Lamington Rd.) | 908-534-4011 | www.rylandinnnj.com

Chef Anthony Bucco (ex New Brunswick's Stage Left) is "breathing new life" into this "venerable" Whitehouse favorite that reopened in 2012 under new management, with "beautiful" American fare sourced from local farms and prepared "with an emphasis on creativity"; the thoroughly renovated 18th-century building affords "elegance" in a "country setting", while a "superb" tasting menu and "attentive" service help make it seem "worth every crazy penny."

Sabor *Nuevo Latino*
24 | 22 | 20 | $47

North Bergen | 8809 River Rd. (bet. Churchill & Old River Rds.) | 201-943-6366 | www.saborlatinbistro.com

"Dark, cozy and sultry" this "swanky" Nuevo Latino "hot spot" in North Bergen keeps the "vibe upbeat" with "authentic" eats like "to-die-for" pork shank, "outstanding" guac and "amazing" skirt steak washed down with "delicious" mojitos and "dangerous" sangria; service is "friendly", and while it's "quiet and pleasant" at lunch, dinner can get "noisy", plus a "fun crowd" comes out to dance on Thursday–Saturday nights.

	FOOD	DECOR	SERVICE	COST

Saddle River Inn 🖼️Ⓜ️ *American/French*   26 | 25 | 25 | $63

Saddle River | 2 Barnstable Ct. (Allendale Rd.) | 201-825-4016 |
www.saddleriverinn.com

"Always top of the class", this "elegant" "gem" in Saddle River is a
"longtime favorite" for "superb", "sophisticated" Americana with
"French flair"; the "cozy", "beautifully restored" barn makes for a
"warm, comfortable atmosphere", and service is "unbelievable",
and though all of this "charm" comes with "pricey" tabs, the BYO
policy helps keep things a bit more "affordable"; P.S. the scores may
not reflect a change in ownership in 2013.

Saffron *Indian*   21 | 19 | 20 | $27

East Hanover | 249 Rte. 10 E. (New Murray Rd.) | 973-599-0700 |
www.saffronnj.com

"Reliably good and authentic" Indian eats keep this East Hanover
strip-mall BYO "popular with locals" thanks to large portions of
"consistent", "tasty" fare, including "lots of vegetarian choices" and
a varied lunch buffet; decor is "a little more upscale" than the average joint, and though some think the service "needs some work",
"reasonable" prices and online coupons make it a "great place
for the family."

Sagami Japanese Restaurant Ⓜ️ *Japanese*   26 | 20 | 23 | $36

Collingswood | 37 W. Crescent Blvd. (bet. Haddon Ave. &
White Horse Pike) | 856-854-9773

"Simply the best" say fans of this Collingswood BYO Japanese,
"an old favorite" for "incredible", "authentic" cuisine – think
"excellent" sushi ,"fresh" sashimi and "delicious" udon; even
if some think the decor "needs sprucing up" and the main dining
room suffers from "short ceilings", the "superior food" is why you'll
"need a reservation."

Sage 🚫 *Mediterranean*   23 | 18 | 22 | $39

Ventnor | 5206 Atlantic Ave. (Weymouth Ave.) | 609-823-2110 |
www.sageventnor.com

"Well-prepared" Mediterranean fare is on order at this "great neighborhood BYO" in Ventnor City; though it's "away from the hubbub of
AC", the rustic Tuscan-inspired digs can get "noisy but tolerable",
and there are no complaints about the service; P.S. don't forget to
stop by the ATM, it only accepts cash.

Sakura *Japanese*   22 | 20 | 21 | $31

Parsippany | 949 Rte. 46 (Beverwyck Rd.) | 973-335-8818 |
www.sakuranj.com

Surf meets turf at this Parsippany Japanese adjacent to the
Ramada Limited where "excellent", "fresh fish" and "creative
rolls" satisfy sushi lovers and hibachi chefs put on a "great show"
for those who prefer their proteins cooked; groups, families and
couples laud the "friendly" staff and "pleasant" atmosphere –
and for those who say it's "too pricey to eat at regularly", the option
to "BYO is appreciated."

	FOOD	DECOR	SERVICE	COST

Sakura Bana ⓜ *Japanese* | 25 | 18 | 21 | $36 |

Ridgewood | 43 Franklin Ave. (Chestnut St.) | 201-447-6525 |
www.sakurabana.com

"A perennial favorite", this "busy, busy" Ridgewood BYO has been
luring locals with "can't-be-any-fresher", "top-notch sushi and
sashimi" and cooked "classic" Japanese dishes since 1984; while
there's not much in the way of atmosphere, the staff makes you "feel
like family", and if some find dinner "pricey", lunchtime bento boxes
are a "great value" – either way, most think the tabs are "worth it."

Salt Creek Grille *American* | 21 | 22 | 21 | $43 |

Rumson | 4 Bingham Ave. (River Rd.) | 732-933-9272
Princeton | Forrestal Village Shopping Ctr. | 1 Rockingham Row
(Village Blvd.) | 609-419-4200
www.saltcreekgrille.com

High ceilings, wooden beams and fire pits set the scene for "laid-
back" "fun" at these American grills serving "solid" (if a "bit
pricey") meat-centric "comfort food"; there's live music weekends at the Princeton outpost, while Rumson offers a "beautiful"
river view, and a "lively", "loud" bar scene attracts a "young" crowd
at both locations.

Salt Gastro Pub ⓜ *American* | 22 | 18 | 20 | $32 |

Stanhope | 109 Rte. 206 (bet. Acorn & Ash Sts.) | 973-347-7258 |
www.saltgastropub.com

Presented by the folks behind the former Bula, this community-
minded, "casual" gastropub in Stanhope boasts an "eclectic menu"
of "darn delicious", locally focused American grub and a "great beer
selection"; with "entertaining", "'60s throwback decor" and "interesting" music on weekends, it's a "lively" "must-stop" – especially
for the "young" and "tattooed."

Salute Brick Oven Bistro ⓜ *Italian* | 22 | 20 | 20 | $37 |

Montclair | 173 Glen Ridge Ave. (Willow St.) | 973-746-2380 |
www.salutebistro.com

Italian "comfort food with an upscale twist" is on the menu at this
"lively" Montclair BYO where the "well-prepared" "inventive" eats
include "interesting specials"; a "friendly" staff presides over the
rustic Tuscan farmhouse–inspired space, but some caution it can
get "painfully loud", so either opt for "outdoor seating in season"
or "forget quiet conversation and just enjoy the food."

Samba Montclair ⓩ *Brazilian* | - | - | - | M |

Montclair | 7 Park St. (Rte. 506) | 973-744-6764 |
www.montclairsamba.com

Don't expect to find a churrascario at this midpriced Montclair BYO
Brazilian from restaurateur Ilson Goncalves (ex Blu, Next Door),
which serves authentic comfort food from southern Brazil, including
dishes such as bobó de camarão (yuca pureé with shrimp and rice)
and feijoada (black bean stew, available Fridays and Saturdays
only); antiques hanging on the walls and vintage tableware give a

rustic feel to the small, high-ceilinged space, which is supplemented by limited sidewalk seating.

Samdan *Turkish*

21 | 17 | 20 | $37

Cresskill | 178 Piermont Rd. (Union Ave.) | 201-816-7343 | www.samdanrestaurant.com

A "longtime classic" appealing to "young and old" alike, this "reliable" Cresskill Turk turns out "huge portions" of kebabs "cooked to perfection", "interesting" breads and more; a staff that "knows the menu" and "reasonable prices" help distract from a "sparse" dining room some say "needs updating", but quiet conditions make it "a dependable spot for a leisurely meal."

Sam Mickail's CUT Steakhouse 🏷 Ⓜ *Steak*

- | - | - | VE

West Orange | 4Sixty6 | 466 Prospect Ave. (Rooney Circle) | 973-474-9896 | www.4sixty6.com

Located on the second floor of West Orange's 4Sixty6 nightclub, this modern steakhouse from chef Sam Mickail serves up a Med-accented menu of dry-aged steaks, signature rack of lamb, seafood and more in a swanky setting complete with chandelier, club chairs and silver-foil ceiling; a sophisticated wine list and handcrafted cocktails complete the pricey picture.

Sammy's Ye Old Cider Mill *Steak*

23 | 14 | 18 | $60

Mendham | 353 Mendham Rd. W. (Oak Knoll Rd.) | 973-543-7675 | www.sammyscidermill.com

"If the Soup Nazi ran a steakhouse", it would resemble the "shtick" of this "pricey" former speakeasy in Mendham where you order upon entering and drink in the "'70s rec room" basement bar until your "huge steaks", "luscious lobsters" and "great french fries" are served at picnic tables in the "bingo hall"–meets-"cafeteria" upstairs; while fans think the "ridiculous waits" and "general pandemonium" are part of the "charm", some "just don't get it."

Sanducci's Trattoria *Italian*

19 | 19 | 19 | $30

River Edge | 620 Kinderkamack Rd. (Van Buren Ave.) | 201-599-0600 | www.sanduccis.com

"Terrific portions" of "solid" Italian "comfort food" make for a "family atmosphere" at this River Edge "neighborhood" "standby" where *amici* say the fare isn't fancy, but "some nights that's just the ticket"; the staff is "friendly" and though the faux-Tuscan farmhouse-like digs can get crowded, "reasonable" prices and a "bargain" lunch buffet help compensate.

San Remo *Italian*

22 | 15 | 20 | $36

Shrewsbury | 37 E. Newman Springs Rd. (Rte. 35) | 732-345-8200 | www.sanremoitaliana.com

Shrewsbury locals seek out this "hidden gem" for "interesting" Italian eats served by a "pleasant" staff; though some suggest "the digs could use some more spice", at least the BYO policy "keeps the price reasonable."

	FOOD	DECOR	SERVICE	COST

Sanzari's New Bridge Inn *Italian*   21 | 22 | 22 | $48

New Milford | 105 Old New Bridge Rd. (New Bridge Rd.) |
201-692-7700 | www.sanzarisnewbridgeinn.com

You'll find "old-world charm" in a "lovely setting" at this "cozy" New
Milford Italian where "lots of options" make for an "enjoyable dining" experience; seating includes a barroom with a "nice fireplace"
and a more formal, "quiet" dining room – either way, the staff is
"nice and helpful", and if some find it "pricey", the Sunday night
prix fixe dinner is a "bargain."

Sapori *Italian*   25 | 22 | 23 | $44

Collingswood | 601 Haddon Ave. (Harvard Ave.) | 856-858-2288 |
www.sapori.info

With "single-minded dedication", chef-owner Franco Lombardo's
Italian BYO "tops all the others" in Collingswood thanks to "terrific"
à la carte offerings and a prix fixe tasting menu, all "wonderfully
prepared" with "incredible fresh, authentic ingredients"; stone-
accented walls create a rustic feel, and the staff is "friendly" and
"knowledgeable" – good thing when there are so many "interesting,
innovative" daily specials to describe.

Satis Ⓜ *European*   24 | 22 | 23 | $49

Jersey City | 212 Washington St. (Sussex St.) | 201-435-5151 |
www.satisbistro.com

A "hidden gem" in Jersey City's Paulus Hook, this bi-level modern
European offers "fine-dining quality" in a "relaxed cafe atmosphere",
with "top-notch food", a salumeria and a "terrific" wine bar; set in a
"charming" brownstone sporting exposed-brick walls, a marble bar,
tile floors and a warm-weather patio, the feel is decidedly "old world" –
add a "knowledgeable" staff that makes you "feel at home" and you
know why many say it's "worth the drive from anywhere."

Savini *Italian*   21 | 21 | 21 | $50

Allendale | 168 W. Crescent Ave. (Hamilton St.) | 201-760-3700 |
www.savininj.com

"Old-world Italian" in a "lovely atmosphere" makes this "comfortable" Allendale "standby" a "go-to" for "well-prepared"
dishes that are perhaps "not innovative" but help make for a
"pleasant" meal; service is "attentive", and while tabs are a "bit
pricey", *The Real Housewives of New Jersey* types at the "lively bar"
prove to be "very entertaining."

Scalini Fedeli Ⓢ *Italian*   27 | 24 | 25 | $73

Chatham | 63 Main St. (bet. Parrott Mill Rd. & Tallmadge Ave.) |
973-701-9200 | www.scalinifedeli.com

What "white-linen Italian should be", this Chatham "special-occasion
destination" from chef Michael Cetrulo is "excellent from start to
finish", with "beautiful presentations" of "creative, delicious" dishes,
"top-notch" service and "elegant" Tuscan decor in an 18th-century
farmhouse; not surprisingly, all this "refinement" is "expensive", but
BYO on weeknights sans corkage "helps to keep the cost down";
P.S. dinner is prix fixe only.

	FOOD	DECOR	SERVICE	COST

Scarborough Fair Ⓜ *American* | 20 | 21 | 21 | $42 |

Sea Girt | 1414 Meetinghouse Rd. (bet. Bernadette Ct. & Rte. 35) | 732-223-6658 | www.scarboroughfairrestaurant.com

Set in an "appealing" 19th-century farmhouse with high ceilings and private alcoves, this "romantic" Sea Girt "hideout" offers "intimate" dining suitable for "special occasions"; the "delicious" seafood-focused New American fare is "presented beautifully", and servers "never rush", making for a "relaxing" meal.

Seabra's Marisqueira *Portuguese/Seafood* | 24 | 18 | 21 | $35 |

Newark | 87 Madison St. (bet. Ferry & Lafayette Sts.) | 973-465-1250 | www.seabrasmarisqueira.com

A "seafood heaven" is what fans call this Portuguese seafooder in Newark Ironbound, where the "food is terrific and authentic" and there's "plenty of it", including octopus that's "done right" and "killer seasonal specials"; the "small", casual storefront sports tiled walls and a bar that reminds some of a "diner", but the service is "friendly and helpful" and tabs are reasonable – "you are in for a treat."

Sea Grass *American* | 24 | 21 | 22 | $36 |

Ocean Grove | 68 Main Ave. (bet. New York Ave. & Pilgrim Pathway) | 732-869-0770 | www.seagrassnj.com

The "seafood-driven" menu also includes "plenty of choices for meat lovers" at this contemporary Ocean Grove American; though the "nautical" decor may not impress, an "outgoing" staff adds to the "lively vibe" (some warn that it "can be noisy"), and BYO helps keep costs "acceptable."

The Sea Grill *Seafood/Steak* | ▽ 21 | 20 | 20 | $43 |

Avalon | 225 21st St. (bet. Dune & Ocean Drs.) | 609-967-5511 | www.seagrillrestaurant.com

Fans laud the "great concept" of this Avalon surf 'n' turfer where you "select your meat or fish" and "tell the chef how you want it cooked", then "help yourself" to the salad bar; the digs are basic and service is largely DIY, and while it's not cheap, most have "no complaints."

Sear House ❶ *Steak* | ▽ 23 | 26 | 21 | $68 |

Closter | 411 Piermont Rd. (bet. Alpine Dr. & Auryansen Ct.) | 201-292-4612 | www.searhouse.com

For "NYC ambiance", there's "no need to cross the bridge", thanks to this "gorgeous", two-story Closter steakhouse where gleaming woods, a Zen-like water feature, "elegant booths" and a "cozy lounge" draw an "upscale clientele" for "great steaks" chops and seafood; thoughts on service range from "incredible" to "subpar", but all agree it's "very expensive" – good thing the early dinner prix fixe special is "a deal."

Seasons 52 *American* | 24 | 24 | 23 | $36 |

Cherry Hill | Cherry Hill Mall | 2000 Rte. 38 (Mall Dr.) | 856-665-1052 | www.seasons52.com

"As the seasons change, so does the menu" at this Cherry Hill link of a "well-priced" national chain where the "sensible portions" of "healthy", "flavorful" and local New American eats – including "signature" flatbreads and "incredible" mini-desserts – come in at under 475 calories; the staff is "helpful and enthusiastic", and the airy, "modern" space boasts a "beautiful piano bar" and outdoor patio – add an "amazing wine list" and you have a "wonderful dining experience."

Sebastian's The Steakhouse ⊠ *Steak*

24	22	22	$56

Morristown | 80 Elm St. (Blachley Pl.) | 973-539-8545 | www.sebastiansthesteakhouse.com

"Much more than a steakhouse", this "hidden gem" in Morristown offers an "interesting menu" of "excellent" prime meats, seafood and Italian-accented specials in a "lovely", historic two-story space with exposed-brick walls, warm woods and alfresco seating; the servers "knows their stuff", and while it's "not inexpensive", many tout it as a "quiet alternative" to the "pick-up scene Downtown."

Segovia *Portuguese/Spanish*

22	16	20	$39

Moonachie | 150 Moonachie Rd. (Maple St.) | 201-641-4266 | www.segoviarestaurant.com

"Delish", "garlicky" Iberian cooking "wakes up the senses" at this Moonachie stalwart where the "spectacular" portions are "easily shared" – and an "excellent value"; "friendly" service is another reason there's "always a crowd", but given the "cramped" seating, just don't be surprised to "hear the next table chewing their food."

Segovia Steakhouse & Seafood *Spanish/Steak*

22	19	20	$46

Little Ferry | 217 Main St. (Vogt Ln.) | 201-814-1100 | www.segoviasteakhouse.com

Little Ferry locals say "you can't beat" the "tasty steaks" and other "decent" eats at this white-tablecloth Spanish chophouse that might be "prettier" than its nearby sibling, Segovia, but its portions are just as "huge"; "crowded" conditions are mitigated by "competitive pricing" and "soft-spoken" service that make it a "reliable" option for a "nice business dinner."

Señorita's Mexican Grill ❶ *Mexican*

19	18	18	$26

Bloomfield | 285 Glenwood Ave. (bet. Bloomfield Ave. & Conger St.) | 973-743-0099
Clark | Hyatt Hills Golf Complex | 1300 Raritan Rd. (bet. Central & Walnut Aves.) | 732-669-9024
www.senoritasmexicangrill.com

Insiders expect "dependable Mexican food and drinks" at these affordable siblings, though some say service can be "random"; you can catch the game on flat-screen TVs in "sports-bar areas" that supplement the "funky", colorful dining rooms, and the Clark location also features "terrific" outdoor seating "next to a golf course."

Serenade *French*

26	25	25	$75

Chatham | 6 Roosevelt Ave. (Main St.) | 973-701-0303 | www.restaurantserenade.com

Offering a "civilized dining experience", this "high-end" Chatham destination "deserves all the accolades" for its "creative presentations" of "phenomenal" French cuisine and "extensive" wine list; though "pants with deep pockets are suggested" given the "expensive" tabs, the "quiet", "romantic" ambiance and "first-class" service make it many diners' "go-to for special occasions."

Sergeantsville Inn Ⓜ *American* | 23 | 24 | 21 | $51 |

Sergeantsville | 601 Rosemont Ringoes Rd. (Stockton Flemington Rd.) | 609-397-3700 | www.sergeantsvilleinn.com

From the "quaint, romantic dining room" to the "cozy" bar, this "charming" Sergeantsville American has "so much atmosphere", thanks to its setting in a "lovely, historic stone building"; "gourmet" fare (including "many game entrees") and "warm, attentive" service make it feel like a "getaway" that justifies the "special-occasion" prices.

Sette Ⓩ *Italian* | 23 | 20 | 22 | $48 |

Bernardsville | 7 Mine Brook Rd. (bet. Mt. Airy Rd. & Quimby Ln.) | 908-502-5054 | www.settecucina.com

The "well-thought-out", "expertly prepared" cuisine wins "raves" at this Bernardsville Italian where a "welcoming" staff is happy to "accommodate", and BYO keeps down slightly "pricey" tabs; since there are "just a few seats" in the "intimate", earth-toned space, *amici* advise "be sure to have a reservation."

Shanghai Jazz Ⓜ *Asian* | 22 | 21 | 23 | $45 |

Madison | 24 Main St. (bet. Central Ave. & Community Pl.) | 973-822-2899 | www.shanghaijazz.com

"Savory", "upscale" Asian fare is served "with a side of jazz" at this "unique" Madison "gem" where "tastefully done" performances from "big-name artists" put it "over the top"; despite "tight quarters" and "high prices" (there's no cover charge but food and drink minimums vary), the "welcoming" service and "lively crowd" can make for a "great night out."

Shipwreck Grill *American/Seafood* | 24 | 19 | 21 | $54 |

Brielle | 720 Ashley Ave. (Rte. 35) | 732-292-9380 | www.shipwreckgrill.com

"Fresh fish is what it's all about" at this Brielle American seafooder boasting "a diverse and sophisticated menu" of "stellar" swimmers and "wonderful" crustaceans plus "perfect" sirloins and filets; service is "attentive", and the "friendly" bar draws "lots of locals" and singles – just be prepared for "stadium-level" noise and "NY prices."

Shogun *Japanese/Steak* | 21 | 19 | 20 | $33 |

East Brunswick | Route 18 Shopping Ctr. | 1020 Rte. 18 N. (bet. Gunia & Main Sts.) | 732-390-1922 | www.shogun18.net
Green Brook | 166 Rte. 22 (bet. Andrew St. & Washington Ave.) | 732-968-3330 | www.shogun22.net
Kendall Park | 3376 Rte. 27 (Sand Hills Rd.) | 732-422-1117 | www.shogun27.com
Toms River | 1536 N. Bay Ave. (Oak Ave.) | 732-286-9888 | www.shogunbeylea.com

(continued)

Shogun Legends *Japanese/Steak*

Wall | 1969 Rte. 34 S. (bet. Allaire & Allenwood Rds.) | 732-449-6696 | www.shogunlegends.com

The "show is what draws the customers" at these "entertaining", teppanyaki-style Japanese steakhouses; even if the decor gets mixed marks and service is just "ok", "solid" eats and moderate prices make for a "fun night out", especially "with a group."

Shumi ⓜ *Japanese*
27 | 16 | 22 | $48

Somerville | 30 S. Doughty Ave. (Veterans Memorial Dr.) | 908-526-8596

"Snag a seat at the convivial bar" and join the "devoted patrons" of this "top-notch" Somerville sushi specialist where the chef is "dedicated to his craft and it shows" in the "quality and freshness" of every morsel; while the no-frills space is in a somewhat "bizarre location" ("one challenge: find it"), and tabs aren't cheap, BYO is a plus and fans say it's "definitely worth the trip."

Siam Garden *Thai*
22 | 21 | 20 | $32

Red Bank | The Galleria | 2 Bridge Ave. (Front St.) | 732-224-1233 | www.siamgardenrestaurant.com

"Busy with loyal locals", this Red Bank BYO dishes up "well-prepared", "authentic" Thai cuisine that's full of "interesting spices"; while service gets mixed marks, "exotic" imported artwork and antiques create a "lovely" atmosphere that's matched by "decent" prices.

Silk Road ⓜ *Afghan*
24 | 20 | 23 | $29

Warren | Village Square Mall | 41 Mountain Blvd. (Primrose Way) | 908-561-8288 | www.silkroadrestaurant.org

"Sublime hand-pulled bread", "moist, tender" kebabs and other "flavorful" Afghan treats are served in "exotically decorated" surrounds reminiscent of a "foreign land" at this "well-priced" Warren BYO; "charmed" devotees appreciate the "warm welcome" from a staff that "works hard to please its patrons."

Simply Vietnamese *Vietnamese*
24 | 14 | 21 | $29

Tenafly | 1 Highwood Ave. (Riveredge Rd.) | 201-568-7770 | www.simplyvietnamese.com

"Large portions" of "light, tasty" Vietnamese fare "attract a savvy crowd of Asian food–lovers" to this midpriced Tenafly BYO staffed by a "helpful" crew; even if there's "not much atmosphere" in the "simple", "unpretentious" storefront setting, insiders say the "food is the reason to go."

Sirena Ristorante *Italian*
22 | 24 | 20 | $53

Long Branch | Pier Vill. | 27 Ocean Ave. (Melrose Terr.) | 732-222-1119 | www.sirenaristorante.com

The "spectacular" "view makes it" say fans of this upscale, oceanfront Italian in Long Branch's Pier Village offering a "well-executed", "varied menu" and "great wine list" in "beautiful" airy digs; while some find it "a bit pricey" and the service "spotty", the "lovely setting" helps ensure it's "always a delight."

	FOOD	DECOR	SERVICE	COST

Siri's Thai French Cuisine Ⓜ *French/Thai* | 24 | 20 | 22 | $36 |

Cherry Hill | 2117 Rte. 70 W. (bet. Beideman & Washington Aves.) | 856-663-6781 | www.siris-nj.com

An "interesting fusion" of Thai and French flavors "tempts the palate" at this "delightful find" in a Cherry Hill strip mall that "defies expectations"; a few grumble about the "outdated" decor, but for loyalists, the "friendly, helpful" service, moderate tabs and BYO contribute to a "pleasant dining experience."

Skylark ❶ *Diner/Eclectic* | 21 | 21 | 20 | $25 |

Edison | 17 Wooding Ave. (Rte. 1) | 732-777-7878 | www.skylarkdiner.com

Skylark on the Hudson *Diner/Eclectic*

Jersey City | 25 River Dr. S. (Town Square Pl.) | 201-533-8989 | www.skylarkonthehudson.com

With a "souped-up" menu that's "more gourmet" than expected, plus a full bar, an interior from *"The Jetsons"* at Edison and Manhattan views at JC, this "upscale" Eclectic duo is "not the typical diner"; service can be "dicey" and a few feel it's "overpriced", but after sundown, it takes on a "nightclub feel" that makes for a "unique experience."

Small World Coffee *Coffeehouse* | 23 | 20 | 22 | $12 |

Princeton | 14 Witherspoon St. (bet. Lincoln Hwy. & Spring St.) | 609-924-4377

Princeton | 254 Nassau St. (Pine St.) | 609-924-4377

www.smallworldcoffee.com

A "knowledgeable" staff serves up "terrific coffee", "beautiful, tasty pastries", wraps and other inexpensive treats at this "funky", "fast-paced" coffee shop duo in Princeton; adorned with local art, the compact spaces can get "crowded", but if you manage to "grab a table", insiders say "just sitting there among Princeton U. students makes you feel smart."

NEW Smashburger *Burgers* | 20 | 17 | 19 | $13 |

East Brunswick | 591 Rte. 18 S. (Summerhill Rd.) | 732-387-2620

North Brunswick | North Village Shopping Ctr. | 975 Rte. 1 S. (Aaron Rd.) | 732-275-8177

Glassboro | 698 N. Delsea Dr. (William L. Dalton Dr.) | 856-229-9393 www.smashburger.com

"A refreshing take on the burger joint", these links of a Denver-based chain dish up "delish", "customizable" patties with a "wide variety" of gourmet toppings, plus "superb seasoned fries", "filling" shakes and more; expect "reasonable" tabs and "quick" service amid a "plain", "modern" setting.

Smithville Inn *American* | 22 | 23 | 23 | $40 |

Smithville | 1 N. New York Rd. (bet. Moss Mill & Old New York Rds.) | 609-652-7777 | www.smithvilleinn.com

Set in an 18th-century inn overlooking a "beautiful" lake and garden, this "lovely", "upscale" "old-style American" in Smithville retains its "original historic charm"; the "polished" staff serves "large portions" of "consistently good" comfort classics, and a "fantastic brunch" fuels visitors for a Sunday stroll through the "quaint" surrounding village.

| | FOOD | DECOR | SERVICE | COST |

Smitty's Clam Bar ⊠Ⓜ *Seafood* — 23 | 16 | 22 | $22

Somers Point | 910 Bay Ave. (Annie Ave.) | 609-927-8783
A "lively crowd" is content to "wait forever" – BYO beers in hand –
for a seat at this Somers Point waterfront clam "shack" serving up
"affordable" fresh fish "without the frills" and signature chowder;
even if there's "no decor to speak of", the "charming" "Shore-town"
vibe is hard to beat, and fans say "summer's not complete" without
a meal here.

Sol-Mar Restaurant ❶ *Portuguese/Seafood* — 24 | 20 | 23 | $38
(aka Vila Nova do Sol-Mar)

Newark | 267 Ferry St. (Niagara St.) | 973-344-3041 |
www.solmar-restaurant.com
Expect "generous portions" of "quality" Portuguese cooking (especially "just-out-of-the-net" seafood) at this moderately priced
Newark "stalwart" where an "attentive" staff ensures a "relaxing" experience; the old world–inspired "fancy restaurant side"
is complemented by an "easygoing" bar area where you can "ab-
sorb the local flavor."

Solo Bella *Italian* — 23 | 20 | 20 | $31

Jackson | 426 Chandler Rd. (Jackson Mills Rd.) | 732-961-0951 |
www.solobella.com
"Great brick-oven pizza", pastas with "freshly prepared sauces" and
other "quality" Italian dishes are a "good value" at this "busy" Jackson
BYO; the staff is "eager to please" but sometimes it can get "overwhelmed" when the wood-accented room gets "crowded" and "loud."

So Moon Nan Jip ❶ *Korean* — 24 | 15 | 19 | $34

Palisades Park | 238 Broad Ave. (Brinkerhoff Ave.) | 201-944-3998
"Real Korean BBQ" is "cooked in front of you" at this midpriced
Palisades Park hangout; insiders say "you don't go for the decor or
service", and it can be "hard to get in", but the reward is "as good as
any restaurant in Koreatown in NYC"; P.S. it's open until 3 AM.

Son Cubano ❶ *Cuban* — 20 | 25 | 20 | $56

West New York | 40-4 Riverwalk Pl. (Port Imperial Blvd.) |
201-399-2020 | www.soncubanonj.com
Manhattan views that "cannot be beat" lure "crowds" of "pretty
people" to this waterfront West New York cousin of an NYC Cuban;
service is solid and the fare's "delicious", but most agree it com-
mands "hefty" prices for its "sexy", "swanky" scene, which includes
live Latin music on the weekends.

Sono Sushi *Japanese* — 26 | 20 | 23 | $35

Middletown | Village Mall | 1098 Rte. 35 S. (bet. New Monmouth Rd. &
Penelope Ln.) | 732-706-3588 | www.sonosushi.net
Fans attest to the "enduring quality" of this Middletown Japanese's
"fresh, flavorful" sushi and "authentic" cooked fare, which makes up
for "strip-mall surroundings" and digs that some find "dated"; "reasonable" prices, a BYO policy, "charming hospitality" and a "kid-
friendly" vibe are further reasons it's been "here for so many years."

	FOOD	DECOR	SERVICE	COST

Sophie's Bistro ⓜ *French*
23 | 20 | 23 | $40

Somerset | 700 Hamilton St. (bet. Douglas & Matilda Aves.) | 732-545-7778 | www.sophiesbistro.net

From "outstanding onion soup" to "falling-off-the-bone lamb shank", this "charming find" in Somerset offers "flavorful" French "comfort food done right"; "attentive", "welcoming" service in "lovely" surrounds makes it a "go-to for a romantic dinner."

Sorrento ⓜ *Italian*
23 | 21 | 21 | $48

East Rutherford | 132 Park Ave. (bet. 1st & 2nd Sts.) | 201-507-0093

A staff that "makes you feel at home" delivers "thoughtfully prepared" traditional fare at this East Rutherford Italian, and BYO helps offset "high" prices ("a real plus"); upholstered seats and hardwood floors accent the "beautiful" dining room, though regulars warn that weekends can get "noisy when crowded."

Spain *Portuguese/Spanish*
22 | 18 | 21 | $39

Newark | 419 Market St. (Raymond Blvd.) | 973-344-0994 | www.spainrestaurant.com

"Superb seafood and steaks" are a "treat" on the "extensive" menu at this "reasonably priced" Ironbound Iberian; while a few feel the "kitschy" traditional setting could use a "renovation", most appreciate the "friendly" service and "inviting" vibe that makes it "fun with a group", and "large portions" mean "no one ever leaves hungry."

Spain 92 *Spanish*
21 | 21 | 22 | $36

Raritan | 1116 Hwy. 202 S. (Vones Ln.) | 908-704-9292 | www.spain92.com

"Plentiful" portions of "tasty paella" and other "authentic" Spanish dishes, backed by "wonderful" sangria, are a "good value" at this Raritan stalwart; "attentive" service and warm wood accents in the white-tablecloth dining room create a "happy" atmosphere, but insiders especially "recommend visiting on one of the special entertainment nights", which often feature live music.

Spanish Manor *Portuguese/Spanish*
∇ 25 | 19 | 22 | $26

Newark | 246 Heller Pkwy. (6th St.) | 973-481-2500 | www.thespanishmanor.com

Expect big portions of "great" Iberian fare for a "reasonable price" at this "must-try" stalwart in Newark; fans who've "been eating here for years" say the welcoming service and spacious, "party"-friendly digs make for a "relaxing" experience.

Spanish Pavillion *Spanish*
23 | 21 | 23 | $38

Harrison | 31 Harrison Ave. (Dey St.) | 973-485-7750 | www.spanishpavillion.com

"Abundant" servings of "reliable" Spanish cuisine washed down with "fabulous" sangria merit "repeat visits" say loyalists of this Harrison "standby" featuring a mahogany bar and an "outdoor patio for the summer months"; service that "makes you feel like family" rounds out a "great deal for the money."

| | FOOD | DECOR | SERVICE | COST |

Spanish Tavern *Spanish*

| 22 | 19 | 21 | $40 |

Mountainside | 1239 Rte. 22 E. (Locust Ave.) | 908-232-2171
Newark | 103 McWhorter St. (Green St.) | 973-589-4959
www.spanishtavern.com

The "hearty Spanish specialties" include "fresh-off-the-boat" sea-food and "terrific" paella at these "festive" siblings in Mountainside and Newark; some say the decor "needs updating", and "enormous crowds" are to be expected, but factoring in "pleasant" service, "reasonable" tabs and "excellent sangria" to boot, most deem it a "worthwhile dining experience."

Spargo's Grille Ⓜ *American*

| 22 | 19 | 21 | $41 |

Manalapan | Andee Plaza | 130 Rte. 33 W. (Millhurst Rd.) | 732-294-9921 | www.spargosgrille.com

An "attentive" staff serves up "clever New American cuisine" show-casing the "creativity in the kitchen" at this Manalapan BYO; regulars say "don't be fooled by the strip-mall location" or discouraged by tabs that are "a little on the pricey side" – early-bird specials and multicourse tasting menus are worthy of "a special night out."

Spice Thai Cuisine Ⓜ *Thai*

| ▽ 24 | 21 | 22 | $27 |

Bloomfield | 26 Belleville Ave. (Willet St.) | 973-748-0056 | www.spicethainj.com

The "delicious" Thai cooking is "absolutely authentic in spice and presentation" boast boosters of this moderately priced Bloomfield BYO; though the "small", "simple" space "can get too crowded on busy nights", "solicitous" service helps smooth things over.

Spike's *Seafood*

| 21 | 13 | 18 | $29 |

Point Pleasant Beach | 415 Broadway (Channel Dr.) | 732-295-9400

"Fresh fish, right off the boat", chowders that "should not be missed" and other "simple", "tasty" seafood dishes served in "huge portions" lure "locals" to this "friendly", midpriced BYO in Point Pleasant Beach; the "shack" is "really just a fish market with a few tables", so you can always buy the daily catch and "take it home to cook."

Spuntino Wine Bar & Italian Tapas ❶ *Italian*

| - | - | - | I |

Clifton | Clifton Commons | 70 Kingsland Rd. (bet. River Rd. & Walnut St.) | 973-661-2435 | www.spuntinowinebar.com

Italian nibbles like bruschetta, homemade meatballs and thin-crust pizzas pair with an all-Boot wine list, including 42 by the glass, at this casual Clifton small-plates specialist; an open kitchen and illu-minated wine racks add interest to the rustic, spacious dining room, though you can also snag a seat at the sleek, marble-topped bar.

Squan Tavern Ⓜ *Italian*

| 20 | 17 | 20 | $29 |

Manasquan | 15 Broad St. (bet. Beams Terr. & Main St.) | 732-223-3324 | www.squantavern.com

"Ample" portions of "stick-to-your-ribs" Southern Italian fare and "wonderful, filling" pizzas pack 'em in to this long-standing Manasquan "mainstay"; some suggest the "casual", dark-wood decor "needs a redo", but that doesn't deter "locals" who praise the "neighborhood bar feel" and "moderate pricing."

Sri Thai *Thai*

22	15	19	$23

Hoboken | 234 Bloomfield St. (3rd St.) | 201-798-4822 | www.srithaihoboken.com

This Hoboken Thai BYO will "restore your faith in good pad Thai", with "spicy" traditional fare at modest prices; "seating is close" in the "tiny", "dated" space, but "the food makes up for it", and many report "good experiences" with the "quick delivery."

Stage House *American*

20	19	19	$38

Scotch Plains | 366 Park Ave. (bet. Front St. & Mountain Ave.) | 908-322-4224 | www.stagehousetavern.com

"Reasonable" tabs are a draw at this Scotch Plains American serving a "straightforward" menu of steaks, seafood and plenty of "pub grub–type food"; set in a "historic, rustic" stagecoach stop, it has a "sedate", "Colonial feel" complemented by a "lively" (and "often loud") tavern plus a "huge outdoor patio" that's "packed" in the summer months.

Stage Left *American*

25	23	25	$69

New Brunswick | 5 Livingston Ave. (George St.) | 732-828-4444 | www.stageleft.com

The "industrious" staff has a "knack" for getting you to performances "on time" at this "sophisticated" New Brunswick "go-to" convenient to the State Theater, where a "wide-ranging yet accessible wine list" accompanies the "delicious" New American fare; while "pricey", fans insist it's "worth every penny" for a "special occasion", and the "mouthwatering burger" makes dining at the bar an appealing "casual option."

Stamna Greek Taverna *Greek*

24	18	21	$32

Bloomfield | 1045 Broad St. (bet. Johnson & Watchung Aves.) | 973-338-5151

NEW **Little Falls** | 66 E. Main St. (bet. Turnberry Rd. & Van Ness Ave.) | 973-256-6400

www.stamnataverna.com

"Fresh fish" and "fall-off-the-bone" lamb shine on the "authentic" Greek menu at this "fairly priced" BYO pair in Bloomfield and Little Falls, but be sure to "save room for homemade dessert" too; despite "sometimes long waits" in a "hole-in-the-wall" setting with "tightly packed" tables, there's a "warm atmosphere" enhanced by a staff that "tries to please."

Steakhouse 85 *Steak*

24	22	23	$65

New Brunswick | 85 Church St. (bet. George & Neilson Sts.) | 732-247-8585 | www.steakhouse85.com

While "juicy" steaks are the specialty of this "special-occasion steakhouse" in New Brunswick, it also offers "excellent" seafood, all delivered by an "attentive", "professional" staff in "lovely", "classy" environs; "eye-popping" prices don't deter carnivores seeking "something special", and the Friday night prix fixe dinner for two "cannot be beat" for "good value."

	FOOD	DECOR	SERVICE	COST

Stella Marina *Italian*
23 | 22 | 19 | $49

Asbury Park | 800 Ocean Ave. (Asbury Ave.) | 732-775-7776 | www.stellamarinarestaurant.com

"Amazing views of the ocean", "better-than-average" Italian cuisine and a "great wine list" are the draws at this "hot spot" on the Asbury Park boardwalk; opinions are divided on the service ("friendly" vs. "spotty"), and the "lively" bar scene and "hip" vibe can sometimes translate into "noise", but most insist "you can never go wrong" here.

Steve & Cookie's By the Bay *American*
27 | 24 | 25 | $53

Margate | 9700 Amherst Ave. (Monroe Ave.) | 609-823-1163 | www.steveandcookies.com

Fans attest "quality is everything" at Cookie Till's "legendary" Margate New American where "well-trained" servers offer "on-target sugges-tions" from the menu of "excellent" locally sourced fare and "exten-sive wine list"; the mood is "upbeat" in the multiroom space that's usually packed with an "'in' crowd", which is why regulars recom-mend "reservations in the summer and on weekends year-round."

St. Eve's Ⓜ *American*
23 | 22 | 22 | $53

Ho-Ho-Kus | 611 N. Maple Ave. (Brookside Ave.) | 201-857-4717 | www.stevesnj.com

A "thoughtful", "attentive" staff delivers "imaginative" New American dishes amid "tasteful", wood-accented surrounds at this Ho-Ho-Kus BYO; it can get "a bit noisy" and some say it's "expensive for the quality", but others deem it their "first choice" for "a nice night out."

Steve's Sizzling Steaks *Steak*
23 | 16 | 21 | $35

Carlstadt | 620 Rte. 17 S. (bet. Berry & Passaic Aves.) | 201-438-9677 | www.stevessizzlingsteaks.net

The "consistently great steaks" are a "good deal for the price" at this Carlstadt "throwback" where solid service ensures a "comfortable" vibe; while the "tiny", "sports-themed" space is certainly "not fancy", it's still usually "packed to the rafters" with admirers.

Stockton Inn *American*
21 | 22 | 21 | $44

Stockton | 1 N. Main St. (bet. Church St. & Stockton Sergeantsville Rd.) | 609-397-1250 | www.stocktoninn.com

"Wonderful comfort foods" fill the menu at this "charming" Stockton New American set in a circa-1710 building with working fireplaces, plus "nice gardens for summer dining"; though some find it "a little overpriced", enthusiasts insist it's a "great place to linger."

Stone House at Stirling Ridge Ⓜ *American*
22 | 25 | 22 | $55

Warren | 50 Stirling Rd. (bet. Dillon Ct. & Stiles Rd.) | 908-754-1222 | www.stonehouseatstirlingridge.com

With an "open kitchen for foodies to admire" and "tasteful" decor, the "beautiful" dining room "has the feel of an upscale ski lodge" at this Warren New American, which is especially "delightful" in the summer when you can start off with a cocktail "outside by the fire pit"; service is solid and the "excellent" eats "rarely disappoint", so while it's not cheap, fans deem the tabs "reasonable."

Stony Hill Inn *Continental/Italian*

FOOD	DECOR	SERVICE	COST
22	23	22	$59

Hackensack | 231 Polifly Rd. (Mary St.) | 201-342-4085 |
www.stonyhillinn.com

A "classy blast from the past", this 19th-century Hackensack "land-mark" promises a "quiet, refined dining experience" that "lends itself to dressing up a bit", with "excellently prepared" Continental-Italian cuisine and "attentive" service; though prices are undoubtedly "high", live music and dancing on weekends helps make it "worth the cost on a special occasion."

Strip House *Steak*

FOOD	DECOR	SERVICE	COST
25	23	23	$67

Livingston | The Westminster Hotel | 550 W. Mt. Pleasant Ave. (bet. Daven Ave. & Microlab Rd.) | 973-548-0050 |
www.striphousenewjersey.com

"Succulent" steaks and "well-mannered" servers seem right at home in the "sexy" "boudoir" setting of this Livingston chophouse in the Westminster Hotel, a destination for those wishing to "hide out with a blind date"; veterans advise "don't look at the prices", but do check out the "well-stocked" bar, and for those rolling really "old school", a "baked Alaska" might hit the spot.

Surf Taco *Mexican*

FOOD	DECOR	SERVICE	COST
21	17	18	$13

Belmar | 1003 Main St. (10th Ave.) | 732-681-3001
Forked River | Fieldcrest Commons | 44 Manchester Ave. (bet. Adams St. & Bob Ct. Ln.) | 609-971-9996
Jackson | 21 Hope Chapel Rd. (bet. Delta Ave. & Veterans Hwy.) | 732-364-8226
Long Branch | 94 Brighton Ave. (2nd Ave.) | 732-229-7873
Manasquan | 121 Parker Ave. (Stockton Lake Blvd.) | 732-223-7757
Point Pleasant Beach | 1300 Richmond Ave. (Washington Ave.) | 732-701-9000
Red Bank | 35 Broad St. (bet. Mechanic & Wallace Sts.) | 732-936-1800
Toms River | 1887 Hooper Ave. (bet. Kettle Creek Rd. & Oak Hill Dr.) | 732-255-3333
www.surftaco.com

"Mexican food meets surfer dudes" at this "inexpensive" chain serving "big portions" of "tasty" fare in "casual", "beach-themed" settings; the "cafeteria-style" setup is "essentially self-serve", but food comes out "fresh and fast", which is why it's the choice of many for a "quick bite before a Shore night out"; P.S. all locations except Jackson are BYO.

Sushi Lounge *Japanese*

FOOD	DECOR	SERVICE	COST
21	20	18	$40

Hoboken | 200 Hudson St. (2nd St.) | 201-386-1117
Totowa | 235 Rte. 46 W. (bet. Riverview Dr. & Union Blvd.) | 973-890-0007
Morristown | 12 Schuyler Pl. (bet. Ann St. & County Rd. 510) | 973-539-1135
www.sushilounge.com

"Creative" maki and "lethal" cocktails draw a "hip", "attractive" crowd to this "trendy" sushi trio where "chic" surrounds become "hopping" lounges at night; some find the fare "overpriced", while others advise "bring your earplugs" because it can get "loud", but those who like a little "social" with their sashimi say it's a "great night out."

	FOOD	DECOR	SERVICE	COST

Sweet Basil's Cafe *American*
23 | **17** | **20** | **$25**

Livingston | 498 S. Livingston Ave. (bet. Concord Dr. & Northfield Rd.) | 973-994-3600 | www.sweetbasilscafe.com

Relocated to Livingston, this "inviting" New American BYO is still serving up "high-quality" brunches (and more) to "ladies who lunch" and others in a "cozy", "bistro-style" space; some find the new surrounds "noisier", but prices remain "reasonable" and service steady, making it an overall "welcome addition" to the neighborhood.

Tabor Road Tavern *American*
22 | **23** | **20** | **$44**

Morris Plains | 510 Tabor Rd. (Mt. Pleasant Ave.) | 973-267-7004 | www.taborroadtavern.com

With its "ski-lodge" surrounds and "eclectic" "comfort food", this Morris Plains American makes a "cozy" spot for a "date" or "family meal", while the "lively" bar hosts a "fortysomethings" scene; some find the food "inconsistent" and "pricey", but factor in "roaring" fireplaces and "friendly" service, and it's no surprise it's "always packed."

Tacconelli's Pizzeria Ⓜ⊘ *Pizza*
21 | **16** | **18** | **$19**

Maple Shade | 450 S. Lenola Rd. (Rotary Way) | 856-638-0338 | www.tacconellispizzerianj.com

"Yummy" pizza is the main event at this Maple Shade offshoot of the famous Philly shops, with "long lines" of devotees waiting for its signature thin-crust pies; basic digs reflect a focus on food alone, but they don't deter fans from "going back every week", and there's no longer a need to "call ahead" to reserve dough; P.S. BYO and cash only.

Taka Ⓜ *Japanese*
25 | **23** | **23** | **$37**

Asbury Park | 632 Mattison Ave. (bet. Bond St. & Cookman Ave.) | 732-775-1020 | www.takaapnj.com

"BYOing doesn't get much better than this in Asbury Park" attest fans of Taka Hirai's midpriced spot, which "executes what it does very well", namely, "innovative, fresh" Japanese cuisine and an "extensive sushi menu"; "congenial" service and a "lovely space" are further reasons many say it's "come into its own as a hot spot" in town.

Taka Sushi *Japanese*
23 | **19** | **20** | **$32**

Summit | 95 Summit Ave. (bet. Franklin Pl. & Springfield Ave.) | 908-277-0886 | www.takasummit.com

"Wonderfully fresh" sushi "never disappoints" at this midpriced Summit Japanese BYO; the "sleek, uncluttered" decor has an "intimate" feel, and while some grouse about "rushed" service, fans say it's still a "reliable" "go to" for the neighborhood.

Tapas de España ◐ *Spanish*
24 | **21** | **22** | **$34**

North Bergen | 7909 Bergenline Ave. (79th St.) | 201-453-1690 | www.tapasnj.com

For those who like to "experiment", the "various" options at this North Bergen Spanish are "out of this world", backed by "awesome" sangria; "polite" servers work the bi-level space distinguished by brick arches and dark woods, and while some warn that "the small plates add up", others find the tabs "reasonable."

Taqueria Downtown *Mexican*

25 | 18 | 18 | $16

Jersey City | 236 Grove St. (Grand St.) | 201-333-3220
"Superb" tacos and other "authentic" dishes make this "funky little" Jersey City taqueria "the real deal", perhaps "to a fault" ("don't ask for guacamole", "chips" or "nachos"); while some are cool to "no-frills" decor and "service with a scowl", diehards deem it all "part of the appeal", or at least tolerable for such "legit", affordable eats.

Taste of Asia Ⓜ *Malaysian*

23 | 17 | 21 | $29

Chatham | 245 Main St. (bet. Fairmount & Passaic Aves.) | 973-701-8821 | www.atasteofasianj.com
Some "like it hot" at this Chatham Malaysian, and the chef will oblige with "flavorful" dishes, including those from other Asian cuisines; a "courteous" staff helps diners "feel welcome" in the basic digs, and moderate prices make it a "good casual dinner choice."

Taverna Mykonos Ⓜ *Greek*

24 | 22 | 23 | $42

Elmwood Park | 238 Broadway (Lyncrest Ave.) | 201-703-9200 | www.tavernamykonos.com
"Transport yourself to the islands" (via Route 4) at this Elmwood Park Greek, a more "casual" sibling of Fair Lawn's Oceanos, serving "first-rate" fare with an emphasis on "simply prepared" seafood; "efficient, friendly" waiters work the "clean", modern space, and many report a "lovely" meal "for a good price."

🆕 Tavro Thirteen *American*

- | - | - | E

Swedesboro | 1301 Kings Hwy. (Ashton Ave.) | 856-467-8413 | www.tavro13.com
'Hip-storic' describes this mod redo of the classic Old Swedes Inn in Swedesboro, where a sumptuous, fireplace-graced dining room is balanced with a rockin' bar and funky lounge; chef Terence Feury (ex NYC's Le Bernardin and Fork in Philly) is making a go at destination dining with his ambitious American fare.

Teak *Asian*

22 | 22 | 19 | $41

Red Bank | 64 Monmouth St. (bet. Broad St. & Maple Ave.) | 732-747-5775 | www.teakrestaurant.com
"Creative" Asian fare and sushi appeal to the "adventurous" at this "hip" Red Bank eatery with a "fun bar", "lively" vibe and "well-done" decor; critics say the "food can be a wild card" and "service can vary", and fume that the "price-to-quantity ratio is out of whack", but fans tout it as a "great date spot" and a "place to see and be seen."

Teplitzky's Ⓜ *Diner*

▽ 19 | 19 | 17 | $27

Atlantic City | Chelsea Hotel | 111 S. Chelsea Ave. (Pacific Ave.) | 609-428-4550 | www.thechelsea-ac.com
"You'll feel like you're at a Hollywood hotel in the '60s" at this midpriced diner in AC's Chelsea Hotel comprising a "quaint" counter section, "retro-chic" lounge area and poolside patio; a "pleasant" staff serves up breakfast fare done "just right", as well as an all-day lunch menu and weekend brunch; P.S. closed Tuesdays and Thursdays.

| | FOOD | DECOR | SERVICE | COST |

Teresa Caffe *Italian*
23 | 19 | 20 | $31

Princeton | Palmer Sq. | 23 Palmer Sq. E. (Hulfish St.) | 609-921-1974 | www.terramomo.com

Always "bustling", this "popular" 20-year-old Princeton trattoria serves "simple", "well-prepared" pastas and pizza, with produce sourced from its own farm, accompanied by a "good" wine list; though the "long waits" (and no reservations) can be "frustrating", the "well-priced" fare keeps it a perennial "favorite."

Terra Nova *American*
21 | 22 | 21 | $33

Sewell | 590 Delsea Dr. (Holly Dell Dr.) | 856-589-8883 | www.terranovawineanddine.com

"Variety" is the hallmark of this Sewell "California-style" American where pastas share the menu with quesadillas, jambalaya and sushi – all "consistently good" and served in a spacious Mission Revival setting; add "great" cocktails and a "fine selection" of wines to the mix, plus moderate prices, and locals have reason to return "several times."

Tewksbury Inn *American*
21 | 20 | 20 | $50

Oldwick | 55 Main St. (King St.) | 908-439-2641 | www.thetewksburyinn.com

A "quaint" "small-town inn" dating to the "stagecoach days", this Oldwick American draws the "horsey set" and other locals for "solid" American standards "with a pinch of creativity"; for those who find the "formal" dining room "fussy", a "rustic" "tavern" room offers a more casual dine plus an "active" "bar crowd", while an outdoor patio provides a place to "watch the world go by"; P.S. "oenophiles" take note: bottles are half-price Mondays.

Thai Chef *French/Thai*
21 | 19 | 20 | $34

Montclair | 664 Bloomfield Ave. (bet. Orange & Valley Rds.) | 973-744-4994

The "elevated" Thai cuisine has a "French accent" at this mid-priced Montclair BYO, where "spicy" is accurately applied and experts advise "save room for the chocolate soufflé"; although some think the fare's "gone downhill" and can seem "overpriced", the "relaxed setting", especially on the patio, earns it a spot on fans' "repeat list."

Thai Kitchen *Thai*
24 | 19 | 22 | $26

Bridgewater | 1351 Prince Rodgers Ave. (bet. Bridge St. & I-287) | 908-231-8822
Bridgewater | Somerset Shopping Ctr. | 327 Hwy. 202 (Thompson St.) | 908-722-8983
Chester | Streets of Chester | 320 Rte. 206 S. (Old Chester Rd.) | 908-879-9800
Hillsborough | Hillsborough Shopping Ctr. | 649 Rte. 206 (bet. Amwell Rd. & Raider Blvd.) | 908-904-8038
www.thaikitchennj.com

"Delicious" Thai fare attracts "many loyal customers" to this "fantastic" BYO foursome, where "exquisite sauces" are seasoned for each "spice tolerance" level (from "mild" to "help, I'm dying"); while the basic decor doesn't warm any hearts, the "quick", "friendly" service does, and with such "affordable" prices, fans say they're a "no brainer."

Thai Thai *Thai*   24 | 18 | 21 | $25

Old Bridge | Village at Town Ctr. | 3843 Rte. 516
(bet Cottrell Rd. & Wisdom Way) | 732-679-4455 |
www.menuthaithaicuisine.com

"Authentic", "tasty" Thai dishes that are "artfully presented" draw Old Bridgers to this "casual" BYO, where a "warm" atmosphere prevails in a spacious, no-frills dining room; vegetarians will find plenty of options here, and "courteous", "quick" service and "reasonable" prices round out a "consistently good experience."

That's Amore Ⓜ *Italian*   22 | 20 | 20 | $33

Collingswood | 690 Haddon Ave. (Collings Ave.) | 856-869-5683 |
www.ilovethatsamore.com

A "varied menu" of "hearty" fare awaits diners at this "homey" Collingswood Italian BYO, where "enormous" portions guarantee another meal to "take home"; while regulars advise you "bring earplugs" to combat the "noise", a "friendly atmosphere" prevails, and with moderate prices, many feel "you can't go wrong here."

Theresa's *Italian*   22 | 19 | 21 | $38

Westfield | 47 Elm St. (bet. Broad St. & North Ave.) |
908-233-9133 | www.theresasrestaurant.com

A "long-standing favorite" on Westfield's Restaurant Row, this "casual" Italian (a sibling of nearby Isabella's and Mojave Grille) "never disappoints" with its "reliable", "straightforward" fare; some knock the "noise" and "no-reservations" policy, and tight seating means you might "hear your neighbor's entire conversation", but outdoor tables and a "friendly staff" add to its appeal, and BYO "helps keep costs down."

Thirty Acres Ⓩ *American*   22 | 19 | 21 | $42

Jersey City | 500 Jersey Ave. (Wayne St.) | 201-435-3100 |
www.thirtyacresrestaurant.com

"Innovative" is how fans describe this Jersey City New American newcomer from Kevin Pemoulie (ex NYC's Momofuku Noodle Bar), whose "fresh", "eclectic" dishes borrow liberally from cuisines of the world and change daily; the "small" corner storefront space is minimalist and can be "noisy", and there's a no-reservations policy for small parties, but fans say it's "worth the wait" for such a "great new addition" to the local scene; P.S. it now serves beer and wine.

3 Forty Grill *American*   21 | 22 | 20 | $42

Hoboken | 340 Sinatra Dr. (4th St.) | 201-217-3406 |
www.3fortygrill.com

A "top-notch" Hudson River view and "tasty" eats headline this "always busy" Hoboken waterfront New American where warm weather outdoor dining and a late-night "lounge atmosphere" add to its "first-date" appeal; an "attentive" staff presides over the "chic, "modern" digs, and while some balk at "NYC prices", others point out "you're paying for the location."

3 West *American*

21 | 22 | 21 | $48

Basking Ridge | Riverwalk Village Ctr. | 665 Martinsville Rd. (Independence Blvd.) | 908-647-3000 | www.3westrest.com

"Reliable" New American fare and an "extensive wine cellar" draw fans to this "happening place" in Basking Ridge – a "pleasant upscale surprise in a strip mall" where the "cozy fireplace", exposed kitchen and a "beautiful dark-wood bar" lend it a "chic" "ski-lodge" feel; a "busy" happy hour filled with "professionals" means it "can get loud", and while some lament "sketchy service" and a "predictable" menu, most call it "a local favorite."

Tick Tock Diner ◑ *Diner*

19 | 17 | 19 | $19

Clifton | 281 Allwood Rd. (bet. Bloomfield & Passaic Aves.) | 973-777-0511 | www.theticktockdiner.com

"When you look up *diner* in the dictionary", you might find a picture of this Clifton "classic" – a "landmark" on Route 3 since 1948 – where fans take the "eat heavy" motto to heart with "gigantic" portions of "decent", if "undistinguished", "comfort food"; it's a "throwback" all right, with "lots of chrome" and mirrors, and waitresses who can cop a "Jersey attitude", but prices are "great" and it's open all night "to satisfy any craving."

Tim McLoone's Supper Club *American*

19 | 22 | 20 | $43

Asbury Park | 1200 Ocean Ave. (bet. 4th & 5th Aves.) | 732-774-1155 | www.timmcloonessupperclub.com

A "unique place to eat and catch a show", this supper club on the Asbury Park boardwalk above McLoone's Asbury Grille offers "nicely prepared" New American dishes in a setting made "lively" with musical acts and the owner's weekly radio talk show; critics who find the fare "standard" and "overpriced" lament that you're "paying for the location", but others insist it's "the place to be."

Tim Schafer's *American*

23 | 19 | 23 | $49

Morristown | 82 Speedwell Ave. (bet. Cattano Ave. & Clinton Pl.) | 973-538-3330 | www.timschafersrestaurant.com

A "longtime" Morristown "favorite", this Downtown BYO takes a "creative" spin through the American cookbook, with an "ambitious" mix of cuisines, including "beer-inspired" dishes; although some suggest "it's slipped a little" and others note "tired" decor, a staff that "could not be nicer" and an overall "intimate" vibe help keep loyalists "going back."

Tina Louise *Asian*

23 | 18 | 22 | $32

Carlstadt | 403 Hackensack St. (bet. Broad St. & Division Ave.) | 201-933-7133 | www.villagerestaurantgroup.com

Sisters Tina and Louise Wong offer an Asian menu filled with "possibilities" and "unexpected flavors" at this "friendly" BYO near the Meadowlands in Carlstadt; it's "tight quarters" in the "small storefront" and there can be a "line", but the "personable" staff and affordable prices secure its status as a local "favorite."

Tisha's Fine Dining *American* | 25 | 21 | 23 | $45 |

Cape May | Washington Street Mall | 322 Washington St. (bet. Jackson & Perry Sts.) | 609-884-9119 | www.tishasfinedining.com

Opinions are mixed on this Cape May BYO's move to its current address in the Washington Street Mall – some feel it "lost some atmosphere moving away from the ocean", while others think the present spot is "convenient", "more real and less foo-foo"; still, most agree the New American cuisine is "top-notch" and the service is "attentive", and deem it an "overall pleasant dining experience."

Toast *American* | 21 | 18 | 20 | $22 |

Montclair | 700 Bloomfield Ave. (bet. Orange Rd. & St Lukes Pl.) | 973-509-8099 | www.toastmontclair.com

Asbury Park | 516 Cookman Ave. (Bangs Ave.) | 732-776-5900 | www.toastasburypark.com

For "comfort food that is pretty darn good", this "charming" American duo with outposts in Montclair and Asbury Park slings "creative and classic" breakfast, brunch and lunch dishes for fans so devoted they're willing to wait in "long lines" on weekends; service is "sporadic" but prices are "good" – just remember to BYO if you want to spike your OJ.

Tokyo Hibachi & Sushi Buffet *Japanese* | 23 | 22 | 21 | $25 |

Deptford | Locust Grove Plaza | 1692 Clements Bridge Rd. (Westville Almonesson Rd.) | 856-848-8289 | www.tokyodeptford.com

Choose from the "fresh seafood" and sushi buffet or go the hibachi route at this Deptford Japanese, which also offers à la carte cooked options; the strip-mall space is "cute" and the staff "friendly", and with "reasonable prices", fans find it "great for family outings."

Tomatoes *Californian/Eclectic* | 23 | 21 | 21 | $49 |

Margate | 9300 Amherst Ave. (Washington Ave.) | 609-822-7535 | www.tomatoesmargate.com

Aficionados advise "don't be deceived by the trendy bar crowd" or DJs at this "happening", upscale "locals' hangout" "right near the bay" in Margate, for it also serves "well-prepared", "tasty" Cal-Eclectic fare and a "good wine selection"; a few find the clientele "pretentious", while impressions of the service vary from "congenial" to "unfriendly", but many report a "good time" here.

Tony Da Caneca *Portuguese* | 22 | 19 | 21 | $38 |

Newark | 72 Elm Rd. (Houston St.) | 973-589-6882 | www.tonydacanecarestaurant.com

A "mainstay" of Newark's Ironbound district since 1965, this "quintessential" Portuguese offers "well-prepared" fare paired with "quality" Iberian wines; it's "off the beaten path", and the "quiet, formal" dining room may be a bit "old-style", but a "convivial" atmosphere prevails, and prices are "fair", especially since ample portions mean you "won't have to eat for the next two days."

	FOOD	DECOR	SERVICE	COST

Tony Luke's *Cheesesteaks* — 23 | 16 | 19 | $14

Atlantic City | Borgata Hotel Casino & Spa | 1 Borgata Way
(Renaissance Point Blvd.) | 609-317-1000
Sicklerville | Crossings at Twin Oaks | 663 Berlin-Crosskeys Rd.
(bet. Johnson Rd. & Redbud Dr.) | 856-875-8700
www.tonylukes.com

With "so much" piled on one bun you "won't be able to walk out",
the "tasty" Philly-style cheesesteaks at these NJ links in an area
chain draw fans with their "fresh rolls" and "juicy" meats – from beef
to roast pork to chicken; counter-service is "friendly", tabs are "cheap"
and even if you're not actually in the City of Brotherly Love, the
mega-sammies are "a must-have."

Tony's Baltimore Grill ● *Pizza* — 22 | 15 | 18 | $19

Atlantic City | 2800 Atlantic Ave. (Iowa Ave.) | 609-345-5766 |
www.tonysbaltimoregrill.com

An "Atlantic City institution", this circa-1927 pizzeria "landmark" is a "must" for a "late-night pizza", dishing out pies as well
as "damn good" meatballs and more until 3 AM, and "inexpensive drinks" from the bar 24/7; prices are "family-friendly" while
the service is "abrupt, but efficient", and even though some think
it needs a "face-lift", it remains a popular spot "for locals and in-
the-know tourists."

Tony's Touch of Italy II *Pizza* — 23 | 15 | 20 | $19

Wayne | Drug Fair Shopping Ctr. | 315 Valley Rd. (MacDonald Dr.) |
973-694-7787 | www.tonystouchofitaly.com

A local "favorite", this Wayne Italian BYO serves up pizza and "great
basic red-sauce dishes" courtesy of chef Anton Testino (who ap-
peared on *Chopped*); though the strip-mall space is not fancy, it has
a "family atmosphere", and moderate prices for "nice portions" make
it a "great value."

Topaz Thai Restaurant *Thai* — ∇ 24 | 17 | 21 | $21

Belleville | Bell Plaza | 137 Washington Ave. (Belleville Ave.) |
973-759-7425 | www.topazthainj.com

"Sit down and let Mama (aka Wanida Reid) take care of you" at
this Belleville Thai BYO, a local "gem" serving some "phenomenal",
"spicy" dishes; it's a "casual", "tiny" storefront, but that doesn't pre-
vent it from "filling up on weekends", and "friendly service", plus
moderate prices, keep loyalists coming back.

The Tortilla Press *Mexican* — 21 | 19 | 20 | $23

Collingswood | 703 Haddon Ave. (Collings Ave.) | 856-869-3345 |
www.thetortillapress.com

Tortilla Press Cantina *Mexican*

Merchantville | 7716 Maple Ave. (bet. Manor & Union Aves.) |
856-356-2050 | www.tortillapresscantina.com

Mexican "with a twist" is the mantra for this pair from chef-owner
Mark Smith, who uses "fresh local ingredients" in his "modern",
"enjoyable" takes on traditional dishes ("don't miss the guacamole"),
including some "good selections" for vegetarians; with their "fun,

colorful" atmosphere, and "reasonable prices", fans say the pair's an overall "good bet"; P.S. Collingswood is BYO, but they'll provide the margarita mix.

Tortuga's Cocina Ⓜ Mexican

`23 | 18 | 21 | $23`

Lambertville | 11½ Church St. (Union St.) | 609-397-7272 | www.tortugascocina.com

Tortuga's Mexican Village ⊘ Mexican

Princeton | 41 Leigh Ave. (bet. John & Witherspoon Sts.) | 609-924-5143 | www.tortugasmv.com

"Simple", "well-prepared" dishes are the draw at this "quaint" Mexican BYO "off the main drag" in Princeton; a new space, across the street from the old, is "larger", if "noisier", but still maintains a "homey" feel, while "friendly" service and "great" (though cash-only) prices make it "well worth a visit"; P.S. the Lambertville sibling serves alcohol, takes plastic and has a back patio.

Toscana Italian

`∇ 24 | 24 | 24 | $29`

Mullica Hill | 127 Bridgeton Pike (bet. Walnut Ln. & Wheatley Blvd.) | 856-478-2288 | www.toscanamullicahill.com

"As homey as a family kitchen", this Mullica Hill Italian BYO serves up wood-fired pizzas and homemade pastas that fans deem "unlike anything outside of Italy"; even if it can be "noisy", the space has a "warm" vibe, aided by a "great" staff and "hands-on" owner, and "reasonable prices" keep regulars returning "again and again."

Trap Rock American

`21 | 22 | 21 | $43`

Berkeley Heights | 279 Springfield Ave. (Kuntz Ave.) | 908-665-1755 | www.traprockrestaurant.net

A brewpub "with gastronomic ambitions", this "cool" Berkeley Heights local offers an "interesting array" of "upscale" "tavern food", with "even better" beer; if "NYC prices" give pause to some, and the dining room can be "noisy", there's a fireplace in the front room for those chilly winter nights, and the prevailing vibe is "relaxed."

Trattoria La Sorrentina Italian

`25 | 18 | 22 | $30`

North Bergen | 7831 Bergenline Ave. (79th St.) | 201-869-8100 | www.sorrentinanb.com

"Outstanding" thin-crust pizza and "delicious" pastas lure locals to this North Bergen Italian "gem", where everyone "seems to know their fellow diners" and "friendly" waiters keep up a "frantic pace" in the simple space (brick walls, tile floors); sadly, it's not a "great little secret" anymore, and you'll probably "have to wait" on weekends, but fans agree it's "worth it" – and a "great bang for your buck."

Trattoria Mediterranea Ⓜ Italian

`22 | 19 | 23 | $39`

Bedminster | 2472 Lamington Rd. (bet. Somerville Rd. & U.S. 206) | 908-781-7131 | www.trattoriamediterranea.com

You might "feel like family" at this Bedminster Italian "charmer", where "solid" "home cooking" has a Calabrian flair; sure, it might seem "old-fashioned" to some, and the scene "can get loud", but a host of "regulars" find it a "nice local" option, and BYO "makes it a bargain."

Trattoria Saporito   *Italian*   23 | 20 | 21 | $38

Hoboken | 328 Washington St. (bet. 3rd & 4th Sts.) | 201-533-1801 | www.trattoriasaporito.com

"Old-World" Italian fare with a "red-sauce" emphasis is the forte of this midpriced Hoboken BYO set in a "nice" storefront on Washington Street; waiters provide "personal attention", and if you "close your eyes", fans say, "you are in Italy."

Tre Amici   *Italian*   22 | 18 | 21 | $45

Long Branch | 628 Ocean Ave. (West End Ct.) | 732-571-8922 | www.treamicinj.com

Chopped winner Matthew Zappoli "knows what he's doing" in the kitchen of this high-end BYO Italian in Long Branch, which showcases his "well-prepared" fare in an "unassuming", "casual" setting; while there's "not much in the way of decor", the vibe is "friendly" and service comes "with a smile."

Tre Famiglia ⓜ *Italian*   25 | 21 | 24 | $36

Haddonfield | 403 N. Haddon Ave. (Hawthorne Ave.) | 856-429-1447 | www.trefamiglia.com

"Everything is carefully made" with "quality ingredients", including "gnocchi light as a cloud", at this "excellent" Haddonfield Italian BYO, a relocation of Philly's century-old Chip's; while some are cool to the "banquet-hall" vibe and "close seating", waiters are "attentive" and at midrange prices, fans find it "worth every penny."

Tre Piani ⓢ *Italian/Mediterranean*   22 | 21 | 22 | $46

Princeton | Princeton Forrestal Vill. | 120 Rockingham Row (Village Blvd.) | 609-452-1515 | www.trepiani.com

Everything is "expansive" at this "fun" Italian-Mediterranean in Princeton's Forrestal Village – from the "wide selection" of "solid" "seasonal" dishes served in "large" portions to the "inviting" tri-level space plus outdoor patio; for something "cozier", there's an adjoining wine bar perfect for "people-watching", and "pricey" tabs don't deter those who find it a "nice surprise."

Trinity ⓜ *American*   22 | 24 | 21 | $44

Keyport | 84 Broad St. (bet. Front & 3rd Sts.) | 732-888-1998 | www.trinitykeyport.com

A converted 19th-century church in Keyport provides a "stunning setting" for this "lovely" American where the "creative" menu includes "long-term favorites", Mediterranean accents and seasonally changing fare; service is "friendly" (though some find it a "bit lackluster" at times), and there's live entertainment on weekends.

Trinity ⓘ *American/Pub Food*   18 | 18 | 18 | $34

Hoboken | 306 Sinatra Dr. (3rd St.) | 201-533-4446 | www.hobokentrinity.com

"Dependable" American fare and a "great beer selection" at "fair prices" make this a "great all around hangout" on the Hoboken waterfront; even if some say the service "could use a boost", the "inviting" space boasts appealing "views of NYC" that help make it feel somewhat "a bit nicer than the typical pub", with an "upscale crowd" to match.

Trio 🛇 Ⓜ *Italian*   ▽ 24 | 21 | 21 | $39

Martinsville | 1938 Washington Valley Rd. (bet. Chimney Rock Rd. & Quarry Ln.) | 732-469-8746 | www.trioofmartinsville.com

An "attentive" staff dishes up "excellent pastas and Italian delicacies" at this "family-friendly" Martinsville Italian; with hardwood floors and white tablecloths, the contemporary dining room has a "quiet", "cozy" atmosphere, and BYO complements the "reasonable" prices.

Triumph Brewing Co. ☾ *American/Eclectic*   19 | 20 | 19 | $30

Princeton | 138 Nassau St. (bet. Tulane St. & Vandeventer Ave.) | 609-924-7855 | www.triumphbrewing.com

"Solid pub food" at "fair" prices makes for a "casual, fun meal" at this Princeton microbrewery, though fans say the "awesome" beer "brewed on the premises" may be the real "reason for going"; even if the "lively bar scene" gets "noisy", "eating alongside the brewing equipment" in the "novel", "modern" space is a definite "attraction."

Tutto a Modo Mio *Italian*   22 | 18 | 22 | $35

Ridgefield | 482 Bergen Blvd. (Ridgefield Terr.) | 201-313-9690 | www.tuttoamodomio.com

"Consistent", "high-quality" Italian cooking is "what really stands out" at this moderately priced neighborhood BYO in Ridgefield; even if the "small, casual" space is simply so-so, regulars give a nod to the "pride and professionalism" of a staff that does "anything to please."

Tuzzio's Ⓜ *Italian*   20 | 15 | 20 | $31

Long Branch | 224 Westwood Ave. (Morris Ave.) | 732-222-9614 | www.tuzzios.com

A "red-gravy" "family restaurant" that "hasn't changed" in years, this "low-key" Long Branch Italian draws "lots of regulars" thanks to "Mack truck"–sized portions of "real-thing" "home cooking" – think pizza, pastas, proteins and a "great" "special salad"; the "active bar" feels like *Cheers*, and with "good" prices and a "friendly" staff, no wonder locals have been "eating here since childhood."

27 Mix 🛇 *Eclectic*   21 | 19 | 21 | $34

Newark | 27 Halsey St. (bet. Bleeker St. & Central Ave.) | 973-648-0643 | www.27mix.com

A "creative" "mix" of Latin, Asian and American fare, "imaginative specials" and "really good drinks" draws a "laid-back crowd" for lunch, happy hour and dinner to this "sophisticated" but "comfortable" Eclectic "steps from the Newark Museum" and NJPAC; a "friendly staff" presides over the "cool", rustic-industrial digs (exposed brick, dark woods), and the warm weather patio "is a nice touch" – especially when the "active noise level" inside gets to be a bit much.

TwoFiftyTwo ⚥ *American* · 20 · 17 · 20 · $42

Bedminster | 252 Somerville Rd. (bet. Main St. & Miller Ln.) |
908-234-9093 | www.twofiftytworestaurant.com

A "charming little restaurant" in a 1922 Arts and Crafts bungalow,
this Bedminster "locavore haunt" serves up "tasty", "seasonal" New
American fare in a "tiny", "cozy dining room"; service is "standard"
and tabs aren't cheap, but BYO's a plus, especially since guests can
stash extra wine in the vintage mailboxes on-site.

Umeya Ⓜ *Japanese* · 23 · 17 · 18 · $37

Cresskill | 156 Piermont Rd. (Allen St.) | 201-816-0511 |
www.umeyasushi.com

The "fish simply melts in your mouth" swoon sushi fans of the "reliable", "authentic" eats at this midpriced Cresskill Japanese; though
the "well-meaning" service can be "slow" in the "intimate", no-frills
space, locals nonetheless consider it a "lovely place to dine."

Under the Moon *Argentinean/Eclectic* · ▽ 23 · 22 · 22 · $24

Bordentown | 210 Farnsworth Ave. (bet. Church & Walnut Sts.) |
609-291-8301 | www.underthemooncafe.com

A Bordentown "must-try", this affordable BYO offers "fantastic"
Argentinean-Eclectic fare delivered by a staff that's "eager to
serve"; while the decor earns solid marks (and reminds some of
"dining in an antiques store"), reservations are a good idea if you
want to snag a table in the "small, cozy" space.

Undici *Italian* · 23 · 24 · 22 · $61

Rumson | 11 W. River Rd. (bet. Lafayette & Washington Sts.) |
732-842-3880 | www.undicirestaurant.com

"*Molto bene*" cry *amici* of this "happening" "upscale" Rumson Italian
where the "charming" Tuscan farm house decor lends a "relaxed"
feel to accompany "very tasty" (and "very pricey") "creative" eats;
a "huge", "busy" bar offers a popular perch for "sublime" thin crust
pizza and vino from the "extensive" wine selection – add an "attentive staff" and you "feel like you've been whisked away" to Firenze.

Union Park Dining Room *American* · 26 · 25 · 24 · $55

Cape May | Hotel Macomber | 727 Beach Ave. (Howard St.) |
609-884-8811 | www.unionparkdiningroom.com

A "fine-dining" "destination" in Cape May, this "romantic" spot in the
Hotel Macomber delivers "memorable", "creative" New American
cuisine in a "charming", "formal" setting with a veranda where you
can "listen to the waves crashing on the beach"; "dependable" service also gets cheers, and while it's "pricey", "BYO is a big plus" (it
also serves a limited selection of local wines).

Uproot ⚥ *American* · 22 · 23 · 22 · $51

Warren | 9 Mt. Bethel Rd. (Mountain Blvd.) | 908-834-8194 |
www.uprootrestaurant.com

Warren locals confess they "make excuses just to go back" to this
"modern, cool" American delivering "loads of atmosphere" along
with its "creative", "tasty" menu and "well-planned" wine list;

"friendly" service further makes it a "treat" that might be "pricey" but still feels like an "awesome value."

Upstairs ●Ⓜ *American* | 24 | 22 | 23 | $47

Upper Montclair | 608 Valley Rd. (bet. Bellevue & Lorraine Aves.) | 973-744-4144 | www.upstairsmontclair.com
Perched atop Montclair "sushi standby Dai-Kichi", this "pricey" New American turns out "creative" small and large plates in a sleek space with a "cool" vibe; "imaginative" bartenders mixing "mean cocktails" at the "modern" bar further make it "stand out" from the crowd.

Urban Table *Eclectic* | 19 | 20 | 19 | $35

Basking Ridge | Riverwalk Village Ctr. | 665 Martinsville Rd. (Independence Blvd.) | 908-647-6007
Morristown | 40 W. Park Pl. (Market St.) | 973-326-9200
www.urbantablerestaurant.com
"Hipsters, blue- and white-collar types and locals alike" pack these midpriced siblings where the Eclectic menu has "something for everyone", including "creative salads and sandwiches", burgers and even sushi; critics say service can be an "issue", while others reason the "noisy", "trendy atmosphere" works for "quick", "casual dining."

Ursino Ⓢ *American* | 24 | 25 | 22 | $61

Union | Stem Bldg. | 1075 Morris Ave. (bet. Kean Dr. & North Ave.) | 908-249-4099 | www.ursinorestaurant.com
"Attention to detail" is evident in the "innovative", "farm-to-table" fare at this "special" New American "hidden in a modern building on campus at Kean University" (it "makes me want to go back to college" muse fans); the "stylish" setting and "competent" service help justify "expensive" tabs, and outdoor seating's a "treat" when it's warm.

Valencia *Steak* | 24 | 20 | 21 | $33

Elizabeth | 665 Monroe Ave. (bet. Louisa St. & North Ave.) | 908-354-2525 | www.valencarestaurantnj.com
"Plentiful" servings of "delicious" Iberian eats at moderate prices make this "a regular place" for Elizabeth locals, but insiders say "nothing beats cooking your own steak" on a hot stone (a house specialty); even if space is "tight" in the wood-accented, white-tablecloth dining room, "friendly" service and a "decent wine list" add appeal.

Valentino's *Italian* | 19 | 18 | 19 | $45

Park Ridge | 103 Spring Valley Rd. (bet. Fremont & Grand Aves.) | 201-391-2230 | www.valentinosnj.com
"Regulars" rely on the "better-than-average" pasta and other "traditional" eats at this "pricey" Park Ridge Italian; if some knock "dated" decor and "mediocre" service, the fact that it's "been around a long time" says a lot.

Varka *Greek/Seafood* | 25 | 23 | 23 | $62

Ramsey | 30 N. Spruce St. (Carol St.) | 201-995-9333 | www.varkarestaurant.com
"Pick your exact piece" from the fresh fish display and the kitchen will "cook it any way you like" at this "upscale" Greek seafooder in

Ramsey that's known for "top-quality, beautifully prepared" dishes (just prepare for the "sticker shock"); insiders say it generally "gets everything right, except the noise level" – though summertime patio dining "eliminates that problem."

Vasili's Taverna 🗷 *Greek*

▽ 20 | 15 | 19 | $35

Teaneck | 365 Queen Anne Rd. (bet. Degraw & Hillside Aves.) | 201-287-1007 | www.vasilistaverna.com

"Solid" Greek "classics" and "especially good seafood" (the "whole grilled fish can't be beat") are a decent "value" at this "popular neighborhood BYO" in Teaneck; if the compact, Mediterranean-themed dining room doesn't earn raves, insiders recommend the "wonderful" patio "when the weather allows."

Ventura's Greenhouse ◐ *Italian*

20 | 18 | 19 | $32

Margate | 106 S. Benson Ave. (Atlantic Ave.) | 609-822-0140 | www.venturasgreenhouse.com

A "Margate staple" for years, this "casual" beachfront Italian hybrid combines a "lively" first-floor pub with a second-floor dining room plus two decks – all with their own menus and "wide selection" of eats, including "great pizza"; fans cheer it's "fun in the summer", especially when dining or ("more importantly") drinking alfresco, and enjoying the view of landmark Lucy the Elephant.

Verjus 🅼 *French*

24 | 19 | 22 | $54

Maplewood | 1790 Springfield Ave. (Rutgers St.) | 973-378-8990 | www.verjusrestaurant.com

An "unexpected" but "delightful" "taste of France" in Maplewood, this "well-run gem" serves up "superb" Gallic cooking, including a "luscious" brunch; some suggest the "quiet, subdued" setting "doesn't live up" to the "price tag", but the "attentive" staff oversees a "relaxing dining experience."

Verve 🗷 *American/French*

22 | 21 | 22 | $44

Somerville | 18 E. Main St. (bet. Bridge & Warren Sts.) | 908-707-8655 | www.vervestyle.com

The "well-executed" French-American menu delivers "a nice variety" at this "lovely little bistro" in Somerville where sidewalk seating supplements the "old-school", white-tablecloth dining room; devotees don't mind tabs "on the expensive side", especially given the "warm, friendly" service and "great bar scene."

Via45 *Italian*

25 | 22 | 23 | $45

Red Bank | 45 Broad St. (bet. Mechanic & Wallace Sts.) | 732-450-9945 | www.via45.com

A "Red Bank gem", this upscale BYO Italian is a "rare treat" where "everything is fresh, fresh, fresh" and "cooked to order", including gluten-free and vegan offerings from a menu that changes daily; the staff is "friendly", and while some caution that it can be "difficult to get in" to the "intimate" space, and the "slow-food" approach "takes a little time", most agree it's "worth the wait."

Vic's ⓜ *Italian/Pizza* | 22 | 15 | 20 | $24

Bradley Beach | 60 Main St. (Evergreen Ave.) | 732-774-8225 |
www.vicspizza.com

Serving up "worth-the-wait" thin-crust pizza and "red-sauce" "comfort food" for over 65 years, this "family-favorite" Bradley Beach "institution" is "so old-school it's cool again", say fans; while the "1950s basement rec room" decor could use "updating", you "can't beat the prices" – "just stick to the standard Italian fare and you won't be disappointed."

Villa Amalfi ⓜ *Italian* | 23 | 21 | 23 | $50

Cliffside Park | 793 Palisade Ave. (Marion Ave.) | 201-886-8626 |
www.villaamalfi.com

"Artfully prepared" Italian specialties and "terrific", "formal" service are "conducive to making memories" at this "classy" Cliffside Park venue that's "been around forever"; even if tabs are "a little high" and critics say it's "time to freshen up" the "old-style" decor, loyalists consider it "something special."

Village Gourmet *Eclectic* | 19 | 18 | 17 | $34

Rutherford | 75 Park Ave. (The Terrace) | 201-438-9404 |
www.villagerestaurantgroup.com

Expect a "huge menu" of Eclectic dishes cooked in "any mix-and-match variation" at this "reliable" stop in Downtown Rutherford; while the service and dark-wood decor strike some as "average in every way", supporters say "big" portions and BYO help make it a "great value" – and it's "nice to be able to buy wine" in the on-site store.

Village Green *American* | 24 | 20 | 23 | $53

Ridgewood | 36 Prospect St. (Hudson St.) | 201-445-2914 |
www.villagegreenrestaurant.com

Regulars rave about the "innovative" tasting menus at this "wonderful" Ridgewood New American where the "delicious, delicate" fare is "beautifully executed"; insiders say bringing your own "favorite bottle of wine" helps "keep the price down a bit", and "attentive" service amid the "cozy" surrounds enhances a "truly memorable" experience.

Village Whiskey *Burgers* | ▽ 24 | 23 | 24 | $38

Atlantic City | REVEL | 500 Boardwalk (bet. Metropolitan &
New Jersey Aves.) | 609-225-9880 | www.revelresorts.com

Iron Chef Jose Garces brings his Philly-based American burger bar to Atlantic City's Revel where "masterfully mixed whiskey cocktails" and an "awesome beer selection" wash down "don't-miss" duck-fat fries, "worth-the-wait" patties and "amazing" pickled veggies; while prices reflect the "upscale casino" locale, the pubby space is "low-key" and the "professional" staff is "happy to help with suggestions."

Villa Vittoria *Italian* | 22 | 20 | 22 | $41

Brick | 2700 Hooper Ave. (Cedar Bridge Ave.) | 732-920-1550 |
www.villavittoria.com

Amici "have been going for years" to this Italian stalwart in Brick for "good red-sauce" fare served by "wonderful" waiters; it's a "little expensive" for some, and others grouse about "too-loud" live music in an otherwise "comfortable" setting, but for fans it remains a default choice for "any big family occasion."

Vincentown Diner *Diner*

FOOD	DECOR	SERVICE	COST
21	17	20	$20

Vincentown | 2357 Rte. 206 (Pemberton Rd.) | 609-267-3033 | www.vincentowndiner.com

"Not your typical diner fare", the "satisfying", "down-home" dishes at this "farm-to-fork" Vincentown pit stop are made with "local, fresh ingredients" that "impress" regulars; even if the decor gets middling scores, "lots of menu choices" and "reasonable prices" boost the "family-friendly" vibe.

Vine ⚄ *American/Mediterranean*

FOOD	DECOR	SERVICE	COST
24	23	24	$58

Basking Ridge | 95 Morristown Rd. (bet. Maple & Parkview Aves.) | 908-221-0017 | www.vinerestaurant.net

The "top-notch" Med–New American cooking "never disappoints" say devotees of this "upscale" Basking Ridge "favorite"; "a hit on all marks", it's a "lovely experience" thanks to the "quiet", contemporary setting and "warm, welcoming" service that "makes everyone feel like a regular."

Walpack Inn ⓜ *American*

FOOD	DECOR	SERVICE	COST
23	24	23	$37

Wallpack Center | Rte. 615 (Rte. 206) | 973-948-3890 | www.walpackinn.com

"Take a ride through the countryside" to reach this "scenic" Traditional American in Wallpack Center where you might spot "deer outside the window" from the "rustic, cabin-style" dining area, and "attentive" service brightens the "wonderful ambiance"; the "hearty" menu has an "emphasis on steaks", and "amazing" homemade bread helps make it a "must-visit."

Wasabi Asian Plates *Japanese*

FOOD	DECOR	SERVICE	COST
22	18	21	$31

Somerville | 12 W. Main St. (bet. Bridge & Maple Sts.) | 908-203-8881

Wasabi House *Japanese*

East Brunswick | Colchester Plaza | 77 Tices Ln. (Rte. 18) | 732-254-9988 | www.wasabieb.com

"If you have the craving" for "old-school" sushi, this "go-to" Japanese duo in East Brunswick and Somerville delivers "fresh servings" at "reasonable prices", plus "interesting hot dishes as well"; though the "accommodating staff strives to please", the settings "can get crowded at times", so insiders say "go early to avoid a wait"; P.S. East Brunswick is BYO.

Washington Inn *American*

FOOD	DECOR	SERVICE	COST
26	25	25	$61

Cape May | 801 Washington St. (Jefferson St.) | 609-884-5697 | www.washingtoninn.com

The "definition of fine dining" for many, this Cape May "classic" "always delivers" with "wonderful" American fare, an "extensive wine list" and "polished" service; set in a "well-preserved", "romantic" Victorian plantation house, it boasts several dining rooms, "each with its own personality", making it "perfect" for a "special dinner", and while it's "pricey", the "lively bar" has a cheaper menu.

	FOOD	DECOR	SERVICE	COST

Waterfront Buffet *Eclectic*
▽ 22 | 20 | 19 | $29

Atlantic City | Harrah's Resort Atlantic City | 777 Harrah's Blvd. (Brigantine Blvd.) | 609-441-5000 | www.harrahs.com

Players "never miss" this Eclectic buffet in AC's Harrah's Resort (especially if they "get comped") for its "amazing variety" of "ethnic and American" dishes, including an "abundance of seafood"; a "cool" vibe and "modern" environs complete the picture.

Waterside *Mediterranean*
20 | 23 | 19 | $55

North Bergen | 7800 River Rd. (77th St.) | 201-861-7767 | www.watersiderestaurantandcatering.com

You "can't beat" the "magnificent" Manhattan views that distinguish the "beautiful" modern setting at this upscale Mediterranean seafooder on the North Bergen waterfront; a few feel the "service leaves a lot to be desired" given the "expensive" tabs, but "the food is more than decent", and "interesting characters" at the bar add to the "fun."

Wayne Steakhouse Ⓜ *Steak*
▽ 25 | 21 | 24 | $58

Wayne | 2230 Hamburg Tpke. (Westview Rd.) | 973-616-0047 | www.waynesteakhouse.com

A "professional" crew comprised of Peter Luger alumni delivers "awesome" dry-aged steaks, seafood dishes and "terrific" sides at this "family"-friendly Wayne BYO steakhouse; some think the "old-world" German ambiance "lacks" in comparison to the cuisine, but there's patio seating for the summer months.

West Lake Seafood *Chinese*
24 | 14 | 18 | $30

Matawan | Pine Crest Plaza | 1016 Rte. 34 (Broad St.) | 732-290-2988 | www.westlakeseafood.com

"As authentic as it gets", this Chinese BYO "strip-mall eatery" in Matawan is like "taking a step into Chinatown" what with "always fresh seafood", "excellent" Peking duck and other "unusual and delicious" dishes; the "complete lack of decor" and erratic service make for a "so-so" ambiance, but "generous portions" and reasonable tabs mean it's "a great place for the family."

What's Your Beef? *Steak*
21 | 15 | 18 | $41

Rumson | 21 W. River Rd. (Lafayette St.) | 732-842-6205 | www.whatsyourbeefrumsonnj.com

"Choose your own cut of meat" and "place your order at the grill" at this Rumson steakhouse that attracts a "nice crowd" from the "neighborhood" with its "old-school menu" and "big salad bar"; some find it "expensive", considering that you "sort of serve yourself", while others say the decor "needs a major makeover", but to regulars it always "feels like coming home" to the "familylike atmosphere."

Whispers *American*
26 | 24 | 25 | $58

Spring Lake | Hewitt Wellington Hotel | 200 Monmouth Ave. (2nd Ave.) | 732-974-9755 | www.whispersrestaurant.com

"Not your mother's average Shore restaurant", this "upscale" New American in Spring Lake's Hewitt Wellington Hotel is "always a treat", thanks to "superb" cuisine and "gracious" service in "cozy"

"Victorian surroundings"; "BYO helps" temper the "high" tabs, and while some caution that "weekends are noisy and crowded", most report a "beautiful dining experience."

Whistlers Inn ● *American/BBQ* — 20 | 17 | 18 | $19

Cinnaminson | 901 Rte. 130 S. (Riverton Rd.) | 856-786-7427 | www.whistlersinnnj.com

For a "classic pub dining experience", Cinnaminson locals "mingle with neighbors" at this affordable watering hole where the "friendly" staff slings "excellent wings and barbecue" from the on-site smokehouse; the "rustic bar atmosphere" gets middling scores, though the spacious outdoor deck "greatly expands the capacity and enjoyment" during the warmer months.

White House *Sandwiches* — 25 | 13 | 17 | $15

Atlantic City | Trump Taj Mahal | 1000 Boardwalk (Virginia Ave.) | 609-345-7827
Atlantic City | 2301 Arctic Ave. (Mississippi Ave.) | 609-345-8599 ⊄ www.whitehousesubshop.net

The "legendary" submarine sandwiches at this Atlantic City "staple" are so "delicious", devotees of the original cash-only Arctic Avenue location have put up with "brusque" service, lines and "divey" digs for years; those in the know say the "cheap", "enormous" hoagies made with "fresh" fillings and "scrumptious", locally baked bread are "just as wonderful" at the newer Trump Taj Mahal locale – plus you can pay with plastic.

White Mana ●⊄ *Burgers* — 18 | 13 | 18 | $11

Jersey City | 470 Tonnele Ave. (Manhattan Ave.) | 201-963-1441

"Wallow in burger heaven" 24/7 at this "cheap", cash-only Jersey City greasy spoon set in "classic 1939 digs" that were originally built for the NY World's Fair; regulars with "wonderful memories" say "forget the decor" and just soak up the "history" – it's "pretty much an institution."

White Manna *Burgers* — 22 | 13 | 18 | $10

Hackensack | 358 River St. (bet. Anderson & Camden Sts.) | 201-342-0914

Fans "can't get enough" of the "delish" sliders at this budget Hackensack "classic", where it's a "real treat" to watch the crowd ranging from "suits to hard hats" "order burgers by the bunch"; the "shoebox-size" spot is "always cramped" (think "10 clowns in a Volkswagen"), service can be "slow" and "you'll smell like onions for hours", but most agree it's "worthy of a trip"; P.S. no relation to JC's White Mana.

NEW WildFlour Bakery/Cafe Ⓜ *Bakery* — - | - | - | I

Lawrenceville | 2691 Main St. (bet. Gordon Ave. & Manning Ln.) | 609-620-1100 | www.wildflourbakery-cafe.com

Fresh breads, pastries and cakes join sweet and savory crêpes, salads and soups on the entirely gluten-free menu at this Lawrenceville bakery/cafe; tucked into a Victorian house on historic Main Street, it's open for breakfast, lunch and weekend brunch, and there's free Wi-Fi for the laptop crowd.

William Douglas Steakhouse 🗷 Ⓜ *Steak* 24 | 24 | 22 | $62

Cherry Hill | Garden State Park | 941 Haddonfield Rd. (bet. Graham & Severn Aves.) | 856-665-6100 | www.williamdouglassteakhouse.com

There's "nothing like a good steak" swoon devotees of the "deluxe, mouthwatering" meat at this "serious" steakhouse that "shares a kitchen with McCormick & Schmick's" in Cherry Hill's former Garden State Park racetrack; some warn the "upscale pricing" might "leave a gaping hole in your wallet", but given the "wonderful" service and "elegant", equestrian-themed atmosphere with frequent live jazz, it's a "superb" setting for "business entertainment"; P.S. closed Sundays and Mondays.

Windansea *Seafood* 20 | 21 | 20 | $39

Highlands | 56 Shrewsbury Ave. (bet. Cornwall & Jackson Sts.) | 732-872-2266 | www.windanseanj.com

The "view is top-notch" at this "casual" Highlands seafooder where "dinner on the water's edge" offers vistas of the Shrewsbury River, Sandy Hook bay and even the "NYC skyline"; while "friendly" staffers serve "reliably good" (if "typical Shore") eats to dock-and-diners and families, it's the "bustling bar trade" and live music that makes the tiki-style deck a twentysomething "party all summer."

The WindMill *Hot Dogs* 19 | 14 | 17 | $12

Hoboken | 79 Hudson St. (bet. Hudson Pl. & Newark St.) | 201-963-0900 ●

Westfield | 256 E. Broad St. (bet. Central Ave. & Elmer St.) | 908-233-2001

Belmar | 1201 River Rd. (K St.) | 732-681-9628 ●

Freehold | 3338 Hwy. 9 (Jackson Mills Rd.) | 732-303-9855

Long Branch | 200 Ocean Avenue N. (bet. Joline & Seaview Aves.) | 732-870-6098

Long Branch | 586 Ocean Blvd. (Montgomery Ave.) | 732-229-9863 ●

Ocean Grove | 18 S. Main St. (bet. Bond St. & Lake Ave.) | 732-988-5277

Red Bank | 22 N. Bridge Ave. (bet. Front & Monmouth Sts.) | 732-747-5958

www.windmillhotdogs.com

For a "relaxing" "quick bite", these "classic" hot dog stands are a "good bet" according to fans who relish the "reliable" red hots with a "slight crunch when you bite", "dependable burgers", fries and more; you pretty much "help yourself" in the "basic" surroundings, and while a few find it "overpriced for what it is", others insist there's "nothing better after a day at the beach."

Witherspoon Grill *Seafood/Steak* 22 | 21 | 20 | $50

Princeton | 57 Witherspoon St. (bet. Hulfish St. & Paul Robeson Pl.) | 609-924-6011 | www.jmgroupprinceton.com

"A true Princeton charmer", this "elegant" but "casual" surf 'n' turfer makes a "good local standby" for its "nice choice of steaks, burgers", "amazing crab cakes" and "great cocktails"; though service can be "absentminded" and "expensive" tabs match the "high noise" level, a "hopping bar scene" and "pleasant" outdoor patio help ease the pain.

	FOOD	DECOR	SERVICE	COST

Wolfgang Puck
American Grille *American*
25 | 22 | 23 | $59

Atlantic City | Borgata Hotel Casino & Spa | 1 Borgata Way (Huron Ave.) |
609-317-1000 | www.theborgata.com

"Wolfgang is one of the best" say fans of chef Puck's "classy, tasty"
New American in AC's Borgata Hotel where the "middle of the casino" locale may be "exposed", but the "comfortable" setting is still
"elegant"; the staff is "attentive", and though "expensive" tabs in
the dining room mean it "helps to be a high roller", some say eating
in the tavern area is "more fun" – plus it "won't break the bank."

Wondee's *Thai*
▽ 22 | 13 | 19 | $23

Hackensack | 296 Main St. (bet. Berry & Camden St.) | 201-883-1700

Enthusiasts exhort "if you like Thai, try" this "simple, storefront" BYO
in Hackensack where the "well-prepared", "different and delicious"
dishes "won't let you down"; though the "very casual" decor "reminds you of a diner", "low prices" and a "helpful staff" distract.

Wonder Seafood *Chinese*
23 | 15 | 18 | $20

Edison | 1984 Rte. 27 (bet. Langstaff Ave. & Municipal Blvd.) |
732-287-6328

"Be adventurous" and "try everything" (even if you "wonder what it
is you are eating") at this "authentic" and inexpensive Cantonese
BYO in Edison lauded for its "huge selection of seafood" and "really
great dim sum"; the "small, tight quarters" are "always busy", and
while some think the staff can be "surly", others praise the recommendations of the host – "he's never let us down."

Xina *Chinese*
▽ 23 | 20 | 23 | $30

Toms River | 3430 Rte. 37 (Douglas St.) | 732-279-6327 |
www.xinarestaurant.com

This midpriced Chinese newcomer in Toms River is quickly becoming
an area "favorite" for its "high-quality" fare, including "appetizers
that are big enough to share", an "extensive sushi bar" and "remarkable" raw bar lineup; "friendly" service and a "large, open dining
room" are further pluses, but for some, the "best part is it's BYO."

Yankee Doodle Tap Room *Pub Food*
17 | 20 | 18 | $34

Princeton | Nassau Inn | 10 Palmer Sq. (Hulfish St.) | 609-688-2600 |
www.nassauinn.com

For "nostalgia" and "tradition" this "old Princeton spot" in the Nassau
Inn is a "cozy" "must-stop" thanks to "photos of illustrious alumni",
"wooden booths" and the namesake Norman Rockwell mural behind
the bar; the "standard" American pub grub is deemed only "fair",
the service "passable" and prices "expensive for hotel food", but
where else can you "eat at a table where Einstein carved his name"?

Ya Ya Noodles *Noodle Shop*
20 | 16 | 18 | $22

Skillman | Montgomery Shopping Ctr. | 1325 Rte. 206 N. (Georgetown
Franklin Tpke.) | 609-921-8551 | www.yayanoodles.com

Serving up "simple, but good" Chinese in the Montgomery Shopping
Center, this "consistent", reasonably priced BYO stays "popular",

especially among moviegoers, due to its "convenient location" and "pretty tasty" eats including "excellent noodles" and bubble teas; the decor is "dated", and while some call it "peaceful", others say "they move you along", but either way it's "worth a try."

Yellow Fin *American*

`25` `19` `20` `$55`

Surf City | 104 24th St. (Long Beach Blvd.) | 609-494-7001
The "innovative dishes are a treat" at this BYO New American "gem" in Surf City, especially "outstanding" seafood; some quip you'll have to "leave your car keys" to settle your tab, and others pan "rushed" service and "noisy", "close quarters", but most say it's "not to be missed."

Yellow Submarine *Cheesesteaks*

`21` `14` `19` `$11`

Maple Shade | 710 N. Forklanding Rd. (Orchard Ave.) | 856-667-2110
"Huge" cheesesteaks (as well as "very good" subs) are on offer at this Maple Shade take-out counter; the digs are "simple", but service is "friendly" and prices are "reasonable."

Yokohama Japanese Restaurant *Japanese*

▽ `25` `24` `24` `$26`

Maple Shade | 300 S. Lenola Rd. (Old Kings Hwy.) | 856-608-8812 | www.yokohamacuisine.com
At this Maple Shade "gem", "delicious, beautifully prepared" sushi and other "high-quality" Japanese dishes are matched by "exceptional" service from "super-nice" servers and owners; "excellent prices" are another reason fans insist "you can't go wrong" here.

Yoshi-Sono *Japanese*

`21` `17` `20` `$30`

West Orange | 643 Eagle Rock Ave. (Pleasant Valley Way) | 973-325-2005 | www.yoshi-sono.com
For most this "quiet" West Orange Japanese is "worth trying to find", thanks to "consistently good" fare, "bargain prices" and "friendly" staffers who "really try hard"; the consensus is that it's "not a bad choice" for "sushi in the 'burbs."

Yumi Ⓢ Ⓜ *Asian*

`26` `20` `22` `$39`

Sea Bright | 1120 Ocean Ave. (bet. Church & New Sts.) | 732-212-0881 | www.yumirestaurant.com
The "quality and presentation" are "as good as it gets" at this Sea Bright Asian BYO where "super-fresh" fish is transformed into "excellent sushi" and "outstanding, creative rolls", while "delicious" fusion dishes "can't be beat"; though some complain the portions are "shrinking and the prices are increasing", for most, "pretty" digs and "friendly" service round out a "fabulous", "memorable meal."

Za *American*

`22` `21` `22` `$47`

Pennington | 147 W. Delaware Ave. (bet. Green St. & Rte. 31) | 609-737-4400 | www.zarestaurants.com
This Pennington BYO is a "special place" where a "limited but excellent", if somewhat "high-priced", seasonal menu of New American fare (including a 'Green Table' selection of less expensive, healthier dishes) is served by "friendly" folk in "quirky" environs featuring a gallery of works by emerging artists inside and an outdoor wisteria garden that's a warm-weather "oasis."

	FOOD	DECOR	SERVICE	COST

Zack's Oak Bar & Restaurant *American* | 21 | 20 | 20 | $30

Hoboken | 232 Willow Ave. (3rd St.) | 201-653-7770 |
www.zackshoboken.com

Hobokenites look to this "homey" tavern for "quick" American pub grub at a "reasonable price"; while most content themselves with "great" burgers and "friendly" service, there are some grumblings of "better options" in the area.

Zafra *Pan-Latin* | 24 | 18 | 20 | $30

Hoboken | 301 Willow Ave. (3rd St.) | 201-610-9801 |
www.zafrakitchens.com

Chef Maricel Presilla's "wonderful" small plates will "excite your taste buds" at this Pan-Latin BYO "gem" that's a "great-value" alternative to sibling Cucharamama; "friendly" service is another plus, and while it's "tiny" inside, you can "sit outside on a nice day" and enjoy "the Hoboken street scene."

Zeppoli *Italian* | 26 | 21 | 23 | $39

Collingswood | 618 Collings Ave. (bet. Richey Ave. & White Horse Pike) | 856-854-2670 | www.zeppolirestaurant.com

"The best in South Jersey, hands down" declare devotees of Vetri alum Joey Baldino's midpriced BYO, which has won Collingswood's heart with his "top-notch" takes on "rustic Sicilian food", served by a solid staff; the "basic" interior boasts a mere 35 seats, so it's "not an easy reservation" and can get "loud and cramped", but most happily jump the hurdles for cooking "the way Italian should be done."

NEW Zinburger Wine & Burger Bar *Burgers* | 21 | 18 | 20 | $25

Clifton | Promenade Shops at Clifton | 853 Rte. 3 W. (bet. Bloomfield & Passaic Aves.) | 973-272-1492
Paramus | 1 Garden State Plaza (Garden State Plaza Pkwy.) | 201-368-8092
www.zinburgernj.com

"Creative", "artisanal burgers" and "unique", "tasty" sides, plus a "nice selection" of wines are a "match made in heaven" for fans of this hamburger chainlet; although a vocal minority finds it "kinda pricey" for what it is, "friendly" staffers and "appealing" decor compensate.

NEW Zoe's Kitchen *Mediterranean* | - | - | - | I

Marlton | 500 Rte. 73 S. (Sagemore Dr.) | 856-334-5615 |
www.zoeskitchen.com

Salads, pita sandwiches and other light, Mediterranean-inspired dishes pack the all-day menu at this Marlton branch of the national fast-casual chain; the colorful, counter-serve setting suits for a quick bite or take-home meal.

Zylo *Steak* | 22 | 25 | 21 | $61

Hoboken | W Hotel | 225 River St. (bet. 2nd & 3rd Sts.) |
201-253-2500 | www.zylorestaurant.com

An "impeccable" view of NYC and "excellent" food draw a "very trendy" crowd to this Tuscan steakhouse in Hoboken's W Hotel; the "beautiful" setting and "above-average" service leave most feeling "happy", but others are "unsure" if it's "worth the high prices."

INDEXES

LOCATION MAPS

Special Features

Listings cover the best in each category and include names, locations and Food ratings. Multi-location restaurants' features may vary by branch.

BREAKFAST

(See also Hotel Dining)

Alice's | **Lake Hopatcong**	20
Country Pancake | **Ridgewood**	19
Eppes Essen | **Livingston**	19
Full Moon | **Lambertville**	20
Hobby's Deli | **Newark**	25
Jack's Café | **Westwood**	22
Janice | **Ho-Ho-Kus**	21
Java Moon | **Jackson**	23
Je's | **Newark**	24
La Isla | **Hoboken**	25
Little Food Cafe | **multi.**	23
Market Roost | **Flemington**	23
Mastoris | **Bordentown**	21
Mustache Bill's | **Barnegat Light**	22
Ponzio's | **Cherry Hill**	20
Pop Shop | **Collingswood**	23
Raymond's | **multi.**	21
Rolling Pin Cafe | **Westwood**	25
Skylark | **multi.**	21
Tick Tock | **Clifton**	19
Tisha's | **Cape May**	25
Toast | **Montclair**	21
Urban Table | **Morristown**	19
Vincentown Diner | **Vincentown**	21
Zafra | **Hoboken**	24

BRUNCH

Amanda's | **Hoboken**	25
Amelia's Bistro | **Jersey City**	20
Avenue | **Long Branch**	22
Blue Morel | **Morristown**	24
Brass Rail | **Hoboken**	19
Brothers Moon | **Hopewell**	24
Chart House | **Weehawken**	22
Court St. Rest.Bar | **Hoboken**	21
Crown Palace | **Middletown**	20
David Burke From. | **Rumson**	25
Dim Sum Dynasty | **Ridgewood**	20
Dining/Anty. David's | **Hoboken**	24
Elements | **Princeton**	25
Elysian Café | **Hoboken**	23
Esty St. | **Park Ridge**	25

Fiddleheads | **Jamesburg**	22
Gables Rest. | **Beach Haven**	25
Harvest Bistro | **Closter**	21
Ho-Ho-Kus Tavern | **Ho-Ho-Kus**	21
KC Prime | **Lawrenceville**	22
Lambertville Stn. | **Lambertville**	20
Levant Grille | **Englewood**	21
Liberty House | **Jersey City**	20
Light Horse Tavern | **Jersey City**	22
Little Food Cafe | **Bayonne**	23
LuNello's Montville | **Montville**	21
Madame Claude | **Jersey City**	22
Madeleine's | **Northvale**	24
Manor | **W Orange**	24
Marco/Pepe | **Jersey City**	23
Maritime Parc | **Jersey City**	23
Moghul | **Edison**	21
Molly Pitcher Inn | **Red Bank**	22
MoonShine Modern | **Millburn**	19
Ninety Acres/Natirar | **Peapack**	25
Park W. Tavern | **Ridgewood**	20
Peacock Inn Rest. | **Princeton**	26
Rat's | **Hamilton**	25
Raymond's | **multi.**	21
Robin's Nest | **Mt Holly**	24
Rob's Bistro | **Madison**	22
Rod's Steak | **Morristown**	22
Satis | **Jersey City**	24
Stone/Stirling Ridge | **Warren**	22
Sweet Basil's | **Livingston**	23
Taqueria D.T. | **Jersey City**	25
Taste/Asia | **Chatham**	23
Tortilla Press | **Collingswood**	21
3 Forty Grill | **Hoboken**	21
3 West | **Basking Ridge**	21
Toast | **Montclair**	21
Urban Table | **Morristown**	19
Verjus | **Maplewood**	24
Villa Amalfi | **Cliffside Pk**	23
W. Lake Seafood | **Matawan**	24
Za | **Pennington**	22
Zafra | **Hoboken**	24

BUFFET

(Check availability)

Aamantran | **Toms River**	21
Akbar | **Edison**	21
Amiya | **Jersey City**	21
Antonia's/Park | **N Bergen**	22
Bernards Inn | **Bernardsville**	25
Bistro 55 | **Rochelle Pk**	19
Bistro/Marino | **Collingswood**	25
Black Forest Inn | **Stanhope**	24
Brick Ln. Curry | **multi.**	23
Capriccio | **A.C.**	24
Chand Palace | **multi.**	22
Cinnamon | **Morris Plains**	21
Cranbury Inn | **Cranbury**	18
David Burke From. | **Rumson**	25
Grain House | **Basking Ridge**	20
Guru Palace | **N Brunswick**	19
Hat Tavern | **Summit**	20
India/Hudson | **Hoboken**	20
Karma Kafe | **Hoboken**	23
Kaya's Kitchen | **Belmar**	25
KC Prime | **Lawrenceville**	22
Kinara | **Edgewater**	21
Lafayette House | **Lafayette**	22
Málaga's | **Hamilton**	26
Manor | **W Orange**	24
Mantra | **Paramus**	21
Martino's | **Somerville**	22
McLoone's | **Long Branch**	19
Mehndi | **Morristown**	23
Mill/Spg. Lake | **Spring Lake Hts**	20
Minado | **multi.**	22
Moghul | **Edison**	21
Molly Pitcher Inn | **Red Bank**	22
Namaskaar | **Englewood**	23
Neelam | **multi.**	21
Old Man Rafferty's | **New Bruns.**	19
Saffron | **E Hanover**	21
Salt Creek Grille | **Rumson**	21
Spargo's | **Manalapan**	22
Villa Amalfi | **Cliffside Pk**	23
Waterfront Buffet | **A.C.**	22

BUSINESS DINING

Acquaviva/Fonti | **Westfield**	20
Adega Grill | **Newark**	21
Aldo/Gianni | **Montvale**	21
Antonia's/Park | **N Bergen**	22

A Toute Heure | **Cranford**	26
Bacari Grill | **Washington Twp**	21
Benihana | **multi.**	20
Bernards Inn | **Bernardsville**	25
Biagio's | **Paramus**	20
Biddy O'Malley's | **Northvale**	20
Blue Morel | **Morristown**	24
Blue2O | **Cherry Hill**	22
Bonefish Grill | **multi.**	21
Blvd. Five 72 | **Kenilworth**	23
Brass Rail | **Hoboken**	19
Café Azzurro | **Peapack**	22
Cafe Emilia | **Bridgewater**	20
Calandra's | **Fairfield**	21
Capital Grille | **Paramus**	25
Cara Mia | **Millburn**	21
Casa Dante | **Jersey City**	22
Cenzino | **Oakland**	25
Char Steak | **Raritan**	23
Chart House | **Weehawken**	22
Chef's Table | **Franklin Lakes**	27
Chez Catherine | **Westfield**	26
Chophouse | **Gibbsboro**	24
Corso 98 | **Montclair**	23
Da Filippo's | **Somerville**	24
Dante's Rist. | **Mendham**	20
Daryl | **New Bruns.**	23
David Burke From. | **Rumson**	25
Dimora | **Norwood**	23
Dino/Harry's | **Hoboken**	24
Due Mari | **New Bruns.**	26
E & V | **Paterson**	24
Eccola Italian | **Parsippany**	22
Edward's Steak | **Jersey City**	21
Egan/Sons | **W Orange**	20
El Cid | **Paramus**	22
Eno Terra | **Kingston**	25
Esty St. | **Park Ridge**	25
Fascino | **Montclair**	26
55 Main | **Flemington**	22
Fiorino | **Summit**	23
Fire/Oak | **Jersey City**	20
Fleming's | **multi.**	23
Franco's Metro | **Fort Lee**	22
Fuji | **Haddonfield**	25
Gallagher's | **A.C.**	23
Giumarello's | **Westmont**	25
Gladstone | **Gladstone**	21
Grand Cafe | **Morristown**	23

Grissini | **Englewood Cliffs**	22
Hamilton/Ward | **Paterson**	24
Harvest Bistro | **Closter**	21
Hat Tavern | **Summit**	20
Highlawn Pavilion | **W Orange**	24
Ho-Ho-Kus Tavern | **Ho-Ho-Kus**	21
Huntley Taverne | **Summit**	22
Iberia | **Newark**	22
Il Capriccio | **Whippany**	25
Il Fiore | **Collingswood**	24
Il Villaggio | **Carlstadt**	24
Ivy Inn | **Hasbrouck Hts**	21
J&K Steak | **Morristown**	22
Just Rest. | **Old Bridge**	24
Kyma | **Somerville**	23
La Campagna | **Morristown**	24
La Dolce Vita | **Belmar**	22
L'Allegria | **Madison**	23
La Strada | **Randolph**	23
Latour | **Ridgewood**	26
Legal Sea Foods | **Paramus**	21
Levant Grille | **Englewood**	21
Liberty House | **Jersey City**	20
Light Horse Tavern | **Jersey City**	22
Lithos | **Livingston**	23
Locale | **Closter**	21
Lotus Cafe | **Hackensack**	21
Luke Palladino | **A.C.**	24
Lu Nello | **Cedar Grove**	25
LuNello's Montvill | **Montville**	21
Madeleine's | **Northvale**	24
Manor | **W Orange**	24
Maritime Parc | **Jersey City**	23
Masina | **Weehawken**	20
McCormick/Schmick's | **Hackensack**	20
Mekong Grill | **Ridgewood**	20
Mill/Spg. Lake | **Spring Lake Hts**	20
MK Valencia | **Ridgefield Pk**	21
Mojave Grille | **Westfield**	21
MoonShine Modern | **Millburn**	19
Morton's | **Hackensack**	25
Nanni Rist. | **Rochelle Pk**	22
Nico Kitchen/Bar | **Newark**	20
Ninety Acres/Natirar | **Peapack**	25
Oceanos | **Fair Lawn**	24
Old Homestead | **A.C.**	26
Oliver a Bistro | **Bordentown**	25
Osteria Giotto | **Montclair**	25

Osteria Morini | **Bernardsville**	24
Palace of Asia | **Cherry Hill**	23
Panico's | **New Bruns.**	21
Park/Orchard | **E Rutherford**	22
Park Steak | **Park Ridge**	24
Park W. Tavern | **Ridgewood**	20
Peacock Inn Rest. | **Princeton**	26
P.F. Chang's | **multi.**	21
Phillips Seafood | **A.C.**	21
Pluckemin Inn | **Bedminster**	25
Ponzio's | **Cherry Hill**	20
Portofino Rist. | **Tinton Falls**	21
Porto Leggero | **Jersey City**	23
Puccini's | **Jersey City**	22
Queen Margherita | **Nutley**	24
Rare | **Little Falls**	23
Raven/Peach | **Fair Haven**	24
River Palm Terrace | **multi.**	25
Rod's Steak | **Morristown**	22
Roots Steak | **Summit**	25
Ruth's Chris | **multi.**	25
Ryland Inn | **Whitehouse**	25
Sam Mickail's CUT | **W Orange**	–
Sanzari's | **New Milford**	21
Scalini Fedeli | **Chatham**	27
Sear House | **Closter**	23
Segovia | **Moonachie**	22
Segovia Steak | **Little Ferry**	22
Serenade | **Chatham**	26
Sirena Rist. | **Long Branch**	22
Son Cubano | **W New York**	20
Sorrento | **E Rutherford**	23
Spain | **Newark**	22
Spanish Pavillion | **Harrison**	23
Spanish Tavern | **multi.**	22
Steakhouse 85 | **New Bruns.**	24
Stone/Stirling Ridge | **Warren**	22
Stony Hill Inn | **Hackensack**	22
Tabor Rd. Tavern | **Morris Plains**	22
Taverna Mykonos | **Elmwood Pk**	24
NEW Tavro 13 | **Swedesboro**	–
Terra Nova | **Sewell**	21
3 Forty Grill | **Hoboken**	21
3 West | **Basking Ridge**	21
Tim Schafer's | **Morristown**	23
Tony/Caneca | **Newark**	22
Ursino | **Union**	24
Valencia | **Elizabeth**	24
Valentino's | **Park Ridge**	19

Vasili's | **Teaneck**	20
Villa Amalfi | **Cliffside Pk**	23
Vine | **Basking Ridge**	24
Wasabi | **Somerville**	22
Waterside | **N Bergen**	20
Wayne Steak | **Wayne**	25
Wm. Douglas | **Cherry Hill**	24
Zack's Oak Bar/Rest. | **Hoboken**	21
Zeppoli | **Collingswood**	26
Zylo | **Hoboken**	22

BYO

Adara | **Montclair**	19
Ah' Pizz | **Montclair**	20
Ajihei | **Princeton**	24
Al Dente Italiana | **Moorestown**	23
A Little Bit/Cuba Dos | **Freehold**	22
A Little Café | **Voorhees**	23
Allen's | **New Gretna**	22
Anna's Italian | **Middletown**	23
Aoyama | **multi.**	23
Aozora | **Montclair**	23
Arturo's | **Maplewood**	24
Arugula | **Sewell**	23
A Taste/Mexico | **Princeton**	20
Athenian Gdn. | **Galloway Twp**	22
A Toute Heure | **Cranford**	26
Avanti | **Pennington**	21
Bamboo Leaf | **multi.**	20
Barone's | **multi.**	23
Baumgart's | **multi.**	18
Belford Bistro | **Belford**	26
Bell/Whistle | **Hopewell**	20
Benito's Trattoria | **Chester**	23
Beyti Kebab | **Union City**	22
Big John's | **W Berlin**	23
Bistro/Marino | **Collingswood**	25
Bistro Olé | **Asbury Pk**	22
Black Duck | **W Cape May**	26
Black-Eyed Susans | **Harvey Cedars**	24
Black Trumpet | **Spring Lake**	22
Blu | **Montclair**	24
Blue Bottle Cafe | **Hopewell**	26
Blue Claw Crab | **Burlington**	24
Blue Fish Grill | **Flemington**	23
Blue Point Grill | **Princeton**	25
Blue Rooster | **Cranbury**	22
Bombay Bistro | **Summit**	21
Brandl | **Belmar**	24

Brian's | **Lambertville**	26
Brick Ln. Curry | **multi.**	23
Brioso | **Marlboro**	23
British Chip Shop | **Haddonfield**	24
Brooklyn's Pizzeria | **multi.**	22
Brothers Moon | **Hopewell**	24
Café Azzurro | **Peapack**	22
Cafe Graziella | **Hillsborough**	22
Cafe Matisse | **Rutherford**	26
Cafe Panache | **Ramsey**	26
Casa Maya | **multi.**	21
Casual Habana | **Hackensack**	25
Chambers Walk | **Lawrenceville**	22
Chao Phaya | **Somerville**	22
Charrito's | **Hoboken**	22
Chef Jon's | **Whippany**	20
Chef's Table | **Franklin Lakes**	27
Chef Vola's | **A.C.**	27
Chinese Mirch | **multi.**	19
Christie's Italian | **Howell**	23
Cinnamon | **Morris Plains**	21
Clementine's | **Avon-by-Sea**	23
Coriander | **Voorhees**	24
Costanera | **Montclair**	24
Country Pancake | **Ridgewood**	19
Cuban Pete's | **Montclair**	20
CulinAriane | **Montclair**	27
Da Filippo's | **Somerville**	24
Da's Kitchen | **Hopewell**	25
Da Soli | **Haddonfield**	25
Dayi'nin Yeri | **Cliffside Pk**	24
DeLorenzo's Pizza | **Hamilton Twp**	25
DeLorenzo's Pies | **Robbinsville**	27
NEW Despaña | **Princeton**	–
Dim Sum Dynasty | **Ridgewood**	20
Dining/Anty. David's | **Hoboken**	24
Di Palma Bros. | **N Bergen**	23
Dish | **Red Bank**	23
D'Jeet? | **Red Bank**	21
Dream Cuisine | **Cherry Hill**	26
Efe's Med. Grill | **multi.**	21
El Azteca | **Mt Laurel**	23
NEW Elbow Room | **Newark**	–
Elements Asia | **Lawrenceville**	23
NEW Elena Wu | **Voorhees**	–
El Mesón Café | **Freehold**	23
El Tule | **Lambertville**	25
Eppes Essen | **Livingston**	19
NEW Escape | **Montclair**	–

Etc. Steak | **Teaneck**	25
NEW Europe Café | **Tenafly**	-
Far East Taste | **Eatontown**	23
Fascino | **Montclair**	26
Fedora Café | **Lawrenceville**	22
Ferry House | **Princeton**	22
Fiddleheads | **Jamesburg**	22
15 Fox Pl. | **Jersey City**	22
55 Main | **Flemington**	22
Fin Raw Bar/Kitchen | **Montclair**	24
Firefly Bistro | **Manasquan**	22
Five Guys | **Brick**	22
Fontana/Trevi | **Leonia**	22
Fresco Steak | **Milltown**	23
Fuji | **Haddonfield**	25
Full Moon | **Lambertville**	20
Gennaro's | **Princeton**	21
Good Karma Cafe | **Red Bank**	22
NEW Grange | **Westwood**	-
Hamilton's Grill | **Lambertville**	24
Harvey Cedars | **multi.**	20
Hummus Elite | **Englewood**	21
I Gemelli Rist. | **S Hackensack**	25
Ikko | **Brick**	25
Il Fiore | **Collingswood**	24
Il Mondo Vecchio | **Madison**	25
IndeBlue | **Collingswood**	25
NEW Indiya | **Collingswood**	-
Isabella's Bistro | **Westfield**	19
It's Greek To Me | **multi.**	19
Jack's Café | **Westwood**	22
J&K Steak | **multi.**	22
Janice | **Ho-Ho-Kus**	21
Java Moon | **Jackson**	23
Jimmy Buff's | **Kenilworth**	20
Joe Pesce | **Collingswood**	25
Joe's Peking Duck | **Marlton**	23
Jose's Mex. Cantina | **multi.**	20
Juanito's | **multi.**	22
Justin's Rist. | **multi.**	22
Kailash | **Ridgewood**	21
Kanji | **Tinton Falls**	24
Kaya's Kitchen | **Belmar**	25
Kevin's Thyme | **Ho-Ho-Kus**	25
Khun Thai | **Short Hills**	22
Khyber Grill | **South Plainfield**	21
Kibitz Room | **Cherry Hill**	24
Kinara | **Edgewater**	21
Konbu | **Manalapan**	23
Krave Café | **Newton**	25
Kuzina/Sofia | **Cherry Hill**	22
Kyma | **Somerville**	23
Labrador | **Normandy Bch**	21
La Campagna | **Morristown**	24
La Cipollina | **Freehold**	21
La Couronne | **Montclair**	23
La Focaccia | **Summit**	23
La Fontana Coast | **Sea Isle City**	23
La Isla | **Hoboken**	25
La Mezzaluna | **Princeton**	22
La Pastaria | **multi.**	21
La Pergola | **Millburn**	20
NEW La Sera | **Wyckoff**	-
La Spiaggia | **Ship Bottom**	23
Latour | **Ridgewood**	26
Latz's/Bay | **Somers Point**	21
Lemongrass | **Morris Plains**	23
Le Rendez-Vous | **Kenilworth**	26
Levant Grille | **Englewood**	21
NEW Lidia's Cuban | **Cranford**	-
Lilly's/Canal | **Lambertville**	20
Limani | **Westfield**	25
NEW Lisa's Med. | **Ridgewood**	-
Little Food Cafe | **Pompton Plains**	23
Little Tuna | **Haddonfield**	22
LoBianco | **Margate**	23
NEW Local Seasonal | **Ramsey**	-
Lola Latin Bistro | **Metuchen**	21
Lorena's | **Maplewood**	28
Lotus Cafe | **Hackensack**	21
LouCás | **Edison**	23
Luca's Rist. | **Somerset**	24
Luke Palladino | **Northfield**	24
Madame Claude | **Jersey City**	22
Main St. | **Kingston**	20
Manon | **Lambertville**	24
Margherita's | **Hoboken**	21
Market Roost | **Flemington**	23
Martino's | **Somerville**	22
Matt's Red Rooster | **Flemington**	26
Meemah | **Edison**	23
Megu Sushi | **multi.**	24
Mekong Grill | **Ridgewood**	20
Mesob | **Montclair**	23
Midori | **Denville**	23
Mie Thai | **Woodbridge**	23
Mikado | **Cherry Hill**	22
NEW Mistral | **Princeton**	-

TwoFiftyTwo | **Bedminster**	20
Under/Moon | **Bordentown**	23
Vasili's | **Teaneck**	20
Village Gourmet | **Rutherford**	19
Vlg. Green | **Ridgewood**	24
Wasabi | **E Brunswick**	22
Wayne Steak | **Wayne**	25
W. Lake Seafood | **Matawan**	24
Whispers | **Spring Lake**	26
Wondee's | **Hackensack**	22
Wonder Seafood | **Edison**	23
Xina | **Toms River**	23
Ya Ya | **Skillman**	20
Yellow Fin | **Surf City**	25
Yokohama | **Maple Shade**	25
Za | **Pennington**	22
Zafra | **Hoboken**	24
Zeppoli | **Collingswood**	26

CELEBRITY CHEFS

Christopher Albrecht	
Eno Terra | **Kingston**	25
Scott Anderson	
Elements | **Princeton**	25
NEW Mistral | **Princeton**	-
Zod Arifai	
Blu | **Montclair**	24
Daryl | **New Bruns.**	23
Next Door | **Montclair**	22
Claude Baills	
Chef's Table | **Franklin Lakes**	27
Joseph Baldino	
Zeppoli | **Collingswood**	26
Anthony Bucco	
Ryland Inn | **Whitehouse**	25
David Burke	
David Burke From. | **Rumson**	25
Gaspard Caloz	
Madeleine's | **Northvale**	24
Humberto Campos	
Lorena's | **Maplewood**	28
Andrea Carbine	
A Toute Heure | **Cranford**	26
Michael Cetrulo	
Il Mondo Vecchio | **Madison**	25
Porto Leggero | **Jersey City**	23
Scalini Fedeli | **Chatham**	27
Sirena Rist. | **Long Branch**	22
Stella Marina | **Asbury Pk**	23

Thomas Ciszak	
Blue Morel | **Morristown**	24
Chakra | **Paramus**	23
Ryan DePersio	
Bar Cara | **Bloomfield**	21
Fascino | **Montclair**	26
Nico Kitchen/Bar | **Newark**	20
Andrew DiCataldo	
Patria | **Rahway**	23
David Drake	
Alice's | **Lake Hopatcong**	20
Ariane Duarte	
CulinAriane | **Montclair**	27
David Felton	
Ninety Acres/Natirar | **Peapack**	25
Terence Feury	
NEW Tavro 13 | **Swedesboro**	-
Bobby Flay	
Bobby Flay Steak | **A.C.**	25
Bobby's Burger | **multi.**	21
Marc Forgione	
American Cut | **A.C.**	24
Jose Garces	
Amada | **A.C.**	26
Village Whiskey | **A.C.**	24
Nicholas Harary	
Nicholas | **Red Bank**	28
Corey Heyer	
Bernards Inn | **Bernardsville**	25
Matt Ito	
Fuji | **Haddonfield**	25
Kevin Kohler	
Cafe Panache | **Ramsey**	26
James Laird	
Serenade | **Chatham**	26
Michael Latour	
Latour | **Ridgewood**	26
Bruce Lefebvre	
Frog & Peach | **New Bruns.**	25
Peter Loria	
Cafe Matisse | **Rutherford**	26
Nelson Martinez	
Bibi'z Rest. | **Westwood**	20
Christine Nunn	
NEW Grange | **Westwood**	-
Luke Palladino	
Luke Palladino | **multi.**	24

Nunzio Patruno
Nunzio Rist. | **Collingswood** 23

Manuel Perez
Peacock Inn Rest. | **Princeton** 26

Georges Perrier
Mia | **A.C.** 24

Anthony Pino
Bin 14 | **Hoboken** 23
Dining/Anty. David's | **Hoboken** 24

Kevin Portscher
Vlg. Green | **Ridgewood** 24

Maricel Presilla
Cucharamama | **Hoboken** 25
Zafra | **Hoboken** 24

Wolfgang Puck
Wolfgang Puck | **A.C.** 25

Daniel Richer
Arturo's | **Maplewood** 24

Chris Scarduzio
Mia | **A.C.** 24

John Schatz
Union Park | **Cape May** 26

Tony Sindaco
Hat Tavern | **Summit** 20

Scott Snyder
Blvd. Five 72 | **Kenilworth** 23

Cesar Sotomayor
NEW Café 37 | **Ridgewood** 25

Angelo Stella
Porto Leggero | **Jersey City** 23

Kevin Takafuji
Blue Morel | **Morristown** 24

Josh Thomsen
NEW Agricola | **Princeton** -

Kenneth Trickilo
Liberty House | **Jersey City** 20

Michael Weisshaupt
Rest. Latour | **Hamburg** 26

Michael White
Due Mari | **New Bruns.** 26
Osteria Morini | **Bernardsville** 24

Robert Wiedmaier
Mussel Bar/Wiedmaier | **A.C.** 24

CHILD-FRIENDLY

(Alternatives to the usual fast-food places; * children's menu available)

Aby's* | **Matawan** 20
A Mano* | **Ridgewood** 22
Axelsson's* | **Cape May** 23

Bamboo Leaf | **Bradley Bch** 20
Bareli's | **Secaucus** 23
Barone's* | **multi.** 23
Baumgart's* | **multi.** 18
Benihana* | **multi.** 20
Beyti Kebab | **Union City** 22
Big Ed's BBQ* | **Matawan** 19
Black Duck | **W Cape May** 26
Black Forest Inn | **Stanhope** 24
Blue Point Grill* | **Princeton** 25
Bobby Chez | **multi.** 23
Braddock's* | **Medford** 24
Brioso | **Marlboro** 23
Cafe Loren | **Avalon** 25
Calandra's* | **Fairfield** 21
Capriccio | **A.C.** 24
Casa Giuseppe | **Iselin** 23
Casa Vasca | **Newark** 24
Cassie's* | **Englewood** 19
Chao Phaya | **Somerville** 22
Cheesecake Factory* | **multi.** 21
Chengdu 46 | **Clifton** 23
Christie's Italian* | **Howell** 23
Cucina Calandra* | **Fairfield** 21
Dai-Kichi | **Upper Montclair** 23
Delicious Hgts.* | **Berkeley Hts** 19
Dock's Oyster | **A.C.** 25
E & V | **Paterson** 24
El Azteca* | **Mt Laurel** 23
El Cid | **Paramus** 22
El Mesón Café* | **Freehold** 23
Espo's* | **Raritan** 22
Far East Taste | **Eatontown** 23
Filomena Rustica* | **W Berlin** 23
Fire/Oak* | **multi.** 20
Five Guys* | **multi.** 22
Fornos/Spain | **Newark** 23
Frankie Fed's* | **Freehold Twp** 22
Frenchtown Inn | **Frenchtown** 22
Harvest Moon Inn* | **Ringoes** 23
Hiram's Roadstand | **Fort Lee** 22
Hobby's Deli | **Newark** 25
Ho-Ho-Kus Tavern* | **Ho-Ho-Kus** 21
Holsten's* | **Bloomfield** 19
Ikko* | **Brick** 25
Inn/Hawke Rest.* | **Lambertville** 18
It's Greek To Me | **multi.** 19
Jack's Café* | **Westwood** 22
Java Moon* | **Jackson** 23

Jose's Mex. Cantina* | **multi.**	20
Kibitz Room* | **Cherry Hill**	24
La Esperanza* | **Lindenwold**	24
Legal Sea Foods* | **multi.**	21
Little Tuna* | **Haddonfield**	22
LouCás* | **Edison**	23
Lu Nello | **Cedar Grove**	25
Margherita's | **Hoboken**	21
Mex. Food Factory* | **Marlton**	21
Mikado | **Cherry Hill**	22
Monster Sushi* | **Summit**	20
Mud City Crab* | **Manahawkin**	23
Nana's Deli* | **Livingston**	23
Nanni Rist. | **Rochelle Pk**	22
Navesink Fishery | **Navesink**	25
Nomad Pizza | **Hopewell**	25
Norma's* | **Cherry Hill**	22
Park/Orchard* | **E Rutherford**	22
P.F. Chang's* | **Marlton**	21
Ponzio's* | **Cherry Hill**	20
Pop Shop* | **Collingswood**	23
Pub* | **Pennsauken**	21
Raimondo's | **Ship Bottom**	24
Ram's Head Inn* | **Galloway**	25
Rat's | **Hamilton**	25
Raymond's* | **multi.**	21
Reservoir Tavern | **Boonton**	23
Robongi | **Hoboken**	22
Rob's Bistro* | **Madison**	22
Saffron | **E Hanover**	21
Sagami | **Collingswood**	26
Señorita's* | **multi.**	19
Shipwreck Grill | **Brielle**	24
Shogun* | **multi.**	21
Siri's Thai French* | **Cherry Hill**	24
Skylark* | **multi.**	21
Sono Sushi* | **Middletown**	26
Stamna* | **multi.**	24
Steve/Cookie's* | **Margate**	27
Surf Taco* | **multi.**	21
Thai Kitchen | **multi.**	24
Theresa's* | **Westfield**	22
Tortilla Press* | **Collingswood**	21
Tick Tock* | **Clifton**	19
Tina Louise | **Carlstadt**	23
Toast* | **Montclair**	21
Urban Table | **Morristown**	19
Verjus | **Maplewood**	24
Wasabi | **multi.**	22

W. Lake Seafood | **Matawan**	24
White House | **A.C.**	25
White Mana | **Jersey City**	18
White Manna | **Hackensack**	22
WindMill* | **multi.**	19
Zafra | **Hoboken**	24

DANCING

Adelphia | **Deptford**	21
Alstarz | **Bordentown**	18
Azúcar | **Jersey City**	22
Busch's Seafood | **Sea Isle City**	21
Casa Dante | **Jersey City**	22
Coastline | **Cherry Hill**	20
Cuba Libre | **A.C.**	21
Cubanu | **Rahway**	20
Delta's | **New Bruns.**	22
Dinallo's | **River Edge**	21
Filomena | **Clementon**	24
Filomena Rustica | **W Berlin**	23
Krogh's | **Sparta**	21
Málaga's | **Hamilton**	26
Manor | **W Orange**	24
Mohawk House | **Sparta**	22
Portobello | **Oakland**	21
Portug. Manor | **Perth Amboy**	23
Rat's | **Hamilton**	25
Sabor | **N Bergen**	24
Skylark | **Edison**	21
Stony Hill Inn | **Hackensack**	22
Villa Amalfi | **Cliffside Pk**	23
Windansea | **Highlands**	20

DESSERT SPECIALISTS

Bar Cara | **Bloomfield**	21
Baumgart's | **multi.**	18
Bent Spoon | **Princeton**	27
Chakra | **Paramus**	23
Cheesecake Factory | **multi.**	21
CulinAriane | **Montclair**	27
Fascino | **Montclair**	26
Fedora Café | **Lawrenceville**	22
Frog & Peach | **New Bruns.**	25
Holsten's | **Bloomfield**	19
Janice | **Ho-Ho-Kus**	21
Lilly's/Canal | **Lambertville**	20
Madeleine's | **Northvale**	24
Old Man Rafferty's | **multi.**	19
Raymond's | **multi.**	21
Robin's Nest | **Mt Holly**	24

Rolling Pin Cafe | **Westwood**	25
Satis | **Jersey City**	24
Small World Coffee | **Princeton**	23
St. Eve's | **Ho-Ho-Kus**	23

ENTERTAINMENT

(Call for types and times
of performances)

Baia | **Somers Point**	19
Bernards Inn | **Bernardsville**	25
Blue Point Grill | **Princeton**	25
Casa Dante | **Jersey City**	22
Chakra | **Paramus**	23
Chef Mike's ABG | **S Seaside Pk**	22
Cubacàn | **Asbury Pk**	22
Da Filippo's | **Somerville**	24
Dock's Oyster | **A.C.**	25
Ebbitt Room | **Cape May**	26
Filomena | **Clementon**	24
Filomena Lake. | **Deptford**	24
Filomena Rustica | **W Berlin**	23
Grand Cafe | **Morristown**	23
Harvest Moon Inn | **Ringoes**	23
Il Capriccio | **Whippany**	25
Makeda | **New Bruns.**	22
Manor | **W Orange**	24
Mattar's Bistro | **Allamuchy**	23
Mohawk House | **Sparta**	22
Molly Pitcher Inn | **Red Bank**	22
Mompou | **Newark**	22
MoonShine Modern | **Millburn**	19
Moonstruck | **Asbury Pk**	24
Nanni Rist. | **Rochelle Pk**	22
Norma's | **Cherry Hill**	22
Peter Shields Inn | **Cape May**	26
Portug. Manor | **Perth Amboy**	23
Ram's Head Inn | **Galloway**	25
Rat's | **Hamilton**	25
Raven/Peach | **Fair Haven**	24
Rumba Cubana | **N Bergen**	22
Ryland Inn | **Whitehouse**	25
Sabor | **N Bergen**	24
Shanghai Jazz | **Madison**	22
Shipwreck Grill | **Brielle**	24
Stage House | **Scotch Plains**	20
Steve/Cookie's | **Margate**	27
Stony Hill Inn | **Hackensack**	22
Sushi Lounge | **Morristown**	21
Tapas/España | **N Bergen**	24
Tim McLoone's | **Asbury Pk**	19

Triumph Brew. | **Princeton**	19
Verve | **Somerville**	22
Villa Amalfi | **Cliffside Pk**	23
Windansea | **Highlands**	20

FIREPLACES

Adega Grill | **Newark**	21
Amanda's | **Hoboken**	25
Anna's Italian | **Middletown**	23
Anton's/Swan | **Lambertville**	22
Arthur's Steak | **N Brunswick**	21
Avenue | **Long Branch**	22
Axia Taverna | **Tenafly**	23
Bareli's | **Secaucus**	23
NEW Bellissimo's | **Little Falls**	–
Bernards Inn | **Bernardsville**	25
Berta's Chateau | **Wanaque**	22
Biagio's | **Paramus**	20
Biddy O'Malley's | **Northvale**	20
Black Forest Inn | **Stanhope**	24
Black Trumpet | **Spring Lake**	22
Bloomfield Stk./Sea | **Bloomfield**	21
Blue Pig Tavern | **Cape May**	21
Blvd. Five 72 | **Kenilworth**	23
Braddock's | **Medford**	24
Bruschetta | **Fairfield**	20
Carpaccio | **Middlesex**	21
Cath. Lombardi | **New Bruns.**	24
Char Steak | **Raritan**	23
Chickie/Pete's | **Egg Harbor Twp**	21
Chophouse | **Gibbsboro**	24
Clydz | **New Bruns.**	23
Crab Trap | **Somers Point**	24
Cranbury Inn | **Cranbury**	18
Da Filippo's | **Somerville**	24
Dauphin Grille | **Asbury Pk**	22
David Burke From. | **Rumson**	25
Delicious Hgts. | **Berkeley Hts**	19
Dimora | **Norwood**	23
Dino's | **Harrington Pk**	21
Doc's Place | **Somers Point**	20
Dublin Sq. | **Cherry Hill**	18
Ebbitt Room | **Cape May**	26
Eno Terra | **Kingston**	25
Esty St. | **Park Ridge**	25
Filomena Lake. | **Deptford**	24
Filomena Rustica | **W Berlin**	23
Gables Rest. | **Beach Haven**	25
Giumarello's | **Westmont**	25

Gladstone | **Gladstone**	21	Shogun | **Kendall Pk**	21
Grain House | **Basking Ridge**	20	Silk Road | **Warren**	24
Grand Cafe | **Morristown**	23	Sirena Rist. | **Long Branch**	22
Grato | **Morris Plains**	22	Smithville Inn | **Smithville**	22
High St. Grill | **Mt Holly**	24	Sol-Mar | **Newark**	24
Ho-Ho-Kus Tavern | **Ho-Ho-Kus**	21	Spain 92 | **Raritan**	21
Huntley Taverne | **Summit**	22	Stage House | **Scotch Plains**	20
Il Michelangelo | **Boonton**	21	Stage Left | **New Bruns.**	25
Inn/Millrace Rest. | **Hope**	22	Steve/Cookie's | **Margate**	27
Inn at Sugar Hill | **Mays Landing**	20	Stone/Stirling Ridge | **Warren**	22
Inn/Hawke Rest. | **Lambertville**	18	Sushi Lounge | **Totowa**	21
Ivy Inn | **Hasbrouck Hts**	21	Tabor Rd. Tavern | **Morris Plains**	22
Knife/Fork Inn | **A.C.**	24	Trap Rock | **Berkeley Hts**	21
Krogh's | **Sparta**	21	Undici | **Rumson**	23
Lafayette House | **Lafayette**	22	Union Park | **Cape May**	26
Library IV | **Williamstown**	24	Uproot | **Warren**	22
Light Horse Tavern | **Jersey City**	22	Urban Table | **Basking Ridge**	19
Lithos | **Livingston**	23	Valentino's | **Park Ridge**	19
Luciano's | **Rahway**	22	Walpack Inn | **Wallpack**	23
LuNello's Montville | **Montville**	21	Washington Inn | **Cape May**	26
Mad Batter | **Cape May**	22	Windansea | **Highlands**	20
Main St. | **Princeton**	20	Wolfgang Puck | **A.C.**	25
Mastoris | **Bordentown**	21	Yankee Doodle | **Princeton**	17
Max's Seafood | **Gloucester**	26		

McLoone's | **W Orange**	19
Metuchen Inn | **Metuchen**	23
Milford Oyster | **Milford**	25
Mohawk House | **Sparta**	22
Molly Pitcher Inn | **Red Bank**	22
Park W. Tavern | **Ridgewood**	20
Peter Shields Inn | **Cape May**	26
Plantation | **Harvey Cedars**	19
Pluckemin Inn | **Bedminster**	25
Pub | **Pennsauken**	21
Ram's Head Inn | **Galloway**	25
Rat's | **Hamilton**	25
Redstone Grill | **Marlton**	22
Remington's | **Manasquan**	21
River Palm Terrace | **Mahwah**	25
Roberto's | **Beach Haven**	23
Salt Creek Grille | **Princeton**	21
Salt Gastro | **Stanhope**	22
Samdan | **Cresskill**	21
Sanzari's | **New Milford**	21
Scarborough Fair | **Sea Girt**	20
Sear House | **Closter**	23
Serenade | **Chatham**	26
Sergeantsville Inn | **Sergeantsville**	23
Shanghai Jazz | **Madison**	22

GREEN/LOCAL/ORGANIC

NEW Agricola | **Princeton**	-
Arturo's (Midland Pk) | **Midland Pk**	23
A Toute Heure | **Cranford**	26
Blue Morel | **Morristown**	24
NEW Escape | **Montclair**	-
Fig Tree | **Hoboken**	24
NEW Grange | **Westwood**	-
NEW Local Seasonal | **Ramsey**	-
Lorena's | **Maplewood**	28
Ninety Acres/Natirar | **Peapack**	25
Pairings | **Cranford**	23
Peacock Inn Rest. | **Princeton**	26
Ryland Inn | **Whitehouse**	25
Serenade | **Chatham**	26
Steve/Cookie's | **Margate**	27
St. Eve's | **Ho-Ho-Kus**	23
Stone/Stirling Ridge | **Warren**	22
Ursino | **Union**	24
Zeppoli | **Collingswood**	26

HISTORIC PLACES

(Year opened; * building)

1676 | Bloomfield Stk./Sea* | **Bloomfield**	21
1710 | Stockton Inn | **Stockton**	21

1714 | Eno Terra* | **Kingston** 25

1734 | Sergeantsville Inn* | 23
Sergeantsville

1737 | Stage House* | **Scotch Plains** 20

1742 | Black Horse Tavern* | 19
Mendham

1750 | Cranbury Inn* | **Cranbury** 18

1768 | Grain House* | 20
Basking Ridge

1770 | Inn/Millrace Rest.* | **Hope** 22

1770 | LuNello's Montville* | 21
Montville

1770 | Rocky Hill Inn* | **Rocky Hill** 19

1787 | Smithville Inn* | **Smithville** 22

1796 | Ho-Ho-Kus Tavern* | 21
Ho-Ho-Kus

1799 | Saddle River Inn* | 26
Saddle River

1800 | Bell's Mansion* | **Stanhope** 20

1800 | Tewksbury Inn* | **Oldwick** 21

1805 | Frenchtown Inn* | 22
Frenchtown

1811 | Harvest Moon Inn* | **Ringoes** 23

1813 | Farnsworth* | **Bordentown** 21

1818 | Stony Hill Inn* | **Hackensack** 22

1823 | Braddock's* | **Medford** 24

1840 | Inn/Hawke Rest.* | 18
Lambertville

1840 | Milford Oyster* | **Milford** 25

1840 | Washington Inn* | 26
Cape May

1843 | Metuchen Inn* | **Metuchen** 23

1847 | Gladstone* | **Gladstone** 21

1850 | David Burke From.* | 25
Rumson

1850 | Delta's* | **New Bruns.** 22

1850 | Light Horse Tavern* | 22
Jersey City

1856 | High St. Grill* | **Mt Holly** 24

1856 | Il Michelangelo* | **Boonton** 21

1857 | Old Bay Rest.* | **New Bruns.** 20

1858 | Trinity (Keyport)* | **Keyport** 22

1863 | Lambertville Stn.* | 20
Lambertville

1864 | Renault Winery Rest.* | 23
Egg Harbor

1870 | Edward's Steak* | **Jersey City** 21

1870 | Ivy Inn* | **Hasbrouck Hts** 21

1879 | Ebbitt Room* | **Cape May** 26

1879 | Sebastian's* | **Morristown** 24

1880 | 410 Bank St.* | **Cape May** 25

1880 | Moonstruck* | **Asbury Pk** 24

1882 | Busch's Seafood | 21
Sea Isle City

1882 | Mad Batter* | **Cape May** 22

1885 | Fish* | **Asbury Pk** 22

1890 | Gables Rest.* | **Beach Haven** 25

1890 | Matt's Red Rooster* | 26
Flemington

1890 | Red* | **Red Bank** 21

1890 | Robin's Nest* | **Mt Holly** 24

1890 | Scarborough Fair* | **Sea Girt** 20

1890 | Whispers* | **Spring Lake** 26

1892 | Black Trumpet* | 22
Spring Lake

1895 | Amanda's* | **Hoboken** 25

1895 | Elysian Café* | **Hoboken** 23

1897 | Dock's Oyster | **A.C.** 25

1900 | Athenian Gdn.* | 22
Galloway Twp

1900 | Elements Cafe* | 23
Haddon Hts

1903 | Columbia Inn* | **Montville** 21

1905 | Casona* | **Collingswood** 22

1909 | Highlawn Pavilion* | 24
W Orange

1912 | Ninety Acres/Natirar* | 25
Peapack

1920 | Harvey Cedars* | 20
Harvey Cedars

1920 | Kubel's | **Barnegat Light** 19

1921 | Chef Vola's | **A.C.** 27

1921 | Federici's | **Freehold** 22

1922 | Lobster House | **Cape May** 22

1924 | Stage Left* | **New Bruns.** 25

1926 | Iberia | **Newark** 22

1926 | Spike's | **Pt. Pleas. Bch** 21

1927 | Berta's Chateau* | **Wanaque** 22

1927 | Krogh's* | **Sparta** 21

1927 | Tony's/Grill* | **A.C.** 22

1928 | Molly Pitcher Inn* | **Red Bank** 22

1928 | Rutt's Hut | **Clifton** 21

1930 | Clementine's* | 23
Avon-by-Sea

1930 | RosaLuca's* | **Asbury** 24

1932 | Hiram's Roadstand | **Fort Lee** 22

1932 | Spanish Tavern | **Newark** 22

1933 | Harry's Lobster | **Sea Bright** 22

1933 | Sammy's/Cider Mill | 23
Mendham

1935 | Angelo's | **A.C.** 21

1936 | Helmers' | **Hoboken** 20

1936 | Reservoir Tavern | **Boonton** 23

1936 | Steve/Cookie's* | **Margate** 27

1936 | Steve's Steaks | **Carlstadt** 23

1937 | Kinchley's Tavern | **Ramsey** 22

1937 | Yankee Doodle | **Princeton** 17

1938 | Mill/Spg. Lake | 20
Spring Lake Hts

1939 | Holsten's | **Bloomfield** 19

1939 | Homestead Inn | **Trenton** 23

1939 | White Manna* | 22
Hackensack

1939 | White Mana | **Jersey City** 18

1940 | Blackbird Dining* | 24
Collingswood

1941 | Walpack Inn* | **Wallpack** 23

1942 | Oyster Creek Inn | 24
Leeds Point

1942 | Tuzzio's* | **Long Branch** 20

1944 | Charlie's | **Somers Point** 21

1945 | Max's Seafood | **Gloucester** 26

1946 | Biggie's Clam Bar | **Hoboken** 20

1946 | White House | **A.C.** 25

1947 | Vic's | **Bradley Bch** 22

1948 | Tick Tock* | **Clifton** 19

1950 | Main St.* | **Princeton** 20

1951 | Pub | **Pennsauken** 21

1951 | Rod's Steak | **Morristown** 22

1956 | Arthur's Tavern | 20
Morris Plains

1956 | Eppes Essen | **Livingston** 19

1956 | Manco/Manco Pizza | 23
Ocean City

1956 | Manor | **W Orange** 24

1956 | Whistlers Inn | **Cinnaminson** 20

1957 | Pete/Elda's | **Neptune City** 24

1959 | Mustache Bill's | 22
Barnegat Light

1960 | Rosie's Trattoria* | **Randolph** 22

1961 | Blue Claw Crab | 24
Burlington

1961 | DeLorenzo's Pizza | 25
Hamilton Twp

1962 | Hobby's Deli | **Newark** 25

1962 | PJ's Pancake | **Princeton** 18

HOTEL DINING

Americas Best Value Inn
Palace of Asia | **Cherry Hill** 23

Bally's Atlantic City
Harry's Oyster | **A.C.** 22

Berkeley Hotel
Dauphin Grille | **Asbury Pk** 22

Bernards Inn, The
Bernards Inn | 25
Bernardsville

Best Western Fairfield
Cucina Calandra | **Fairfield** 21

Blue Bay Inn
Copper Canyon | 24
Atlantic Highlands

Borgata Hotel Casino & Spa
Bobby Flay Steak | **A.C.** 25
Fornelletto | **A.C.** 23
Izakaya | **A.C.** 23
Old Homestead | **A.C.** 26
Tony Luke's | **A.C.** 23
Wolfgang Puck | **A.C.** 25

Caesars Atlantic City
Atlantic Grill | **A.C.** 21
Mia | **A.C.** 24

Carroll Villa Hotel
Mad Batter | **Cape May** 22

Chelsea Hotel
Chelsea Prime | **A.C.** 24
Teplitzky's | **A.C.** 19

Congress Hall Hotel
Blue Pig Tavern | **Cape May** 21

Courtyard by Marriott
Fire/Oak | **Montvale** 20

Crystal Springs Resort
Rest. Latour | **Hamburg** 26

DoubleTree Mount Laurel
GG's | **Mt Laurel** 23

Gables Inn
Gables Rest. | **Beach Haven** 25

Golden Nugget Hotel
Chart House | **A.C.** 22

Grand Summit Hotel
Hat Tavern | **Summit** 20

Grand Victorian Hotel
Black Trumpet | 22
Spring Lake

Hampton Inn & Suites
Calandra's | **Fairfield** 21

Harrah's Resort Atlantic City
Dos Caminos | **A.C.** 22
Luke Palladino | **A.C.** 24
McCormick/Schmick's | **A.C.** 20
Waterfront Buffet | **A.C.** 22

Heldrich Hotel
Christopher's | **New Bruns.** [20]
Daryl | **New Bruns.** [23]
Hewitt Wellington Hotel
Whispers | **Spring Lake** [26]
Hilton Parsippany
Ruth's Chris | **Parsippany** [25]
Hotel Macomber
Union Park | **Cape May** [26]
Inn at Millrace Pond
Inn/Millrace Rest. | **Hope** [22]
Inn at Sugar Hill
Inn at Sugar Hill | [20]
Mays Landing
Inn on Main Hotel
Firefly Bistro | **Manasquan** [22]
Madison Hotel
Rod's Steak | **Morristown** [22]
Molly Pitcher Inn
Molly Pitcher Inn | **Red Bank** [22]
Nassau Inn
Yankee Doodle | **Princeton** [17]
Ocean Club Condos
Girasole (AC) | **A.C.** [23]
Olde Mill Inn
Grain House | **Basking Ridge** [20]
Peacock Inn
Peacock Inn Rest. | **Princeton** [26]
Quarter at the Tropicana
Carmine's | **A.C.** [22]
Cuba Libre | **A.C.** [21]
The Palm | **A.C.** [24]
P.F. Chang's | **A.C.** [21]
Renault Winery Resort & Golf
Renault Winery Rest. | [23]
Egg Harbor
Resorts Casino & Hotel
Capriccio | **A.C.** [24]
Gallagher's | **A.C.** [23]
REVEL
Amada | **A.C.** [26]
American Cut | **A.C.** [24]
Azure/Allegretti | **A.C.** [23]
Mussel Bar/Wiedmaier | **A.C.** [24]
Village Whiskey | **A.C.** [24]
Sheraton Lincoln Harbor
Masina | **Weehawken** [20]
Tropicana Casino & Resort
Fin | **A.C.** [25]

Trump Taj Mahal
Il Mulino | **A.C.** [25]
Virginia Hotel
Ebbitt Room | **Cape May** [26]
Westin Governor Morris
Blue Morel | **Morristown** [24]
Westin Jersey City Newport
Fire/Oak | **Jersey City** [20]
Westminster Hotel
Strip House | **Livingston** [25]
W Hotel
Zylo | **Hoboken** [22]

JACKET REQUIRED

Manor | **W Orange** [24]
Molly Pitcher Inn | **Red Bank** [22]

LATE DINING

(Weekday closing hour)
Adelphia | 1 AM | **Deptford** [21]
Alchemist/Barrister | 12 AM | [18]
Princeton
Alstarz | varies | **Bordentown** [18]
Barnacle Bill's | 2 AM | **Rumson** [20]
Benny Tudino's | 12:45 AM | [20]
Hoboken
Biagio's | 3 AM | **Paramus** [20]
Biddy O'Malley's | 2 AM | [20]
Northvale
Biggie's Clam Bar | 1 AM, [20]
12:30 AM | **multi.**
Black Horse Diner | 24 hrs. | [20]
Mount Ephraim
Brasilia | 12 AM | **Newark** [21]
Brennen's Steak | 12 AM | [22]
Neptune City
Brick City Bar/Grill | 12 AM | [19]
Newark
Brickwall Tavern | 1 AM | **Asbury Pk** [20]
NEW Bro. Jimmy's | 2 AM | [-]
New Bruns.
Cath. Lombardi | varies | [24]
New Bruns.
Cenzino | 1 AM | **Oakland** [25]
Chakra | varies | **Paramus** [23]
Charlie's | 2 AM | **Somers Point** [21]
Chickie/Pete's | varies | **multi.** [21]
Cinders Grill | 12 AM | **Mine Hill** [20]
Clydz | 1:30 AM | **New Bruns.** [23]
Coastline | 3 AM | **Cherry Hill** [20]
Cubanu | varies | **Rahway** [20]

Danny's | 1 AM | **Red Bank** <u>22</u>

Delicious Hgts. | 2 AM | <u>19</u>
Berkeley Hts

Delta's | varies | **New Bruns.** <u>22</u>

Dinallo's | 2 AM | **River Edge** <u>21</u>

Dong Bang | 12 AM | **Fort Lee** <u>20</u>

Dublin Sq. | 2 AM | **multi.** <u>18</u>

Efe's Med. Grill | 12 AM | **multi.** <u>21</u>

Egan/Sons | 1:30 AM | **multi.** <u>20</u>

Famous/King of Pizza | 12 AM | <u>22</u>
Berlin

Farnsworth | varies | **Bordentown** <u>21</u>

Gam Mee Ok | 24 hrs. | **Fort Lee** <u>22</u>

Hamburgao | 12 AM | **multi.** <u>21</u>

Hollywood Cafe | 2 AM | <u>22</u>
Woodbury Heights

Hotoke | 2 AM | **New Bruns.** <u>20</u>

Ibby's | 12 AM | **Jersey City** <u>20</u>

Iberia | 1:30 AM | **Newark** <u>22</u>

Irish Pub/Inn | 24 hrs. | **A.C.** <u>21</u>

Jack Baker's | 2 AM | **Toms River** <u>20</u>

Kinchley's Tavern | 12 AM | **Ramsey** <u>22</u>

Krogh's | 1 AM | **Sparta** <u>21</u>

Kubel's | 12 AM | **Long Beach** <u>19</u>

Landmark Americana | 2 AM | <u>22</u>
Glassboro

Las Palmas | 12 AM | **W New York** <u>24</u>

Library III | 12 AM | **Egg Harbor Twp** <u>25</u>

Library II | varies | **Voorhees** <u>24</u>

Mantra | varies | **Paramus** <u>21</u>

Masina | 1 AM | **Weehawken** <u>20</u>

Mastoris | 1 AM | **Bordentown** <u>21</u>

Mattar's Bistro | 12 AM | <u>23</u>
Allamuchy

Mehndi | 12 AM | **Morristown** <u>23</u>

Metro Diner | 12 AM | **Brooklawn** <u>20</u>

Miller's Ale House | 2 AM | <u>21</u>
Mt Laurel

MK Valencia | 2 AM | **Ridgefield Pk** <u>21</u>

MoonShine Modern | 2 AM | <u>19</u>
Millburn

Morton's | 12 AM | **A.C.** <u>25</u>

Nicholas | 12 AM | **Red Bank** <u>28</u>

Novita Bistro | 12 AM | **Metuchen** <u>20</u>

Old Bay Rest. | 2 AM | **New Bruns.** <u>20</u>

Orange Squirrel | 1 AM | **Bloomfield** <u>21</u>

Pete/Elda's | 12 AM | <u>24</u>
Neptune City

Phily Diner | 12 AM | **Runnemede** <u>20</u>

NEW Pig/Prince | 1:30 AM | <u>20</u>
Montclair

Pino's La Forchetta | 12 AM | <u>20</u>
Marlboro

P.J. Whelihan's | varies | **multi.** <u>21</u>

Porta | varies | **Asbury Pk** <u>24</u>

Red | 2 AM | **Red Bank** <u>21</u>

Redstone Grill | varies | **Marlton** <u>22</u>

Reservoir Tavern | varies | **Boonton** <u>23</u>

River Grille | 1:30 AM | **Chatham** <u>-</u>

Royal Warsaw | varies | <u>23</u>
Elmwood Pk

Sear House | 12 AM | **Closter** <u>23</u>

Señorita's | varies | **multi.** <u>19</u>

Skylark | 1 AM | **Edison** <u>21</u>

Sol-Mar | 1 AM | **Newark** <u>24</u>

So Moon Nan Jip | 3 AM | <u>24</u>
Palisades Pk

Spuntino | 12 AM | **Clifton** <u>-</u>

Tapas/España | 12:30 AM | <u>24</u>
N Bergen

Tick Tock | 24 hrs. | **Clifton** <u>19</u>

Tony's/Grill | 3 AM | **A.C.** <u>22</u>

Trinity (Hoboken) | varies | <u>18</u>
Hoboken

Triumph Brew. | varies | **Princeton** <u>19</u>

Upstairs | varies | **Upper Montclair** <u>24</u>

Ventura's | 1 AM | **Margate** <u>20</u>

Whistlers Inn | 2 AM | <u>20</u>
Cinnaminson

White Mana | 24 hrs. | **Jersey City** <u>18</u>

WindMill | varies | **multi.** <u>19</u>

MEET FOR A DRINK

Adega Grill | **Newark** <u>21</u>

Alice's | **Lake Hopatcong** <u>20</u>

Alstarz | **Bordentown** <u>18</u>

Amada | **A.C.** <u>26</u>

Amelia's Bistro | **Jersey City** <u>20</u>

Arturo's (Midland Pk) | **Midland Pk** <u>23</u>

Avenue | **Long Branch** <u>22</u>

Bacari Grill | **Washington Twp** <u>21</u>

Bar Cara | **Bloomfield** <u>21</u>

Barnacle Bill's | **Rumson** <u>20</u>

Basil T's | **Red Bank** <u>21</u>

Biagio's | **Paramus** <u>20</u>

Bibi'z Rest. | **Westwood** <u>20</u>

Biddy O'Malley's | **Northvale** <u>20</u>

Bin 14 | **Hoboken** <u>23</u>

Bistro 55 | **Rochelle Pk** <u>19</u>

Black Horse Tavern | **Mendham** <u>19</u>

Blue Morel | **Morristown** <u>24</u>

Rumba Cubana | **N Bergen**	22
Ruth's Chris | **multi.**	25
Ryland Inn | **Whitehouse**	25
Salt Creek Grille | **Rumson**	21
Sear House | **Closter**	23
Sergeantsville Inn | **Sergeantsville**	23
Sirena Rist. | **Long Branch**	22
Son Cubano | **W New York**	20
Stage Left | **New Bruns.**	25
Stella Marina | **Asbury Pk**	23
Stone/Stirling Ridge | **Warren**	22
Stony Hill Inn | **Hackensack**	22
Sushi Lounge | **multi.**	21
Tabor Rd. Tavern | **Morris Plains**	22
NEW Tavro 13 | **Swedesboro**	-
Teak | **Red Bank**	22
Terra Nova | **Sewell**	21
Tewksbury Inn | **Oldwick**	21
3 Forty Grill | **Hoboken**	21
Tortilla Press | **Merchantville**	21
Trap Rock | **Berkeley Hts**	21
Trinity (Keyport) | **Keyport**	22
Trinity (Hoboken) | **Hoboken**	18
Triumph Brew. | **Princeton**	19
27 Mix | **Newark**	21
Undici | **Rumson**	23
Uproot | **Warren**	22
Upstairs | **Upper Montclair**	24
Ursino | **Union**	24
Verve | **Somerville**	22
Villa Amalfi | **Cliffside Pk**	23
Village Whiskey | **A.C.**	24
Vine | **Basking Ridge**	24
Waterside | **N Bergen**	20
Windansea | **Highlands**	20
Witherspoon | **Princeton**	22
Wolfgang Puck | **A.C.**	25
Yankee Doodle | **Princeton**	17
Zack's Oak Bar/Rest. | **Hoboken**	21
Zylo | **Hoboken**	22

MICROBREWERIES

Basil T's | **Red Bank**	21
Egan/Sons | **multi.**	20
Iron Hill | **Maple Shade**	22
Krogh's | **Sparta**	21
Trap Rock | **Berkeley Hts**	21
Triumph Brew. | **Princeton**	19

NEWCOMERS

Acanto Rist. | **Tenafly**	-
Agricola | **Princeton**	-
Ama Rist. | **Sea Bright**	25
Bat Barry's | **Westwood**	-
Bellissimo's | **Little Falls**	-
Blue Fig | **Moorestown**	-
Bro. Jimmy's | **New Bruns.**	-
Burgerwood | **Englewood**	-
Café 37 | **Ridgewood**	25
Central Kitchen | **Englewood Cliffs**	-
Despaña | **Princeton**	-
Diwani | **Ridgewood**	-
Due | **Ridgewood**	-
Elbow Room | **Newark**	-
Elena Wu | **Voorhees**	-
Escape | **Montclair**	-
Europe Café | **Tenafly**	-
G Grab & Go | **Edison**	-
Giulia's Kitchen | **Cliffside Pk**	-
Grange | **Westwood**	-
Indiya | **Collingswood**	-
La Sera | **Wyckoff**	-
Lidia's Cuban | **Cranford**	-
Local Seasonal | **Ramsey**	-
Mistral | **Princeton**	-
North End Bistro | **Princeton**	-
Nuovo Trattoria | **Manalapan**	-
The Pass | **Rosemont**	-
Pig/Prince | **Montclair**	20
Red Knot | **Kenilworth**	-
Smashburger | **multi.**	20
Tavro 13 | **Swedesboro**	-
WildFlour | **Lawrenceville**	-
Zoe's Kitchen | **Marlton**	-

OFFBEAT

Adara | **Montclair**	19
Augustino's | **Hoboken**	24
Baumgart's | **multi.**	18
Belmont Tavern | **Belleville**	22
Beyti Kebab | **Union City**	22
Bistro/Cherry Hill | **Cherry Hill**	23
Blue Danube | **Trenton**	23
Brick Ln. Curry | **multi.**	23
British Chip Shop | **Haddonfield**	24
Chef Vola's | **A.C.**	27
Clydz | **New Bruns.**	23
Cuban Pete's | **Montclair**	20

Cubby's BBQ	**Hackensack**	20
Dayi'nin Yeri	**Cliffside Pk**	24
Di Palma Bros.	**N Bergen**	23
El Mesón Café	**Freehold**	23
Fedora Café	**Lawrenceville**	22
Flirt Sushi	**Allendale**	22
Full Moon	**Lambertville**	20
Garlic Rose	**multi.**	20
Guru Palace	**N Brunswick**	19
Homestead Inn	**Trenton**	23
Hummus Elite	**Englewood**	21
Jack's Café	**Westwood**	22
JBJ Soul Kit.	**Red Bank**	21
Kinara	**Edgewater**	21
Lilly's/Canal	**Lambertville**	20
Makeda	**New Bruns.**	22
Málaga's	**Hamilton**	26
Mantra	**multi.**	21
Meemah	**Edison**	23
Mehndi	**Morristown**	23
Mesob	**Montclair**	23
Minado	**multi.**	22
Ming	**Edison**	22
Monster Sushi	**Summit**	20
Namaskaar	**Englewood**	23
Orange Squirrel	**Bloomfield**	21
Pamir	**Morristown**	21
Pho Anh Dao	**Edison**	22
Pop Shop	**Collingswood**	23
Pub	**Pennsauken**	21
Risotto House	**Rutherford**	22
Rolling Pin Cafe	**Westwood**	25
Royal Warsaw	**Elmwood Pk**	23
Sammy's/Cider Mill	**Mendham**	23
Satis	**Jersey City**	24
Shanghai Jazz	**Madison**	22
Skylark	**multi.**	21
Spain 92	**Raritan**	21
Strip House	**Livingston**	25
Thirty Acres	**Jersey City**	22
Tim Schafer's	**Morristown**	23
Tony's/Grill	**A.C.**	22
Trinity (Keyport)	**Keyport**	22
Upstairs	**Upper Montclair**	24
Vincentown Diner	**Vincentown**	21
White Mana	**Jersey City**	18
White Manna	**Hackensack**	22
Zinburger	**Clifton**	21

OUTDOOR DINING

Chart House	**Weehawken**	22
Elysian Café	**Hoboken**	23
Frog & Peach	**New Bruns.**	25
Gables Rest.	**Beach Haven**	25
Girasole (Bound Brook)	**Bound Brook**	24
Highlawn Pavilion	**W Orange**	24
Ho-Ho-Kus Tavern	**Ho-Ho-Kus**	21
La Fontana Coast	**Sea Isle City**	23
Le Rendez-Vous	**Kenilworth**	26
Lilly's/Canal	**Lambertville**	20
Maritime Parc	**Jersey City**	23
Mill/Spg. Lake	**Spring Lake Hts**	20
Moonstruck	**Asbury Pk**	24
Rat's	**Hamilton**	25
Raven/Peach	**Fair Haven**	24
Rebecca's	**Edgewater**	23
Robongi	**Hoboken**	22
Ruth's Chris	**Weehawken**	25
Sirena Rist.	**Long Branch**	22
Stage House	**Scotch Plains**	20
Stage Left	**New Bruns.**	25
Stella Marina	**Asbury Pk**	23
Stone/Stirling Ridge	**Warren**	22
Tisha's	**Cape May**	25
Windansea	**Highlands**	20
Za	**Pennington**	22
Zafra	**Hoboken**	24

PEOPLE-WATCHING

Bacari Grill	**Washington Twp**	21
Bernards Inn	**Bernardsville**	25
Bin 14	**Hoboken**	23
Bistro 55	**Rochelle Pk**	19
Bistro/Cherry Hill	**Cherry Hill**	23
Blue2O	**Cherry Hill**	22
Bobby Flay Steak	**A.C.**	25
Brio	**Cherry Hill**	21
Buddakan	**A.C.**	25
Cafe Madison	**Riverside**	23
Caffe/Lamberti	**Cherry Hill**	24
Chart House	**Weehawken**	22
Chickie/Pete's	**Bordentown**	21
Clydz	**New Bruns.**	23
Continental	**A.C.**	23
Cubacàn	**Asbury Pk**	22
Cuba Libre	**A.C.**	21
Cucharamama	**Hoboken**	25

Daryl | **New Bruns.**	23
Delta's | **New Bruns.**	22
Dino/Harry's | **Hoboken**	24
Eccola Italian | **Parsippany**	22
Egan/Sons | **W Orange**	20
Elysian Café | **Hoboken**	23
Esty St. | **Park Ridge**	25
Fire/Oak | **multi.**	20
Fleming's | **multi.**	23
Fuji | **Haddonfield**	25
Grato | **Morris Plains**	22
Grissini | **Englewood Cliffs**	22
Highlawn Pavilion | **W Orange**	24
Hollywood Cafe | **Woodbury Heights**	22
Hotoke | **New Bruns.**	20
Huntley Taverne | **Summit**	22
Langosta Lounge | **Asbury Pk**	20
Light Horse Tavern | **Jersey City**	22
Lilly's/Canal | **Lambertville**	20
Lu Nello | **Cedar Grove**	25
Madame Claude | **Jersey City**	22
Makeda | **New Bruns.**	22
Marco/Pepe | **Jersey City**	23
Megu Sushi | **multi.**	24
Metro Diner | **Brooklawn**	20
Mia | **A.C.**	24
MK Valencia | **Ridgefield Pk**	21
Molly Pitcher Inn | **Red Bank**	22
Mompou | **Newark**	22
MoonShine Modern | **Millburn**	19
Nunzio Rist. | **Collingswood**	23
Oliver a Bistro | **Bordentown**	25
Peacock Inn Rest. | **Princeton**	26
Phily Diner | **Runnemede**	20
Pluckemin Inn | **Bedminster**	25
Ponzio's | **Cherry Hill**	20
Pop Shop | **Collingswood**	23
Pub | **Pennsauken**	21
Rumba Cubana | **N Bergen**	22
Sabor | **N Bergen**	24
Salt Creek Grille | **Rumson**	21
Sammy's/Cider Mill | **Mendham**	23
Small World Coffee | **Princeton**	23
Son Cubano | **W New York**	20
Tabor Rd. Tavern | **Morris Plains**	22
Tapas/España | **N Bergen**	24
🆕 Tavro 13 | **Swedesboro**	–
Teak | **Red Bank**	22

3 West | **Basking Ridge**	21
Trinity (Hoboken) | **Hoboken**	18
27 Mix | **Newark**	21
Undici | **Rumson**	23
Witherspoon | **Princeton**	22
Wolfgang Puck | **A.C.**	25
Zeppoli | **Collingswood**	26

POWER SCENES

Basilico | **Millburn**	23
Bernards Inn | **Bernardsville**	25
Blue Morel | **Morristown**	24
Bobby Flay Steak | **A.C.**	25
Caffe/Lamberti | **Cherry Hill**	24
Capital Grille | **multi.**	25
Casa Dante | **Jersey City**	22
Cath. Lombardi | **New Bruns.**	24
Chakra | **Paramus**	23
Chez Catherine | **Westfield**	26
Cuba Libre | **A.C.**	21
Daryl | **New Bruns.**	23
David Burke From. | **Rumson**	25
Edward's Steak | **Jersey City**	21
Fascino | **Montclair**	26
Fleming's | **multi.**	23
410 Bank St. | **Cape May**	25
Gallagher's | **A.C.**	23
Grain House | **Basking Ridge**	20
Grand Cafe | **Morristown**	23
Hamilton/Ward | **Paterson**	24
Highlawn Pavilion | **W Orange**	24
Il Mondo Vecchio | **Madison**	25
Morton's | **multi.**	25
Nico Kitchen/Bar | **Newark**	20
Ninety Acres/Natirar | **Peapack**	25
Old Homestead | **A.C.**	26
Park Steak | **Park Ridge**	24
Peacock Inn Rest. | **Princeton**	26
Phillips Seafood | **A.C.**	21
Ponzio's | **Cherry Hill**	20
Porto Leggero | **Jersey City**	23
Redstone Grill | **Marlton**	22
Rest. Latour | **Hamburg**	26
River Palm Terrace | **Edgewater**	25
Roots Steak | **Summit**	25
Ryland Inn | **Whitehouse**	25
Saddle River Inn | **Saddle River**	26
Scalini Fedeli | **Chatham**	27
Serenade | **Chatham**	26

Stony Hill Inn | **Hackensack**	22
NEW Tavro 13 | **Swedesboro**	–
Undici | **Rumson**	23
Washington Inn | **Cape May**	26
Wm. Douglas | **Cherry Hill**	24
Wolfgang Puck | **A.C.**	25

PRIVATE ROOMS

(Restaurants charge less at off times; call for capacity)

Alice's | **Lake Hopatcong**	20
Amanda's | **Hoboken**	25
Andre's | **Newton**	25
Antonia's/Park | **N Bergen**	22
Arturo's (Midland Pk) | **Midland Pk**	23
Barone's | **Moorestown**	23
Bernards Inn | **Bernardsville**	25
Bistro Olé | **Asbury Pk**	22
Black Duck | **W Cape May**	26
Black Forest Inn | **Stanhope**	24
Blue Morel | **Morristown**	24
Blvd. Five 72 | **Kenilworth**	23
Buddakan | **A.C.**	25
Cafe Matisse | **Rutherford**	26
Cafe Panache | **Ramsey**	26
Caffe/Lamberti | **Cherry Hill**	24
Cenzino | **Oakland**	25
Chakra | **Paramus**	23
Chelsea Prime | **A.C.**	24
Chez Catherine | **Westfield**	26
Chophouse | **Gibbsboro**	24
Daryl | **New Bruns.**	23
Dimora | **Norwood**	23
Edward's Steak | **Jersey City**	21
Charrito's | **Weehawken**	22
Elements | **Princeton**	25
Eno Terra | **Kingston**	25
Fascino | **Montclair**	26
Fiorino | **Summit**	23
Fleming's Steakhouse | **Marlton**	23
Frenchtown Inn | **Frenchtown**	22
Frog & Peach | **New Bruns.**	25
Gables Rest. | **Beach Haven**	25
Giumarello's | **Westmont**	25
Grand Cafe | **Morristown**	23
Hamilton's Grill | **Lambertville**	24
Harvest Bistro | **Closter**	21
Highlawn Pavilion | **W Orange**	24
Ho-Ho-Kus Tavern | **Ho-Ho-Kus**	21
Iberia | **Newark**	22

Il Capriccio | **Whippany**	25
Il Villaggio | **Carlstadt**	24
Inn/Millrace Rest. | **Hope**	22
Liberty House | **Jersey City**	20
Lithos | **Livingston**	23
Luciano's | **Rahway**	22
LuNello's Montville | **Montville**	21
Madeleine's | **Northvale**	24
Manor | **W Orange**	24
Maritime Parc | **Jersey City**	23
Mattar's Bistro | **Allamuchy**	23
Mediterra | **Princeton**	22
Mehndi | **Morristown**	23
Nauvoo Grill | **Fair Haven**	19
Nicholas | **Red Bank**	28
Nico Kitchen/Bar | **Newark**	20
Ninety Acres/Natirar | **Peapack**	25
Oceanos | **Fair Lawn**	24
Pairings | **Cranford**	23
Pluckemin Inn | **Bedminster**	25
Porto Leggero | **Jersey City**	23
Pub | **Pennsauken**	21
Rare | **Little Falls**	23
Rest. Latour | **Hamburg**	26
River Palm Terrace | **multi.**	25
Ryland Inn | **Whitehouse**	25
Saddle River Inn | **Saddle River**	26
Serenade | **Chatham**	26
Stage House | **Scotch Plains**	20
Stage Left | **New Bruns.**	25
Stone/Stirling Ridge | **Warren**	22
Stony Hill Inn | **Hackensack**	22
Tomatoes | **Margate**	23
Villa Amalfi | **Cliffside Pk**	23
Washington Inn | **Cape May**	26
Waterside | **N Bergen**	20

PRIX FIXE MENUS

(Call for prices and times)

Adara | **Montclair**	19
Amanda's | **Hoboken**	25
Andre's | **Newton**	25
Arturo's | **Maplewood**	24
Bernards Inn | **Bernardsville**	25
Brian's | **Lambertville**	26
Cafe Matisse | **Rutherford**	26
Chez Catherine | **Westfield**	26
Court St. Rest.Bar | **Hoboken**	21
David Burke From. | **Rumson**	25
Dream Cuisine | **Cherry Hill**	26

Drew's Bistro | **Keyport**	27
Eccola Italian | **Parsippany**	22
Edward's Steak | **Jersey City**	21
Esty St. | **Park Ridge**	25
Fascino | **Montclair**	26
Fig Tree | **Hoboken**	24
Filomena | **Clementon**	24
Frog & Peach | **New Bruns.**	25
Fuji | **Haddonfield**	25
Gables Rest. | **Beach Haven**	25
Girasole (AC) | **A.C.**	23
Highlawn Pavilion | **W Orange**	24
J&K Steak | **Morristown**	22
Komegashi | **Jersey City**	23
Latour | **Ridgewood**	26
Liberty House | **Jersey City**	20
Lithos | **Livingston**	23
Madeleine's | **Northvale**	24
Manon | **Lambertville**	24
Mikado | **multi.**	22
Nicholas | **Red Bank**	28
Norma's | **Cherry Hill**	22
Nunzio Rist. | **Collingswood**	23
Oliver a Bistro | **Bordentown**	25
Pluckemin Inn | **Bedminster**	25
Rat's | **Hamilton**	25
Rest. Latour | **Hamburg**	26
Rocca | **Glen Rock**	23
Rosemary/Sage | **Riverdale**	24
Ryland Inn | **Whitehouse**	25
Sapori | **Collingswood**	25
Scalini Fedeli | **Chatham**	27
Sear House | **Closter**	23
Serenade | **Chatham**	26
Stage Left | **New Bruns.**	25
Stone/Stirling Ridge | **Warren**	22
Verjus | **Maplewood**	24
Vlg. Green | **Ridgewood**	24
Wasabi | **Somerville**	22

QUICK BITES

Aby's | **Matawan**	20
Ah' Pizz | **Montclair**	20
Alchemist/Barrister | **Princeton**	18
Baumgart's | **multi.**	18
Bobby Chez | **multi.**	23
Bobby's Burger | **multi.**	21
British Chip Shop | **Haddonfield**	24
Brooklyn's Pizzeria | **multi.**	22

Casa Maya | **Gillette**	21
Cassie's | **Englewood**	19
Chickie/Pete's | **Bordentown**	21
Continental | **A.C.**	23
Cubby's BBQ | **Hackensack**	20
Dauphin Grille | **Asbury Pk**	22
DeLorenzo's Pizza | **Hamilton Twp**	25
DeLorenzo's Pies | **Robbinsville**	27
Egan/Sons | **W Orange**	20
Eppes Essen | **Livingston**	19
Five Guys | **multi.**	22
Franco's Metro | **Fort Lee**	22
Full Moon | **Lambertville**	20
Grimaldi's | **Hoboken**	23
Grub Hut | **Manville**	21
Hamburgao | **multi.**	21
Harold's N.Y. Deli | **Edison**	22
Hiram's Roadstand | **Fort Lee**	22
Hobby's Deli | **Newark**	25
Holsten's | **Bloomfield**	19
Hummus Elite | **Englewood**	21
Ibby's | **multi.**	20
Irish Pub/Inn | **A.C.**	21
It's Greek To Me | **multi.**	19
Jack's Café | **Westwood**	22
Kibitz Room | **Cherry Hill**	24
Kinchley's Tavern | **Ramsey**	22
La Tapatia | **Asbury Pk**	24
Little Food Cafe | **multi.**	23
Locale | **Closter**	21
Luigi's Pizza | **Marlton**	21
Mastoris | **Bordentown**	21
Mex. Food Factory | **Marlton**	21
Mustache Bill's | **Barnegat Light**	22
Nana's Deli | **Livingston**	23
Napoli's Pizza | **Hoboken**	21
Nha Trang Place | **Jersey City**	23
Pic-Nic | **E Newark**	24
Ponzio's | **Cherry Hill**	20
Pop's Garage | **Asbury Pk**	21
Pop Shop | **Collingswood**	23
Raymond's | **multi.**	21
Rolling Pin Cafe | **Westwood**	25
Rumba Cubana | **Jersey City**	22
Rutt's Hut | **Clifton**	21
Salute Brick Oven | **Montclair**	22
Skylark | **multi.**	21
Small World Coffee | **Princeton**	23
Taqueria D.T. | **Jersey City**	25

Tick Tock | **Clifton**	19
Toast | **Montclair**	21
Tony Luke's | **A.C.**	23
Tony's Touch/Italy | **Wayne**	23
Tortilla Press | **Merchantville**	21
Trattoria/Sorrentina | **N Bergen**	25
Trinity (Hoboken) | **Hoboken**	18
Urban Table | **Morristown**	19
White Mana | **Jersey City**	18
White Manna | **Hackensack**	22
Windansea | **Highlands**	20
WindMill | **multi.**	19
Witherspoon | **Princeton**	22
Wondee's | **Hackensack**	22
Zinburger | **Clifton**	21

QUIET CONVERSATION

Adega Grill | **Newark**	21
Amarone | **Teaneck**	21
Biagio's | **Paramus**	20
Black Trumpet | **Spring Lake**	22
Blue Morel | **Morristown**	24
Braddock's | **Medford**	24
BV Tuscany | **Teaneck**	24
Cafe Madison | **Riverside**	23
Cafe Matisse | **Rutherford**	26
Calandra's | **Fairfield**	21
Chao Phaya | **multi.**	22
Chef's Table | **Franklin Lakes**	27
Chez Catherine | **Westfield**	26
Classic Quiche | **Teaneck**	23
Corso 98 | **Montclair**	23
Da Filippo's | **Somerville**	24
Davia | **Fair Lawn**	22
Dino's | **Harrington Pk**	21
Elements | **Princeton**	25
Eppes Essen | **Livingston**	19
Etc. Steak | **Teaneck**	25
Farnsworth | **Bordentown**	21
Fascino | **Montclair**	26
Fiddleheads | **Jamesburg**	22
55 Main | **Flemington**	22
Fiorino | **Summit**	23
Fontana/Trevi | **Leonia**	22
Franco's Metro | **Fort Lee**	22
Frenchtown Inn | **Frenchtown**	22
Giumarello's | **Westmont**	25
Grand Cafe | **Morristown**	23
Grimaldi's | **Hoboken**	23

Guru Palace | **N Brunswick**	19
Highlawn Pavilion | **W Orange**	24
Huntley Taverne | **Summit**	22
Il Capriccio | **Whippany**	25
Inn at Sugar Hill | **Mays Landing**	20
Ivy Inn | **Hasbrouck Hts**	21
Kinara | **Edgewater**	21
Krave Café | **Newton**	25
La Strada | **Randolph**	23
Latour | **Ridgewood**	26
Levant Grille | **Englewood**	21
Locale | **Closter**	21
Lotus Cafe | **Hackensack**	21
Luciano's | **Rahway**	22
Madeleine's | **Northvale**	24
Molly Pitcher Inn | **Red Bank**	22
Namaskaar | **Englewood**	23
Nico Kitchen/Bar | **Newark**	20
Palace of Asia | **Cherry Hill**	23
Park Steak | **Park Ridge**	24
Peacock Inn Rest. | **Princeton**	26
Peter Shields Inn | **Cape May**	26
Pluckemin Inn | **Bedminster**	25
Rat's | **Hamilton**	25
Rest. Latour | **Hamburg**	26
Rocca | **Glen Rock**	23
Rocky Hill Inn | **Rocky Hill**	19
Ryland Inn | **Whitehouse**	25
Saddle River Inn | **Saddle River**	26
Segovia Steak | **Little Ferry**	22
Sergeantsville Inn | **Sergeantsville**	23
Smithville Inn | **Smithville**	22
Sorrento | **E Rutherford**	23
Stone/Stirling Ridge | **Warren**	22
Stony Hill Inn | **Hackensack**	22
Tewksbury Inn | **Oldwick**	21
Tony/Caneca | **Newark**	22
Umeya | **Cresskill**	23
Vasili's | **Teaneck**	20
Verjus | **Maplewood**	24
Villa Amalfi | **Cliffside Pk**	23
Vlg. Green | **Ridgewood**	24
Whispers | **Spring Lake**	26
Wm. Douglas | **Cherry Hill**	24

RAW BARS

Akai | **Englewood**	24
Avenue | **Long Branch**	22
Bahrs Landing | **Highlands**	19

Big Fish Seafood | **Princeton**	20
Black Whale | **Beach Haven**	22
Blue Morel | **Morristown**	24
Blue Point Grill | **Princeton**	25
Blue2O | **Cherry Hill**	22
Bobby Flay Steak | **A.C.**	25
Caffe/Lamberti | **Cherry Hill**	24
Char Steak | **Raritan**	23
Chef Mike's ABG | **S Seaside Pk**	22
Costanera | **Montclair**	24
Crab Trap | **Somers Point**	24
Dock's Oyster | **A.C.**	25
Edward's Steak | **Jersey City**	21
Fin | **A.C.**	25
Fin Raw Bar/Kitchen | **Montclair**	24
Fish | **Asbury Pk**	22
Halcyon Brasserie | **Montclair**	22
Hamilton/Ward | **Paterson**	24
Harvest Bistro | **Closter**	21
Harvey Cedars | **Beach Haven**	20
Il Capriccio | **Whippany**	25
Jack Baker's | **Toms River**	20
Klein's | **Belmar**	23
La Focaccia | **Summit**	23
La Griglia | **Kenilworth**	23
Legal Sea Foods | **multi.**	21
Liberty House | **Jersey City**	20
Limani | **Westfield**	25
Little Tuna | **Haddonfield**	22
Lobster House | **Cape May**	22
LouCás | **Edison**	23
Maritime Parc | **Jersey City**	23
McCormick/Schmick's | **Hackensack**	20
McLoone's | **Long Branch**	19
MK Valencia | **Ridgefield Pk**	21
Nero's Grille | **Livingston**	19
Oceanos | **Fair Lawn**	24
Old Homestead | **A.C.**	26
Oyster Creek Inn | **Leeds Point**	24
Park Steak | **Park Ridge**	24
Park W. Tavern | **Ridgewood**	20
Phillips Seafood | **A.C.**	21
Pino's La Forchetta | **Marlboro**	20
Plantation | **Harvey Cedars**	19
Portobello | **Oakland**	21
Red's Lobster Pot | **Pt. Pleas. Bch**	23
Rooney's | **Long Branch**	21
Rosie's Trattoria | **Randolph**	22
Shipwreck Grill | **Brielle**	24
Spike's | **Pt. Pleas. Bch**	21
Stage House | **Scotch Plains**	20
Stella Marina | **Asbury Pk**	23
Steve/Cookie's | **Margate**	27
3 Forty Grill | **Hoboken**	21
Varka | **Ramsey**	25
Waterside | **N Bergen**	20
Wayne Steak | **Wayne**	25

ROMANTIC PLACES

Acquaviva/Fonti | **Westfield**	20
Adega Grill | **Newark**	21
Amanda's | **Hoboken**	25
Andre's | **Newton**	25
Anton's/Swan | **Lambertville**	22
Arugula | **Sewell**	23
Avenue | **Long Branch**	22
Bell's Mansion | **Stanhope**	20
Bernards Inn | **Bernardsville**	25
Bistro/Marino | **Collingswood**	25
Black Trumpet | **Spring Lake**	22
Blue Morel | **Morristown**	24
Cafe Madison | **Riverside**	23
Cafe Matisse | **Rutherford**	26
Cara Mia | **Millburn**	21
Cath. Lombardi | **New Bruns.**	24
Chakra | **Paramus**	23
Chef Mike's ABG | **S Seaside Pk**	22
CulinAriane | **Montclair**	27
David Burke From. | **Rumson**	25
Ebbitt Room | **Cape May**	26
Elements | **Princeton**	25
Eno Terra | **Kingston**	25
Esty St. | **Park Ridge**	25
55 Main | **Flemington**	22
Fig Tree | **Hoboken**	24
Flirt Sushi | **Allendale**	22
Frenchtown Inn | **Frenchtown**	22
Frog & Peach | **New Bruns.**	25
Fuji | **Haddonfield**	25
Gables Rest. | **Beach Haven**	25
Giumarello's | **Westmont**	25
Gladstone | **Gladstone**	21
Grand Cafe | **Morristown**	23
Guru Palace | **N Brunswick**	19
Harvest Bistro | **Closter**	21
Harvest Moon Inn | **Ringoes**	23
Highlawn Pavilion | **W Orange**	24

Ho-Ho-Kus Tavern | **Ho-Ho-Kus**	21
Huntley Taverne | **Summit**	22
Il Capriccio | **Whippany**	25
Il Villaggio | **Carlstadt**	24
Inn/Millrace Rest. | **Hope**	22
Ivy Inn | **Hasbrouck Hts**	21
Jose's Mex. Cantina | **multi.**	20
Komegashi | **Jersey City**	23
Krave Café | **Newton**	25
La Cipollina | **Freehold**	21
L'Allegria | **Madison**	23
Langosta Lounge | **Asbury Pk**	20
Latour | **Ridgewood**	26
Le Rendez-Vous | **Kenilworth**	26
Liberty House | **Jersey City**	20
Lilly's/Canal | **Lambertville**	20
Lola's | **Hoboken**	22
Lorena's | **Maplewood**	28
Manor | **W Orange**	24
Maritime Parc | **Jersey City**	23
Mehndi | **Morristown**	23
Metuchen Inn | **Metuchen**	23
Mia | **A.C.**	24
Ming | **Morristown**	22
MK Valencia | **Ridgefield Pk**	21
Molly Pitcher Inn | **Red Bank**	22
Mompou | **Newark**	22
MoonShine Modern | **Millburn**	19
Ninety Acres/Natirar | **Peapack**	25
Oliver a Bistro | **Bordentown**	25
Pairings | **Cranford**	23
Patria | **Rahway**	23
Peacock Inn Rest. | **Princeton**	26
Peter Shields Inn | **Cape May**	26
Pino's La Forchetta | **Marlboro**	20
Pluckemin Inn | **Bedminster**	25
Ram's Head Inn | **Galloway**	25
Rat's | **Hamilton**	25
Raven/Peach | **Fair Haven**	24
Rebecca's | **Edgewater**	23
Rest. Latour | **Hamburg**	26
Rod's Steak | **Morristown**	22
Ryland Inn | **Whitehouse**	25
Saddle River Inn | **Saddle River**	26
Scalini Fedeli | **Chatham**	27
Scarborough Fair | **Sea Girt**	20
Sear House | **Closter**	23
Serenade | **Chatham**	26
Sergeantsville Inn | **Sergeantsville**	23

Sette | **Bernardsville**	23
Sirena Rist. | **Long Branch**	22
Son Cubano | **W New York**	20
Stone/Stirling Ridge | **Warren**	22
Stony Hill Inn | **Hackensack**	22
Taka | **Asbury Pk**	25
Tewksbury Inn | **Oldwick**	21
Ursino | **Union**	24
Washington Inn | **Cape May**	26
Waterside | **N Bergen**	20
Whispers | **Spring Lake**	26
Za | **Pennington**	22

SENIOR APPEAL

Antonia's/Park | **N Bergen**	22
Athenian Gdn. | **Galloway Twp**	22
Bahrs Landing | **Highlands**	19
Baumgart's | **multi.**	18
Bistro/Marino | **Collingswood**	25
Blue Danube | **Trenton**	23
Bonefish Grill | **multi.**	21
Brio | **Cherry Hill**	21
British Chip Shop | **Haddonfield**	24
Café Azzurro | **Peapack**	22
Cafe Madison | **Riverside**	23
Calandra's | **Fairfield**	21
Carmine's | **A.C.**	22
Casa Dante | **Jersey City**	22
Cath. Lombardi | **New Bruns.**	24
Chez Catherine | **Westfield**	26
Chophouse | **Gibbsboro**	24
Classic Quiche | **Teaneck**	23
Country Pancake | **Ridgewood**	19
Crab Trap | **Somers Point**	24
Davia | **Fair Lawn**	22
Di Palma Bros. | **N Bergen**	23
Don Pepe | **multi.**	22
Don Pepe's Steak | **Pine Brook**	22
E & V | **Paterson**	24
Edward's Steak | **Jersey City**	21
El Cid | **Paramus**	22
Eppes Essen | **Livingston**	19
55 Main | **Flemington**	22
Fleming's | **multi.**	23
Fornos/Spain | **Newark**	23
Franco's Metro | **Fort Lee**	22
Gallagher's | **A.C.**	23
Grand Cafe | **Morristown**	23
Grimaldi's | **Hoboken**	23

Harold's N.Y. Deli | **Edison**	22
Helmers' | **Hoboken**	20
Highlawn Pavilion | **W Orange**	24
Hiram's Roadstand | **Fort Lee**	22
Hobby's Deli | **Newark**	25
Ho-Ho-Kus Tavern | **Ho-Ho-Kus**	21
Holsten's | **Bloomfield**	19
Iberia | **Newark**	22
Il Capriccio | **Whippany**	25
Il Fiore | **Collingswood**	24
Il Villaggio | **Carlstadt**	24
It's Greek To Me | **multi.**	19
Ivy Inn | **Hasbrouck Hts**	21
Jack Baker's | **multi.**	20
Java Moon | **Jackson**	23
Joe Pesce | **Collingswood**	25
Kibitz Room | **Cherry Hill**	24
Klein's | **Belmar**	23
Knife/Fork Inn | **A.C.**	24
Krave Café | **Newton**	25
Kuzina/Sofia | **Cherry Hill**	22
La Couronne | **Montclair**	23
La Dolce Vita | **Belmar**	22
Lafayette House | **Lafayette**	22
Legal Sea Foods | **Short Hills**	21
Library IV | **Williamstown**	24
Little Tuna | **Haddonfield**	22
Lobster House | **Cape May**	22
Lotus Cafe | **Hackensack**	21
LouCás | **Edison**	23
Madeleine's | **Northvale**	24
Manor | **W Orange**	24
Mastoris | **Bordentown**	21
McCormick/Schmick's | **multi.**	20
Mesón Madrid | **Palisades Pk**	20
Mill/Spg. Lake | **Spring Lake Hts**	20
Nanni Rist. | **Rochelle Pk**	22
Nunzio Rist. | **Collingswood**	23
Oceanos | **Fair Lawn**	24
Octopus's Gdn. | **West Creek**	23
Oliver a Bistro | **Bordentown**	25
Patsy's | **Fairview**	22
Pete/Elda's | **Neptune City**	24
P.F. Chang's | **Marlton**	21
Phily Diner | **Runnemede**	20
Pop Shop | **Collingswood**	23
Portobello | **Oakland**	21
Portug. Manor | **Perth Amboy**	23
Pub | **Pennsauken**	21

Renault Winery Rest. | **Egg Harbor**	23
Rio Rodizio | **Union**	21
Rod's Steak | **Morristown**	22
Sanducci's | **River Edge**	19
Segovia Steak | **Little Ferry**	22
Smithville Inn | **Smithville**	22
Spain | **Newark**	22
Spanish Tavern | **multi.**	22
Stone/Stirling Ridge | **Warren**	22
Stony Hill Inn | **Hackensack**	22
Trattoria Saporito | **Hoboken**	23
Tutto/Modo Mio | **Ridgefield**	22
Valentino's | **Park Ridge**	19
Varka | **Ramsey**	25
Verjus | **Maplewood**	24
Villa Amalfi | **Cliffside Pk**	23
Villa Vittoria | **Brick**	22
Waterfront Buffet | **A.C.**	22
WindMill | **multi.**	19
Wm. Douglas | **Cherry Hill**	24
Wolfgang Puck | **A.C.**	25

SINGLES SCENES

Adega Grill | **Newark**	21
Alice's | **Lake Hopatcong**	20
Avenue | **Long Branch**	22
Bibi'z Rest. | **Westwood**	20
Bin 14 | **Hoboken**	23
Bistro 55 | **Rochelle Pk**	19
Blue Pig Tavern | **Cape May**	21
Brass Rail | **Hoboken**	19
Brooklyn's Pizzeria | **Ridgewood**	22
Bruschetta | **Fairfield**	20
Buddakan | **A.C.**	25
Cenzino | **Oakland**	25
Chakra | **Paramus**	23
Char Steak | **Raritan**	23
Chef Mike's ABG | **S Seaside Pk**	22
Chickie/Pete's | **Bordentown**	21
Clydz | **New Bruns.**	23
Continental | **A.C.**	23
Copper Canyon | **Atlantic Highlands**	24
Cuba Libre | **A.C.**	21
Cucharamama | **Hoboken**	25
Daryl | **New Bruns.**	23
Delicious Hgts. | **Berkeley Hts**	19
Egan/Sons | **W Orange**	20
Fire/Oak | **multi.**	20
Fleming's | **Edgewater**	23

Grissini | **Englewood Cliffs**	22
Hat Tavern | **Summit**	20
Huntley Taverne | **Summit**	22
Inlet Café | **Highlands**	20
Krogh's | **Sparta**	21
Langosta Lounge | **Asbury Pk**	20
Light Horse Tavern | **Jersey City**	22
Luke Palladino | **A.C.**	24
Metropolitan Cafe | **Freehold**	21
Mia | **A.C.**	24
Mill/Spg. Lake | **Spring Lake Hts**	20
MK Valencia | **Ridgefield Pk**	21
Mompou | **Newark**	22
Old Man Rafferty's | **multi.**	19
Orange Squirrel | **Bloomfield**	21
P.J. Whelihan's | **multi.**	21
Plantation | **Harvey Cedars**	19
Quiet Man | **Dover**	23
Red | **Red Bank**	21
Redstone Grill | **Marlton**	22
Rooney's | **Long Branch**	21
Sabor | **N Bergen**	24
Sage | **Ventnor**	23
Salt Creek Grille | **multi.**	21
Shipwreck Grill | **Brielle**	24
Son Cubano | **W New York**	20
Sushi Lounge | **multi.**	21
Tabor Rd. Tavern | **Morris Plains**	22
Teak | **Red Bank**	22
3 Forty Grill | **Hoboken**	21
3 West | **Basking Ridge**	21
Tomatoes | **Margate**	23
Trap Rock | **Berkeley Hts**	21
Trinity (Hoboken) | **Hoboken**	18
Urban Table | **Basking Ridge**	19
Verve | **Somerville**	22
Waterside | **N Bergen**	20
Windansea | **Highlands**	20
Witherspoon | **Princeton**	22

SLEEPERS

(Good food, but little known)

Assaggini/Roma | **Newark**	24
Blackbird Dining | **Collingswood**	24
British Chip Shop | **Haddonfield**	24
Cafe Loren | **Avalon**	25
Chelsea Prime | **A.C.**	24
Coriander | **Voorhees**	24
Da's Kitchen | **Hopewell**	25
Da Soli | **Haddonfield**	25

Dayi'nin Yeri | **Cliffside Pk**	24
Depot Mkt. Cafe | **Cape May**	24
Diving Horse | **Avalon**	25
Dream Cuisine | **Cherry Hill**	26
El Tule | **Lambertville**	25
Etc. Steak | **Teaneck**	25
Giuseppe | **N Haledon**	24
Hamilton/Ward | **Paterson**	24
High St. Grill | **Mt Holly**	24
Hunkar Rest. | **Carlstadt**	25
I Gemelli Rist. | **S Hackensack**	25
IndeBlue | **Collingswood**	25
Je's | **Newark**	24
Joe Pesce | **Collingswood**	25
Jo-Sho | **Somerset**	25
Just Rest. | **Old Bridge**	24
Kanji | **Tinton Falls**	24
Kaya's Kitchen | **Belmar**	25
La Primavera | **W Orange**	24
Las Palmas | **W New York**	24
La Tapatia | **Asbury Pk**	24
Málaga's | **Hamilton**	26
Max's Seafood | **Gloucester**	26
Monsoon | **Mt Laurel**	25
Pic-Nic | **E Newark**	24
RosaLuca's | **Asbury**	24
Satis | **Jersey City**	24
Spanish Manor | **Newark**	25
Spice Thai | **Bloomfield**	24
Topaz Thai | **Belleville**	24
Toscana | **Mullica Hill**	24
Trio | **Martinsville**	24
Wayne Steak | **Wayne**	25
Yokohama | **Maple Shade**	25

SPECIAL OCCASIONS

Adara | **Montclair**	19
Amanda's | **Hoboken**	25
Anton's/Swan | **Lambertville**	22
Bacari Grill | **Washington Twp**	21
Bernards Inn | **Bernardsville**	25
Blue Morel | **Morristown**	24
Bobby Flay Steak | **A.C.**	25
Brandl | **Belmar**	24
Buddakan | **A.C.**	25
Cafe Matisse | **Rutherford**	26
Cafe Panache | **Ramsey**	26
Cara Mia | **Millburn**	21
Chakra | **Paramus**	23

Chart House | **Weehawken**	22
Chef's Table | **Franklin Lakes**	27
Chengdu 46 | **Clifton**	23
Chez Catherine | **Westfield**	26
Cucharamama | **Hoboken**	25
CulinAriane | **Montclair**	27
Daryl | **New Bruns.**	23
David Burke From. | **Rumson**	25
Esty St. | **Park Ridge**	25
55 Main | **Flemington**	22
Fiorino | **Summit**	23
Fleming's Steakhouse | **Marlton**	23
Frenchtown Inn | **Frenchtown**	22
Frog & Peach | **New Bruns.**	25
Gallagher's | **A.C.**	23
Girasole (AC) | **A.C.**	23
Girasole (Bound Brook) | **Bound Brook**	24
Giumarello's | **Westmont**	25
Grand Cafe | **Morristown**	23
Guru Palace | **N Brunswick**	19
Harvest Bistro | **Closter**	21
Harvest Moon Inn | **Ringoes**	23
Highlawn Pavilion | **W Orange**	24
Ho-Ho-Kus Tavern | **Ho-Ho-Kus**	21
Hotoke | **New Bruns.**	20
Il Capriccio | **Whippany**	25
Il Villaggio | **Carlstadt**	24
Inn/Millrace Rest. | **Hope**	22
La Cipollina | **Freehold**	21
Latour | **Ridgewood**	26
Liberty House | **Jersey City**	20
Locale | **Closter**	21
Lorena's | **Maplewood**	28
Luciano's | **Rahway**	22
Lu Nello | **Cedar Grove**	25
Madeleine's | **Northvale**	24
Málaga's | **Hamilton**	26
Manor | **W Orange**	24
Maritime Parc | **Jersey City**	23
Mattar's Bistro | **Allamuchy**	23
Mehndi | **Morristown**	23
Mill/Spg. Lake | **Spring Lake Hts**	20
MoonShine Modern | **Millburn**	19
Nicholas | **Red Bank**	28
Ninety Acres/Natirar | **Peapack**	25
Nunzio Rist. | **Collingswood**	23
Pairings | **Cranford**	23
The Palm | **A.C.**	24

Park Steak | **Park Ridge**	24
Peacock Inn Rest. | **Princeton**	26
Peter Shields Inn | **Cape May**	26
Piccola Italia | **Ocean Twp**	25
Pluckemin Inn | **Bedminster**	25
Ram's Head Inn | **Galloway**	25
Rat's | **Hamilton**	25
Raven/Peach | **Fair Haven**	24
Rebecca's | **Edgewater**	23
Rest. Latour | **Hamburg**	26
River Palm Terrace | **multi.**	25
Rod's Steak | **Morristown**	22
Roots Steak | **Summit**	25
RosaLuca's | **Asbury**	24
Ryland Inn | **Whitehouse**	25
Saddle River Inn | **Saddle River**	26
Scalini Fedeli | **Chatham**	27
Scarborough Fair | **Sea Girt**	20
Sear House | **Closter**	23
Serenade | **Chatham**	26
Shanghai Jazz | **Madison**	22
Son Cubano | **W New York**	20
Stage House | **Scotch Plains**	20
Stage Left | **New Bruns.**	25
Stone/Stirling Ridge | **Warren**	22
Stony Hill Inn | **Hackensack**	22
3 West | **Basking Ridge**	21
Trinity (Keyport) | **Keyport**	22
Villa Amalfi | **Cliffside Pk**	23
Washington Inn | **Cape May**	26
Wm. Douglas | **Cherry Hill**	24
Wolfgang Puck | **A.C.**	25

TASTING MENUS

Adara | **Montclair**	19
Arturo's | **Maplewood**	24
Bernards Inn | **Bernardsville**	25
Blvd. Five 72 | **Kenilworth**	23
Cafe Matisse | **Rutherford**	26
Chez Catherine | **Westfield**	26
Cuba Libre | **A.C.**	21
Da Filippo's | **Somerville**	24
Dauphin Grille | **Asbury Pk**	22
Due Mari | **New Bruns.**	26
Ebbitt Room | **Cape May**	26
Elements | **Princeton**	25
Etc. Steak | **Teaneck**	25
Fascino | **Montclair**	26
Frog & Peach | **New Bruns.**	25

Fuji | **Haddonfield**	25
Gables Rest. | **Beach Haven**	25
Komegashi | **Jersey City**	23
Kuzina/Sofia | **Cherry Hill**	22
La Cipollina | **Freehold**	21
Le Rendez-Vous | **Kenilworth**	26
Limani | **Westfield**	25
Nicholas | **Red Bank**	28
Ninety Acres/Natirar | **Peapack**	25
Norma's | **Cherry Hill**	22
Nunzio Rist. | **Collingswood**	23
Pairings | **Cranford**	23
Peacock Inn Rest. | **Princeton**	26
Pluckemin Inn | **Bedminster**	25
Rest. Latour | **Hamburg**	26
Rosemary/Sage | **Riverdale**	24
Ryland Inn | **Whitehouse**	25
Serenade | **Chatham**	26
Spargo's | **Manalapan**	22
Stage Left | **New Bruns.**	25
Ursino | **Union**	24
Vlg. Green | **Ridgewood**	24
Vine | **Basking Ridge**	24

TRENDY

Adara | **Montclair**	19
Alice's | **Lake Hopatcong**	20
Amada | **A.C.**	26
American Cut | **A.C.**	24
Aozora | **Montclair**	23
A Toute Heure | **Cranford**	26
Bar Cara | **Bloomfield**	21
Bibi'z Rest. | **Westwood**	20
Bin 14 | **Hoboken**	23
Bistro 55 | **Rochelle Pk**	19
Blu | **Montclair**	24
Blue Bottle Cafe | **Hopewell**	26
Blue2O | **Cherry Hill**	22
Bobby Flay Steak | **A.C.**	25
Blvd. Five 72 | **Kenilworth**	23
Buddakan | **A.C.**	25
Cafe Matisse | **Rutherford**	26
Cafe Metro | **Denville**	21
Chakra | **Paramus**	23
Char Steak | **Raritan**	23
Chef Mike's ABG | **S Seaside Pk**	22
Clydz | **New Bruns.**	23
Continental | **A.C.**	23
Cuba Libre | **A.C.**	21

Cubanu | **Rahway**	20
Cucharamama | **Hoboken**	25
Daryl | **New Bruns.**	23
David Burke From. | **Rumson**	25
Drew's Bistro | **Keyport**	27
Fascino | **Montclair**	26
Fig Tree | **Hoboken**	24
Fin | **A.C.**	25
Fin Raw Bar/Kitchen | **Montclair**	24
Fire/Oak | **multi.**	20
Flirt Sushi | **Allendale**	22
Girasole (Bound Brook) | **Bound Brook**	24
Grato | **Morris Plains**	22
Guru Palace | **N Brunswick**	19
Hotoke | **New Bruns.**	20
Hummus Elite | **Englewood**	21
Huntley Taverne | **Summit**	22
Iron Hill | **Maple Shade**	22
Jack's Café | **Westwood**	22
Just Rest. | **Old Bridge**	24
Komegashi | **Jersey City**	23
Labrador | **Normandy Bch**	21
Langosta Lounge | **Asbury Pk**	20
Lemongrass | **Morris Plains**	23
Levant Grille | **Englewood**	21
Light Horse Tavern | **Jersey City**	22
Lorena's | **Maplewood**	28
Madame Claude | **Jersey City**	22
Makeda | **New Bruns.**	22
Mantra | **multi.**	21
Marco/Pepe | **Jersey City**	23
Maritime Parc | **Jersey City**	23
Mehndi | **Morristown**	23
Metropolitan Cafe | **Freehold**	21
Mia | **A.C.**	24
MK Valencia | **Ridgefield Pk**	21
Mompou | **Newark**	22
MoonShine Modern | **Millburn**	19
Nico Kitchen/Bar | **Newark**	20
Ninety Acres/Natirar | **Peapack**	25
Nomad Pizza | **Hopewell**	25
Old Homestead | **A.C.**	26
Orange Squirrel | **Bloomfield**	21
Osteria Morini | **Bernardsville**	24
Pairings | **Cranford**	23
Pho Anh Dao | **Edison**	22
Pop's Garage | **Asbury Pk**	21
Rat's | **Hamilton**	25

Red | **Red Bank**	21	
Rob's Bistro | **Madison**	22	
Rolling Pin Cafe | **Westwood**	25	
Rosa Mexicano | **Hackensack**	22	
Rumba Cubana | **N Bergen**	22	
Sabor | **N Bergen**	24	
Sage | **Ventnor**	23	
Satis | **Jersey City**	24	
Shanghai Jazz | **Madison**	22	
Shumi | **Somerville**	27	
Simply Vietnamese | **Tenafly**	24	
Sirena Rist. | **Long Branch**	22	
Skylark | **multi.**	21	
Son Cubano | **W New York**	20	
Steakhouse 85 | **New Bruns.**	24	
Stella Marina | **Asbury Pk**	23	
Steve/Cookie's | **Margate**	27	
St. Eve's | **Ho-Ho-Kus**	23	
Sushi Lounge | **multi.**	21	
Taqueria D.T. | **Jersey City**	25	
Taverna Mykonos | **Elmwood Pk**	24	
NEW Tavro 13 | **Swedesboro**	–	
Teak | **Red Bank**	22	
Terra Nova | **Sewell**	21	
Theresa's | **Westfield**	22	
Thirty Acres | **Jersey City**	22	
3 Forty Grill | **Hoboken**	21	
3 West | **Basking Ridge**	21	
Trap Rock | **Berkeley Hts**	21	
Trinity (Hoboken) | **Hoboken**	18	
27 Mix | **Newark**	21	
Undici | **Rumson**	23	
Uproot | **Warren**	22	
Upstairs | **Upper Montclair**	24	
Urban Table | **Morristown**	19	
Ursino | **Union**	24	
Verve | **Somerville**	22	
Vincentown Diner | **Vincentown**	21	
Vine | **Basking Ridge**	24	
Waterside | **N Bergen**	20	
Witherspoon | **Princeton**	22	
Wolfgang Puck | **A.C.**	25	
Yellow Fin | **Surf City**	25	
Zafra | **Hoboken**	24	
Zylo | **Hoboken**	22	

VIEWS

NEW Ama Rist. | **Sea Bright**	25	
Avenue | **Long Branch**	22	
Bahrs Landing | **Highlands**	19	
Baumgart's | **Edgewater**	18	
Chart House | **Weehawken**	22	
Chelsea Prime | **A.C.**	24	
Continental | **A.C.**	23	
Crab House | **Edgewater**	19	
Crab Trap | **Somers Point**	24	
Cubacàn | **Asbury Pk**	22	
Fish | **Asbury Pk**	22	
Fleming's | **Edgewater**	23	
Highlawn Pavilion | **W Orange**	24	
Hunkar Rest. | **Carlstadt**	25	
Inlet Café | **Highlands**	20	
Krogh's | **Sparta**	21	
La Fontana Coast | **Sea Isle City**	23	
Lambertville Stn. | **Lambertville**	20	
Langosta Lounge | **Asbury Pk**	20	
Liberty House | **Jersey City**	20	
Maritime Parc | **Jersey City**	23	
Martini Beach | **Cape May**	22	
Masina | **Weehawken**	20	
McLoone's | **Long Branch**	19	
Milford Oyster | **Milford**	25	
Mill/Spg. Lake | **Spring Lake Hts**	20	
Molly Pitcher Inn | **Red Bank**	22	
Moonstruck | **Asbury Pk**	24	
Phillips Seafood | **A.C.**	21	
Plantation | **Harvey Cedars**	19	
Rat's | **Hamilton**	25	
Rest. Latour | **Hamburg**	26	
Smithville Inn | **Smithville**	22	
Son Cubano | **W New York**	20	
Stella Marina | **Asbury Pk**	23	
3 Forty Grill | **Hoboken**	21	
Tim McLoone's | **Asbury Pk**	19	
Ventura's | **Margate**	20	
Walpack Inn | **Wallpack**	23	
Waterside | **N Bergen**	20	
Windansea | **Highlands**	20	
Zylo | **Hoboken**	22	

VISITORS ON EXPENSE ACCOUNT

Adara | **Montclair**	19	
American Cut | **A.C.**	24	
Avenue | **Long Branch**	22	
Bernards Inn | **Bernardsville**	25	
Blue Morel | **Morristown**	24	
Blue2O | **Cherry Hill**	22	

Bobby Flay Steak | **A.C.**	25
Blvd. Five 72 | **Kenilworth**	23
Brennen's Steak | **Neptune City**	22
Buddakan | **A.C.**	25
Cafe Emilia | **Bridgewater**	20
Cafe Madison | **Riverside**	23
Cafe Matisse | **Rutherford**	26
Capriccio | **A.C.**	24
Cath. Lombardi | **New Bruns.**	24
Chakra | **Paramus**	23
Char Steak | **Raritan**	23
Chart House | **Weehawken**	22
Chef's Table | **Franklin Lakes**	27
Chelsea Prime | **A.C.**	24
Chez Catherine | **Westfield**	26
CulinAriane | **Montclair**	27
David Burke From. | **Rumson**	25
Dino/Harry's | **Hoboken**	24
Esty St. | **Park Ridge**	25
Fascino | **Montclair**	26
Fleming's | **multi.**	23
Gables Rest. | **Beach Haven**	25
Gallagher's | **A.C.**	23
Girasole (AC) | **A.C.**	23
Grand Cafe | **Morristown**	23
Grissini | **Englewood Cliffs**	22
Hamilton/Ward | **Paterson**	24
Harry's Lobster | **Sea Bright**	22
Highlawn Pavilion | **W Orange**	24
Il Capriccio | **Whippany**	25
Il Mulino | **A.C.**	25
Il Villaggio | **Carlstadt**	24
Knife/Fork Inn | **A.C.**	24
La Mezzaluna | **Princeton**	22
Liberty House | **Jersey City**	20
Luke Palladino | **A.C.**	24
Lu Nello | **Cedar Grove**	25
Mantra | **Paramus**	21
Maritime Parc | **Jersey City**	23
Mia | **A.C.**	24
Morton's | **Hackensack**	25
Nicholas | **Red Bank**	28
Ninety Acres/Natirar | **Peapack**	25
Old Homestead | **A.C.**	26
Panico's | **New Bruns.**	21
Park Steak | **Park Ridge**	24
Pluckemin Inn | **Bedminster**	25
Portofino Rist. | **Tinton Falls**	21
Porto Leggero | **Jersey City**	23

Ram's Head Inn | **Galloway**	25
Rest. Latour | **Hamburg**	26
River Palm Terrace | **multi.**	25
Rod's Steak | **Morristown**	22
Roots Steak | **multi.**	25
Ruth's Chris | **multi.**	25
Ryland Inn | **Whitehouse**	25
Saddle River Inn | **Saddle River**	26
Scalini Fedeli | **Chatham**	27
Sear House | **Closter**	23
Serenade | **Chatham**	26
Sirena Rist. | **Long Branch**	22
Stage Left | **New Bruns.**	25
Stone/Stirling Ridge | **Warren**	22
Strip House | **Livingston**	25
3 West | **Basking Ridge**	21
Undici | **Rumson**	23
Uproot | **Warren**	22
Varka | **Ramsey**	25
Villa Amalfi | **Cliffside Pk**	23
Waterside | **N Bergen**	20
Wolfgang Puck | **A.C.**	25

WARM WELCOME

Adega Grill | **Newark**	21
Alice's | **Lake Hopatcong**	20
Amanda's | **Hoboken**	25
Angelo's | **A.C.**	21
A Toute Heure | **Cranford**	26
Benito's Trattoria | **Chester**	23
Berta's Chateau | **Wanaque**	22
Biddy O'Malley's | **Northvale**	20
Cafe Emilia | **Bridgewater**	20
Calandra's | **Fairfield**	21
Casa Giuseppe | **Iselin**	23
Cenzino | **Oakland**	25
Chez Catherine | **Westfield**	26
Cinnamon | **Morris Plains**	21
Corso 98 | **Montclair**	23
Cucharamama | **Hoboken**	25
Da Filippo's | **Somerville**	24
Dai-Kichi | **Upper Montclair**	23
Di Palma Bros. | **N Bergen**	23
Far East Taste | **Eatontown**	23
Fascino | **Montclair**	26
Fernandes Steak | **Newark**	25
Fiddleheads | **Jamesburg**	22
Greek Taverna | **multi.**	21
Huntley Taverne | **Summit**	22

Il Capriccio | **Whippany**	25	Edward's Steak | **Jersey City**	21
Labrador | **Normandy Bch**	21	Esty St. | **Park Ridge**	25
Langosta Lounge | **Asbury Pk**	20	Fin | **A.C.**	25
Latour | **Ridgewood**	26	Fleming's | **multi.**	23
Le Rendez-Vous | **Kenilworth**	26	Frog & Peach | **New Bruns.**	25
Levant Grille | **Englewood**	21	Giumarello's | **Westmont**	25
Madeleine's | **Northvale**	24	Gladstone | **Gladstone**	21
Nana's Deli | **Livingston**	23	Hamilton/Ward | **Paterson**	24
Oceanos | **Fair Lawn**	24	Harvest Moon Inn | **Ringoes**	23
Osteria Giotto | **Montclair**	25	Liberty House | **Jersey City**	20
Plantation | **Harvey Cedars**	19	Manor | **W Orange**	24
Pop's Garage | **Asbury Pk**	21	Mediterra | **Princeton**	22
Quiet Man | **Dover**	23	Mia | **A.C.**	24
Risotto House | **Rutherford**	22	Nicholas | **Red Bank**	28
Rolling Pin Cafe | **Westwood**	25	Nico Kitchen/Bar | **Newark**	20
RosaLuca's | **Asbury**	24	Ninety Acres/Natirar | **Peapack**	25
Sage | **Ventnor**	23	Osteria Morini | **Bernardsville**	24
Taqueria D.T. | **Jersey City**	25	Park/Orchard | **E Rutherford**	22
Trattoria Saporito | **Hoboken**	23	Pluckemin Inn | **Bedminster**	25
Verjus | **Maplewood**	24	Rat's | **Hamilton**	25

WINNING WINE LISTS

American Cut | **A.C.**	24	Rest. Latour | **Hamburg**	26
Bernards Inn | **Bernardsville**	25	River Palm Terrace | **multi.**	25
Berta's Chateau | **Wanaque**	22	River Winds | **West Deptford**	24
Bin 14 | **Hoboken**	23	Ryland Inn | **Whitehouse**	25
Black Forest Inn | **Stanhope**	24	Salt Creek Grille | **Rumson**	21
Blue Morel | **Morristown**	24	Scalini Fedeli | **Chatham**	27
Bobby Flay Steak | **A.C.**	25	Serenade | **Chatham**	26
Brass Rail | **Hoboken**	19	Stage House | **Scotch Plains**	20
Cafe Madison | **Riverside**	23	Stage Left | **New Bruns.**	25
Capital Grille | **Cherry Hill**	25	Stone/Stirling Ridge | **Warren**	22
Cath. Lombardi | **New Bruns.**	24	Tabor Rd. Tavern | **Morris Plains**	22
Chakra | **Paramus**	23	Terra Nova | **Sewell**	21
Chengdu 46 | **Clifton**	23	Tewksbury Inn | **Oldwick**	21
Court St. Rest.Bar | **Hoboken**	21	3 West | **Basking Ridge**	21
Cucharamama | **Hoboken**	25	Tre Piani | **Princeton**	22
Daryl | **New Bruns.**	23	Ursino | **Union**	24
David Burke From. | **Rumson**	25	Washington Inn | **Cape May**	26
Due Mari | **New Bruns.**	26	Witherspoon | **Princeton**	22
		Wm. Douglas | **Cherry Hill**	24
		Wolfgang Puck | **A.C.**	25

Cuisines

Includes names, locations and Food ratings.

AFGHAN

Pamir | **Morristown**	21
Silk Road | **Warren**	24

AMERICAN

Acacia | **Lawrenceville**	22
Adelphia | **Deptford**	21
NEW Agricola | **Princeton**	-
Alchemist/Barrister | **Princeton**	18
Alice's | **Lake Hopatcong**	20
Amanda's | **Hoboken**	25
Amelia's Bistro | **Jersey City**	20
Andre's | **Newton**	25
Anton's/Swan | **Lambertville**	22
A Toute Heure | **Cranford**	26
The Backyard | **Stone Harbor**	24
Barnacle Bill's | **Rumson**	20
NEW Bat Barry's | **Westwood**	-
Baumgart's | **multi.**	18
Belford Bistro | **Belford**	26
Bell's Mansion | **Stanhope**	20
Bernards Inn | **Bernardsville**	25
Biddy O'Malley's | **Northvale**	20
Biggie's Clam Bar | **multi.**	20
Bistro 55 | **Rochelle Pk**	19
Bistro/Cherry Hill | **Cherry Hill**	23
Black-Eyed Susans | **Harvey Cedars**	24
Black Horse Diner | **Mount Ephraim**	20
Black Horse Tavern | **Mendham**	19
Black Trumpet | **Spring Lake**	22
Black Whale | **Beach Haven**	22
Blu | **Montclair**	24
Blue Bottle Cafe | **Hopewell**	26
Blue Morel | **Morristown**	24
Blue Pig Tavern | **Cape May**	21
Blue Rooster | **Cranbury**	22
Bonefish Grill | **multi.**	21
Blvd. Five 72 | **Kenilworth**	23
Braddock's | **Medford**	24
Brandl | **Belmar**	24
Brass Rail | **Hoboken**	19
Brick City Bar/Grill | **Newark**	19
Brickwall Tavern | **Asbury Pk**	20
Brothers Moon | **Hopewell**	24
Cafe Loren | **Avalon**	25
Cafe Madison | **Riverside**	23

NEW Café 37 | **Ridgewood**	25
NEW Central Kitchen | **Englewood Cliffs**	-
Chakra | **Paramus**	23
Chambers Walk | **Lawrenceville**	22
Charley's Ocean Grl. | **Long Branch**	19
Charlie's | **Somers Point**	21
Cheesecake Factory | **multi.**	21
Chef Mike's ABG | **S Seaside Pk**	22
Chickie/Pete's | **Egg Harbor Twp**	21
Chimney Rock Inn | **multi.**	19
Christopher's | **New Bruns.**	20
Clydz | **New Bruns.**	23
Coastline | **Cherry Hill**	20
Country Pancake | **Ridgewood**	19
Cranbury Inn | **Cranbury**	18
CulinAriane | **Montclair**	27
Daryl | **New Bruns.**	23
Dauphin Grille | **Asbury Pk**	22
David Burke From. | **Rumson**	25
Delicious Hgts. | **multi.**	19
Depot Mkt. Cafe | **Cape May**	24
Dish | **Red Bank**	23
D'Jeet? | **Red Bank**	21
Doc's Place | **Somers Point**	20
Drew's Bistro | **Keyport**	27
Ebbitt Room | **Cape May**	26
Elements | **Princeton**	25
Elements Cafe | **Haddon Hts**	23
Esty St. | **Park Ridge**	25
Ferry House | **Princeton**	22
Fiddleheads | **Jamesburg**	22
55 Main | **Flemington**	22
Fig Tree | **Hoboken**	24
Fire/Oak | **multi.**	20
Firefly Bistro | **Manasquan**	22
Frog & Peach | **New Bruns.**	25
GG's | **Mt Laurel**	23
Gladstone | **Gladstone**	21
Grain House | **Basking Ridge**	20
NEW Grange | **Westwood**	-
Harvest Moon Inn | **Ringoes**	23
Hat Tavern | **Summit**	20
Highlawn Pavilion | **W Orange**	24
High St. Grill | **Mt Holly**	24

CUISINES

Ho-Ho-Kus Tavern | **Ho-Ho-Kus**	21
Hollywood Cafe | **Woodbury Heights**	22
Holsten's | **Bloomfield**	19
Hotel Tides | **Asbury Pk**	22
Huntley Taverne | **Summit**	22
Inn/Millrace Rest. | **Hope**	22
Inn at Sugar Hill | **Mays Landing**	20
Iron Hill | **multi.**	22
Isabella's Bistro | **Westfield**	19
Ivy Inn | **Hasbrouck Hts**	21
Jack Baker's | **multi.**	20
Jack's Café | **Westwood**	22
Janice | **Ho-Ho-Kus**	21
Java Moon | **Jackson**	23
JBJ Soul Kit. | **Red Bank**	21
Just Rest. | **Old Bridge**	24
Kevin's Thyme | **Ho-Ho-Kus**	25
Krave Café | **Newton**	25
Krogh's | **Sparta**	21
Kubel's | **Long Beach**	19
Lafayette House | **Lafayette**	22
Lambertville Stn. | **Lambertville**	20
Landmark Americana | **Glassboro**	22
Latz's/Bay | **Somers Point**	21
Laurel | **Maplewood**	21
Liberty House | **Jersey City**	20
Library IV | **Williamstown**	24
Light Horse Tavern | **Jersey City**	22
LoBianco | **Margate**	23
Lucky Bones | **Cape May**	21
LuNello's Montville | **Montville**	21
Mad Batter | **Cape May**	22
Main St. | **multi.**	20
Manor | **W Orange**	24
Marco/Pepe | **Jersey City**	23
Maritime Parc | **Jersey City**	23
Mattar's Bistro | **Allamuchy**	23
Matt's Red Rooster | **Flemington**	26
McLoone's | **multi.**	19
Merion Inn | **Cape May**	22
Metro Diner | **Brooklawn**	20
Metuchen Inn | **Metuchen**	23
Miller's Ale House | **Mt Laurel**	21
Mill/Spg. Lake | **Spring Lake Hts**	20
MK Valencia | **Ridgefield Pk**	21
Mockingbird | **Basking Ridge**	22
Mohawk House | **Sparta**	22
Molly Pitcher Inn | **Red Bank**	22

MoonShine Modern | **Millburn**	19
Moonstruck | **Asbury Pk**	24
Nauvoo Grill | **Fair Haven**	19
Next Door | **Montclair**	22
Nicholas | **Red Bank**	28
Ninety Acres/Natirar | **Peapack**	25
NEW North End Bistro | **Princeton**	–
Old Man Rafferty's | **multi.**	19
One 53 | **Rocky Hill**	24
Orange Squirrel | **Bloomfield**	21
Oyster Creek Inn | **Leeds Point**	24
Pairings | **Cranford**	23
Park W. Tavern | **Ridgewood**	20
Peacock Inn Rest. | **Princeton**	26
Peter Shields Inn | **Cape May**	26
Phily Diner | **Runnemede**	20
Pig/Prince | **Montclair** **NEW**	20
PJ's Pancake | **Princeton**	18
Plantation | **Harvey Cedars**	19
Pluckemin Inn | **Bedminster**	25
Pop Shop | **Collingswood**	23
Prickly Pear | **Hackettstown**	22
Ram's Head Inn | **Galloway**	25
Raven/Peach | **Fair Haven**	24
Raymond's | **multi.**	21
Red | **Red Bank**	21
Redstone Grill | **Marlton**	22
Remington's | **Manasquan**	21
Renault Winery Rest. | **Egg Harbor**	23
Rest. Latour | **Hamburg**	26
River Grille | **Chatham**	–
River Winds | **West Deptford**	24
Robin's Nest | **Mt Holly**	24
Rocky Hill Inn | **Rocky Hill**	19
Rolling Pin Cafe | **Westwood**	25
Rosemary/Sage | **Riverdale**	24
Ryland Inn | **Whitehouse**	25
Saddle River Inn | **Saddle River**	26
Salt Creek Grille | **multi.**	21
Salt Gastro | **Stanhope**	22
Scarborough Fair | **Sea Girt**	20
Sea Grass | **Ocean Grove**	24
Seasons 52 | **Cherry Hill**	24
Sergeantsville Inn | **Sergeantsville**	23
Shipwreck Grill | **Brielle**	24
Smithville Inn | **Smithville**	22
Spargo's | **Manalapan**	22
Stage House | **Scotch Plains**	20
Stage Left | **New Bruns.**	25

Steve/Cookie's	**Margate**	27
St. Eve's	**Ho-Ho-Kus**	23
Stockton Inn	**Stockton**	21
Stone/Stirling Ridge	**Warren**	22
Sweet Basil's	**Livingston**	23
Tabor Rd. Tavern	**Morris Plains**	22
NEW Tavro 13	**Swedesboro**	–
Terra Nova	**Sewell**	21
Tewksbury Inn	**Oldwick**	21
Thirty Acres	**Jersey City**	22
3 Forty Grill	**Hoboken**	21
3 West	**Basking Ridge**	21
Tim McLoone's	**Asbury Pk**	19
Tim Schafer's	**Morristown**	23
Tisha's	**Cape May**	25
Toast	**multi.**	21
Trap Rock	**Berkeley Hts**	21
Trinity (Hoboken)	**Hoboken**	18
Triumph Brew.	**Princeton**	19
TwoFiftyTwo	**Bedminster**	20
Union Park	**Cape May**	26
Uproot	**Warren**	22
Upstairs	**Upper Montclair**	24
Ursino	**Union**	24
Verve	**Somerville**	22
Vlg. Green	**Ridgewood**	24
Vine	**Basking Ridge**	24
Walpack Inn	**Wallpack**	23
Washington Inn	**Cape May**	26
Whispers	**Spring Lake**	26
Wolfgang Puck	**A.C.**	25
Yellow Fin	**Surf City**	25
Za	**Pennington**	22
Zack's Oak Bar/Rest.	**Hoboken**	21
Zinburger	**Paramus**	21

ARGENTINEAN

| Under/Moon | **Bordentown** | 23 |

ASIAN

Aoyama	**multi.**	23
Baumgart's	**multi.**	18
Buddakan	**A.C.**	25
NEW Elena Wu	**Voorhees**	–
Hotoke	**New Bruns.**	20
Ming	**Morristown**	22

BAKERIES

| Bucu | **Paramus** | 19 |
| Mastoris | **Bordentown** | 21 |

| Ponzio's | **Cherry Hill** | 20 |
| **NEW** WildFlour | **Lawrenceville** | – |

BARBECUE

Big Ed's BBQ	**Matawan**	19
NEW Bro. Jimmy's	**New Bruns.**	–
Cubby's BBQ	**Hackensack**	20
Dinosaur BBQ	**Newark**	23
Grub Hut	**Manville**	21
Memphis Pig Out	**Atlantic Highlands**	21
Whistlers Inn	**Cinnaminson**	20

BELGIAN

| Mussel Bar/Wiedmaier | **A.C.** | 24 |

BRAZILIAN

Brasilia	**Newark**	21
Hamburgao	**multi.**	21
Rio Rodizio	**multi.**	21
Samba Montclair	**Montclair**	–

BRITISH

| British Chip Shop | **Haddonfield** | 24 |

BURGERS

Bobby's Burger	**multi.**	21
Bucu	**Paramus**	19
NEW Burgerwood	**Englewood**	–
Five Guys	**multi.**	22
Hiram's Roadstand	**Fort Lee**	22
Kubel's	**Barnegat Light**	19
Pop Shop	**Collingswood**	23
Rutt's Hut	**Clifton**	21
NEW Smashburger	**multi.**	20
Urban Table	**Basking Ridge**	19
Village Whiskey	**A.C.**	24
White Mana	**Jersey City**	18
White Manna	**Hackensack**	22
Zinburger	**multi.**	21

CAJUN

| Old Bay Rest. | **New Bruns.** | 20 |

CARIBBEAN

| 410 Bank St. | **Cape May** | 25 |

CHEESESTEAKS

Big John's	**W Berlin**	23
Gaetano's	**Berlin**	21
Tony Luke's	**multi.**	23
Yellow Sub.	**Maple Shade**	21

CUISINES

CHINESE

(* dim sum specialist)

Cathay 22 | **Springfield**	21
Chef Jon's | **Whippany**	20
Chengdu 46 | **Clifton**	23
Chinese Mirch | **multi.**	19
Crown Palace* | **multi.**	20
Dim Sum Dynasty* | **Ridgewood**	20
Elements Asia | **Lawrenceville**	23
Far East Taste | **Eatontown**	23
Hanami | **multi.**	18
Hunan Chinese | **Morris Plains**	22
Hunan Taste | **Denville**	24
Joe's Peking Duck* | **Marlton**	23
Lotus Cafe | **Hackensack**	21
Meemah | **Edison**	23
Ming | **Edison**	22
Mr. Chu | **E Hanover**	21
P.F. Chang's | **multi.**	21
W. Lake Seafood | **Matawan**	24
Wonder Seafood* | **Edison**	23
Xina | **Toms River**	23
Ya Ya | **Skillman**	20

COFFEEHOUSES

Small World Coffee | **Princeton**	23

CONTINENTAL

Black Forest Inn | **Stanhope**	24
Court St. Rest.Bar | **Hoboken**	21
Farnsworth | **Bordentown**	21
Inn/Millrace Rest. | **Hope**	22
Main St. | **multi.**	20
Stony Hill Inn | **Hackensack**	22

CREOLE

410 Bank St. | **Cape May**	25
Old Bay Rest. | **New Bruns.**	20

CUBAN

A Little Bit/Cuba Dos | **Freehold**	22
Azúcar | **Jersey City**	22
Casona | **Collingswood**	22
Casual Habana | **Hackensack**	25
Cubacàn | **Asbury Pk**	22
Cuba Libre | **A.C.**	21
Cuban Pete's | **Montclair**	20
Cubanu | **Rahway**	20
Cucharamama | **Hoboken**	25
La Isla | **Hoboken**	25

Las Palmas | **W New York**	24
NEW Lidia's Cuban | **Cranford**	-
Martino's | **Somerville**	22
Mi Bandera | **Union City**	23
Rebecca's | **Edgewater**	23
Rumba Cubana | **multi.**	22
Son Cubano | **W New York**	20
Zafra | **Hoboken**	24

DELIS

(see also Sandwiches)

Eppes Essen | **Livingston**	19
Harold's N.Y. Deli | **Edison**	22
Hobby's Deli | **Newark**	25
Kibitz Room | **Cherry Hill**	24
Nana's Deli | **Livingston**	23

DINER

Black Horse Diner | **Mount Ephraim**	20
Mastoris | **Bordentown**	21
Metro Diner | **Brooklawn**	20
Mustache Bill's | **Barnegat Light**	22
Phily Diner | **Runnemede**	20
Ponzio's | **Cherry Hill**	20
Skylark | **multi.**	21
Teplitzky's | **A.C.**	19
Tick Tock | **Clifton**	19
Vincentown Diner | **Vincentown**	21

EASTERN EUROPEAN

Blue Danube | **Trenton**	23

ECLECTIC

Adara | **Montclair**	19
A Little Café | **Voorhees**	23
Alstarz | **Bordentown**	18
Avenue Bistro | **Verona**	21
Bibi'z Rest. | **Westwood**	20
Bistro/Red Bank | **Red Bank**	21
Black Duck | **W Cape May**	26
Cafe Matisse | **Rutherford**	26
Cafe Panache | **Ramsey**	26
Chakra | **Paramus**	23
Classic Quiche | **Teaneck**	23
Continental | **A.C.**	23
Fedora Café | **Lawrenceville**	22
Frenchtown Inn | **Frenchtown**	22
Full Moon | **Lambertville**	20
Gables Rest. | **Beach Haven**	25
Garlic Rose | **multi.**	20

Grand Lux	**multi.**	20
Jack's Café	**Westwood**	22
Labrador	**Normandy Bch**	21
Langosta Lounge	**Asbury Pk**	20
Lilly's/Canal	**Lambertville**	20
Market Roost	**Flemington**	23
Martini Beach	**Cape May**	22
Metropolitan Cafe	**Freehold**	21
NEW Mistral	**Princeton**	-
Nico Kitchen/Bar	**Newark**	20
Oliver a Bistro	**Bordentown**	25
Park/Orchard	**E Rutherford**	22
Skylark	**multi.**	21
Tomatoes	**Margate**	23
27 Mix	**Newark**	21
Urban Table	**multi.**	19
Village Gourmet	**Rutherford**	19
Waterfront Buffet	**A.C.**	22

ETHIOPIAN

Makeda	**New Bruns.**	22
Mesob	**Montclair**	23

EUROPEAN

Patria	**Rahway**	23
Satis	**Jersey City**	24

FRENCH

Aozora	**Montclair**	23
Blackbird Dining	**Collingswood**	24
Brian's	**Lambertville**	26
Chef's Table	**Franklin Lakes**	27
Chez Catherine	**Westfield**	26
Dream Cuisine	**Cherry Hill**	26
NEW Elena Wu	**Voorhees**	-
Ferry House	**Princeton**	22
Grand Cafe	**Morristown**	23
Latour	**Ridgewood**	26
Lorena's	**Maplewood**	28
Madeleine's	**Northvale**	24
Manon	**Lambertville**	24
Origin	**multi.**	24
NEW The Pass	**Rosemont**	-
Rat's	**Hamilton**	25
Saddle River Inn	**Saddle River**	26
Serenade	**Chatham**	26
Siri's Thai French	**Cherry Hill**	24
Thai Chef	**Montclair**	21
Verjus	**Maplewood**	24
Verve	**Somerville**	22

FRENCH (BISTRO)

Elysian Café	**Hoboken**	23
Harvest Bistro	**Closter**	21
Le Rendez-Vous	**Kenilworth**	26
Madame Claude	**Jersey City**	22
Rob's Bistro	**Madison**	22
Sophie's Bistro	**Somerset**	23

FRENCH (BRASSERIE)

Avenue	**Long Branch**	22

GERMAN

Black Forest Inn	**Stanhope**	24
Helmers'	**Hoboken**	20

GREEK

Athenian Gdn.	**Galloway Twp**	22
Axia Taverna	**Tenafly**	23
Greek Taverna	**multi.**	21
It's Greek To Me	**multi.**	19
Kuzina/Sofia	**Cherry Hill**	22
Kyma	**Somerville**	23
Limani	**Westfield**	25
Lithos	**Livingston**	23
Pithari/Ouzo	**multi.**	23
Stamna	**multi.**	24
Taverna Mykonos	**Elmwood Pk**	24
Varka	**Ramsey**	25
Vasili's	**Teaneck**	20

HOT DOGS

Hiram's Roadstand	**Fort Lee**	22
Jimmy Buff's	**multi.**	20
Rutt's Hut	**Clifton**	21
WindMill	**multi.**	19

ICE CREAM PARLORS

Baumgart's	**Ridgewood**	18
Bent Spoon	**Princeton**	27
Holsten's	**Bloomfield**	19

INDIAN

Aamantran	**Toms River**	21
Akbar	**Edison**	21
Amiya	**multi.**	21
Bombay Bistro	**Summit**	21
Brick Ln. Curry	**multi.**	23
Chand Palace	**multi.**	22
Chinese Mirch	**Edgewater**	19
Cinnamon	**Morris Plains**	21
Coriander	**Voorhees**	24
Guru Palace	**N Brunswick**	19

CUISINES

IndeBlue | **Collingswood**	25
India/Hudson | **Hoboken**	20
NEW Indiya | **Collingswood**	-
Kailash | **Ridgewood**	21
Karma Kafe | **Hoboken**	23
Khyber Grill | **South Plainfield**	21
Kinara | **Edgewater**	21
Mantra | **multi.**	21
Mehndi | **Morristown**	23
Ming | **Edison**	22
Moghul | **Edison**	21
Monsoon | **Mt Laurel**	25
Namaskaar | **Englewood**	23
Neelam | **multi.**	21
Palace of Asia | **multi.**	23
Saffron | **E Hanover**	21

IRISH

Biddy O'Malley's | **Northvale**	20
Dublin Sq. | **multi.**	18
Egan/Sons | **multi.**	20
Irish Pub/Inn | **A.C.**	21
Quiet Man | **Dover**	23

ITALIAN

(N=Northern; S=Southern)

NEW Acanto Rist. | **Tenafly**	-
Acquaviva/Fonti | **Westfield**	20
Al Dente | N | **Piscataway**	22
Al Dente Italiana | **Moorestown**	23
Aldo/Gianni | **Montvale**	21
NEW Ama Rist. | **Sea Bright**	25
Amarone | N | **Teaneck**	21
Amici Milano | N | **Trenton**	21
Andiamo | **Haworth**	21
Angelo's | **A.C.**	21
Anna's Italian | **Middletown**	23
Anna's Rist. | **Summit**	20
Antonia's/Park | **N Bergen**	22
Arturo's (Midland Pk) | S | **Midland Pk**	23
Arugula | **Sewell**	23
Assaggini/Roma | **Newark**	24
A Tavola | **Old Bridge**	21
Augustino's | **Hoboken**	24
Avanti | **Pennington**	21
Bacari Grill | **Washington Twp**	21
Baia | **Somers Point**	19
Bar Cara | **Bloomfield**	21
Bareli's | **Secaucus**	23

Barone's | **multi.**	23
Basilico | **Millburn**	23
Basil T's | **Red Bank**	21
Bazzarelli | **Moonachie**	20
NEW Bellissimo's | **Little Falls**	-
Belmont Tavern | **Belleville**	22
Benito's Trattoria | N | **Chester**	23
Berta's Chateau | N | **Wanaque**	22
Biagio's | **Paramus**	20
Bin 14 | **Hoboken**	23
Bistro/Marino | **Collingswood**	25
Blackbird Dining | **Collingswood**	24
Brian's | **Lambertville**	26
Brio | **multi.**	21
Brioso | **Marlboro**	23
Bruno's | **Haddonfield**	21
Bruschetta | **Fairfield**	20
BV Tuscany | N | **Teaneck**	24
Café Azzurro | N | **Peapack**	22
Cafe Bello | **Bayonne**	23
Cafe Emilia | **Bridgewater**	20
Cafe Graziella | **Hillsborough**	22
Cafe 2825 | **A.C.**	24
Caffe/Lamberti | **Cherry Hill**	24
Capriccio | **A.C.**	24
Cara Mia | **Millburn**	21
Carmine's | **A.C.**	22
Carpaccio | **Middlesex**	21
Casa Dante | **Jersey City**	22
Casa Giuseppe | N | **Iselin**	23
Cassie's | **Englewood**	19
Cath. Lombardi | **New Bruns.**	24
Cenzino | **Oakland**	25
Chef Vola's | **A.C.**	27
Christie's Italian | **Howell**	23
Columbia Inn | **Montville**	21
Corso 98 | **Montclair**	23
Cucina Calandra | S | **Fairfield**	21
Da Filippo's | **Somerville**	24
Dante's Rist. | **Mendham**	20
Da Soli | **Haddonfield**	25
Davia | **Fair Lawn**	22
DeAnna's | **Lambertville**	22
Dimora | **Norwood**	23
Dinallo's | **River Edge**	21
Dining/Anty. David's | N | **Hoboken**	24
Dino's | **Harrington Pk**	21
Di Palma Bros. | **N Bergen**	23
Domenico's | **Ventnor**	23

NEW Due	N	**Ridgewood**	–
Due Mari	**New Bruns.**	26
E & V	**Paterson**	24
Eccola Italian	**Parsippany**	22
Eno Terra	**Kingston**	25
Espo's	S	**Raritan**	22
Fascino	**Montclair**	26
15 Fox Pl.	**Jersey City**	22
Filomena	S	**Clementon**	24
Filomena Rustica	S	**W Berlin**	23
Fiorino	N	**Summit**	23
Fontana/Trevi	**Leonia**	22
Fornelletto	**A.C.**	23
Franco's Metro	**Fort Lee**	22
Frankie Fed's	**Freehold Twp**	22
Frescos	**Cape May**	23
Gennaro's	**Princeton**	21
Girasole (AC)	S	**A.C.**	23
Girasole (Bound Brook)	**Bound Brook**	24
Giumarello's	N	**Westmont**	25
GoodFellas	**Garfield**	23
Grato	**Morris Plains**	22
Grissini	**Englewood Cliffs**	22
Homestead Inn	**Trenton**	23
I Gemelli Rist.	**S Hackensack**	25
Il Capriccio	**Whippany**	25
Il Fiore	**Collingswood**	24
Il Michelangelo	**Boonton**	21
Il Mondo Vecchio	**Madison**	25
Il Mulino	**A.C.**	25
Il Villaggio	**Carlstadt**	24
Janice	**Ho-Ho-Kus**	21
Jimmy's	S	**Asbury Pk**	23
Joe Pesce	**Collingswood**	25
Justin's Rist.	**multi.**	22
Kinchley's Tavern	**Ramsey**	22
La Campagna	**Morristown**	24
La Cipollina	**Freehold**	21
La Couronne	**Montclair**	23
La Dolce Vita	**Belmar**	22
La Focaccia	N	**Summit**	23
La Fontana Coast	**Sea Isle City**	23
La Griglia	**Kenilworth**	23
L'Allegria	N	**Madison**	23
La Mezzaluna	**Princeton**	22
La Pastaria	**multi.**	21
La Pergola	N	**Millburn**	20
La Primavera	**W Orange**	24

La Riviera	**Clifton**	26
NEW La Sera	**Wyckoff**	–
La Spiaggia	**Ship Bottom**	23
La Strada	**Randolph**	23
La Vecchia	**Edgewater**	22
Locale	**Closter**	21
LouCás	**Edison**	23
Luca's Rist.	**Somerset**	24
Luciano's	**Rahway**	22
Luigi's	**E Hanover**	22
Luigi's Pizza	**multi.**	21
Luke Palladino	**multi.**	24
Lu Nello	**Cedar Grove**	25
LuNello's Montville	**Montville**	21
Margherita's	**Hoboken**	21
Masina	**Weehawken**	20
Metro North	**Princeton**	19
Mia	**A.C.**	24
MK Valencia	**Ridgefield Pk**	21
Nanni Rist.	**Rochelle Pk**	22
Nick's Pizza/Steak	**multi.**	23
Novita Bistro	**Metuchen**	20
Nunzio Rist.	**Collingswood**	23
NEW Nuovo Trattoria	**Manalapan**	–
Osteria Giotto	**Montclair**	25
Osteria Morini	**Bernardsville**	24
Paisano's Rest.	**Rutherford**	22
Palazzo	**Montclair**	20
Panico's	**New Bruns.**	21
Passariello's	**multi.**	22
Patsy's	**Fairview**	22
Piccola Italia	**Ocean Twp**	25
Piero's	**Union Beach**	22
Pino's La Forchetta	**Marlboro**	20
Porta	**Asbury Pk**	24
Portobello	N	**Oakland**	21
Portofino Rist.	**Tinton Falls**	21
Portofino's	**Morristown**	21
Porto Leggero	**Jersey City**	23
Puccini's	**Jersey City**	22
Queen Margherita	**Nutley**	24
Raimondo's	**Ship Bottom**	24
Reservoir Tavern	**Boonton**	23
Risotto House	**Rutherford**	22
Rist. Giorgia	**Rumson**	25
Roberto's	N	**Beach Haven**	23
Rocca	**Glen Rock**	23
RosaLuca's	**Asbury**	24

CUISINES

Rosie's Trattoria | **Randolph**	22
Salute Brick Oven | **Montclair**	22
Sanducci's | **River Edge**	19
San Remo | **Shrewsbury**	22
Sanzari's | **New Milford**	21
Sapori | **Collingswood**	25
Savini | **Allendale**	21
Scalini Fedeli | N | **Chatham**	27
Sette | **Bernardsville**	23
Sirena Rist. | **Long Branch**	22
Solo Bella | **Jackson**	23
Sorrento | **E Rutherford**	23
Squan Tavern | S | **Manasquan**	20
Stella Marina | **Asbury Pk**	23
Stony Hill Inn | **Hackensack**	22
Teresa Caffe | **Princeton**	23
That's Amore | **Collingswood**	22
Theresa's | **Westfield**	22
Tony's/Grill | **A.C.**	22
Tony's Touch/Italy | **Wayne**	23
Toscana | **Mullica Hill**	24
Trattoria/Sorrentina | **N Bergen**	25
Trattoria Med. | **Bedminster**	22
Trattoria Saporito | **Hoboken**	23
Tre Amici | **Long Branch**	22
Tre Famiglia | **Haddonfield**	25
Tre Piani | **Princeton**	22
Trio | N | **Martinsville**	24
Tutto/Modo Mio | **Ridgefield**	22
Tuzzio's | **Long Branch**	20
Undici | **Rumson**	23
Valentino's | **Park Ridge**	19
Ventura's | **Margate**	20
Via45 | **Red Bank**	25
Vic's | **Bradley Bch**	22
Villa Amalfi | **Cliffside Pk**	23
Villa Vittoria | **Brick**	22
Zeppoli | S | **Collingswood**	26
Zylo | N | **Hoboken**	22

JAPANESE

(* sushi specialist)

Ajihei* | **Princeton**	24
Akai* | **Englewood**	24
Aozora | **Montclair**	23
Benihana | **multi.**	20
Dai-Kichi* | **Upper Montclair**	23
Danny's* | **Red Bank**	22
Elements Asia | **Lawrenceville**	23

Flirt Sushi* | **Allendale**	22
Fuji | **Haddonfield**	25
Hanami | **multi.**	18
Ikko* | **Brick**	25
Izakaya | **A.C.**	23
Jo-Sho* | **Somerset**	25
Kanji* | **Tinton Falls**	24
Kiku* | **multi.**	21
Kimchi Hana* | **South Plainfield**	23
Komegashi* | **Jersey City**	23
Konbu* | **Manalapan**	23
Megu Sushi* | **multi.**	24
Midori* | **Denville**	23
Mikado* | **multi.**	22
Minado* | **multi.**	22
Monster Sushi* | **Summit**	20
Nagoya | **Mahwah**	24
Nikko* | **Whippany**	24
Nori | **multi.**	21
Robongi | **multi.**	22
Sagami* | **Collingswood**	26
Sakura | **Parsippany**	22
Sakura Bana* | **Ridgewood**	25
Shogun* | **multi.**	21
Shumi* | **Somerville**	27
Sono Sushi* | **Middletown**	26
Sushi Lounge* | **multi.**	21
Taka* | **Asbury Pk**	25
Taka Sushi* | **Summit**	23
Tokyo Hibachi* | **Deptford**	23
Umeya* | **Cresskill**	23
Wasabi* | **multi.**	22
Yokohama* | **Maple Shade**	25
Yoshi-Sono* | **W Orange**	21

JEWISH

Eppes Essen | **Livingston**	19
Harold's N.Y. Deli | **Edison**	22
Hobby's Deli | **Newark**	25
Hummus Elite | **Englewood**	21
Kibitz Room | **Cherry Hill**	24
Nana's Deli | **Livingston**	23

KOREAN

(* barbecue specialist)

Dong Bang* | **Fort Lee**	20
Gam Mee Ok | **Fort Lee**	22
Kimchi Hana* | **South Plainfield**	23
So Moon Nan Jip* | **Palisades Pk**	24

KOSHER/ KOSHER-STYLE

Etc. Steak | **Teaneck**	25
Hummus Elite | **Englewood**	21

MALAYSIAN

Meemah | **Edison**	23
Penang | **multi.**	22
Taste/Asia | **Chatham**	23

MEDITERRANEAN

NEW Blue Fig | **Moorestown**	–
Calandra's | **Fairfield**	21
Efe's Med. Grill | **multi.**	21
Fig Tree | **Hoboken**	24
Frescos | **Cape May**	23
Hamilton's Grill | **Lambertville**	24
Hummus Elite | **Englewood**	21
Levant Grille | **Englewood**	21
NEW Lisa's Med. | **Ridgewood**	–
Mediterra | **Princeton**	22
NEW Mistral | **Princeton**	–
Moonstruck | **Asbury Pk**	24
Sage | **Ventnor**	23
Tre Piani | **Princeton**	22
Trinity (Keyport) | **Keyport**	22
Vine | **Basking Ridge**	24
Waterside | **N Bergen**	20
NEW Zoe's Kitchen | **Marlton**	–

MEXICAN

Aby's | **Matawan**	20
A Taste/Mexico | **Princeton**	20
Casa Maya | **multi.**	21
Charrito's | **multi.**	22
Dos Caminos | **A.C.**	22
El Azteca | **Mt Laurel**	23
El Mesón Café | **Freehold**	23
El Tule | **Lambertville**	25
Grub Hut | **Manville**	21
Jose's Mex. Cantina | **multi.**	20
Juanito's | **multi.**	22
La Esperanza | **Lindenwold**	24
La Tapatia | **Asbury Pk**	24
Los Amigos | **multi.**	21
Mex. Food Factory | **Marlton**	21
Pop's Garage | **multi.**	21
Rosa Mexicano | **Hackensack**	22
Señorita's | **multi.**	19
Surf Taco | **multi.**	21

Taqueria D.T. | **Jersey City**	25
Tortilla Press | **multi.**	21
Tortuga's | **multi.**	23

MIDDLE EASTERN

Ibby's | **multi.**	20
Norma's | **Cherry Hill**	22

NUEVO LATINO

Cubacàn | **Asbury Pk**	22
Sabor | **N Bergen**	24

PAN-LATIN

Cucharamama | **Hoboken**	25
Lola Latin Bistro | **Metuchen**	21
Patria | **Rahway**	23
Zafra | **Hoboken**	24

PERSIAN

Levant Grille | **Englewood**	21

PERUVIAN

Costanera | **Montclair**	24
El Tule | **Lambertville**	25

PIZZA

Ah' Pizz | **Montclair**	20
A Mano | **Ridgewood**	22
Anthony's | **multi.**	21
Arturo's | **Maplewood**	24
Bar Cara | **Bloomfield**	21
Benny Tudino's | **Hoboken**	20
Brooklyn's Pizzeria | **multi.**	22
CPK | **multi.**	19
Carluccio's Pizza | **Northfield**	25
Cassie's | **Englewood**	19
Columbia Inn | **Montville**	21
Conte's | **Princeton**	23
DeLorenzo's Pizza | **Hamilton Twp**	25
DeLorenzo's Pies | **Robbinsville**	27
Famous/King of Pizza | **multi.**	22
Federici's | **Freehold**	22
Frankie Fed's | **Freehold Twp**	22
Gaetano's | **Berlin**	21
Grimaldi's | **Hoboken**	23
Kinchley's Tavern | **Ramsey**	22
Luigi's Pizza | **multi.**	21
Manco/Manco Pizza | **Ocean City**	23
Margherita's | **Hoboken**	21
Napoli's Pizza | **Hoboken**	21

CUISINES

Nick's Pizza/Steak | **multi.**	23
Nomad Pizza | **Hopewell**	25
Osteria Procaccini | **multi.**	24
Passariello's | **multi.**	22
Pete/Elda's | **Neptune City**	24
Porta | **Asbury Pk**	24
Reservoir Tavern | **Boonton**	23
Solo Bella | **Jackson**	23
Tacconelli's | **Maple Shade**	21
Tony's/Grill | **A.C.**	22
Tony's Touch/Italy | **Wayne**	23
Trattoria/Sorrentina | **N Bergen**	25
Vic's | **Bradley Bch**	22

POLISH

Royal Warsaw | **Elmwood Pk**	23

PORTUGUESE

Adega Grill | **Newark**	21
Allegro Seafood | **Newark**	23
Bistro Olé | **Asbury Pk**	22
Don Pepe | **multi.**	22
Europa South | **Pt. Pleas. Bch**	23
Fernandes Steak | **Newark**	25
Iberia | **Newark**	22
Pic-Nic | **E Newark**	24
Portug. Manor | **Perth Amboy**	23
Seabra's Marisqueira | **Newark**	24
Segovia | **Moonachie**	22
Sol-Mar | **Newark**	24
Spain | **Newark**	22
Spanish Manor | **Newark**	25
Tony/Caneca | **Newark**	22

PUB FOOD

Biddy O'Malley's | **Northvale**	20
Black Horse Tavern | **Mendham**	19
Brick City Bar/Grill | **Newark**	19
Brickwall Tavern | **Asbury Pk**	20
Chickie/Pete's | **multi.**	21
Dublin Sq. | **multi.**	18
Inn/Hawke Rest. | **Lambertville**	18
Irish Pub/Inn | **A.C.**	21
Iron Hill | **multi.**	22
Landmark Americana | **Glassboro**	22
Light Horse Tavern | **Jersey City**	22
Miller's Ale House | **Mt Laurel**	21
Park W. Tavern | **Ridgewood**	20
P.J. Whelihan's | **multi.**	21
Quiet Man | **Dover**	23

Rocky Hill Inn | **Rocky Hill**	19
Trinity (Hoboken) | **Hoboken**	18
Yankee Doodle | **Princeton**	17

SANDWICHES

(See also Delis)
Big John's | **W Berlin**	23
NEW G Grab & Go | **Edison**	-
Little Food Cafe | **multi.**	23
PrimoHoagies | **multi.**	21
Rolling Pin Cafe | **Westwood**	25
White House | **A.C.**	25

SEAFOOD

Allen's | **New Gretna**	22
Atlantic Grill | **A.C.**	21
Axelsson's | **Cape May**	23
Azure/Allegretti | **A.C.**	23
Bahrs Landing | **Highlands**	19
Big Fish Seafood | **Princeton**	20
Biggie's Clam Bar | **multi.**	20
Black Whale | **Beach Haven**	22
Bloomfield Stk./Sea | **Bloomfield**	21
Blue Claw Crab | **Burlington**	24
Blue Fish Grill | **Flemington**	23
Blue Point Grill | **Princeton**	25
Blue2O | **Cherry Hill**	22
Bobby Chez | **multi.**	23
Bonefish Grill | **multi.**	21
Brandl | **Belmar**	24
Busch's Seafood | **Sea Isle City**	21
Caffe/Lamberti | **Cherry Hill**	24
Charley's Ocean Grl. | **Long Branch**	19
Chart House | **multi.**	22
Chef Mike's ABG | **S Seaside Pk**	22
Chophouse | **Gibbsboro**	24
Crab House | **Edgewater**	19
Crab Trap | **Somers Point**	24
Da Filippo's | **Somerville**	24
Diving Horse | **Avalon**	25
Dock's Oyster | **A.C.**	25
Due Mari | **New Bruns.**	26
Fin | **A.C.**	25
Fin Raw Bar/Kitchen | **Montclair**	24
Fish | **Asbury Pk**	22
Fresco Steak | **Milltown**	23
Halcyon Brasserie | **Montclair**	22
Harry's Lobster | **Sea Bright**	22
Harry's Oyster | **A.C.**	22
Harvey Cedars | **multi.**	20

Il Villaggio	**Carlstadt**	24
Inlet Café	**Highlands**	20
Jack Baker's	**multi.**	20
Joe Pesce	**Collingswood**	25
Klein's	**Belmar**	23
Knife/Fork Inn	**A.C.**	24
Kubel's	**Barnegat Light**	19
Kyma	**Somerville**	23
La Dolce Vita	**Belmar**	22
La Griglia	**Kenilworth**	23
Legal Sea Foods	**multi.**	21
Limani	**Westfield**	25
Little Tuna	**Haddonfield**	22
Lobster House	**Cape May**	22
Maritime Parc	**Jersey City**	23
Max's Seafood	**Gloucester**	26
McCormick/Schmick's	**multi.**	20
Mike's Seafood	**Sea Isle City**	21
Milford Oyster	**Milford**	25
Minado	**multi.**	22
Mud City Crab	**Manahawkin**	23
Navesink Fishery	**Navesink**	25
Oceanos	**Fair Lawn**	24
Octopus's Gdn.	**West Creek**	23
Oyster Creek Inn	**Leeds Point**	24
Park Steak	**Park Ridge**	24
Phillips Seafood	**A.C.**	21
Red's Lobster Pot	**Pt. Pleas. Bch**	23
Ritz Seafood	**Voorhees**	24
River Palm Terrace	**multi.**	25
Rod's Steak	**Morristown**	22
Rooney's	**Long Branch**	21
Seabra's Marisqueira	**Newark**	24
Sea Grill	**Avalon**	21
Shipwreck Grill	**Brielle**	24
Smitty's Clam Bar	**Somers Point**	23
Sol-Mar	**Newark**	24
Spike's	**Pt. Pleas. Bch**	21
Steakhouse 85	**New Bruns.**	24
Varka	**Ramsey**	25
W. Lake Seafood	**Matawan**	24
Windansea	**Highlands**	20
Witherspoon	**Princeton**	22

SMALL PLATES

(See also Spanish tapas specialist)

Bin 14	Italian	**Hoboken**	23
Cinders Grill	Eclectic	**Mine Hill**	20
NEW Mistral	Eclectic	**Princeton**	-
Upstairs	Amer.	**Upper Montclair**	24

SOUTHERN

Bell/Whistle	**Hopewell**	20
Delta's	**New Bruns.**	22
NEW Escape	**Montclair**	-
Je's	**Newark**	24

SOUTHWESTERN

Copper Canyon	**Atlantic Highlands**	24
Los Amigos	**multi.**	21
Mojave Grille	**Westfield**	21

SPANISH

(* tapas specialist)

Adega Grill	**Newark**	21
Amada	**A.C.**	26
Bistro Olé	**Asbury Pk**	22
Casa Vasca	**Newark**	24
Chateau/Spain	**Newark**	22
NEW Despaña*	**Princeton**	-
Don Pepe	**multi.**	22
El Cid	**Paramus**	22
Europa South	**Pt. Pleas. Bch**	23
Fernandes Steak	**Newark**	25
Fornos/Spain	**Newark**	23
Iberia	**Newark**	22
Lola's*	**Hoboken**	22
Málaga's	**Hamilton**	26
Mesón Madrid	**Palisades Pk**	20
Mompou*	**Newark**	22
Pic-Nic	**E Newark**	24
Portug. Manor	**Perth Amboy**	23
Segovia	**Moonachie**	22
Segovia Steak	**Little Ferry**	22
Spain	**Newark**	22
Spain 92	**Raritan**	21
Spanish Manor	**Newark**	25
Spanish Pavillion	**Harrison**	23
Spanish Tavern	**multi.**	22
Tapas/España*	**N Bergen**	24

STEAKHOUSES

American Cut	**A.C.**	24
Arthur's Steak	**N Brunswick**	21
Arthur's Tavern	**Morris Plains**	20
Atlantic Grill	**A.C.**	21
Bloomfield Stk./Sea	**Bloomfield**	21
Bobby Flay Steak	**A.C.**	25
Brennen's Steak	**Neptune City**	22
Capital Grille	**multi.**	25
Char Steak	**multi.**	23

CUISINES

Chelsea Prime | **A.C.**	24
Chophouse | **Gibbsboro**	24
Cinders Grill | **Mine Hill**	20
Danny's | **Red Bank**	22
Dino/Harry's | **Hoboken**	24
Don Pepe's Steak | **Pine Brook**	22
Edward's Steak | **Jersey City**	21
Etc. Steak | **Teaneck**	25
Fernandes Steak | **Newark**	25
Fleming's | **multi.**	23
Fresco Steak | **Milltown**	23
Gallagher's | **A.C.**	23
Hamilton/Ward | **Paterson**	24
J&K Steak | **multi.**	22
KC Prime | **Lawrenceville**	22
Kiku | **multi.**	21
Knife/Fork Inn | **A.C.**	24
Library IV | **Williamstown**	24
Library III | **Egg Harbor Twp**	25
Library II | **Voorhees**	24
Morton's | **multi.**	25
Nero's Grille | **Livingston**	19
Old Homestead | **A.C.**	26
The Palm | **A.C.**	24
Park Steak | **Park Ridge**	24
Pub | **Pennsauken**	21
Rare | **Little Falls**	23
Rio Rodizio | **Newark**	21
River Palm Terrace | **multi.**	25
Rod's Steak | **Morristown**	22
Roots Steak | **multi.**	25
Ruth's Chris | **multi.**	25
Sammy's/Cider Mill | **Mendham**	23
Sea Grill | **Avalon**	21
Sear House | **Closter**	23
Sebastian's | **Morristown**	24
Segovia Steak | **Little Ferry**	22
Shogun | **multi.**	21
Steakhouse 85 | **New Bruns.**	24
Steve's Steaks | **Carlstadt**	23
Strip House | **Livingston**	25
Valencia | **Elizabeth**	24
Wayne Steak | **Wayne**	25
What's/Beef? | **Rumson**	21
Witherspoon | **Princeton**	22
Wm. Douglas | **Cherry Hill**	24
Zylo | **Hoboken**	22

THAI

Bamboo Leaf | **multi.**	20
Bangkok Gdn. | **Hackensack**	23
Chao Phaya | **multi.**	22
Da's Kitchen | **Hopewell**	25
Far East Taste | **Eatontown**	23
Khun Thai | **Short Hills**	22
Lemongrass | **Morris Plains**	23
Mie Thai | **Woodbridge**	23
Origin | **multi.**	24
Pad-Thai Auth. | **Highland Pk**	22
Penang | **multi.**	22
Ridge Thai | **Ridgewood**	21
Siam Garden | **Red Bank**	22
Siri's Thai French | **Cherry Hill**	24
Spice Thai | **Bloomfield**	24
Sri Thai | **Hoboken**	22
Thai Chef | **Montclair**	21
Thai Kitchen | **multi.**	24
Thai Thai | **Old Bridge**	24
Topaz Thai | **Belleville**	24
Wondee's | **Hackensack**	22

TURKISH

Beyti Kebab | **Union City**	22
Dayi'nin Yeri | **Cliffside Pk**	24
Efe's Med. Grill | **multi.**	21
NEW Europe Café | **Tenafly**	–
Hunkar Rest. | **Carlstadt**	25
Istanbul Rest./Patis. | **N Brunswick**	22
Levant Grille | **Englewood**	21
NEW Lisa's Med. | **Ridgewood**	–
Samdan | **Cresskill**	21

VEGETARIAN

(* vegan)

Chand Palace | **Piscataway**	22
Good Karma Cafe* | **Red Bank**	22
Kaya's Kitchen* | **Belmar**	25

VIETNAMESE

Bamboo Leaf | **multi.**	20
Lemongrass | **Morris Plains**	23
Mekong Grill | **Ridgewood**	20
Nha Trang Place | **Jersey City**	23
Pho Anh Dao | **Edison**	22
Simply Vietnamese | **Tenafly**	24

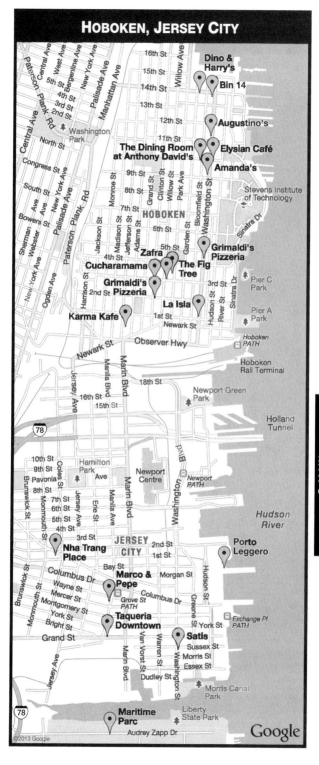

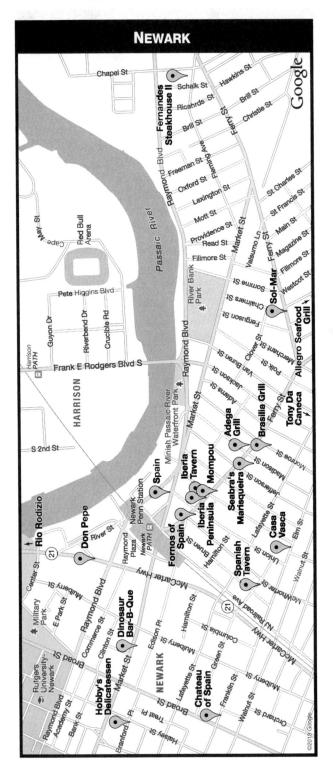

NEWARK

Chapel St

Schalk St

Hawkins St

Fernandes Steakhouse II

Ricahrds St

Brill St

Brill St

Christie St

Ferry St

Raymond Blvd

Freeman St

Oxford St

Fleming Ave

St Charles St

Lexington St

St Francis St

Mott St

Main St

Providence St

Market St

Magazine St

Read St

Valsumo Ln

Fillmore St

Somme St

Fillmore St

River Bank Park

Chalmers St

Sol-Mar

Westcot St

Ferguson St

Merchant St

Allegro Seafood Grill

Passaic River

Red Bull Arena

May St

Cape

Pete Higgins Blvd

Guyon Dr

Riverbend Dr

Crucible Rd

Frank E Rodgers Blvd S

Raymond Blvd

Harrison PATH

HARRISON

S 2nd St

Minish Passaic River Waterfront Park

Raymond Blvd

Polk St

Van Buren St

Clover St

Jackson St

Adams St

Ferry St

Brasillia Grill

Tony Da Caneca

Monroe St

Market St

Adega Grill

Spain

Iberia Tavern

Mompou

Seabra's Marisqueira

Madison St

Jefferson St

Iberia Peninsula

Fornos of Spain

Van Buren St

Newark Penn Station

Lafayette St

Casa Vasca

Elm St

Spanish Tavern

Hamilton St

Union St

Walnut St

Rio Rodizio

Don Pepe

River St

Raymond Plaza

Newark PATH

McCarter Hwy

McWhorter St

NJ Railroad Ave

Center St

Military Park

E Park St

Mulberry St

Raymond Blvd

Commerce St

Clinton Ave

Dinosaur Bar-B-Que

Edison Pl

Hamilton St

Mulberry St

Columbia St

Green St

McCarter Hwy

Rutgers University-Newark

Hobby's Delicatessen

Broad St

Market St

NEWARK

Lafayette St

Chateau of Spain

Mulberry St

Orchard St

Walnut St

Raymond Blvd

Academy St

Bank St

Treat Pl

Halsey St

Branford Pl

Broad St

Franklin St

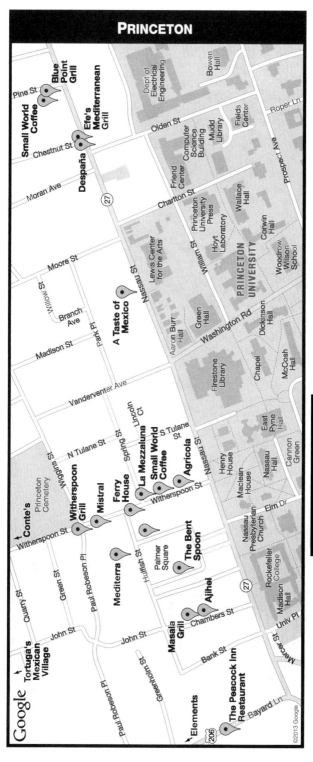

Bowen Hall

Dept. of Electrical Engineering

Roper Ln

Fields Center

Pine St

Blue Point Grill

Small World Coffee

Efe's Mediterranean Grill

Olden St

Mudd Library

Computer Science Building

Chestnut St

Despaña

(27)

Friend Center

Charlton St

Moran Ave

Princeton University Press

Wallace Hall

Lewis Center for the Arts

William St

Hoyt Laboratory

Corwin Hall

Moore St

Willow St

A Taste of Mexico

Nassau St

Green Hall

PRINCETON UNIVERSITY

Woodrow Wilson School

Branch Ave

Park Pl

Aaron Burr Hall

Washington Rd

Dickinson Hall

Madison St

Firestone Library

McCosh Hall

Vanderventer Ave

Chapel

East Pyne Hall

Lincoln Ct

S. Tulane St

Spring St

N Tulane St

La Mezzaluna

Small World Coffee

Agricola

Nassau St

Henry House

Nassau Hall

Cannon Green

Wiggins St

Witherspoon Grill

Mistral

Ferry House

Witherspoon St

Maclean House

Conte's

Princeton Cemetery

Elm Dr

Witherspoon St

Paul Robeson Pl

Mediterra

Huffish St

Palmer Square

The Bent Spoon

Nassau Presbyterian Church

Rockefeller College

Green St

Quarry St

John St

(27)

Ajihei

Madison Hall

Univ Pl

Masala Grill

Chambers St

John St

Bank St

Mercer St

Greenholm St

Tortuga's Mexican Village

Paul Robeson Pl

Elements

(206)

The Peacock Inn Restaurant

Bayard Ln

Google

©2013 Google

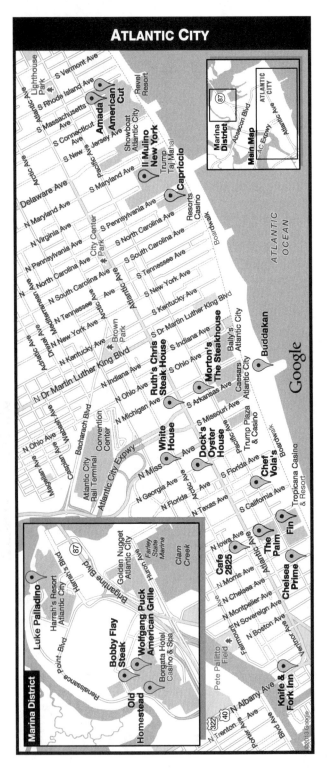

ATLANTIC CITY

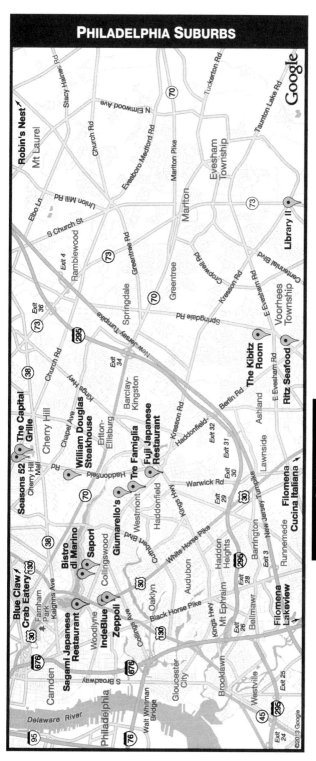

PHILADELPHIA SUBURBS

Locations

Includes names, cuisines and Food ratings.

Metro New York Area

ALLENDALE

Flirt Sushi	*Japanese*	22
Savini	*Italian*	21

ALPINE

Kiku	*Japanese*	21

BAYONNE

Cafe Bello	*Italian*	23
Little Food Cafe	*Sandwiches*	23

BELLEVILLE

Belmont Tavern	*Italian*	22
Topaz Thai	*Thai*	24

BERKELEY HEIGHTS

Delicious Hgts.	*Amer.*	19
Neelam	*Indian*	21
Trap Rock	*Amer.*	21

BLOOMFIELD

Bar Cara	*Italian*	21
Bloomfield Stk./Sea	*Seafood/Steak*	21
Holsten's	*Amer.*	19
Orange Squirrel	*Amer.*	21
Señorita's	*Mex.*	19
Spice Thai	*Thai*	24
Stamna	*Greek*	24

CALDWELL

Nori	*Asian*	21

CARLSTADT

Biggie's Clam Bar	*Amer.*	20
Hunkar Rest.	*Turkish*	25
Il Villaggio	*Italian/Seafood*	24
Steve's Steaks	*Steak*	23
Tina Louise	*Asian*	23

CEDAR GROVE

Lu Nello	*Italian*	25

CLARK

Señorita's	*Mex.*	19

CLIFFSIDE PARK

Dayi'nin Yeri	*Turkish*	24
NEW Giulia's Kitchen	*Amer.*	-
Villa Amalfi	*Italian*	23

CLIFTON

Anthony's	*Pizza*	21
Chengdu 46	*Chinese*	23
It's Greek To Me	*Greek*	19
La Riviera	*Italian*	26
Rutt's Hut	*Hot Dogs*	21
Spuntino	*Italian*	-
Tick Tock	*Diner*	19
Zinburger	*Burgers*	21

CLOSTER

Harvest Bistro	*Amer./French*	21
Locale	*Italian*	21
Sear House	*Steak*	23

CRANFORD

A Toute Heure	*Amer.*	26
Garlic Rose	*Eclectic*	20
NEW Lidia's Cuban	*Cuban*	-
Pairings	*Amer.*	23

CRESSKILL

Hanami	*Chinese/Japanese*	18
Samdan	*Turkish*	21
Umeya	*Japanese*	23

EAST NEWARK

Pic-Nic	*Portug./Spanish*	24

EAST RUTHERFORD

Park/Orchard	*Eclectic*	22
Sorrento	*Italian*	23

EDGEWATER

Baumgart's	*Amer./Asian*	18
Brooklyn's Pizzeria	*Pizza*	22
Chinese Mirch	*Asian*	19
Crab House	*Seafood*	19
Fleming's	*Steak*	23
Greek Taverna	*Greek*	21
Ibby's	*Mideastern*	20
Kinara	*Indian*	21

La Vecchia	*Italian*	22
Rebecca's	*Cuban*	23
River Palm Terrace	*Steak*	25

ELIZABETH

Valencia	*Steak*	24

ELMWOOD PARK

Royal Warsaw	*Polish*	23
Taverna Mykonos	*Greek*	24

ENGLEWOOD

Akai	*Japanese*	24
Baumgart's	*Amer./Asian*	18
NEW Burgerwood	*Burgers*	-
Cassie's	*Italian*	19
Hummus Elite	*Med.*	21
It's Greek To Me	*Greek*	19
Levant Grille	*Med.*	21
Namaskaar	*Indian*	23

ENGLEWOOD CLIFFS

NEW Central Kitchen	*Amer.*	-
Grissini	*Italian*	22

FAIRFIELD

Bruschetta	*Italian*	20
Calandra's	*Med.*	21
Cucina Calandra	*Italian*	21

FAIR LAWN

Davia	*Italian*	22
Oceanos	*Seafood*	24
River Palm Terrace	*Steak*	25

FAIRVIEW

Patsy's	*Italian*	22

FORT LEE

Dong Bang	*Korean*	20
Franco's Metro	*Italian*	22
Gam Mee Ok	*Korean*	22
Hiram's Roadstand	*Hot Dogs*	22
It's Greek To Me	*Greek*	19

FRANKLIN LAKES

Chef's Table	*French*	27

GARFIELD

GoodFellas	*Italian*	23

GLEN ROCK

Greek Taverna	*Greek*	21
Rocca	*Italian*	23

HACKENSACK

Bangkok Gdn.	*Thai*	23
Brooklyn's Pizzeria	*Pizza*	22
Casual Habana	*Cuban*	25
Cheesecake Factory	*Amer.*	21
Cubby's BBQ	*BBQ*	20
Five Guys	*Burgers*	22
Lotus Cafe	*Chinese*	21
McCormick/Schmick's	*Seafood*	20
Morton's	*Steak*	25
P.F. Chang's	*Chinese*	21
Rosa Mexicano	*Mex.*	22
Stony Hill Inn	*Continental*	22
White Manna	*Burgers*	22
Wondee's	*Thai*	22

HARRINGTON PARK

Dino's	*Italian*	21

HARRISON

Spanish Pavillion	*Spanish*	23

HASBROUCK HEIGHTS

Ivy Inn	*Amer.*	21

HAWORTH

Andiamo	*Italian*	21

HAWTHORNE

Justin's Rist.	*Italian*	22

HOBOKEN

Amanda's	*Amer.*	25
Augustino's	*Italian*	24
Benny Tudino's	*Pizza*	20
Biggie's Clam Bar	*Amer.*	20
Bin 14	*Italian*	23
Brass Rail	*Amer.*	19
Charrito's	*Mex.*	22
Court St. Rest.Bar	*Continental*	21
Cucharamama	*S Amer.*	25
Dining/Anty. David's	*Italian*	24
Dino/Harry's	*Steak*	24
Elysian Café	*French*	23
Fig Tree	*Amer.*	24
Grimaldi's	*Pizza*	23
Helmers'	*German*	20
India/Hudson	*Indian*	20
It's Greek To Me	*Greek*	19

Karma Kafe	*Indian*	23
La Isla	*Cuban*	25
Lola's	*Spanish*	22
Margherita's	*Italian*	21
Napoli's Pizza	*Pizza*	21
Robongi	*Japanese*	22
Sri Thai	*Thai*	22
Sushi Lounge	*Japanese*	21
3 Forty Grill	*Amer.*	21
Trattoria Saporito	*Italian*	23
Trinity (Hoboken)	*Amer./Pub*	18
WindMill	*Hot Dogs*	19
Zack's Oak Bar/Rest.	*Amer.*	21
Zafra	*Pan-Latin*	24
Zylo	*Steak*	22

HO-HO-KUS

Ho-Ho-Kus Tavern	*Amer.*	21
Janice	*Amer./Italian*	21
Kevin's Thyme	*Amer.*	25
St. Eve's	*Amer.*	23

JERSEY CITY

Amelia's Bistro	*Amer.*	20
Amiya	*Indian*	21
Azúcar	*Cuban*	22
Casa Dante	*Italian*	22
Edward's Steak	*Steak*	21
15 Fox Pl.	*Italian*	22
Fire/Oak	*Amer.*	20
Five Guys	*Burgers*	22
Ibby's	*Mideast.*	20
It's Greek To Me	*Greek*	19
Komegashi	*Japanese*	23
Liberty House	*Amer.*	20
Light Horse Tavern	*Amer.*	22
Madame Claude	*French*	22
Mantra	*Indian*	21
Marco/Pepe	*Amer.*	23
Maritime Parc	*Amer./Seafood*	23
Nha Trang Place	*Viet.*	23
Porto Leggero	*Italian*	23
Puccini's	*Italian*	22
Rumba Cubana	*Cuban*	22
Satis	*European*	24
Skylark	*Diner/Eclectic*	21
Taqueria D.T.	*Mex.*	25
Thirty Acres	*Amer.*	22
White Mana	*Burgers*	18

KEARNY

Hamburgao	*Brazilian*	21

KENILWORTH

Blvd. Five 72	*Amer.*	23
Jimmy Buff's	*Hot Dogs*	20
La Griglia	*Italian/Seafood*	23
Le Rendez-Vous	*French*	26
NEW Red Knot	*Amer.*	-

LEONIA

Fontana/Trevi	*Italian*	22

LITTLE FALLS

NEW Bellissimo's	*Italian*	-
Rare	*Steak*	23
Stamna	*Greek*	24

LITTLE FERRY

Minado	*Japanese*	22
Segovia Steak	*Spanish*	22

LIVINGSTON

Baumgart's	*Amer./Asian*	18
Eppes Essen	*Deli*	19
Lithos	*Greek*	23
Nana's Deli	*Deli*	23
Nero's Grille	*Steak*	19
Strip House	*Steak*	25
Sweet Basil's	*Amer.*	23

LODI

Penang	*Malaysian/Thai*	22

MAHWAH

Nagoya	*Japanese*	24
River Palm Terrace	*Steak*	25

MAPLEWOOD

Arturo's	*Pizza*	24
Laurel	*Amer.*	21
Lorena's	*French*	28
Verjus	*French*	24

MIDLAND PARK

Arturo's (Midland Pk)	*Italian*	23

MILLBURN

Basilico	*Italian*	23
Cara Mia	*Italian*	21
Five Guys	*Burgers*	22

La Pergola | *Italian* 20
MoonShine Modern | *Amer.* 19

MINE HILL

Cinders Grill | *Eclectic* 20

MONTCLAIR

Adara | *Eclectic* 19
Ah' Pizz | *Pizza* 20
Aozora | *French/Japanese* 23
Blu | *Amer.* 24
Corso 98 | *Italian* 23
Costanera | *Peruvian* 24
Cuban Pete's | *Cuban* 20
CulinAriane | *Amer.* 27
Egan/Sons | *Irish* 20
NEW Escape | *Southern* -
Fascino | *Italian* 26
Fin Raw Bar/Kitchen | *Seafood* 24
Greek Taverna | *Greek* 21
Halcyon Brasserie | *Seafood* 22
J&K Steak | *Steak* 22
La Couronne | *Italian* 23
Mesob | *Ethiopian* 23
Next Door | *Amer.* 22
Nori | *Asian* 21
Osteria Giotto | *Italian* 25
Palazzo | *Italian* 20
NEW Pig/Prince | *Amer.* 20
Raymond's | *Amer.* 21
Salute Brick Oven | *Italian* 22
Samba Montclair | *Brazilian* -
Thai Chef | *French/Thai* 21
Toast | *Amer.* 21

MONTVALE

Aldo/Gianni | *Italian* 21
Fire/Oak | *Amer.* 20

MOONACHIE

Bazzarelli | *Italian* 20
Segovia | *Portug./Spanish* 22

MOUNTAINSIDE

Spanish Tavern | *Spanish* 22

NEWARK

Adega Grill | *Portug./Spanish* 21
Allegro Seafood | *Portug.* 23
Assaggini/Roma | *Italian* 24

Brasilia | *Brazilian* 21
Brick City Bar/Grill | *Pub* 19
Casa Vasca | *Spanish* 24
Chateau/Spain | *Spanish* 22
Dinosaur BBQ | *BBQ* 23
Don Pepe | *Portug./Spanish* 22
NEW Elbow Room | *Amer.* -
Fernandes Steak | *Portug.* 25
Fornos/Spain | *Spanish* 23
Hamburgao | *Brazilian* 21
Hobby's Deli | *Deli* 25
Iberia | *Portug./Spanish* 22
Je's | *Southern* 24
Mompou | *Spanish* 22
Nico Kitchen/Bar | *Eclectic* 20
Rio Rodizio | *Brazilian* 21
Seabra's Marisqueira | *Portug.* 24
Sol-Mar | *Portug.* 24
Spain | *Portug./Spanish* 22
Spanish Manor | *Spanish* 25
Spanish Tavern | *Spanish* 22
Tony/Caneca | *Portug.* 22
27 Mix | *Eclectic* 21

NEW MILFORD

Sanzari's | *Italian* 21

NEW PROVIDENCE

Jose's Mex. Cantina | *Mex.* 20

NORTH BERGEN

Antonia's/Park | *Italian* 22
Di Palma Bros. | *Italian* 23
Rumba Cubana | *Cuban* 22
Sabor | *Nuevo Latino* 24
Tapas/España | *Spanish* 24
Trattoria/Sorrentina | *Italian* 25
Waterside | *Med.* 20

NORTH HALEDON

Giuseppe | *Italian* 24

NORTHVALE

Biddy O'Malley's | *Amer.* 20
Madeleine's | *French* 24

NORWOOD

Dimora | *Italian* 23

NUTLEY

Queen Margherita | *Italian* 24

OAKLAND

Cenzino | Italian — 25
Portobello | Italian — 21

PALISADES PARK

Mesón Madrid | Spanish — 20
So Moon Nan Jip | Korean — 24

PARAMUS

Biagio's | Italian — 20
Bobby's Burger | Burgers — 21
Bonefish Grill | Seafood — 21
Bucu | Bakery/Burgers — 19
CPK | Pizza — 19
Capital Grille | Steak — 25
Chakra | Amer./Eclectic — 23
El Cid | Spanish — 22
Grand Lux | Eclectic — 20
Kiku | Japanese — 21
Legal Sea Foods | Seafood — 21
Mantra | Indian — 21
Zinburger | Burgers — 21

PARK RIDGE

Esty St. | Amer. — 25
Park Steak | Seafood/Steak — 24
Valentino's | Italian — 19

PATERSON

E & V | Italian — 24
Hamilton/Ward | Steak — 24

RAHWAY

Cubanu | Cuban — 20
Luciano's | Italian — 22
Patria | Pan-Latin — 23

RAMSEY

Anthony's | Pizza — 21
Cafe Panache | Eclectic — 26
Kinchley's Tavern | Pizza — 22
NEW Local Seasonal | Amer. — -
Varka | Greek/Seafood — 25

RIDGEFIELD

Tutto/Modo Mio | Italian — 22

RIDGEFIELD PARK

MK Valencia | Amer./Italian — 21

RIDGEWOOD

A Mano | Pizza — 22
Baumgart's | Amer./Asian — 18

Brick Ln. Curry | Indian — 23
Brooklyn's Pizzeria | Pizza — 22
NEW Café 37 | Amer. — 25
Country Pancake | Amer. — 19
Dim Sum Dynasty | Chinese — 20
NEW Diwani | Indian — -
NEW Due | Italian — -
It's Greek To Me | Greek — 19
Kailash | Indian — 21
Latour | French — 26
NEW Lisa's Med. | Med. — -
Mekong Grill | Viet. — 20
Park W. Tavern | Amer. — 20
Raymond's | Amer. — 21
Ridge Thai | Thai — 21
Sakura Bana | Japanese — 25
Vlg. Green | Amer. — 24

RIVER EDGE

Dinallo's | Italian — 21
Sanducci's | Italian — 19

ROCHELLE PARK

Bistro 55 | Amer. — 19
Nanni Rist. | Italian — 22

RUTHERFORD

Cafe Matisse | Eclectic — 26
Paisano's Rest. | Italian — 22
Risotto House | Italian — 22
Village Gourmet | Eclectic — 19

SADDLE RIVER

Saddle River Inn | Amer./French — 26

SCOTCH PLAINS

Stage House | Amer. — 20

SECAUCUS

Bareli's | Italian — 23

SHORT HILLS

Benihana | Japanese — 20
CPK | Pizza — 19
Cheesecake Factory | Amer. — 21
Khun Thai | Thai — 22
Legal Sea Foods | Seafood — 21

SOUTH HACKENSACK

I Gemelli Rist. | Italian — 25

SOUTH ORANGE

Neelam | *Indian*   21

SPRINGFIELD

Cathay 22 | *Chinese*   21

SUMMIT

Anna's Rist. | *Italian*   20
Bombay Bistro | *Indian*   21
Fiorino | *Italian*   23
Hat Tavern | *Amer.*   20
Huntley Taverne | *Amer.*   22
La Focaccia | *Italian*   23
La Pastaria | *Italian*   21
Monster Sushi | *Japanese*   20
Roots Steak | *Steak*   25
Taka Sushi | *Japanese*   23

TEANECK

Amarone | *Italian*   21
BV Tuscany | *Italian*   24
Classic Quiche | *Eclectic*   23
Etc. Steak | *Kosher/Steak*   25
Vasili's | *Greek*   20

TENAFLY

NEW Acanto Rist. | *Italian*   -
Axia Taverna | *Greek*   23
NEW Europe Café | *Turkish*   -
Simply Vietnamese | *Viet.*   24

TOTOWA

Sushi Lounge | *Japanese*   21

UNION

Rio Rodizio | *Brazilian*   21
Ursino | *Amer.*   24

UNION CITY

Beyti Kebab | *Turkish*   22
Mi Bandera | *Cuban*   23

UPPER MONTCLAIR

Brick Ln. Curry | *Indian*   23
Dai-Kichi | *Japanese*   23
Upstairs | *Amer.*   24

VERONA

Avenue Bistro | *Eclectic*   21

WANAQUE

Berta's Chateau | *Italian*   22

WASHINGTON TOWNSHIP

Bacari Grill | *Italian*   21

WAYNE

Brio | *Italian*   21
CPK | *Pizza*   19
Cheesecake Factory | *Amer.*   21
Tony's Touch/Italy | *Pizza*   23
Wayne Steak | *Steak*   25

WEEHAWKEN

Chart House | *Seafood*   22
Charrito's | *Mex.*   22
Masina | *Italian*   20
Robongi | *Japanese*   22
Ruth's Chris | *Steak*   25

WESTFIELD

Acquaviva/Fonti | *Italian*   20
Chez Catherine | *French*   26
Isabella's Bistro | *Amer.*   19
Limani | *Greek*   25
Mojave Grille | *SW*   21
Theresa's | *Italian*   22
WindMill | *Hot Dogs*   19

WEST NEW YORK

Las Palmas | *Cuban*   24
P.F. Chang's | *Chinese*   21
Son Cubano | *Cuban*   20

WEST ORANGE

Egan/Sons | *Irish*   20
Highlawn Pavilion | *Amer.*   24
Jimmy Buff's | *Hot Dogs*   20
La Primavera | *Italian*   24
Manor | *Amer.*   24
McLoone's | *Amer.*   19
Sam Mickail's CUT | *Steak*   -
Yoshi-Sono | *Japanese*   21

WESTWOOD

NEW Bat Barry's | *Amer.*   -
Bibi'z Rest. | *Eclectic*   20
NEW Grange | *Amer.*   -
Hanami | *Chinese/Japanese*   18
It's Greek To Me | *Greek*   19
Jack's Café | *Amer./Eclectic*   22
Rolling Pin Cafe | *Amer.*   25

WOOD-RIDGE

Justin's Rist. | *Italian* — 22

WYCKOFF

Aoyama | *Asian* — 23
NEW La Sera | *Italian* — –

Central

BASKING RIDGE

Grain House | *Amer.* — 20
Mockingbird | *Amer.* — 22
Origin | *French/Thai* — 24
3 West | *Amer.* — 21
Urban Table | *Eclectic* — 19
Vine | *Amer./Med.* — 24

BEDMINSTER

Delicious Hgts. | *Amer.* — 19
Pluckemin Inn | *Amer.* — 25
Trattoria Med. | *Italian* — 22
TwoFiftyTwo | *Amer.* — 20

BERNARDSVILLE

Bernards Inn | *Amer.* — 25
Osteria Morini | *Italian* — 24
Sette | *Italian* — 23

BOONTON

Il Michelangelo | *Italian* — 21
Reservoir Tavern | *Italian* — 23

BOUND BROOK

Chimney Rock Inn | *Amer.* — 19
Girasole (Bound Brook) | *Italian* — 24

BRIDGEWATER

Cafe Emilia | *Italian* — 20
CPK | *Pizza* — 19
Cheesecake Factory | *Amer.* — 21
McCormick/Schmick's | *Seafood* — 20
Thai Kitchen | *Thai* — 24

CHATHAM

River Grille | *Amer.* — –
Scalini Fedeli | *Italian* — 27
Serenade | *French* — 26
Taste/Asia | *Malaysian* — 23

CHESTER

Benito's Trattoria | *Italian* — 23
Thai Kitchen | *Thai* — 24

CRANBURY

Blue Rooster | *Amer.* — 22
Cranbury Inn | *Amer.* — 18

DENVILLE

Cafe Metro | *Eclectic* — 21
Hunan Taste | *Chinese* — 24
Midori | *Japanese* — 23

DOVER

Quiet Man | *Pub* — 23

EAST BRUNSWICK

Bonefish Grill | *Seafood* — 21
Shogun | *Japanese/Steak* — 21
NEW Smashburger | *Burgers* — 20
Wasabi | *Japanese* — 22

EAST HANOVER

Luigi's | *Italian* — 22
Mr. Chu | *Chinese* — 21
Penang | *Malaysian/Thai* — 22
Saffron | *Indian* — 21

EDISON

Akbar | *Indian* — 21
Anthony's | *Pizza* — 21
Benihana | *Japanese* — 20
Cheesecake Factory | *Amer.* — 21
Five Guys | *Burgers* — 22
NEW G Grab & Go | *Sandwiches* — –
Harold's N.Y. Deli | *Jewish/Deli* — 22
LouCás | *Italian* — 23
Meemah | *Chinese/Malaysian* — 23
Ming | *Asian* — 22
Moghul | *Indian* — 21
Pho Anh Dao | *Viet.* — 22
Skylark | *Diner/Eclectic* — 21
Wonder Seafood | *Chinese* — 23

FORDS

McLoone's | *Amer.* — 19

GILLETTE

Casa Maya | *Mex.* — 21
Chimney Rock Inn | *Amer.* — 19

GLADSTONE

Gladstone | *Amer.* — 21

GREEN BROOK

Bonefish Grill | *Seafood* — 21
Shogun | *Japanese/Steak* — 21

HIGHLAND PARK

Pad-Thai Auth.	*Thai*	22
Pithari/Ouzo	*Greek*	23

HILLSBOROUGH

Cafe Graziella	*Italian*	22
Old Man Rafferty's	*Amer.*	19
Thai Kitchen	*Thai*	24

ISELIN

Bonefish Grill	*Seafood*	21
Casa Giuseppe	*Italian*	23

JAMESBURG

Fiddleheads	*Amer.*	22

KENDALL PARK

Shogun	*Japanese/Steak*	21

KINGSTON

Eno Terra	*Italian*	25
Main St.	*Amer./Continental*	20
Osteria Procaccini	*Pizza*	24

LAKE HOPATCONG

Alice's	*Amer.*	20

MADISON

Garlic Rose	*Eclectic*	20
Il Mondo Vecchio	*Italian*	25
L'Allegria	*Italian*	23
Rob's Bistro	*French*	22
Shanghai Jazz	*Asian*	22

MANVILLE

Grub Hut	*BBQ/Mex.*	21

MARTINSVILLE

Aoyama	*Asian*	23
Trio	*Italian*	24

MENDHAM

Aoyama	*Asian*	23
Black Horse Tavern	*Amer.*	19
Dante's Rist.	*Italian*	20
Sammy's/Cider Mill	*Steak*	23

METUCHEN

Lola Latin Bistro	*Pan-Latin*	21
Metuchen Inn	*Amer.*	23
Novita Bistro	*Italian*	20

MIDDLESEX

Carpaccio	*Italian*	21

MILLTOWN

Fresco Steak	*Seafood/Steak*	23

MONROE TOWNSHIP

Pithari/Ouzo	*Greek*	23

MONTVILLE

Columbia Inn	*Italian*	21
LuNello's Montville	*Amer.*	21

MORRIS PLAINS

Arthur's Tavern	*Steak*	20
Cinnamon	*Indian*	21
Grato	*Italian*	22
Hunan Chinese	*Chinese*	22
Lemongrass	*Thai/Viet.*	23
Minado	*Japanese*	22
Tabor Rd. Tavern	*Amer.*	22

MORRISTOWN

Blue Morel	*Amer.*	24
Grand Cafe	*French*	23
J&K Steak	*Steak*	22
La Campagna	*Italian*	24
Mehndi	*Indian*	23
Ming	*Asian*	22
Origin	*French/Thai*	24
Pamir	*Afghan*	21
Portofino's	*Italian*	21
Rod's Steak	*Seafood/Steak*	22
Roots Steak	*Steak*	25
Sebastian's	*Steak*	24
Sushi Lounge	*Japanese*	21
Tim Schafer's	*Amer.*	23
Urban Table	*Eclectic*	19

NEW BRUNSWICK

NEW Bro. Jimmy's	*Amer./BBQ*	–
Cath. Lombardi	*Italian*	24
Christopher's	*Amer.*	20
Clydz	*Amer.*	23
Daryl	*Amer.*	23
Delta's	*Southern*	22
Due Mari	*Italian*	26
Efe's Med. Grill	*Med.*	21
Frog & Peach	*Amer.*	25
Hotoke	*Asian*	20

Makeda	*Ethiopian*	22
Old Bay Rest.	*Cajun/Creole*	20
Old Man Rafferty's	*Amer.*	19
Panico's	*Italian*	21
Stage Left	*Amer.*	25
Steakhouse 85	*Steak*	24

NORTH BRUNSWICK

Arthur's Steak	*Steak*	21
Chinese Mirch	*Asian*	19
Guru Palace	*Indian*	19
Istanbul Rest./Patis.	*Turkish*	22
NEW Smashburger	*Burgers*	20

OLD BRIDGE

A Tavola	*Italian*	21
Just Rest.	*Amer.*	24
Thai Thai	*Thai*	24

PARSIPPANY

Amiya	*Indian*	21
Chand Palace	*Indian*	22
Eccola Italian	*Italian*	22
Five Guys	*Burgers*	22
Ruth's Chris	*Steak*	25
Sakura	*Japanese*	22

PEAPACK

Café Azzurro	*Italian*	22
Ninety Acres/Natirar	*Amer.*	25

PERTH AMBOY

Portug. Manor	*Portug.*	23

PINE BROOK

Bonefish Grill	*Seafood*	21
Don Pepe	*Portug./Spanish*	22
Don Pepe's Steak	*Steak*	22

PISCATAWAY

Al Dente	*Italian*	22
Chand Palace	*Indian*	22

POMPTON PLAINS

Little Food Cafe	*Sandwiches*	23

RANDOLPH

La Strada	*Italian*	23
Rosie's Trattoria	*Italian*	22

RARITAN

Char Steak	*Steak*	23
Espo's	*Italian*	22
Spain 92	*Spanish*	21

RIVERDALE

Rosemary/Sage	*Amer.*	24

ROCKY HILL

One 53	*Amer.*	24
Rocky Hill Inn	*Amer.*	19

SKILLMAN

Ya Ya	*Noodles*	20

SOMERSET

Chao Phaya	*Thai*	22
Jo-Sho	*Japanese*	25
Luca's Rist.	*Italian*	24
Sophie's Bistro	*French*	23

SOMERVILLE

Chao Phaya	*Thai*	22
Da Filippo's	*Italian/Seafood*	24
Kyma	*Greek/Seafood*	23
Martino's	*Cuban*	22
Origin	*French/Thai*	24
Shumi	*Japanese*	27
Verve	*Amer./French*	22
Wasabi	*Japanese*	22

SOUTH PLAINFIELD

Khyber Grill	*Indian*	21
Kimchi Hana	*Japanese*	23

WARREN

Jose's Mex. Cantina	*Mex.*	20
Silk Road	*Afghan*	24
Stone/Stirling Ridge	*Amer.*	22
Uproot	*Amer.*	22

WATCHUNG

Five Guys	*Burgers*	22

WHIPPANY

Chef Jon's	*Chinese*	20
Il Capriccio	*Italian*	25
Nikko	*Japanese*	24

WOODBRIDGE

Mie Thai	*Thai*	23

North Shore

ASBURY

RosaLuca's | *Italian* 24

ASBURY PARK

Bistro Olé | *Portug./Spanish* 22
Brickwall Tavern | *Pub* 20
Cubacàn | *Cuban* 22
Dauphin Grille | *Amer.* 22
Fish | *Seafood* 22
Hotel Tides | *Amer.* 22
Jimmy's | *Italian* 23
Langosta Lounge | *Eclectic* 20
La Tapatia | *Mex.* 24
McLoone's | *Amer.* 19
Moonstruck | *Amer./Med.* 24
Old Man Rafferty's | *Amer.* 19
Pop's Garage | *Mex.* 21
Porta | *Pizza* 24
Stella Marina | *Italian* 23
Taka | *Japanese* 25
Tim McLoone's | *Amer.* 19
Toast | *Amer.* 21

ATLANTIC HIGHLANDS

Copper Canyon | *SW* 24
Memphis Pig Out | *BBQ* 21

AVON-BY-THE-SEA

Clementine's | *Creole* 23

BARNEGAT LIGHT

Kubel's | *Seafood* 19
Mustache Bill's | *Diner* 22

BEACH HAVEN

Black Whale | *Seafood* 22
Chicken/Egg | *Amer.* 21
Gables Rest. | *Eclectic* 25
Harvey Cedars | *Seafood* 20
Roberto's | *Italian* 23

BELFORD

Belford Bistro | *Amer.* 26

BELMAR

Brandl | *Amer.* 24
Kaya's Kitchen | *Veg.* 25

Klein's | *Seafood* 23
La Dolce Vita | *Italian/Seafood* 22
Surf Taco | *Mex.* 21
WindMill | *Hot Dogs* 19

BRADLEY BEACH

Bamboo Leaf | *Thai/Viet.* 20
Vic's | *Italian/Pizza* 22

BRICK

Bonefish Grill | *Seafood* 21
Five Guys | *Burgers* 22
Ikko | *Japanese* 25
Villa Vittoria | *Italian* 22

BRIELLE

Shipwreck Grill | *Amer./Seafood* 24

EATONTOWN

Bobby's Burger | *Burgers* 21
Far East Taste | *Chinese/Thai* 23

FAIR HAVEN

Nauvoo Grill | *Amer.* 19
Raven/Peach | *Amer.* 24

FORKED RIVER

Surf Taco | *Mex.* 21

FREEHOLD

A Little Bit/Cuba Dos | *Cuban* 22
Bobby's Burger | *Burgers* 21
Brio | *Italian* 21
Cheesecake Factory | *Amer.* 21
El Mesón Café | *Mex.* 23
Federici's | *Pizza* 22
Ibby's | *Mideast.* 20
La Cipollina | *Italian* 21
Metropolitan Cafe | *Eclectic* 21
P.F. Chang's | *Chinese* 21
WindMill | *Hot Dogs* 19

FREEHOLD TOWNSHIP

Frankie Fed's | *Italian* 22

HARVEY CEDARS

Black-Eyed Susans | *Amer.* 24
Harvey Cedars | *Seafood* 20
Plantation | *Amer.* 19

LOCATIONS

NORTH SHORE

HIGHLANDS

Bahrs Landing | *Seafood* | 19
Inlet Café | *Seafood* | 20
Windansea | *Seafood* | 20

HOLMDEL

It's Greek To Me | *Greek* | 19

HOWELL

Bamboo Leaf | *Thai/Viet.* | 20
Christie's Italian | *Italian* | 23
Juanito's | *Mex.* | 22

JACKSON

Java Moon | *Amer.* | 23
Solo Bella | *Italian* | 23
Surf Taco | *Mex.* | 21

KEYPORT

Drew's Bistro | *Amer.* | 27
Trinity (Keyport) | *Amer.* | 22

LONG BEACH TOWNSHIP

Kubel's | *Seafood* | 19

LONG BRANCH

Avenue | *French* | 22
Charley's Ocean Grl. | *Amer.* | 19
It's Greek To Me | *Greek* | 19
McLoone's | *Amer.* | 19
Rooney's | *Seafood* | 21
Sirena Rist. | *Italian* | 22
Surf Taco | *Mex.* | 21
Tre Amici | *Italian* | 22
Tuzzio's | *Italian* | 20
WindMill | *Hot Dogs* | 19

MANAHAWKIN

Mud City Crab | *Seafood* | 23

MANALAPAN

Konbu | *Japanese* | 23
NEW Nuovo Trattoria | *Italian* | -
Spargo's | *Amer.* | 22

MANASQUAN

Firefly Bistro | *Amer.* | 22
Remington's | *Amer.* | 21
Squan Tavern | *Italian* | 20
Surf Taco | *Mex.* | 21

MARLBORO

Brioso | *Italian* | 23
Crown Palace | *Chinese* | 20
Pino's La Forchetta | *Italian* | 20
PrimoHoagies | *Sandwiches* | 21

MATAWAN

Aby's | *Mex.* | 20
Big Ed's BBQ | *BBQ* | 19
W. Lake Seafood | *Chinese* | 24

MIDDLETOWN

Anna's Italian | *Italian* | 23
Crown Palace | *Chinese* | 20
Neelam | *Indian* | 21
Sono Sushi | *Japanese* | 26

NAVESINK

Navesink Fishery | *Seafood* | 25

NEPTUNE CITY

Brennen's Steak | *Steak* | 22
Pete/Elda's | *Pizza* | 24

NORMANDY BEACH

Labrador | *Eclectic* | 21

OAKHURST/ OCEAN TOWNSHIP

Piccola Italia | *Italian* | 25

OCEAN GROVE

Sea Grass | *Amer.* | 24
WindMill | *Hot Dogs* | 19

POINT PLEASANT BEACH

Europa South | *Portug./Spanish* | 23
Jack Baker's | *Amer./Seafood* | 20
Red's Lobster Pot | *Seafood* | 23
Spike's | *Seafood* | 21
Surf Taco | *Mex.* | 21

RED BANK

Basil T's | *Italian* | 21
Bistro/Red Bank | *Eclectic* | 21
Bonefish Grill | *Seafood* | 21
Char Steak | *Steak* | 23
Danny's | *Steak* | 22
Dish | *Amer.* | 23
D'Jeet? | *Amer.* | 21

Good Karma Cafe	*Veg.*	22
JBJ Soul Kit.	*Amer.*	21
Juanito's	*Mex.*	22
La Pastaria	*Italian*	21
Molly Pitcher Inn	*Amer.*	22
Nicholas	*Amer.*	28
Red	*Amer.*	21
Siam Garden	*Thai*	22
Surf Taco	*Mex.*	21
Teak	*Asian*	22
Via45	*Italian*	25
WindMill	*Hot Dogs*	19

RUMSON

Barnacle Bill's	*Burgers*	20
David Burke From.	*Amer.*	25
Rist. Giorgia	*Italian*	25
Salt Creek Grille	*Amer.*	21
Undici	*Italian*	23
What's/Beef?	*Steak*	21

SEA BRIGHT

NEW Ama Rist.	*Italian*	25
Harry's Lobster	*Seafood*	22
Yumi	*Asian*	26

SEA GIRT

Scarborough Fair	*Amer.*	20

SHIP BOTTOM

La Spiaggia	*Italian*	23
Raimondo's	*Italian*	24

SHREWSBURY

Pop's Garage	*Mex.*	21
San Remo	*Italian*	22

SOUTH SEASIDE PARK

Chef Mike's ABG	*Amer.*	22

SPRING LAKE

Black Trumpet	*Amer.*	22
Whispers	*Amer.*	26

SPRING LAKE HEIGHTS

Mill/Spg. Lake	*Amer.*	20

SURF CITY

Yellow Fin	*Amer.*	25

TINTON FALLS

Kanji	*Japanese*	24
Portofino Rist.	*Italian*	21

TOMS RIVER

Aamantran	*Indian*	21
Five Guys	*Burgers*	22
Jack Baker's	*Amer./Seafood*	20
Shogun	*Japanese/Steak*	21
Surf Taco	*Mex.*	21
Xina	*Chinese*	23

UNION BEACH

Piero's	*Italian*	22

WALL

Shogun	*Japanese/Steak*	21

WEST CREEK

Octopus's Gdn.	*Seafood*	23

Delaware Valley

ALLAMUCHY

Mattar's Bistro	*Amer.*	23

CLAYTON

Nick's Pizza/Steak	*Italian*	23

FLEMINGTON

Blue Fish Grill	*Seafood*	23
55 Main	*Amer.*	22
Market Roost	*Eclectic*	23
Matt's Red Rooster	*Amer.*	26

FRENCHTOWN

Frenchtown Inn	*Eclectic/French*	22

HACKETTSTOWN

Prickly Pear	*Amer.*	22

HAMBURG

Rest. Latour	*Amer.*	26

HAMILTON

Málaga's	*Spanish*	26
Rat's	*French*	25

HAMILTON TOWNSHIP

DeLorenzo's Pizza	*Pizza*	25

HIGH BRIDGE

Casa Maya | *Mex.* — 21

HOPE

Inn/Millrace Rest. | *Amer.* — 22

HOPEWELL

Bell/Whistle | *Amer./Southern* — 20
Blue Bottle Cafe | *Amer.* — 26
Brothers Moon | *Amer.* — 24
Da's Kitchen | *Thai* — 25
Nomad Pizza | *Pizza* — 25

LAFAYETTE

Lafayette House | *Amer.* — 22

LAMBERTVILLE

Anton's/Swan | *Amer.* — 22
Brian's | *French/Italian* — 26
DeAnna's | *Italian* — 22
El Tule | *Mex./Peruvian* — 25
Full Moon | *Eclectic* — 20
Hamilton's Grill | *Med.* — 24
Inn/Hawke Rest. | *Amer.* — 18
Lambertville Stn. | *Amer.* — 20
Lilly's/Canal | *Eclectic* — 20
Manon | *French* — 24
Tortuga's | *Mex.* — 23

LAWRENCEVILLE

Acacia | *Amer.* — 22
Chambers Walk | *Amer.* — 22
Elements Asia | *Asian* — 23
Fedora Café | *Eclectic* — 22
KC Prime | *Steak* — 22
Palace of Asia | *Indian* — 23
NEW WildFlour | *Bakery* — -

MILFORD

Milford Oyster | *Seafood* — 25

NEWTON

Andre's | *Amer.* — 25
Krave Café | *Amer.* — 25

OLDWICK

Tewksbury Inn | *Amer.* — 21

PENNINGTON

Avanti | *Italian* — 21
Osteria Procaccini | *Pizza* — 24
Za | *Amer.* — 22

PRINCETON

NEW Agricola | *Amer.* — -
Ajihei | *Japanese* — 24
Alchemist/Barrister | *Amer.* — 18
A Taste/Mexico | *Mex.* — 20
Bent Spoon | *Ice Cream* — 27
Big Fish Seafood | *Seafood* — 20
Blue Point Grill | *Seafood* — 25
Bobby's Burger | *Burgers* — 21
Conte's | *Pizza* — 23
NEW Despaña | *Spanish* — -
Efe's Med. Grill | *Med.* — 21
Elements | *Amer.* — 25
Ferry House | *Amer./French* — 22
Gennaro's | *Italian* — 21
La Mezzaluna | *Italian* — 22
Main St. | *Amer./Continental* — 20
Mediterra | *Med.* — 22
Metro North | *Italian* — 19
NEW Mistral | *Eclectic* — -
NEW North End Bistro | *Amer.* — -
Peacock Inn Rest. | *Amer.* — 26
Penang | *Malaysian/Thai* — 22
P.F. Chang's | *Chinese* — 21
PJ's Pancake | *Amer.* — 18
Ruth's Chris | *Steak* — 25
Salt Creek Grille | *Amer.* — 21
Small World Coffee | *Coffee* — 23
Teresa Caffe | *Italian* — 23
Tortuga's | *Mex.* — 23
Tre Piani | *Italian/Med.* — 22
Triumph Brew. | *Amer./Eclectic* — 19
Witherspoon | *Seafood/Steak* — 22
Yankee Doodle | *Pub* — 17

RINGOES

Harvest Moon Inn | *Amer.* — 23

ROBBINSVILLE

DeLorenzo's Pies | *Pizza* — 27

ROSEMONT

NEW The Pass | *French* — -

SERGEANTSVILLE

Sergeantsville Inn | *Amer.* — 23

SPARTA

Krogh's | *Amer.* — 21
Mohawk House | *Amer.* — 22

STANHOPE

Bell's Mansion	*Amer.*	20
Black Forest Inn	*German*	24
Salt Gastro	*Amer.*	22

STOCKTON

Stockton Inn	*Amer.*	21

TRENTON

Amici Milano	*Italian*	21
Blue Danube	*E Euro.*	23
Homestead Inn	*Italian*	23

WALLPACK CENTER

Walpack Inn	*Amer.*	23

WHITEHOUSE

Ryland Inn	*Amer.*	25

South Shore

ATLANTIC CITY

Amada	*Spanish*	26
American Cut	*Steak*	24
Angelo's	*Italian*	21
Atlantic Grill	*Seafood*	21
Azure/Allegretti	*Seafood*	23
Bobby Flay Steak	*Steak*	25
Buddakan	*Asian*	25
Cafe 2825	*Italian*	24
Capriccio	*Italian*	24
Carmine's	*Italian*	22
Chart House	*Seafood*	22
Chef Vola's	*Italian*	27
Chelsea Prime	*Steak*	24
Continental	*Eclectic*	23
Cuba Libre	*Cuban*	21
Dock's Oyster	*Seafood*	25
Dos Caminos	*Mex.*	22
Fin	*Seafood*	25
Fornelletto	*Italian*	23
Gallagher's	*Steak*	23
Girasole (AC)	*Italian*	23
Harry's Oyster	*Seafood*	22
Il Mulino	*Italian*	25
Irish Pub/Inn	*Pub*	21
Izakaya	*Japanese*	23
Knife/Fork Inn	*Amer.*	24
Los Amigos	*Mex./SW*	21
Luke Palladino	*Italian*	24
McCormick/Schmick's	*Seafood*	20
Mia	*Italian*	24

Morton's	*Steak*	25
Mussel Bar/Wiedmaier	*Belgian*	24
Old Homestead	*Steak*	26
The Palm	*Steak*	24
P.F. Chang's	*Chinese*	21
Phillips Seafood	*Seafood*	21
Ruth's Chris	*Steak*	25
Teplitzky's	*Diner*	19
Tony Luke's	*Cheesestks.*	23
Tony's/Grill	*Pizza*	22
Village Whiskey	*Burgers*	24
Waterfront Buffet	*Eclectic*	22
White House	*Sandwiches*	25
Wolfgang Puck	*Amer.*	25

AVALON

Cafe Loren	*Amer.*	25
Diving Horse	*Seafood*	25
PrimoHoagies	*Sandwiches*	21
Sea Grill	*Seafood/Steak*	21

CAPE MAY

Axelsson's	*Seafood*	23
Blue Pig Tavern	*Amer.*	21
Depot Mkt. Cafe	*Amer.*	24
Ebbitt Room	*Amer.*	26
410 Bank St.	*Carib./Creole*	25
Frescos	*Italian/Med.*	23
Lobster House	*Seafood*	22
Lucky Bones	*Amer.*	21
Mad Batter	*Amer.*	22
Martini Beach	*Eclectic*	22
Merion Inn	*Amer.*	22
Peter Shields Inn	*Amer.*	26
Tisha's	*Amer.*	25
Union Park	*Amer.*	26
Washington Inn	*Amer.*	26

EGG HARBOR

Bonefish Grill	*Seafood*	21
Chickie/Pete's	*Pub*	21
Library III	*Steak*	25
Renault Winery Rest.	*Amer.*	23

GALLOWAY

Ram's Head Inn	*Amer.*	25

GALLOWAY TOWNSHIP

Athenian Gdn.	*Greek*	22

HAMMONTON

PrimoHoagies | *Sandwiches*   21

LEEDS POINT

Oyster Creek Inn | *Seafood*   24

MARGATE

Bobby Chez | *Seafood*   23
LoBianco | *Amer.*   23
Steve/Cookie's | *Amer.*   27
Tomatoes | *Cal./Eclectic*   23
Ventura's | *Italian*   20

MAYS LANDING

Inn at Sugar Hill | *Amer.*   20

NEW GRETNA

Allen's | *Seafood*   22

NORTHFIELD

Carluccio's Pizza | *Pizza*   25
Luke Palladino | *Italian*   24

OCEAN CITY

Manco/Manco Pizza | *Pizza*   23

RIO GRANDE

PrimoHoagies | *Sandwiches*   21

SEA ISLE CITY

Busch's Seafood | *Seafood*   21
La Fontana Coast | *Italian*   23
Mike's Seafood | *Seafood*   21

SICKLERVILLE

Nick's Pizza/Steak | *Italian*   23
Tony Luke's | *Cheesestks.*   23

SMITHVILLE

Smithville Inn | *Amer.*   22

SOMERS POINT

Baia | *Italian*   19
Charlie's | *Amer.*   21
Crab Trap | *Seafood*   24
Doc's Place | *Amer.*   20
Latz's/Bay | *Amer.*   21
Smitty's Clam Bar | *Seafood*   23

STONE HARBOR

The Backyard | *Amer.*   24

VENTNOR

Domenico's | *Italian*   23
Sage | *Med.*   23

VENTOR CITY

Megu Sushi | *Japanese*   24

WEST CAPE MAY

Black Duck | *Eclectic*   26

Suburban Philly Area

BERLIN

Famous/King of Pizza | *Pizza*   22
Gaetano's | *Cheesestks.*   21

BORDENTOWN

Alstarz | *Eclectic*   18
Chickie/Pete's | *Pub*   21
Dublin Sq. | *Irish/Pub*   18
Farnsworth | *Continental*   21
Mastoris | *Diner*   21
Oliver a Bistro | *Eclectic*   25
Under/Moon | *Argent./Eclectic*   23

BROOKLAWN

Metro Diner | *Amer./Diner*   20

BURLINGTON

Blue Claw Crab | *Seafood*   24
Luigi's Pizza | *Italian/Pizza*   21
PrimoHoagies | *Sandwiches*   21

CHERRY HILL

Bistro/Cherry Hill | *Amer.*   23
Blue2O | *Seafood*   22
Bobby Chez | *Seafood*   23
Bobby's Burger | *Burgers*   21
Brio | *Italian*   21
Caffe/Lamberti | *Italian*   24
CPK | *Pizza*   19
Capital Grille | *Steak*   25
Cheesecake Factory | *Amer.*   21
Coastline | *Amer.*   20
Dream Cuisine | *French*   26
Dublin Sq. | *Irish/Pub*   18
Famous/King of Pizza | *Pizza*   22
Grand Lux | *Eclectic*   20
Kibitz Room | *Deli*   24
Kuzina/Sofia | *Greek*   22
McCormick/Schmick's | *Seafood*   20

Megu Sushi	*Japanese*	24
Mikado	*Japanese*	22
Norma's	*Mideast.*	22
Palace of Asia	*Indian*	23
P.J. Whelihan's	*Pub*	21
Ponzio's	*Diner*	20
PrimoHoagies	*Sandwiches*	21
Seasons 52	*Amer.*	24
Siri's Thai French	*French/Thai*	24
Wm. Douglas	*Steak*	24

CINNAMINSON

PrimoHoagies	*Sandwiches*	21
Whistlers Inn	*Amer./BBQ*	20

CLEMENTON

Filomena	*Italian*	24

COLLINGSWOOD

Barone's	*Italian*	23
Bistro/Marino	*Italian*	25
Blackbird Dining	*French/Italian*	24
Bobby Chez	*Seafood*	23
Casona	*Cuban*	22
Il Fiore	*Italian*	24
IndeBlue	*Indian*	25
NEW Indiya	*Indian*	-
Joe Pesce	*Italian/Seafood*	25
Nunzio Rist.	*Italian*	23
Pop Shop	*Amer.*	23
Sagami	*Japanese*	26
Sapori	*Italian*	25
That's Amore	*Italian*	22
Tortilla Press	*Mex.*	21
Zeppoli	*Italian*	26

DEPTFORD

Adelphia	*Amer.*	21
Bonefish Grill	*Seafood*	21
Filomena Lake.	*Italian*	24
Tokyo Hibachi	*Japanese*	23

GIBBSBORO

Chophouse	*Seafood/Steak*	24

GLASSBORO

Landmark Americana	*Amer.*	22
Nick's Pizza/Steak	*Italian*	23
NEW Smashburger	*Burgers*	20

GLOUCESTER

Max's Seafood	*Seafood*	26

HADDONFIELD

British Chip Shop	*British*	24
Bruno's	*Italian*	21
Da Soli	*Italian*	25
Fuji	*Japanese*	25
Little Tuna	*Seafood*	22
P.J. Whelihan's	*Pub*	21
Tre Famiglia	*Italian*	25

HADDON HEIGHTS

Elements Cafe	*Amer.*	23

LINDENWOLD

La Esperanza	*Mex.*	24

MAPLE SHADE

Iron Hill	*Amer./Pub*	22
Mikado	*Japanese*	22
P.J. Whelihan's	*Pub*	21
Tacconelli's	*Pizza*	21
Yellow Sub.	*Cheesestks.*	21
Yokohama	*Japanese*	25

MARLTON

Bonefish Grill	*Seafood*	21
Brio	*Italian*	21
Fleming's Steakhouse	*Steak*	23
Joe's Peking Duck	*Chinese*	23
Luigi's Pizza	*Italian/Pizza*	21
Mex. Food Factory	*Mex.*	21
Mikado	*Japanese*	22
P.F. Chang's	*Chinese*	21
Redstone Grill	*Amer.*	22
NEW Zoe's Kitchen	*Med.*	-

MEDFORD

Braddock's	*Amer.*	24

MEDFORD LAKES

P.J. Whelihan's	*Pub*	21

MERCHANTVILLE

Tortilla Press	*Mex.*	21

MOORESTOWN

Al Dente Italiana	*Italian*	23
Barone's	*Italian*	23
NEW Blue Fig	*Med.*	-

LOCATIONS

SUB. PHILLY AREA

Megu Sushi | *Japanese* | 24
Passariello's | *Italian/Pizza* | 22

MOUNT EPHRAIM

Black Horse Diner | *Diner* | 20
Five Guys | *Burgers* | 22

MOUNT HOLLY

High St. Grill | *Amer.* | 24
Robin's Nest | *Amer.* | 24

MOUNT LAUREL

Bobby Chez | *Seafood* | 23
El Azteca | *Mex.* | 23
GG's | *Amer.* | 23
Miller's Ale House | *Pub* | 21
Monsoon | *Indian* | 25
PrimoHoagies | *Sandwiches* | 21

MULLICA HILL

Toscana | *Italian* | 24

PENNSAUKEN

Benihana | *Japanese* | 20
Pub | *Steak* | 21

RIVERSIDE

Cafe Madison | *Amer.* | 23

RUNNEMEDE

Phily Diner | *Diner* | 20

SEWELL

Arugula | *Italian* | 23
Bobby Chez | *Seafood* | 23
P.J. Whelihan's | *Pub* | 21
Terra Nova | *Amer.* | 21

SWEDESBORO

PrimoHoagies | *Sandwiches* | 21
NEW Tavro 13 | *Amer.* | -

VINCENTOWN

Vincentown Diner | *Diner* | 21

VOORHEES

A Little Café | *Eclectic* | 23
Coriander | *Indian* | 24
NEW Elena Wu | *Asian* | -
Five Guys | *Burgers* | 22
Iron Hill | *Amer./Pub* | 22
Library II | *Steak* | 24
Passariello's | *Italian/Pizza* | 22
PrimoHoagies | *Sandwiches* | 21
Ritz Seafood | *Seafood* | 24

WEST BERLIN

Big John's | *Cheesestks.* | 23
Filomena Rustica | *Italian* | 23
Los Amigos | *Mex./SW* | 21

WEST DEPTFORD

River Winds | *Amer.* | 24

WESTMONT

Giumarello's | *Italian* | 25

WILLIAMSTOWN

Library IV | *Steak* | 24
Nick's Pizza/Steak | *Italian* | 23

WOODBURY HEIGHTS

Hollywood Cafe | *Amer.* | 22

ZAGAT
2014

New Jersey Map

Most Popular Restaurants

Listed in order of popularity within each category; map coordinates follow names (numbers preceding chains correspond only to map markers). For multi-location restaurants, only flagship or central locations are plotted. Sections A-K show the entire state (see adjacent). Sections L-S show the Metro New York area (see reverse side of map).

1 Nicholas (E-6)

2 Ninety Acres at Natirar (L-5)

3 CulinAriane (Q-3)

4 Amanda's (S-3)

5 Cafe Panache (B-6)

6 Cafe Matisse (R-2)

7 River Palm Terrace† (S-2)

8 Scalini Fedeli (O-4)

9 410 Bank Street (K-3)

10 Highlawn Pavilion (P-3)

11 A Toute Heure (P-5)

12 Bernards Inn (M-4)

13 Pluckemin Inn (L-5)

14 Adelphia (G-3)

15 Fascino (Q-3)

16 3 Forty Grill (R-4)

17 Serenade (O-4)

18 Cuban Pete's (P-3)

19 Don Pepe* (O-2)

20 Elements* (E-4)

21 The Frog and the Peach* (E-5)

22 Osteria Giotto (P-3)

23 Saddle River Inn (B-6)

24 Rat's (F-4)

25 Arthur's Tavern (M-3)

26 Fornos of Spain (Q-4)

27 Lorena's* (P-4)

28 The Manor (P-3)

29 Old Man Rafferty's† (D-5)

30 Harold's New York Deli (O-7)

31 Carmine's (I-5)

32 David Burke Fromagerie* (E-7)

33 Washington Inn* (K-3)

34 Blue Point Grill (E-5)

35 McLoone's† (O-7)

36 Chef Vola's (I-5)

37 Due Mari* (D-5)

38 Bobby Flay Steak (I-5)

39 It's Greek To Me† (S-2)

40 Stage Left* (E-5)

Most Popular Chains

41 Cheesecake Factory† (P-2)

42 Bonefish Grill† (I-5)

43 Five Guys† (O-2)

44 P.F. Chang's China Bistro† (R-1)

45 Ruth's Chris Steak House† (R-3)

46 Bobby's Burger Palace† (E-6)

47 Chart House (I-5, S-3)

48 The Capital Grille (G-3, R-1)

49 Legal Sea Foods (O-4, R-1)

50 Benihana† (O-4)

*Indicates tie with above   †Indicates multiple branches